Edited by Thomas F. Best

Baptism Today

Understanding, Practice, Ecumenical Implications

Faith and Order Paper No. 207

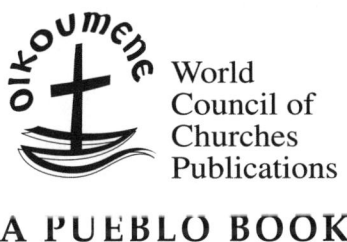
World Council of Churches Publications

A PUEBLO BOOK

Liturgical Press   Collegeville, Minnesota
www.litpress.org

Faith and Order Paper No. 207

WCC Publications
World Council of Churches
P.O. Box 2100, 150 Route de Ferney
1211 Geneva 2, Switzerland
http://www.oikoumene.org

A Pueblo Book published by Liturgical Press

Cover design by Ann Blattner

Excerpts from documents of the Second Vatican Council are from *Vatican Council II: The Basic Sixteen Documents*, by Austin Flannery, OP © 1996 (Costello Publishing Company, Inc.). Used with permission.

Scripture texts in this work are taken from the *New Revised Standard Version Bible* © 1989, Division of Christian Education of the National Council of the Churches of Christ in the United States of America. Used by permission. All rights reserved.

For permissions on liturgical texts included, see pages 437–39.

© 2008 by Order of Saint Benedict, Collegeville, Minnesota. All rights reserved. No part of this book may be reproduced in any form, by print, microfilm, microfiche, mechanical recording, photocopying, translation, or by any other means, known or yet unknown, for any purpose except brief quotations in reviews, without the previous written permission of Liturgical Press, Saint John's Abbey, P.O. Box 7500, Collegeville, Minnesota 56321-7500. Printed in the United States of America.

Library of Congress Cataloging-in-Publication Data

    Baptism today : understanding, practice, ecumenical implications / Thomas F. Best, editor.
        p.   cm.
    Includes bibliographical references and index.
    ISBN 978-0-8146-6221-2 (pbk.)
    1. Baptism.   I. Best, Thomas F.

BV811.3.B37 2008
265'.1—dc22

2008015319

Contents

Introduction
 Thomas F. Best   vii

Part I: Commentaries

Chapter 1: Baptism: Sacrament of the Kingdom
 Boris Bobrinskoy (Eastern Orthodox)   3

Chapter 2: The Sacrament of Holy Baptism
 in the Armenian Apostolic Church
 Mesrob Tashjian (Oriental Orthodox)   15

Chapter 3: The Baptismal Liturgy
 of the Malankara Orthodox Syrian Church
 Jacob Kurien (Oriental Orthodox)   23

Chapter 4: Rite[s] of Baptism in the Catholic Church:
 A Theological-Pastoral Commentary
 James F. Puglisi, SA (Catholic)   29

Chapter 5: The Rite of Holy Baptism in the *Lutheran Book of Worship*
 Jeffrey A. Truscott (Lutheran)   45

Chapter 6: Baptism in the Anglican Communion
 Paul F. Bradshaw (Anglican)   55

Chapter 7: Baptism in the Presbyterian and Reformed Tradition
 Martha Moore-Keish (Presbyterian)   63

Chapter 8: The Baptism of Believers
 Paul Fiddes (Baptist)   73

Chapter 9: Baptism and the Quaker Tradition
 Janet Scott (Quaker)   81

Chapter 10: Baptismal Practice among North American Mennonites
 Rebecca Slough (Mennonite)   89

Chapter 11: The Initiatory Rites of the United Methodist Church
 Karen B. Westerfield Tucker (Methodist)   99

iii

Chapter 12: Baptismal Understanding and Practice
in the Christian Church (Disciples of Christ)
Keith Watkins (Christian Church [Disciples of Christ])   109

Chapter 13: The Baptismal Liturgy
of the Mar Thoma Syrian Church of Malabar
George Mathew (Mar Thoma)   115

Chapter 14: Baptism in the Uniting Church in Australia:
The Liturgy, with Commentary and Reflections
Robert Gribben (United)   133

Chapter 15: Witness in the Waters:
Baptism and Pentecostal Spirituality
Daniel Albrecht (Pentecostal)   147

Chapter 16: Christian Baptism: A Seventh-day Adventist Appraisal
Bert Beach and George Reid (Seventh-day Adventist)   169

Chapter 17: A Salvation Army Perspective on Baptism:
Theological Understanding and Liturgical Practice
Earl Robinson (Salvation Army)   173

Chapter 18: Water Baptism in African Independent Churches:
The Paradigm of Christ Holy Church International
Thomas Oduro (African Instituted Churches)   181

Part II: Survey Articles

Chapter 1: Toward Mutual Recognition of Baptism
Paul Meyendorff (Eastern Orthodox)   195

Chapter 2: Unity in Diversity:
Convergence in the Churches' Baptismal Practices
James F. Puglisi, SA (Catholic)   207

Chapter 3: Convergence and Divergence: Baptism Today
Karen B. Westerfield Tucker (Methodist)   213

Part III: Signs of Recognition

Chapter 1: Mutual Recognition of Baptism Agreement: Germany

Introduction
Thomas F. Best   227

Christian Baptism   228

Chapter 2: Common Baptismal Certificate: Australia

> Australia's Common Baptismal Certificate:
> Its History and Significance
> *Robert Gribben* 231

> Certificate of Baptism 233

Chapter 3: "Baptismal Practice in an Ecumenical Context" Document: Massachusetts, USA

> The Genesis of an Ecumenical Text
> *Gordon White* 235

> Baptism: Baptismal Practice in an Ecumenical Context 236

Part IV: Special Issues

Chapter 1: Baptism in a Post-"State Church" Situation: The Case of the Church of Sweden
Bo Larsson (Lutheran) 247

Chapter 2: Interrogating Christian Practices: Popular Religiosity across the Ocean
J. Jayakiran Sebastian (United) 255

Part V: Baptismal Services

Chapter 1: Rite of Christian Initiation (Eastern Orthodox) 269

Chapter 2: The Canon of the Sacrament of Holy Baptism (Oriental Orthodox) 289

Chapter 3: Text of the Mystery of Holy Baptism (Oriental Orthodox) 303

Chapter 4: Rite of Christian Initiation of Adults and Rite of Baptism for Several Children (Catholic) 319

Chapter 5: Holy Baptism (Lutheran) 359

Chapter 6: The Baptism of Children (Lutheran) 365

Chapter 7: An Anglican Service of Baptism and Confirmation (Anglican) 371

Chapter 8: The Sacrament of Baptism (Presbyterian) 381

Chapter 9: The Baptism of Believers (Baptist)   393

Chapter 10: The Rite of Baptism (Mennonite)   401

Chapter 11: The Baptismal Covenant I (Methodist)   409

Chapter 12: A Representative Disciples Rite of Christian Baptism
 (Christian Church [Disciples of Christ])   417

Chapter 13: Order of Holy Baptism and Chrismation
 (Mar Thoma)   423

List of Contributors   433

Acknowledgments   437

Index   441

Introduction

Thomas F. Best

BAPTISM TODAY:
SHOWING FORTH OUR UNITY IN CHRIST

We belong to Christ: we are his and no other's. This fact is the foundation of our identity as persons, and our unity as Christians, experienced and expressed first in our baptism in Christ and into Christ's body, the Church. In our baptism Christ has claimed each of us for his own, and thus made all of us one in him. The unity we share in Christ is greater than all the differences—historical, theological, cultural—which divide Christians and the churches today: unity is our birthright, shown forth brightly in our common baptism.

It is thus no surprise that baptism is foundational for the modern ecumenical movement. To give two examples: many Protestant churches have long understood that their common baptism reflects a unity which is more fundamental than their differences in the understanding and practice of the rite itself.[1] And it was the statement on baptism from the Second Vatican Council[2] that, perhaps more than any other text, signaled the entry of the Roman Catholic Church into the ecumenical movement.

In the multilateral and conciliar contexts, the section on baptism was the most positively received part of the Faith and Order convergence text *Baptism, Eucharist and Ministry* (BEM);[3] and a common affirmation of baptism is central to the ecclesiology text "Called to be the One Church" adopted by the member churches of the World Council of Churches at its Assembly in Porto Alegre, Brazil, in 2006.[4] The bilateral discussions have, for the most part, not focused on baptism precisely because in most cases it does not pose an obstacle to mutual recognition among the churches concerned.[5] The situation with regard to baptism today is best captured in the text "Ecclesiological and Ecumenical Implications of a Common Baptism: A JWG Study," produced recently by the Joint Working Group between the Roman Catholic Church and the World Council of Churches.[6] Meanwhile the Faith and Order text-in-process "One Baptism: Towards Mutual Recognition" is pressing the discussion forward, stressing the relation of baptism to the process of the believer's lifelong growth into Christ, and exploring the relation of the faith of the believer to the faith of the Christian community as a whole.[7]

Where churches are able to recognize one another's baptisms, variations in practice and understanding are seen as reflecting common, underlying convictions about the life of faith and how one enters into it. Yet in other cases, divergent practices and positions reveal fundamental fault lines in the understanding of the faith. For example, differences over the relation of the believer's faith to that of the Church, and the relation of particular churches to the one Church, lead to some churches rebaptizing (or, in their understanding, baptizing) persons already baptized in another church.[8]

To take another area of concern: baptism with water in the name of the Father, Son, and Holy Spirit has emerged, on both biblical and traditional grounds, as the norm for churches within the ecumenical movement. Yet there are ecumenically engaged churches that, on certain biblical grounds, baptize in the name of Jesus only, and others that baptize without water. Some churches with a distinguished history of Christian witness effect entry into the Christian community without baptismal rites. Questions arise on different grounds as some churches, seeking to inculturate baptism so that its meaning may be evident in their cultural context, substitute other substances for water or use language other than the traditional Trinitarian formula.

Other expressions of nonrecognition—or simply the failure to put into practice the recognition which already exists—also distort and obscure the unity that is already ours in Christ. And this occurs not only between confessional families but between churches within the same confessional family. For all these reasons, then, many churches are divided not only at the Lord's Table but also at the baptistery and at the font. This is intolerable, not least because it denies Christ's will for our unity and his initiative in making us one in him.

Beyond the ecumenical imperative for unity, work on baptism is important for a host of liturgical and theological reasons. The practice and understanding of baptism is intimately related to a church's apprehension of central elements of the Christian faith, including the meaning of salvation and how it is received and experienced; the relation of the individual to the Christian community, both locally and universally; the relation of the faith of the individual to the faith of the Church; the role of liturgy in the life of the individual and of the

Christian community; the importance of Christian nurture, for both the believer and the community as a whole; and the understanding of sacrament and the relation of the Christian and the Church to creation. Lack of clarity about the meaning and practice of baptism has implications for all these areas of the faith and life of each church.

Just as acutely, baptism stands today at the center of a host of complex and sensitive pastoral questions: How may I, baptized as an infant and now an adult, have the actual "experience" of that baptismal event? Should I, as a parent, bring my infant children for baptism—or wait, so that they can make their own decision in the matter? Should my church admit non-baptized children to the Lord's Table? What is the role of sponsors or godparents in the baptismal rite, and afterward, and what relation must they have to the church? What is the role of baptism in relation to cultural identity, especially in situations of secularization and religious pluralism? These are questions that are on the agenda of many churches today, and that sometimes divide churches, not only from one another but also within themselves. For all these reasons a host of issues related to baptism call for study and clarification by the churches, both individually and ecumenically.

BAPTISM TODAY:
THE INTENTION AND ORGANIZATION OF THIS BOOK

Mindful of all these factors, *Baptism Today* offers a survey of the understanding and practice of baptism in a wide range of Christian churches and contexts today. The collection is guided by the conviction that the *understanding* and the *practice* of baptism are inseparable, that the rite itself and its meaning for both the believer and the Christian community can be understood only when the two are held together: the theology of baptism does not exist apart from its liturgical expression, and the liturgy shows forth the faith of the church.

My aims in gathering this material are several: 1) to provide information, presented by persons from the church or tradition concerned, on baptism as perceived and performed across the spectrum of Christian churches and contexts today; 2) to offer, wherever practicable, not only each church's account of baptism but also the (or a) baptismal liturgy in use in that church today; 3) to strengthen awareness of baptism as the foundation of our unity within the one body of Christ; 4) to encourage reflection on the relation between the various theological understandings of baptism, and the actual baptismal practices of the churches today; 5) to promote understanding among Christians of their own baptismal life, and that of other churches, as a contribution to the greater mutual recognition of baptism among the churches today; 6) to contribute to overcoming divisive differences in the baptismal understanding and practice of the churches today; and 7) thereby to promote the renewal of the churches in their common confession, worship, witness, and service today.

The book is organized in the following way. Section I, Commentaries, includes articles on baptism as understood and practiced today. These move from the ancient foundations, both East and West, through the churches of the Reformation and the Anglican tradition, through the historic free churches, to those founded in the nineteenth century and later, and embracing the spectrum from Eastern Orthodox to African Instituted Churches, not forgetting Quakers and Pentecostals on the way. The collection embraces not only the classic ecumenically engaged churches but also voices not so often heard in the ecumenical discussion.

Section II, Survey Articles, offers reflections on the collection as a whole by three seasoned liturgists representing Orthodox, Roman Catholic, and Protestant perspectives. The authors were asked to address, in the way they thought best, three broad areas of concern: 1) to identify lines of convergence—and continuing divergence—among the churches in respect to baptism today; 2) to suggest how churches might build on the mutual recognition of baptism (so far as it exists) to strengthen their common confession, worship, witness, and service; and 3) to suggest concrete steps which might help the churches overcome the remaining divisive differences in their perception and performance of baptism today. Thus the aim is not detailed analysis of the various commentaries and liturgical texts, but rather a review and analysis of the overall situation today with respect to baptism.

Section III, Signs of Recognition, presents three practical examples (each preceded by an introduction indicating its ecumenical and cultural context) of how churches are making visible their baptismal unity in Christ. The most recent, from Germany in 2007, is an official declaration by eleven churches at the national level of the mutual recognition of baptism. The second, from Australia in 1983, is a certificate of baptism which is recognized at the national level by ten churches. The third, from Massachusetts, USA, in 2000, identifies "points of baptismal practice" that can be affirmed by a wide range of churches. This text was agreed to at the state level by the member churches of the Massachusetts Commission on Christian Unity (now part of the

Massachusetts Council of Churches). Significantly, each text stresses the centrality of the use of water and the Trinitarian formula (the Massachusetts text allows for the possibility of other language being used in addition to—but not instead of—the traditional formula). Each text makes plain, in its own way, the fact that baptism is into the one body of Christ—and not into a particular part of it.

Section IV, Special Issues, explores the complex variety of challenges facing the churches in their baptismal practice and understanding in several very different cultural and religious contexts today. Authors from Sweden and India explore issues such as the relation of baptism and church membership to cultural identity and the meaning of baptism in an age marked by both radical secularization and lively religious pluralism.

Section V, Baptismal Services, concludes the book with a collection of services in use today in a wide variety of churches around the world. These have been supplied by the authors of the respective commentaries or other articles, to which they form an indispensable complement. (The sources of these services, as of the "Signs of Recognition" mentioned above, may be found in the acknowledgments at the end of this book.) Through these services one can enter more completely into the actual baptismal practice—and the baptismal understanding embodied in the practice—of the churches and confessions here represented. Not every author supplied a corresponding baptismal service, either because the church concerned does not have a set form of words for the service, or because the author felt that his or her commentary made the practice sufficiently clear. In the case of the Uniting Church in Australia, the author has incorporated the baptismal service into the commentary.

BEYOND *BAPTISM TODAY* . . .

In conclusion, it is important to stress that baptism has implications for many aspects of the life of the churches, and for the ecumenical movement, particularly in relation to the eucharist. Because baptism is the basis of our unity within the one body of Christ, baptism points beyond itself:[9] it yearns to be completed in the full eucharistic fellowship of all the members of Christ's body. Indeed, in discussions of baptism among laypersons, the most commonly asked question is: If we *do* have a common baptism, then why not a common eucharist? Thus the mutual recognition of baptism, and all work on baptism, calls the churches to renewed efforts toward full ecclesial communion, in order that the unity which is theirs in Christ through the waters of the one baptism may find its fulfillment at his one table.

Finally, it is my pleasure to thank each of the contributors to this volume for their engagement and their patience in seeing the project through to its conclusion. I would like to thank in particular Alexander Freeman for his work in preparing the manuscript for publication, as well as Katherine Pastukhova for her efforts in collecting the material, and Carolyn McComish for her work in the earlier stages of the process. Thanks are due also to the publications staff of the World Council of Churches and to the staff at Liturgical Press for their commitment to the project as well as to Brian Flanagan for his work in preparing the index. I offer thanks also to James Puglisi, SA, for his encouragement in this and many other matters over the years.

Notes

[1] See, for example, (embodying a long tradition): "1972: The Pullach Report" [Anglican–Lutheran], in *Growth in Agreement I: Reports and Agreed Statements of Ecumenical Conversations on a World Level, 1972–1982*, eds. Harding Meyer and Lukas Visher, Faith and Order paper No. 108 (Geneva: World Council of Churches, second printing, 2007), pars. 64–66, 22.

[2] "Baptism, therefore, establishes a sacramental bond of unity among all who through it are reborn": *Unitatis Redintegratio*, par. 22.

[3] Faith and Order Paper No. 111, 25th anniversary printing with added intro. (Geneva: WCC Publications, 1982; 2007), 1–7. For the churches' official responses to BEM see Max Thurian, ed., *Churches Respond to BEM: Official Responses to the "Baptism, Eucharist and Ministry" Text*, Vols. I–VI, Faith and Order Papers Nos. 129, 132, 135, 137, 143, 144 (Geneva: World Council of Churches, 1986–1988); and for Faith and Order's analysis of these responses see *Baptism, Eucharist & Ministry 1982–1990: Report on the Process and Responses*, Faith and Order Paper No. 149 (Geneva: WCC Publications, 1990).

[4] See Luis N. Rivera-Pagán, ed., *God, in Your Grace . . . : Official Report of the Ninth Assembly of the World Council of Churches* (Geneva: WCC Publications, 2007), pars. 8–9 and 14(c), 258 and 260. See also the current Faith and Order ecclesiology study document *The Nature and Mission of the Church: A Stage on the Way to a Common Statement*, Faith and Order Paper No. 198 (Geneva: World Council of Churches, 2005), pars. 74–77, 44–46.

[5] See the surveys of the treatment of baptism in the bilateral dialogues by André Birmelé, "Baptism in Ecumenical Dialogues," in *Dialogue between the Community of Protestant Churches in Europe (CPCE) and the European Baptist Federation (EBF) on the Doctrine and Practice of Baptism*, eds. Wilhelm Hüffmeier and Tony Peck, Leuenberg Documents 9 (Frankfurt am Main: Verlag Otto

Lembeck, 2005), 79–103, citation 79; and the previous version, "Baptism and the Unity of the Church in Ecumenical Dialogues," in *Baptism & the Unity of the Church*, eds. Michael Root and Risto Saarinen (Grand Rapids, MI, and Geneva: Wm. B. Eerdmans and WCC Publications, 1998), 104–29.

⁶ See *Eighth Report: Joint Working Group between the Roman Catholic Church and the World Council of Churches, Geneva-Rome, 2005* (WCC Publications: 2005), Appendix C, 45–72.

⁷ This text-in-progress, which is not yet an official text of the Faith and Order Commission, is available in *Minutes of the Standing Commission on Faith and Order, 12–19 June 2007, Crans-Montana, Switzerland*, Faith and Order Paper No. 206 (Geneva: Faith and Order, 2007), Appendix V, 57–81, or directly from Faith and Order, WCC, 150, Rte. de Ferney, 1211 Geneva, Switzerland. This text is especially sensitive to the liturgical dimensions of the rite of baptism. Some results from this study have already been incorporated in the Joint Working Group text; see, for example, "Ecclesiological and Ecumenical Implications of a Common Baptism: A JWG Study," pars. 52, 57.

⁸ The recent Anglican–Baptist bilateral dialogue has tackled this and related issues directly; see "Conversations around the World: Report of the International Conversations between the Anglican Communion and the Baptist World Alliance," in *Growth in Agreement III: International Dialogue Texts and Agreed Statements, 1998–2005*, eds. Jeffrey Gros, FSC, Thomas F. Best, and Lorelei F. Fuchs, SA, Faith and Order Paper No. 204 (Geneva: WCC Publications and Grand Rapids, MI: Wm. B. Eerdmans, 2007), pars. 40–52, 342–347.

⁹ This paragraph incorporates material from the Faith and Order text-in-progress, "One Baptism: Towards Mutual Recognition," par. 109, 81.

Part I

Commentaries

Chapter 1

Baptism: Sacrament of the Kingdom

Boris Bobrinskoy

INTRODUCTION

The very title of this essay indicates my concern to pay homage to the person of Father Alexander Schmemann on the twentieth anniversary of his death—twenty years during which the seed sown in the earth is not dead but has born abundant fruit. Father Alexander was, and remains, a witness to the kingdom of God. He was such throughout his entire life and in all of his work, from his youth through his death and well beyond the limits of his earthly life.

To Father Schmemann's mind, the kingdom of God is manifested and inaugurated in the Church. The Church is the very epiphany of the kingdom, as he so liked to say, and it is such at every moment of its existence, through its various sacramental, hierarchical, liturgical, pastoral, and doctrinal structures. He believed firmly that the Church both proclaims and reveals the kingdom of God despite the deficiencies of its members and of the ecclesial institution itself. Nevertheless, Father Alexander rejected every form of confessional or ecclesiastical triumphalism. He never hesitated to characterize Orthodoxy as being in a state of crisis with regard to the exercise of conciliarity and collegiality, as well as with regard to eucharistic understanding and practice and the general way in which the sacraments are celebrated.

This brings us to our subject of baptism as sacrament of the kingdom. First of all, I would like to offer several quotations from Father Alexander's study on baptism titled *Of Water and the Spirit*. The introductory chapter of this work invites the reader "To Rediscover Baptism." This title is significant in that it reveals Father Alexander's acute awareness of the fact that there is a veritable "absence" of baptism in our lives: "[T]o put it very simply," he asserts:

> Baptism is *absent* from our life. It is, to be sure, still accepted by all as a self-evident necessity. It is not opposed, not even questioned. It is

performed all the time in our churches. It is, in other terms, "taken for granted." Yet, in spite of all this, I dare to affirm that in a very real sense it is absent, and this "absence" is at the root of many tragedies of the Church today.[1]

Father Alexander continues by showing that baptism is absent from the ecclesial liturgy of the community as a whole, in that it "has become a private family celebration performed as a rule outside the corporate worship of the Church, precisely outside its *leitourgia*." "Is it not true," he asks, "that one can be a regular church-goer for years and years without having attended one Baptism, without even knowing how it is performed?"

Yet he goes still further in his critique:

> Being thus absent from liturgy, Baptism then is naturally absent from our *piety*. . . . [T]oday's Christian does not relate either himself or the Church to Baptism. He knows, of course, that he was baptized and that Baptism is a necessary condition for his membership in the Church. But this knowledge remains abstract. It is not referred to the Church as the very community of those who died with Christ and who therefore were given a new life in Him. . . . Finally, having ceased to feed Christian piety, Baptism obviously has lost its power to shape our Christian worldview. . . . A Christian of the past knew not only intellectually but with his entire being that through Baptism he was placed into a radically new relationship with all aspects of life and with the "world" itself; that he received, along with his faith, a radically new understanding of life. Baptism for him was the starting point and also the foundation of a Christian "philosophy of life," of a permanent sense of direction guiding him firmly throughout his entire existence, supplying answers to all questions, solving all problems.

"This foundation," he adds, "is still here with us. Baptism is performed. But it has ceased to be comprehended as the door leading into a new life and as the power to fight for this new life's preservation and growth in us." These passages are exceptionally important, even decisive, in leading toward an authentic "rediscovery" of Christian baptism as participation in the paschal mystery, which is the essence of life within the Church.

THEOLOGICAL PRINCIPLES IN REGARD TO BAPTISM

I would like to take these words of Father Alexander as a point of departure for the remarks I want to make here. Rather than limit myself to purely practical considerations, I would like as well to recall several fundamental theological principles concerning the Trinitarian and ecclesiastical nature of all sacramental life, particularly in regard to baptism.

Basing its reflection on the insights of Father Georges Florovsky, modern Orthodox theology stresses just how much the Church is torn between the two fundamental dimensions of its life, both of which are eschatological. On the one hand, the Church is *in statu viae*, that is, engaged in a continual pilgrimage toward the kingdom of God. On the other hand, it is *in statu patriae*, that is, the Church both inaugurates and manifests in the here and now the Trinitarian kingdom to come. The tension between these two states of the Church's being is fruitful. But that fruitfulness is purchased at the price of a great deal of suffering, because throughout its history the Church is weighed down by the limitations and deficiencies of its members, to the detriment of its witness within the world.

As a "sacrament of the kingdom" the Church is, above all, the locus of Trinitarian communion, revealed and communicated within the divine economy. We owe it especially to St. Basil of Caesarea, following St. Irenaeus, to have shown the importance of the idea of *koinonia* regarding both the inner life of the Godhead and God's presence and activity in the world. On the one hand, *koinonia* expresses the full unity of nature and honor that the Spirit shares with the Father and the Son in the domain of inner-Trinitarian life itself, what is frequently referred to as the "immanent Trinity" or Trinity *ad intra*. On the other hand, *koinonia* refers to the life of human persons renewed by the grace of the Holy Spirit in the sacramental life of the Church. Thus the "communion of the Holy Spirit" stands as a central theme of St. Basil's pneumatology of salvation in the specific sense of the *gift* of the Spirit. As Basil declares, "The Holy Spirit shares with the Father and the Son the communion [*koinonia*] of nature and communion in all things, a union which is unbreakable, proper [to divine life], natural and inseparable."[2]

In the divine economy by which the faithful become sanctified, this same Spirit, Basil says, "renders [us] spiritual through communion with Himself, reintroduces us into Paradise, leads us to the kingdom of heaven and to adoption as children of God, grants us the confidence to address God as 'Father,' to share [*koinonein*] in the grace of Christ, to be called a child of light, and to have a share in eternal glory."[3]

It is significant that the same term, "communion," can express both the ineffable mystery of the unity of the Trinitarian hypostases and indicate as well the pathway of divine condescension toward the human creature who is called to participate in divine life. St. Basil reminds us that this Trinitarian communion is above all a gift of the Spirit, in whom and by whom we unite ourselves to Christ—Christ through whom we receive the gift of divine sonship. "Under the influence of the illuminating power of the Spirit," Basil affirms, "we set our eyes on the beauty of the divine Image of the invisible God (that is, the Son of God), and thereby we are raised to the radiant vision of the Archetype (God the Father)."[4]

ECCLESIAL AND EUCHARISTIC COMMUNION

It is important, in this regard, to note the multiple and entirely complementary dimensions of ecclesial and eucharistic communion.

1. *Communion in the Body of Christ.*

Underlying this theme is the Pauline theology of the Church as Body of Christ, the Church of which we are members and Christ is the Head. The entire economy of salvation is included in this theme. In the eucharistic celebration, the Church "remembers" and thereby renders present the entire work of salvation until the glorious Second Coming of Christ.

2. *Communion in the Holy Spirit*

The same Spirit who from all eternity proceeds from the Father and rests upon the Son is sent by the Father and the Son to rest (*menein*) upon the Body of Christ, of which we are the members, in order to confer upon us filial adoption and to lead us to "theosis" or deification.

3. *Communion in Christ in a Relation at Once Fraternal and Nuptial*

That is, Christ introduces us into a personal relationship with himself. "Listen! I am standing at the door, knocking" (Rev 3:20). The intimacy of that relation is such that the apostle does not hesitate to affirm, "It is no longer I who live, but it is Christ who lives in me" (Gal 2:20).

4. *Ecclesial Communion within the Unity that Marks Every Dimension of the Church's Life*

Ecclesial communion belongs within the unity of the Church's life, particularly of the Church celestial or triumphant. The expression "real presence" of Christ is very often understood in a way that is too limited, focusing on a "personal" Christ. This notion needs to be extended as well to the entire ecclesial body. For within the eucharistic mystery the entire assembly of the saints is present.

5. Communion in the Entire Ecclesial Assembly

Here we touch upon the very heart of our subject. We shall see that baptismal initiation introduces us into every aspect of ecclesial communion, including the conscience of the Church and its faith, which we confess from liturgy to liturgy.

6. Ecclesial Communion Both Open and Closed

Our communion in the Church is, on the one hand, "closed," reserved to those who have been initiated into the faith. On the other hand, it is open insofar as it constitutes the "sacrament of the brother" (according to the expression of St. John Chrysostom). This latter aspect includes compassion for the poor beyond every boundary, since the redeeming sacrifice of Christ rendered present through every eucharistic celebration is offered "for the life of the world" (John 6:51).

BAPTISM, NEW LIFE IN CHRIST, AND THE CHURCH

Fundamental to our faith is the fact that our life in and through Christ—our existence within the life of the Holy Trinity—is an actual incorporation into Christ's death and resurrection. The entire sacramental and liturgical life of the Church enables us to participate in his redemptive Pascha. This is a possibility offered to us from our birth until our death, that is, until our ultimate Pascha. The various stages of our human life are assumed under the direction of the Church by means of the sacraments, by which the light of the kingdom penetrates into the sphere of our human, earthly existence.

At this point I would like to underscore the centrality of the mysteries of baptismal initiation, chrismation, and Eucharist. Together, these three constitute a unique and permanent foundation of new birth in the Spirit. Yet the three are also permanent elements of the entire Christian life. (I shall come back to the importance of the permanent, essential link that unites these three sacramental acts.)

Trinitarian faith introduces the catechumen into the ecclesial community. It creates, renews, and perpetuates the Church, since the Trinity reveals itself precisely in and through the Church. Conversely, it is in the Trinity that the Church finds its source and ground, that it lives, moves, and has its being (cf. Acts 17:28). Orthodox theology is highly sensitive to the "Trinitarian ontology" of the Church: the fact that the Church lives in the image of the Trinity, and that the same love which reveals the ineffable and eternal being of God constitutes the ultimate mystery of the Church. The Eucharist thus represents the advent of the kingdom of the Father, Son, and Holy Spirit, into which we have access through Trinitarian baptism. But the Eucharist also represents the locus where the Church reveals and renews itself. Baptism, then, is both the gift of new life in the Spirit, the source of Trinitarian grace, and the entryway into the Church, where the sacrament of initiation is fulfilled.[5]

Allow me for a moment to focus more specifically on the permanent dimension of baptism in the whole of Christian life: that of the individual believer but also within the entire ecclesial Body. Some years ago the Reverend Father Camelot, one of the foremost initiators of liturgical renewal in France, devoted an entire work to what he called *The Spirituality of Baptism*.[6] He very rightly reminded us that "baptism is the symbol and the anticipation of all that should constitute every spiritual life: throughout his spiritual pilgrimage in this life, the Christian is called to do nothing other than to develop and actualize the potential he has been given in baptism, 'the entryway into spiritual life.'"[7]

With Father Camelot, we can affirm that baptism is truly the "source of every spiritual life." It is enough to read through the rituals of baptismal initiation to discover in them the basic, permanent structures of "the life in Christ." These include the repeated renunciation of Satan and all his works; the several affirmations of "belonging to Christ"; the immersion into Christ's death and rising up in his resurrection; the "putting on" of Christ by vesting with the baptismal garment; the seal of the Spirit through chrismation, which confers on the newly baptized the charism of "royal priesthood"; and finally, the eschatological fruit of baptismal initiation, which is communion in the Holy Eucharist, the sacrament and manifestation of the kingdom of God.

Baptism also inaugurates for the Christian, as for the entire ecclesial community, a time of spiritual warfare. In this struggle against the principalities and powers, the paschal victory in Christ comes not only at the end of our earthly sojourn. It is already given from the very beginning. The Christian is called, therefore, to preserve the purity of the baptismal garment and to renew that purity again and again in the blood of the Lamb.

From the very beginning, baptism has been experienced as an event of the Church, one that concerns and involves the entire eucharistic community. Both the *Didache* and St. Justin Martyr bear witness to the participation of the Christian assembly in the preparation and unfolding of the baptismal rite. Similarly, the *Apostolic Tradition* of Hippolytus of Rome attests to the fact that baptismal initiation finds its fulfillment in eucharistic communion.[8] Finally, St. John Chrysostom exhorts the newly baptized to concern themselves with every aspect of Church life: "Don't be satisfied," he says, "with the fact that you are well yourself, and that you have been liberated from evil. Take care and concern yourself as well with the well-being of those who are members of the same Body as you are, that they too might avoid the ravages of evil. For we are members of one another."[9]

ASPECTS OF THE BAPTISMAL RITE

Let us consider now in more detail the essential aspects of the baptismal rite.

1. The Rejection of Satan

The struggle and rejection of Satanic seductions is the daily affair of the entire Church. When the celebrant asks the catechumen, "Do you renounce Satan?" he questions not only the catechumen and his or her sponsors. The entire ecclesial community renews its baptismal commitment and reaffirms its willingness to struggle in the name of Christ.

2. Commitment to Faith: The Creed

The same thing must be said for the commitment of faithfulness to Christ the Lord, affirmed in the reading of the Nicene Creed, our "symbol of faith." In this regard, it is necessary to stress that the ecclesiological perspective of the Creed is threefold, a point that has fundamental significance for our theme.

   a. In the first place, the Creed or Confession of Faith is that *of the Church* in its entirety. The catechumen professes that faith and makes it his or her own. This confession is then literally taken up again in the anaphora of the eucharistic liturgy—and it is proclaimed by the entire Church.[10]

   b. This confession of faith is also fulfilled *within the Church*, which is the locus, the "sacred space" of the Spirit, in which the newly baptized are reborn to new life and to Trinitarian faith.

   c. Finally, the baptismal confession is a confession of faith *about the Church*: expressed not only in the ecclesiological article dealing with the Church as such but also in the entire Creed, which affirms that the mystery of the Church is coextensive with the Trinitarian economy of salvation.

3. Signification of Death and Resurrection

Baptismal immersion signifies the very real death of the Old Adam and his resurrection in Christ, the New Adam. In the paschal mystery and in his ascension, Christ recapitulates sinful humanity in its entirety; then he gathers that humanity in his own Body, risen from the dead and seated at the right hand of the Father. "And I, when I am lifted up from the earth," Jesus declares, "will draw all people to myself" (John 12:32). This notion brings into play the entire theology of Augustine and Chrysostom concerning *Christus totus*, the "whole Christ," with all of its ecclesial dimensions worked out so well by Georges Florovsky and his disciple, Metropolitan John Zizioulas.

4. The Marriage of the Church to Christ

The nuptial Covenant of the newly baptized person with the divine Bridegroom, symbolized by the triple procession around the baptismal font, is wholly integrated into the mystery of the spiritual "marriage" of the entire Church to Christ. That mystery is recalled and reactualized by every baptismal celebration.

5. Chrismation, the Seal of the Spirit

The chrismation with Holy Unction—the "seal of the Spirit"—should never be dissociated from baptism: neither in liturgical action nor in theological meaning. From the most ancient times, chrismation always stood as an integral part of the sacrament of baptismal initiation. Chrismation serves as the fulfillment and provides the fullness—the very "confirmation"—of baptism. We should point out that the Syriac tradition of the Church in Antioch, represented especially by St. John Chrysostom, knew of no such "post-baptismal" unction even at the end of the fourth century. Nonetheless, that does not at all diminish the Church's consciousness of the perfective or fulfilling action of the Holy Spirit. The Syriac tradition underscores all the more the *prior* action of the Spirit, who sanctifies the baptismal waters and renders the candidate capable of renouncing Satanic powers and confessing Christ as Lord.

The Spirit sanctifies the entire pathway of the baptized Christians, from their most secret inner conversion, through their entire conscious ecclesial commitment, through their death and resurrection "in water and the Spirit," through their growth in eucharistic communion at the chalice of "fire and the Spirit," to culminate in the "fruits of the Spirit," which are a foretaste of the fullness of the kingdom.[11]

6. The Culmination of Baptism: the Eucharist

Baptism finally culminates in the Eucharist, from which it is theologically inseparable. Perhaps I should have begun these reflections by recalling the principles of eucharistic ecclesiology and the centrality of the Eucharist as a true fulfillment of all ecclesial sacramentality. Then I could have proceeded backwards, as it were, to show that the pathway of Christian initiation leads necessarily to its culmination, its ultimate truth. But conversely, it is necessary to insist with just as much force that the baptismal aspect is inherent in every Eucharist, since baptism is indeed the indispensable, permanent, and unique entryway into the nuptial chamber of the eucharistic banquet.

THE ROLE OF GODPARENTS

It would be appropriate at this point to say a few words about the indispensable and many-faceted role of *godparents*.

1. First of all, the godparents represent the entire eucharistic community, for whom they assume responsibility for the authenticity of the commitment assumed by the one to be baptized.

2. I would add to that the fact that in reality it is the entire ecclesial community who supports the newly baptized and speaks both for and with him or her.

3. Yet the ecclesial community not only supports the newly baptized in his or her struggle to continually renounce Satan and reaffirm faithfulness to Christ as Lord. It also relives and, as a body, reactualizes the baptism of each of its members. The entire body of the faithful present at the baptismal ceremony should lift its voice to reaffirm the commitment of each member to Christ. This is the very meaning of the baptismal confession of faith taken up by the community as a whole during the eucharistic celebration.

4. Finally, when it is a matter of the baptism of children, the godparents' role is not only to represent the entire Church. It is also to be the spokespersons for those who cannot yet speak, yet who are mysteriously reborn into a newness of life by the power of the Holy Spirit.

BAPTISM AND THE EUCHARIST:
AN ISSUE IN LITURGICAL PRACTICE TODAY

Given the present circumstances of Orthodoxy, it is not possible to return directly, insistently, and regularly to the ancient practice of baptism celebrated during the course of the eucharistic liturgy. This is for several reasons:

1. First, because there is an enormous amount of reeducation that must be done, not only of the people of God but also of our pastors themselves regarding the enduring, ecclesial meaning of the baptismal liturgy.

2. Then again, introducing the sacraments of initiation into the framework of the eucharistic liturgy can only occur in those communities that are truly prepared, where there is a profound consciousness of the communal reality of the eucharist. In very large churches it is difficult to develop this consciousness. Moreover, too great a number of baptisms within the Divine Liturgy would seriously compromise the "normal" celebration of the Sunday Eucharist.

3. I am very pleased to see the deep convergence and unity in eucharistic baptismal practice among churches on the American continent as well as in certain parishes in France and England. The schema suggested by Father Alexander at the end of his book on baptismal initiation corresponds directly with the practice in my parish. This practice is spreading like oil on water to influence quite a number of Orthodox communities in the West. I can add that I reported on our practice at the last pastoral assembly of the clergy of our diocese in June 2002, where our bishops were present. In fact, for more than thirty years our bishops have given us their blessing to maintain this practice, which by now has become quite customary.

4. Finally, I can mention a directive of Patriarch Alexis II of Moscow, dated November 18, 1993, in which he encourages the sacramental practice which places the baptismal service in the context of the Eucharist. It should be noted, however, that there are a certain number of differences between their practice and ours concerning the larger integration of baptism and chrismation into the eucharistic liturgy.[12]

5. Father Alexander was insistent that prudence and collegial reflection be exercised in this regard, particularly in relation to our hierarchs. He states:

The only adequate solution consists . . . in reinstating *baptismal liturgies*, i.e., the celebration of Baptism before the Divine Liturgy yet in organic liturgical connection with it. How to achieve this must be the object of careful study, discussion and ultimately approval by the hierarchy, without whose sanction, permission and blessing, nothing ought to be done in the Church. Therefore, [my] suggestions are made tentatively, as a starting point of a much needed liturgical and pastoral discussion.[13]

CONCLUSION

Whatever our efforts to rediscover in liturgical practice the ecclesial meaning of baptism—and of all sacramental life—we can only conclude by recalling again the words of Father Alexander:

Obviously none of these "recoveries"—the theological, the liturgical, the spiritual—can be instantaneous, the fruit of merely external reforms and "adjustments." We need much patient study, much pastoral concern, and much love. And above all we need a deepening of our Church consciousness, of the very *mind* of the Church, truly a thirst and hunger for "living water." But I am absolutely convinced that such recovery is not only desirable and possible, but that indeed only in it, only by a common "rediscovery" of the true meaning of Baptism, of its fullness, beauty, power and joy, can we again make our faith "the victory that conquers the world" (1 John 5:4).[14]

Notes

[1] The following quotes from Father Alexander's work are found in: Alexander Schmemann, *Of Water and the Spirit. A Liturgical Study of Baptism* (New York: St Vladimir's Seminary Press, 1974), 8–10.

[2] St. Basil, *Treatise on the Holy Spirit*, 13.30; 24.55; 26.63.

[3] Ibid., 9.23; 15.36.

[4] Ibid., 18.47.

[5] See B. Bobrinskoy, "Le mystère pascal du baptême" (Paris, 1971), 128–129; reprinted in *Communion du Saint-Esprit* (Abbaye de Belfontaine, coll. "Spiritualité Orientale," no. 56, 1992): 103–60.

[6] *La spiritualité du baptême*, 2e éd. (Paris: Les Editions du Cerf, 1993).

[7] Ibid., 11.

[8] *AT* 21.

[9] Baptismal Catechism, 5.14.

[10] See B. Bobrinskoy, "La Liturgie, expression de la foi," in *Communion du Saint-Esprit*, 193–203.

[11] See B. Bobrinskoy, "Onction baptismale et Trinité dans la tradition syrienne," in *Communion du Saint-Esprit*, 161–92.

[12] In Russia the catechumenate is performed during or before the *proskomedia*, and the celebrating priest pronounces the opening benediction, "Blessed is the Kingdom . . . ," in front of the altar table.

The deacon chants the Great Litany of the liturgy of the catechumens in front of the baptismal font, and this is followed by the petitions of the baptismal ritual. The priest at this time says silently the prayer of the first antiphon, which is then sung by the choir. Then comes the great prayer for the blessing of the water. The second antiphon follows, with the hymn "Only Begotten Son," and this is followed by the blessing of oil and the pre-baptismal anointing. Then the Beatitudes are sung.

The priest enters the sanctuary and completes the Lesser Entrance. After the singing of the *troparia* there follows the baptismal immersion and clothing of the newly baptized in the white garment. Then come the prayer and unction of chrismation. The priest utters the *ekphonesis*, "For You are holy, O our God . . . ," and the deacon, from the *ambon*, completes it with "and unto ages of ages."

Then follows the triple procession around the baptismal font, with the singing of "As many as have been baptized into Christ. . . ." This is followed by the *prokeimeon*, then the epistle and the gospel of baptism. After the supplication litany, the deacon adds the petitions of the baptismal litany. The litany of the catechumens is omitted.

Following the communion of the clergy, there comes the "churching" of the newly baptized and his or her communion. At the close of the service, after the dismissal, the priest reads the prayers of the eighth day and completes the ablutions and the tonsuring.

[13] Alexander Schmemann, *Of Water and the Spirit*, 169.

[14] Ibid., 154.

Chapter 2

The Sacrament of Holy Baptism in the Armenian Apostolic Church

Mesrob Tashjian

HISTORICAL AND THEOLOGICAL BACKGROUND

During the first three centuries of Christianity, in Armenia the Scriptures had to be read in Syriac and Greek due to the lack of an Armenian alphabet. It was only after this was invented (in AD 404–406), that the Armenian Church Fathers translated the Holy Scriptures into Armenian from the Greek Septuagint. The indisputable accuracy and beauty of the translation into classical Armenian urged Professor Henry S. Gehman at Princeton to say, "The Armenian language is so well adapted to render the Greek literally that an Armenian codex has almost the same value for the critic as the Greek original on which it is based."[1]

New horizons opened up before the translators, who were skillful theologians careful to reproduce the slightest details of the original; they respect its meaning rather than its form. With the same penetration and mastery, the Armenian church fathers translated the valuable works of the early church fathers, including their liturgies and among them the Liturgy of Baptism. The Armenian church fathers were also familiar with the Didache, or Teaching of the Apostles, which is the earliest description of baptism that we have outside the New Testament.

The central theme of the Armenian catechism attributed to St. Gregory is salvation. St. Gregory says in his commentary on the baptism of Christ, "Then [Christ] came and was Himself baptized by John; undertaking to write an eternal covenant and sealing it with his own blood [cf. Heb 13:20], to give life to all by the illuminating and life-giving baptism, He ordered all men born from the earth, all humans, to imitate the divine image of salvation."[2] The Armenian Church teaches her faithful that the only way to be united with Christ (Gal 3:27) and to enter into the kingdom of God is to be born anew of the Spirit (John 3:5). Baptism brings the baptized person into relationship with the once-for-all saving act of God in Christ. Through faith and baptism all those who are baptized will share in what happened to Christ and in what he has achieved for us.

THE PROCESS OF BAPTISM

According to the ritual of the Armenian Church, the baptismal process goes through the following stations:

1. *The Preparation of the Catechumen*

We open the ceremony with the Lord's Prayer followed by the reading of Psalm 51, which implores God to have mercy upon us, blot out our transgressions, wash us thoroughly from our iniquity, and cleanse us from our sins. A hymn dedicated to the Holy Spirit is sung: "The indivisible Trinity and the power shone forth as a light upon the world; let us praise Him with song." In the following prayer the priest beseeches God to have mercy on the catechumen, to expel and keep away the thoughts, words, and deeds, and all deceptions of the evil one who is accustomed to deceive human beings and make them perish: "Fill this child with your heavenly grace and grant him or her the joy to be named a Christian and make him or her worthy of baptism of the second birth of the holy Font." Then the godfather, holding the child in his arms, will bow three times, saying: "Upon thee was I cast from my birth, and since my mother bore me thou have been my God."

In the Armenian Church baptism has nothing to do with age. Each person, regardless of his or her age, is the child of God. Following the apostles' instructions and examples, the Church of Armenia adopted the baptism of infants. Saint Cyprian (d. 258) says: "Let baptism be confessed as early as possible, not even waiting the customary eight days."[3] His reason was that infants, although without sin, nonetheless bear the sin of Adam. Origen (185–254), the great Alexandrian school theologian and homilist, justifies infant baptism theologically because of the fall of humankind in Adam in his *Homilies on St. Luke*. No mature person should be forced to be baptized against his will; in the case of an infant's baptism, the parents are simply obeying the command of Christ Jesus.

What is the role and function of the godfather in the baptismal service and afterward? The godfather is the spiritual parent of the child. He should be responsible for his or her Christian education. He should know the teachings of the Church and teach the same to his godchildren. For our church, only a male person may be a godfather; he should of course be an adult and not a child. For baptism there should be only one godfather. A person who is not baptized cannot become a godfather; in case of adult baptism, a person cannot become the godfather of his fiancée or wife. The Armenian Church forbids the marriage of a godfather with his goddaughter. Parents cannot become godparents of their children. The godmother plays the role of assisting the godfather in undressing and dressing the child but, as noted, cannot assume the role of the godfather.

2. The Renunciation of Satan and Confession of the Faith

At this point everyone at the church is asked to turn to the west for the renunciation from Satan, which will be said thrice by the godfather while holding the baby in his arms: "We renounce Satan and his every deceit, his wiles, his deliberations, his course, his evil will, his evil angels, his evil ministers, his evil agents, and his every power renouncing, we renounce." Then turning to the east, the priest shall say: "We turn to the light of the knowledge of God." Then the Confession of Faith will be recited in the following way:

> We believe in the all-holy Trinity, in the Father, and in the Son, and in the Holy Spirit. We believe in the annunciation of Gabriel, in the Nativity of Christ, in His Baptism, in His Passion, in His Crucifixion, in His three days burial, in His Resurrection, in His Ascension, in His sitting at the right hand of the Father and His awesome and glorious Second Coming. We confess and we believe.

A gospel passage will be then read (Matt 28:16-20), to be followed by a hymn.

3. The Consecration of the Water

Now the priest, while pouring water into the font crosswise, recites Psalm 29:3-4. Before the consecration the Armenian Church has the following biblical readings: a passage from the prophet Ezekiel (36:25-28), a reading from the Epistle of St. Paul to the Galatians (3:24-29), and the Gospel of Jesus Christ according to John (3:1-8). Following the chanting of the gospel, the priest says the prayer over the water:

> Lord, our God Jesus Christ, you who are the holiest and exempt from every sin, we beseech you, send your Holy Spirit to this water and

cleanse it as you have done to the waters of river Jordan by your descent in it, setting that as an example to this baptismal Font of rebirth of all mankind. Grant through this water, where he/she is being baptized now, the forgiveness of sins and the acceptance of the Holy Spirit, so that he/she may be adopted by your heavenly Father and inherit the kingdom of heavens. Thus, being cleansed from all sins, he/she might live according to your inexhaustible blessings with all your saints, joyfully giving thanks and always praising you, with the Father, and the Holy Spirit now and always, and forever and ever. Amen.

At this point the godfather takes the baby to be undressed. Undressing signifies the putting off of the old nature with its practices, and the putting on of the new nature, which is being renewed in knowledge after the image of its Creator (Col 3:9-10). After chanting "Amen. Alleluia, alleluia, alleluia," the priest takes the container of the Holy Muron (chrism) and, making the sign of the cross over the water, chants: "May this water be blessed and sanctified by the sign of the Holy Cross, and by the Holy Gospel, and by the Holy Muron, and by the grace of this day, in the name of the Father, and of the Son, and of the Holy Spirit, now and always and forever and ever. Amen" (repeated 3 times).

Then the priest, while pouring the Holy Muron crosswise in the water, sings the hymn dedicated to the descent of the Holy Spirit on the day of Pentecost. The Holy Muron, which is prepared from forty-three different fragrant flowers, is blessed by Catholicoses only once every seven years and generally on the feast of Pentecost. The use of the flowers signifies that the child should become a good "odor" of Christ, spreading the fragrance of the knowledge of faith everywhere as a perfume diffuses its sweetness (2 Cor 2:14).

Now that the water is blessed and the Holy Muron poured, thus symbolizing the descent of the Holy Spirit, the Priest says the following prayer:

> We beseech you, O Lord, to call this your servant to the purification and enlightenment of the baptism. We beseech you, O Lord, to make this your servant worthy of your most precious grace. Cleanse him/her from old sins and renew him/her in a new life. Fill this child with the power of the Holy Spirit so that he/she may have the renewal of the glory of your Christ. And to you the Mighty One, and to your Only Begotten Son, and to the liberating Holy Spirit is befitting dominion and honor, now and always and forever and ever. Amen.

At this point the godfather, who as noted above is the spiritual parent, professes the faith of the infant when asked by the priest: "What is the request of this child?" The godfather replies: "Faith, hope, love and baptism. To be baptized and justified; to be cleansed of sins; to be freed from demons and to serve God" (repeated three times). Then the priest shall say: "Be it onto you according to your faith."

4. The Mode of Baptism in the Armenian Church

In the Armenian Church the mode of baptism is threefold immersion, signifying the three days of Jesus' burial. This custom is based on the teaching of St. Paul, as explained in the Epistle to the Romans (6:3-4). Tertullian (160–220), one of the greatest theologians of the Western Church, speaks in his treatise on baptism about the renunciation of Satan, the blessing of water with the Holy Spirit, the threefold immersion, and the anointing with oil. As does Cyril of Jerusalem (315–386), St. Gregory the Illuminator (239–325/6) strongly affirms the central role of the doctrine of salvation in the sacrament of baptism. According to St. Gregory, the catechumens who have been enrolled have become "the sons and the daughters" of one mother, the Church. He celebrates the greatness of baptism that is offered to them, that is, the ransom for captives, the remission of offense, the death of sin, and the generation of the soul.

Hence in the Armenian Church the priest immerses the infant three times in the water, saying, "(Name), the servant of God, coming from the state of catechumen to baptism, is now being baptized in the Name of the Father, and of the Son, and of the Holy Spirit. Redeemed by the Blood of Christ from the servitude of sin, he/she becomes an adopted child of the heavenly Father, a co-heir with Christ and a temple of the Holy Spirit."

And then, taking the child out of the font, the priest says, "Once you have been enlightened to Christ, you have put on Christ. Alleluia. Once you have been enlightened in the Father, the Holy Spirit shall rejoice in you. Alleluia. Glory be to the Father, to the Son and to the Holy Spirit, now and always and forever and ever. Amen."

5. The Sacrament of Holy Confirmation

Confirmation is closely related to the theology of baptism. A few outstanding Church Fathers have written treatises on baptism, expressing the same fundamental views about the rite. In the Eastern tradition there are St. Cyril of Jerusalem (315–386) and St. Ephraim

(306–373); in the Western tradition, Tertullian (160–220) and St. Ambrose of Milan (339–397). All four fathers in their writings on baptism have agreed that there should be the renunciation from Satan and his works; the blessing of the water; baptism by triple immersion; and anointing with oil or chrism. For these fathers, faith and baptism are truly inextricable. In the Armenian Church the sacrament of confirmation completes the sacrament of baptism through anointing the newly baptized with the Holy Muron (chrism), symbolizing the Holy Spirit. Thus, while baptism gives spiritual birth to the catechumen who becomes the adopted child of God, the anointing with oil or chrism (confirmation) gives strength, courage, and the presence and grace of the Holy Spirit, enabling the baptized person to develop the virtues that have been promised to him or her.

Thus after the baptism the priest pours Holy Muron in his palm and begins anointing, crosswise with his thumb, the nine parts of the baptized person's body, saying:

> For the Forehead: "This sweet oil, which is poured upon your forehead in the name of Jesus Christ, be a seal of incorruptible heavenly gifts."
>
> For the Eyes: "May this seal in the name of Jesus Christ enlighten your eyes, so that you may never sleep onto death."
>
> For the Ears: "May with this holy ointment you hear the divine commandments of God."
>
> For the Nostrils: "May this seal in the name of Jesus Christ be to you sweet smell from life to life."
>
> For the Mouth: "May this seal in the name of Jesus Christ guard your mouth and be a strong door for your lips."
>
> For the Hands: "May this seal in the name of Jesus Christ be a cause for benevolence and for all-virtuous deeds and behavior."
>
> For the Heart: "May this divine seal cleanse your heart and establish an upright spirit within you."
>
> For the Back: "May this seal in the name of Jesus Christ be for you a shield of strength."
>
> For the Feet: "May this divine seal direct your journey towards eternal life so that you may not be shaken."
>
> Then the Priest says: "Peace unto you, O saved one of God. Peace unto you, O anointed one of God."

6. The Presentation of the Neophyte to the Main Altar

Reciting Psalm 43, the priest takes the neophyte to the main altar, saying three times: "(Name), servant of Christ, coming from the state of catechumen to baptism, and from baptism to worship, now worships before this holy Table, before this holy Altar and before this holy Font, for he/she has renounced iniquity and has put on the light of the knowledge of God" (repeated 3 times).

7. The Administration of the Holy Eucharist

In the Holy Eucharist the neophyte receives spiritual nourishment, the Body and Blood of our Lord Jesus Christ. In the history of the Christian Church it has been a widespread custom that baptism, confirmation, and Eucharist (communion) are administered one after the other. The three sacraments together form an integral ceremony initiating a new birth in Christ, sanctifying the soul with the gifts of the Holy Spirit, and, finally, making the baptized neophyte a shrine of Christ's presence and a temple of the Holy Spirit. In its own baptismal understanding and practice, the Armenian Apostolic Church has remained faithful to the tradition of the early Church.

Notes

[1] Henry S. Gehman with F. G. Kenyon, "Greek Versions of the OT," in *Hastings Dictionary of the Bible*, 2nd ed., rev. by Frederick C. Grant and H. H. Rowley (Edinburgh: T and T Clark, 1963), 352.

[2] Agat' angeghos, *The Teaching of St. Gregory: An Early Armenian Catechism*, trans. and commentary by Robert W. Thomson, Harvard Armenian Texts and Studies 3 (Cambridge, MA: Harvard University Press, 1970), section 410, 88.

[3] *The Letters of Cyprian of Carthage, translated and annotated by G. W. Clarke*, vol. 3, letters 55–66 (New York: Newman Press, 1986), letter 64, esp. section 2.1, p. 110.

Chapter 3

The Baptismal Liturgy of the Malankara Orthodox Syrian Church

Jacob Kurien

The Malankara Orthodox Syrian Church, one of the oriental Orthodox Churches, follows in general the west-Syrian liturgical tradition. There are at least three phases in the history of liturgical development of the Malankara Orthodox Church: the early phase of indigenous liturgical forms until the sixth century; the middle phase of east-Syrian or Chaldean liturgical influences; and the present phase of adoptions from the west-Syrian or Antiochene liturgical tradition from the seventeenth century.

LITURGICAL, THEOLOGICAL, AND ECCLESIOLOGICAL SIGNIFICANCE

Among the adoptions from the west-Syrian or Antiochene liturgical tradition, the baptismal liturgy is one of the earliest. The current baptismal liturgy is believed to have been written originally by Severus of Antioch (d. 538) in the Greek language, which was translated to Syriac by Jacob of Edessa (d. 708). This was further modified and fixed in the present form by Bar Hebrews, who is also known as Gregorios Abul Farag, in the thirteenth century.

The current text of the baptismal liturgy has eight parts:

1. Preparation, including Scriptural Instructions
2. Exorcism
3. Faith Proclamation
4. Anointing with the Oil of Gladness
5. Immersion in Water Mixed with Chrism (Myron)
6. Anointing with Chrism (Myron)
7. Entry to the Sanctuary and Crowning
8. Benediction and Dismissal

There is no separate prayer or indication in the text of the baptismal liturgy regarding the administration of Holy Communion to the newly baptized. However, there is a verse in the hymn of entry to the sanctuary that hints at the giving of "the fruit of life" to the mouth of the baptized. This could very well imply that Holy Communion was originally considered not as a part of the baptismal text, but rather that the baptismal liturgy as a whole was part of the eucharistic celebration. Naturally, there evolved two options for the administration of baptism: the first, conducting baptism prior to the eucharistic liturgy and giving communion to the newly baptized along with the administration of Holy Communion to all the faithful who are participating in the eucharistic celebration; and the second, conducting baptism after the eucharistic celebration and administering Holy Communion to the newly baptized along with the entry to the altar and crowning.

Although according to the present text of the baptismal liturgy it is implied that the crown given to the newly baptized will be detached after seven days with a special prayer, this is not practiced currently and the detachment of the crown is done immediately after the crowning.

THE PROCESS OF BAPTISM

1. *Preparation, including Scriptural Instruction*

   This part of the baptismal liturgy has three main constituents:

   a. Introductory prayers and exhortation, along with readings from the epistle (Rom 5:20–6:4) and gospels (Luke 3:15-16 and John 3:5-6);

   b. Writing the name of the baptized in the baptismal register, symbolizing entry into the book of life (Phil 4:3; Rev 3:5);

   c. Breathing on the candidate, symbolizing giving new life (Gen 1:2; John 20:22), and stamping three times on the forehead in the name of the Holy Trinity.

2. *Exorcism*

   Casting off evil (whether spirits, influences, or associations) and taking an oath of dissociation from evil constitute this section. The minister and the baptismal candidate (whether by himself or herself, or through the godfather or godmother) address the evil one. The minister makes the sign of the cross nine times on the candidate and commands the evil one to depart forever. The candidate addresses the evil one and makes a public denunciation.

3. Faith Proclamation

This involves principally two acts: first, the candidate professing faith in Jesus Christ by declaring allegiance to the teachings handed over by the fathers, apostles, and prophets; and second, the recital of the Nicene-Constantinopolitan Creed.

4. Anointing with the Oil of Gladness

In the name of the Holy Trinity, the minister stamps on the forehead of the candidate with the oil of gladness.

5. Immersion in Water Mixed with Chrism (Myron)

A set of prayers and actions constitutes this part. Prayers include private and public prayers mainly invoking the Holy Spirit. Among the actions the most important are opening the baptismal font, the mixing of warm and cold water, the sanctifying of water by the invocation of the Holy Spirit, pouring and mixing holy chrism in water, blessing of the chrism-mixed water, and the immersion of the candidate in water in the name of the Holy Trinity. After the immersion the candidate is garbed in a white garment.

6. Anointing with Chrism (Myron)

The candidate is chrismated in two ways: the minister stamps holy chrism on the forehead three times in the name of the Holy Trinity; the minister takes some chrism in the hand and anoints the candidate's entire body.

7. Entry to the Altar and Crowning

If the baptism is done after the celebration of Eucharist, Holy Communion is given either before or after the crowning. After the giving of communion, the baptized one is taken to kiss the holy altar. The newly baptized is then crowned to signify participation in the holy and royal priesthood of the new dispensation (1 Pet 2:5-9).

8. Benediction and Dismissal

Finally the crown is detached from the head of the baptized one as a prayer is given; this is followed by the final benediction and dismissal.

THEOLOGICAL AND ECCLESIOLOGICAL FOUNDATION

The foundation of the baptismal liturgy, both theological and ecclesiological, includes the following five aspects:

1. The Term "Baptism"

Baptism is *mamodeeso* in Syriac, meaning "immersion" in water; therefore the practice of baptism by immersion is followed in the Malankara Orthodox Syrian Church. Baptism has been defined as a *mamodeeso rosonoito*, or "mysterious baptism," in the introductory prayer known as *prumion* in the baptismal liturgy. *Roso*, or "mystery," is a term with even more implications than the word "sacrament": "mystery" refers to a level of life beyond the earthly. More specifically, in the light of Christian theology "mystery" refers to the quality of life in the kingdom of God. Baptism is therefore the beginning of a new order of life and it is open to all, to children as well as grownups.

2. Theological and Ecclesiological Expressions of Baptism

There are many usages in the baptismal liturgy which have profound meaning, interpreting baptism as "birth from above" (*maulodo d'men d'reesh*), a usage which has its basis in John 3:3, 7.

3. Baptism and the Church, as Sisters

In our understanding there is an intimate relation between baptism and the church, so intimate that they are characterized as sisters. This relation is put in terms of birth and subsequent nurture, expressed in the phrase "baptism gives birth and her sister, the Church, feeds those who have been baptized."

4. The Baptized One is the Son or Daughter of Light

The symbolism of light is dominant in the baptismal liturgy, and the one who is baptized is qualified as a son or daughter of light. This usage too has deep roots in biblical texts and in the tradition of the church.

5. The Holy Chrism (Myron) Signifies Three Things

The anointing prayer identifies three qualities which characterize the chrism: the fragrance of the anointed; the sign and stamp of the true faith; and the indwelling of the Holy Spirit and the perfection of the gifts of the Holy Spirit.

SIGNIFICANT COMMONALITIES AND DIFFERENCES IN UNDERSTANDING AND PRACTICE

1. Infant and Adult Baptismal Liturgies

In the Malankara Orthodox Syrian Church, the same baptismal liturgy is used for infant and adult baptism. In this regard, our ancient Eastern church reflects a practice which is now growing in the churches of the West.

2. Combination of Elements of Faith and of "Mediation"

Baptism is considered as a sign of faith on the part of the candidate. This faith is a gift from God (Eph 2:8) that is available to all, both infant and adult, provided that there is a suitable disposition on the part of the candidate. When the candidate is a child, the suitable disposition is expressed through the parents' willingness to commit the child to Christ (Mark 10:14). The mediatory role of the godparent further strengthens and maintains the disposition of the child toward God.

3. Exhortation to the Godparent

Though not directly specified within the baptismal liturgy, in practice there is always an exhortation to the godparent to be diligent in pursuing the Christian upbringing of the newly baptized. This reflects an increasing awareness of the role of formation within the faith and the importance of godparents within this process.

4. Entry to the Sanctuary for Both Men and Women

Following the decision of the episcopal synod of the Malankara Orthodox Syrian Church, the entry to the sanctuary after baptism is now being granted also to female children under the age of five (formerly this was reserved for masculine children).

CONCLUSION

As this discussion shows, the baptismal understanding and practice of the Malankara Orthodox Syrian Church is a distinctive blend of fidelity to the ancient tradition and the application of this tradition to life today. In baptism, as in other areas of Christian faith and life, we seek both to be faithful to the gospel message and to affirm its relevance for contemporary life.

Chapter 4

Rite[s] of Baptism in the Catholic Church: A Theological-Pastoral Commentary

James F. Puglisi, SA

INTRODUCTION

At the outset of this commentary, an important question needs to be posed: Is there only one baptism? One may ask: why raise this issue, since all Christians confess their belief in "one baptism for the forgiveness of sins"? Our dilemma in writing this article is that, in reality, three rites for baptism exist within the Catholic Church: the rite of baptism for infants; the rite that terminates the process of Christian initiation of adults (and for children of catechetical age); and, finally, the rite of baptism in the oriental Catholic churches. It is true that the actual rites for baptism in each case resemble each other, but there is clearly a different theological understanding that undergirds each, as well as differing pastoral practices that are used in their preparation. Therefore, we must discern the unity to be found within the diversity of understanding and practice: we can only respond to our opening question by asserting that indeed there *is* one baptism, but it is celebrated in different ways.

Another important observation to be made here is that historically the Western church has used basically one ritual for baptism since the fifth century, a ritual employed for both adults and children. It was this ritual that remained basically unchanged until the Second Vatican Council, which asked for the elaboration of a proper ritual of baptism for infants.[1]

In the case of infants, the parents and godparents responded at the profession of faith for the child. However, it is important to note that the response offered changed from the time of Augustine to that of Thomas Aquinas, who represents the situation that has obtained from the Middle Ages until our own time.[2] There was a shift from the subject actually confessing his or her personal faith to that of the Christian parents asking baptism of the Church for their child and assuming the responsibility to educate that child in the faith of the Church.[3] Infants, therefore, are baptized in the faith of the Church, as proclaimed by the parents and godparents who represent the local church and the communion of the saints and faithful. In the words of Augustine, it is the entire Church that births each and every one.[4]

In this commentary we will describe what some call the "normative rite" of Christian initiation (of adults) and add a word concerning the rite of baptism for infants. We will also restrict ourselves here to the rites in use in the Latin Catholic Church.

CHRISTIAN INITIATION

The *Praenotanda* and the liturgical texts are places that contain a clear teaching about the sacraments. For this reason we now turn our attention to the liturgical celebration in order to understand better the doctrine of Christian initiation in the Catholic Church.

1. The Process of Christian Initiation
(Rite of Christian Initiation of Adults or RCIA)

The first two numbers of the general introduction to the RCIA lay out for us the doctrine of Christian initiation.[5]

> 1. In the sacraments of Christian initiation we are freed from the power of darkness and joined to Christ's death, burial, and resurrection. We receive the Spirit of filial adoption and are part of the entire people of God in the celebration of the memorial of the Lord's death and resurrection.[6]
>
> 2. Baptism incorporates us into Christ and forms us into God's people. This first sacrament pardons all our sins, rescues us from the power of darkness, and brings us to the dignity of adopted children,[7] a new creation through water and the Holy Spirit. Hence we are called and are indeed the children of God.[8]
>
> By signing us with the gift of the Spirit, confirmation makes us more completely the image of the Lord and fills us with the Holy Spirit, so that we may bear witness to him before all the world and work to bring the Body of Christ to its fullness as soon as possible.[9]
>
> Finally, coming to the table of the eucharist, we eat the flesh and drink the blood of the Son of Man so that we may have eternal life[10] and show forth the unity of God's people. By offering ourselves with

Christ, we share in the universal sacrifice, that is, the entire community of the redeemed offered to God by their High Priest,[11] and we pray for a greater outpouring of the Holy Spirit, so that the whole human race may be brought into the unity of God's family.[12]

3. Thus the three sacraments of Christian initiation closely combine to bring us, the faithful of Christ, to his full stature and to enable us to carry out the mission of the entire people of God in the Church and in the world.[13]

It may be seen from this that the process of becoming a Christian parallels natural human development. As a human individual is formed in the context of a community, so we too become a Christian within the context of the Christian community of the faithful. The introduction to the RCIA describes this journey according to steps or stages, leading from periods of inquiry and growth (evangelization and the precatechumenate), to the sacraments of initiation (acceptance into the catechumenate, the period of the catechumenate, election, the period of purification and enlightenment, the celebration of the sacraments of Christian initiation), and, finally, to the period of mystagogy.[14] Each of the stages has attached to it a ritual moment, which brings to closure the process of growth into the Christian faith and requires each individual to ask to proceed to the next stage.

2. The Stages of the Catechumenate

The first stage, called the precatechumenate, helps the individual examine the motive for requesting baptism and deals with the conversion experience. Usually the individual seeks a Christian friend (or "sponsor") who will guide him or her through this period of inquiry and reflection.

The second stage is called the catechumenate proper, whereby the individual enters a period of time (from two to three years) of instruction in the Christian faith. This stage is marked by a rite of acceptance into the order of catechumens. Here the individuals are formally presented to the Christian community. After a prayer of thanksgiving each one is signed with the cross on the forehead and led into the church. At the conclusion of the Liturgy of the Word each one is presented with a copy of the New Testament and another sign (such as a cross). Their names are then entered into the list of catechumens. During this period the catechumens will be present at the Liturgy of the Word each Sunday and will meet on a regular basis to pray together and study the Scriptures and faith of the Church. Also during this period the catechumens will seek out a responsible Christian to be their godparent.

The third stage is the final preparation or election. This takes place at the beginning of Lent (the first Sunday of Lent) where the catechumens are enrolled as candidates for baptism, which will take place at the end of the six-week preparation in the annual celebration of the Easter Vigil. The importance of this stage is seen in the fact that the bishop of the diocese presides over this election, which is done in the cathedral church. This period is marked also by the fact that the Christian community enters into a penitential preparation for the celebration of Easter and thereby accompanies the elect in their intense preparation for entrance into the Church by their baptism during the vigil on Holy Saturday. The rite of election consists of the presentation of the candidates and the testimony of their godparents; questioning of the candidates as to their intention to receive the sacraments of initiation; enrollment of their names in a special book; and acceptance by the godparents of their responsibility to assist the elect in their intention. A prayer of intercession for the elect and a blessing concludes this rite.

The following six-week period (Lent) is a "period of purification and enlightenment" during which several rites are celebrated. The first of these is called "scrutinies" or exorcisms. Their purpose is to allow the elect to become aware of the human weakness that they are seeking to leave behind and to strengthen them in their resolve to renounce the Evil One and follow Christ more closely. This is done by means of silent prayer and intercessions, accompanied by the imposition of hands in the presence of the Christian community. The prayer of the community for them is an essential part of their own renewal and reaffirmation of their faith.

As this period draws to a conclusion the rites intensify the experience of the elect's intention to renounce the glamour of this world and embrace the consequences of following Christ. These rites include the affirmation of faith when the elect is presented with the Creed and the Lord's Prayer. On the morning of Holy Saturday, the elect have finally arrived at the moment for which they have been preparing and waiting. In very brief ceremonies they "give back" the Creed and Lord's Prayer by reciting them by heart and briefly explaining them. Concluding these rites is the "Ephpheta," or the unstopping of the ears and mouth. Two other rites may be included in this ritual: choosing a new baptismal name (symbolically representing the new person about to be born), and anointing with the oil of catechumens. With this, the elect are ready to come before the community gathered in prayer and fasting at the Easter Vigil late on Holy Saturday evening, make their profession of faith, and be baptized.

Following this brief presentation of the catechumenate and its significance, we may now turn our attention to the actual rites of Christian initiation, focusing on the rites of baptism and confirmation.

3. Baptism

The rite of baptism follows the following sequence:

a. The context

b. Easter Vigil

c. Litany of the Saints

d. Benediction of water

e. Renunciation

f. Profession of faith

g. Baptism

h. Post-baptismal anointing with chrism (only when confirmation does not follow immediately)

i. Giving of a white garment

j. Giving of the lighted candle

The context. This is the same as for all sacramental celebrations and consists of the presence of the assembly presided over by an ordained minister, the Book of Scriptures from which one or more readings are taken, and a homily or preaching based on the proclaimed Word of God. This reflects the fact that all sacraments are ecclesial events at which the whole People of God is assembled and celebrates. The ancient rule of worship that "all celebrate and one presides in the name of all" is most clearly seen in liturgical celebrations in which the ordained minister presides over the celebration of all, with each taking his or her specific role.

The Easter Vigil. The Easter Vigil celebrates the victory of Christ over sin and death and the incorporation of new members through the waters of baptism into the Body of Christ, built up into the living temple of the Holy Spirit where all praise and glory of God is to resound. This is the liturgical celebration which recalls the mystery of God's saving love for his creation. The Church gathers to keep vigil, awaiting the rising Son of salvation with fasting, readings, and prayers. This vigil's Liturgy of the Word contains at least three readings (but it is highly recommended that the community proclaim all seven of the Easter Vigil readings). In the Liturgy of the Word the origins of humanity and humanity's salvation are recounted, and Christians appropriate their authentic identity as God's chosen people. At the conclusion of the liturgy, the maternal womb of the Church brings forth new life as the elect are reborn of water and the Holy Spirit. This has traditionally been the context for celebrating baptism, and it is in this celebration that all adults coming to the faith are to be initiated.

The baptismal liturgy begins after the homily with the presentation of the elect and the *Litany of the Saints*. This is an invocation to those holy men and women who have heroically lived their baptismal commitment, some becoming martyrs for the faith. This prayer allows us to see how our communion goes beyond this earthly life.

The *blessing of water* "declares the religious meaning of water as God's creation and the sacramental use of water in the unfolding of the paschal mystery."[15] The symbolism of baptismal water shows the ambivalence of the symbol of immersion: "When we plunge our head into the water, as in a sepulcher, the old person is immersed, buried completely; when we come up out of the water, the new person appears simultaneously."[16] The scriptural images contained in the blessing are not merely a mythic symbolism, but one of a real passage toward creation and re-creation (Gen 1), of passing through the Red Sea, of Jesus' baptism in the water of the Jordan River, of his passage from death to life in the Resurrection. "What is more extraordinary than the passage of the Jewish people through the sea than to speak of baptism? It is a passage and therefore the Pasch; each one makes it their passage, that from sin to life, from fault to grace, from sinfulness to sanctity."[17]

The prayer ends with an epiclesis asking the descent of the Spirit, so that the baptism will be a true re-creation of the person in the image of God. Hence at the very beginning of the baptismal rite there is a Trinitarian invocation, calling to mind the mystery of God's love from the beginning of the world to its salvation by Christ's death and the pouring out of the Holy Spirit. In this way the newness of Christian baptism is emphasized, by which we share in Christ's own death and resurrection and receive the holiness of God himself. A relation between spirit and water found in the Scriptures (John 7:37-39; Matt 3:11; Ezek 36:16-38) is expressed in the texts of the prayer—for which there are three options—thereby expressing the spiritual efficacy of baptism which depends on the Spirit.

The renunciation of sin and profession of faith represent a rite of passage from a negative moment to a positive one. Practiced in all the ancient churches, the renunciation of Satan, all his works, seductions, and cults—the giving up of all that goes contrary to the Gospel—is an appropriate way of expressing the death and leaving behind of the old person in the waters of baptism.

Following on the renunciation is the *profession of faith*. The other side of the medallion is the profession of faith, which was always considered essential for baptism. There is nothing intellectually abstract about this, since we symbolically do what we say: in fact, it is when the candidate goes down into the pool that the celebrant asks the three questions relative to the Trinitarian faith of the Church. To the three-fold "Do you believe?" the elect will answer three times "I believe" and be visibly plunged under the water. One is really baptized into the *faith* of the Church, and the triple immersion was seen by St. Augustine as the "visible word" of Trinitarian faith.

The dialogical structure of this rite (a triple question asked by the Church and the triple response of each baptized) is symbolically important. No one can proclaim himself or herself a Christian. Only the Church can do this, since it is the Church which asks the baptized not for their "opinions about God," but whether they enter into the Trinitarian faith that has been received from the apostles. Neither can we "self-baptize" ourselves, since Christian faith does not come from one's own opinions. If becoming Christian requires a sacrament, it is precisely because the sacrament is never reducible to its dimensions of interior conversion and a personal decision. It cannot be effected outside of ecclesial mediation.

Next comes the actual *baptism*. The actual place of baptism is important especially when adults are involved. The preferred method is by immersion, although infusion (but not sprinkling or aspersion) is also acceptable. Several types of baptismal pools are now in use and becoming more common: the octagonal pool that symbolizes the fullness of salvation that comes through baptism or, as another option, a cross-shaped pool to symbolize crossing from one side (west) to come out on the other (east)—namely, from darkness to light.

One is baptized with the Trinitarian formula, which should be linked to the Trinitarian formula used in the blessing of the water. The act of baptizing should not only represent purification but also unification to Christ's dying and rising. Baptism is always administered by another who acts in the name of the Church. This makes it a sacrament: the action of God in the action of the Church. Whether it be Peter or Judas who baptizes, it is always *Christ* who baptizes (Augustine).

A *post-baptismal anointing* with chrism does not ordinarily take place unless confirmation does not follow immediately (as is usually the case for infants and children of catechetical age). This anointing is a sign of the royal priesthood of the baptized and the fact that they are now numbered in the company of the people of God.

The *clothing with a white garment*. With the removal of clothes at the time of baptism we may see a symbol of divesting oneself of the old self, the old Adam, and of sin which entered through him (Rom 5:12-21). The giving of the white garment signifies the neophytes' new dignity as a new creation, dressed in the clothes of salvation and a tunic of joy.[18] The cloth of light is a mark of a new exigency required of the life of the baptized.

The *presentation of a lighted candle* shows that the newly baptized are called to walk as befits the children of light, since they have become witnesses of the Gospel whose message they carry in their bodies as in clay vases (2 Cor 4:7).

4. Confirmation

For adults the sacrament of confirmation is to follow immediately, completing baptism. In the case of infants and children of catechetical age this is postponed until a suitable age.

The conjunction of *confirmation*[19] and baptism signifies "the unity of the paschal mystery, the close link between the mission of the Son and the outpouring of the Holy Spirit, and the connection between the two sacraments through which the Son and the Holy Spirit come with the father to those who are baptized."[20] The rite is very simple, consisting of the imposition of hands and anointing with chrism.

The *imposition of hands* is a gesture meaning many things: blessing (Gen 48:13-16; Luke 24:50); consecration for a charge (Deut 34:9; Num 27:18-23), for a ministry (Acts 6:6; 13:3; 2 Tim 1:6); symbolic identification with the one offering sacrifice and the offered victim (Lev 1:4; 3:2;16:21ff.); and healing (Luke 13:13; Mark 8:25). The relation between this gesture and the Spirit is noted in the New Testament (Acts 9:17; 19:5ff.).

Attached to this sign is the *unction with chrism*, a highly perfumed oil. From the prayer of blessing of the oil celebrated on Holy Thursday by the bishop, we come to see the meaning attributed to anointing with this oil. This has to do with the very name of Christ, meaning "anointed one." In relation to the sacraments of initiation, the baptized are seen to share in the mission of Jesus when the Spirit is bestowed on them to make them members of his body. This happens according to the grace given to each, and in order that the Church may grow until it reaches the fullness of Trinitarian faith. The biblical allusion to the perfumed oil reminds us that the disciple must spread abroad the fragrance of Christ.[21] At the conclusion of this rite is the *greeting of peace* which the celebrant offers to each neophyte as a sign of welcome into the Church.

5. The Eucharist

The third of the sacraments of initiation is the Eucharist. The rite of Christian initiation underscores the unity among the sacraments, their close relationship to the mission of the Church, and the responsibility of the local church to share in the catechumen's growth in faith. As we have seen above, the general introduction to the rite indicates succinctly the reality of Catholic belief about the Eucharist when it states:

> . . . coming to the table of the eucharist, we eat the flesh and drink the blood of the Son of Man so that we may have eternal life and show forth the unity of God's people. By offering ourselves with Christ, we share in the universal sacrifice, that is, the entire community of the redeemed offered to God by their High Priest, and we pray for a greater outpouring of the Holy Spirit, so that the whole human race may be brought into the unity of God's family.[22]

The neophytes, or newly baptized, are mentioned by name during the intercessions in the eucharistic prayer and they receive the Eucharist under both species, that is, both bread and wine.

Saint Augustine probably best expresses the relationship between the Eucharist and the Church in the spirit of the Pauline writings. In a series of sermons or mystagogia explaining the rites of Christian initiation, he says:

You ought to know what you have received, what you are going to receive, and what you ought to receive daily. That bread which you see on the altar, consecrated by the word of God, is the Body of Christ. That chalice, or rather, what the chalice holds, consecrated by the word of God, is the Blood of Christ. If you have received worthily, you are what you have received, for the Apostle says: "Because there is one bread, we who are many are one body" (1 Cor 10:17).[23]

The Apostle says: "Whoever, therefore, eats the bread or drinks the cup of the Lord in an unworthy manner, will be answerable for the body and blood of the Lord" (1 Cor 11:27). . . . The mystery that you are lies there on the table; it is your own mystery that you receive. . . . Be what you see, and receive what you are. He explained to the neophytes that when they approached to receive the sanctified bread, they would hear the words "Body of Christ," and they would reply, "Amen." This meant: "It is to what you yourselves are that you reply, 'Amen'; . . . Be therefore truly a member of Christ's body, that your 'Amen' may be sincere."[24]

6. The Period of Post-baptismal Catechesis or Mystagogia

From Easter to Pentecost, the period of the "Great Fifty Days," the neophytes continue their Christian formation. This happens by way of instruction, meetings for prayer, and explanation of the meaning of the various rites they have experienced firsthand in the process of Christian initiation. The neophytes take their rightful place in the liturgical assembly and are engaged in living out their Christian commitment in the life and mission of the Church.

It should be noted that when children of a catechetical age are initiated by means of the catechumenal experience, the period of mystagogia may extend over a longer period until their confirmation, which should then be followed immediately by their receiving the Eucharist. In initiating such children there is, however, a tendency to keep all three of the sacraments of initiation together in their proper progression of baptism—confirmation—Eucharist.

A NOTE ON INFANT BAPTISM

If the sacrament is an expression or an act of faith, how can we baptize newly born infants who, by definition, cannot yet believe in the Gospel and confess their faith? The practice of infant baptism has long been established, as testified by Origen: "The Church has received the tradition of giving baptism to the very young from the apostles themselves."[25] In spite of this opinion, questions were raised early in the history of the church's baptismal practice—as is illustrated by Tertullian, who believed that children should reach the age of reason before being baptized.[26]

It was not, however, the opinion of Tertullian that prevailed. Cyprian of Carthage and Augustine of Hippo and the reflections that came from North Africa led the way. Augustine's argument was that it was not the personal sins of the infant that needed to be remitted but, rather, the sin he or she had inherited. Augustine developed the discussion further, especially through the theme of original sin. Here the solidarity of all human beings in sin influenced his thought. Together with this Augustine envisioned another positive solidarity, namely, that of the infant with the Church. He wrote:

> The infant is presented not so much in the arms that carry it, even though it is also the case when these are of true believers, but by the assembly of all the saints and faithful. . . . consequently it is Mother Church as a whole who is at work in all the saints. As a whole, she is constituted by all. The Church is at once the mother of all and the mother of each.[27]

This means that one is baptized in the faith of the Church and it is the Church that embraces, with its faith, a child who cannot by himself or herself make a confession of faith. At the basis of this reflection is the double solidarity found in the Pauline writings, namely, the solidarity in Adam and the solidarity in Christ (Rom 5).[28]

At this point we need to note what the rite for the baptism of children says. It first defines who "children" are: "they are those who have not yet reached the age of discernment and therefore cannot have or profess personal faith."[29] Next follows an important affirmation:

> To fulfill the true meaning of the sacrament, children must later be formed in the faith in which they have been baptized. The foundation of this formation will be the sacrament itself, which they have already received. Christian formation, which is their due, seeks to lead them gradually to learn God's plan in Christ, so that they may ultimately accept for themselves the faith in which they have been baptized.[30]

This means that the baptism is not an automatic act, but that the parents and godparents of the child, together with the Church, pledge themselves to form the child in faith and its confession.

Throughout the rite of baptism for children we see the important role of the Christian assembly. It must assume its responsibility for assisting the parents and godparents in the expression of the common faith of the Church, on behalf of the child to be baptized. This is why the introduction indicates that the time for the baptism is in the Easter Vigil, or at least on Sunday so that the entire community may be present.[31] That is, care is to be taken that there is a faith context within which the child may grow and develop. This responsibility is, then, primarily that of the parents and godparents—but also that of the community of the faithful. Most parishes offer courses necessary for the parents and godparents, covering their duties and obligations for educating their children in the faith and on the meaning of baptism and the faith of the Church. In this way the Church seeks to respect the integrity of the sacrament and the faith of the Church.

CONCLUSION

We have attempted to present Catholic practice regarding the sacraments of Christian initiation. The relation of baptism to Eucharist is grounded in the nature of both sacraments as uniting one to Christ and giving an ecclesial identity at the same time as a responsibility for evangelical witness. Baptism and Eucharist are together the "sacraments of faith"; the latter nourishes the faith received in the former. Baptism enables the baptized to worship God in Spirit and truth, by giving them a new and permanent status before God and before the community—the status of an adopted child of God and heir to the kingdom of the Lord. To celebrate the Eucharist means that one puts into practice the capacity received in baptism[32] and participates in the eschatological eruption of the kingdom yet to be fulfilled, by joining their witness to that of the saints.

From what has been said it can be seen that the Eucharist is not a thing or an "object" but rather an intimate relationship of loving service in the Lord. It is not by chance that the washing of the feet replaces the institution of the Eucharist in the thirteenth chapter of the Gospel of John—concluded by the command of Jesus to do this "in remembrance of" him. Through the memorial action of the Eucharist we are present to the saving events of the paschal mystery, and we proclaim these events each time we put them into practice in our lives.

Comparison of the rites of baptism for adults and for infants	
Sacraments of Initiation for Adults	**Rite of Baptism for Infants**

SERVICE OF LIGHT	INTRODUCTORY RITES
	  Greeting of the community assembled for the baptism
	  Dialogue with the parents and godparents
	  Signing of the child with the cross

LITURGY OF THE WORD	LITURGY OF THE WORD
	  Readings and homily
	  Intercessions
	  Prayer of exorcism
	  Anointing with the oil of catechumens or imposition of hands

CELEBRATION OF BAPTISM
  Presentation of the candidates
  Invitation to prayer
  Litany of the Saints
  Prayer over the water
  Profession of faith
    - Renunciation of sin
    - Profession of faith
  Baptism
  Explanatory rites
    - [Anointing after baptism]
    - [Clothing with a baptismal garment]
    - Presentation of a lighted candle
	CELEBRATION OF BAPTISM
	  Blessing of the baptismal water
	  Renunciation of sin and profession of faith [done by parents and godparents in the name of the child]
	  Baptism
	  Explanatory rites
	    - Anointing with chrism
	    - Clothing with baptismal garment
	    - Giving of lighted baptismal candle
	    - Rite of Ephpheta

CELEBRATION OF CONFIRMATION
  Invitation
  Laying on of hands
  Anointing with chrism
	CONCLUDING RITES
	  Concluding address
	  The Lord's Prayer
	  Blessing and closing hymn

LITURGY OF THE EUCHARIST	

Notes

[1] See the Constitution on the Sacred Liturgy, *Sacrosanctum Concilium*, 67: "The rite for the Baptism of infants is to be revised. The revision should take into account the fact that those to be baptized are babies. The roles of parents and godparents, and also their duties, should be brought out more clearly in the rite itself."

[2] It appears that in Augustine's times the parents and godparents simply responded to the question on faith: "He or she believes." This was changed sometime after Augustine since Thomas Aquinas notes that the response to the question is "I believe" since no one can predict that the child will become a believer by the age of reason. Rather it is the faith of the Church which is professed in the person of the child (*in persona pueri*). For Augustine see *Sermon* 294, 12; *Epistula* 98 (to Boniface) *PL* 33, 360ff. and for Thomas Aquinas, *Summa theologica*, III, q. 71, a.1, ad 3. For more details consult the work of J. C. Didier, "Faut-il baptiser les enfants? La réponse de la tradition," *Chrétiens de tous les temps 21* (Paris: Cerf, 1967).

[3] It should be noted that the Code of Canon Law in canon 868, 2 states that for the baptism of an infant to be licit there needs to "be a founded hope that the infant will be brought up in the Catholic religion."

[4] Augustine, *Epistula* 98, 5.

[5] *RCIA: Rite of Christian Initiation of Adults*, Study edition, prepared by the International Commission on English in the Liturgy (Collegeville, MN: Liturgical Press, 1988), xvi. All citations from the *RCIA* are taken from this edition, cited as RCIA with the paragraph number.

[6] See Vatican Council II, Decree on the Church's Missionary Activity, *Ad gentes*, no. 14.

[7] See Colossians 1:13; Romans 8:15; Galatians 4:5. See also Council of Trent, sess. 6, *Decr. De justificatione*, cap. 4: Denz.-Schön. 1524.

[8] See 1 John 3:1.

[9] See Vatican II, Decree on the Church's Missionary Activity, *Ad gentes*, no. 36.

[10] See John 6:55.

[11] See Augustine, *De civitate Dei* 10, 6: PL 41, 282. Vatican Council II, Dogmatic Constitution on the Church, *Lumen gentium* no. 11; Decree on the Ministry and Life of Priests, *Presbyterorum ordinis*, no. 2.

[12] See Vatican II, Dogmatic Constitution on the Church, *Lumen gentium*, no. 28.

[13] See *ibid.*, no. 31.

[14] *RCIA*, Introduction, no. 7.

[15] *RCIA*, par. 210.

[16] John Chrysostom, *Homilia* 25, 2.

[17] Ambrose of Milan, *De Sacr.* I, 12.

[18] Cyril of Jerusalem, *Cat. Myst.* 4, 8; cf. Isa 61:10.

¹⁹ The *Catechism of the Catholic Church* treats the question of confirmation basically in three points: 1) that confirmation is a gift of God's grace which increases and deepens baptismal grace (*Catechism of the Catholic Church*, 2nd ed. rev. in accordance with the official Latin text (Vatican City: Libreria Editrice Vaticana, 2000), 1303, hereafter cited as *CCC* followed by the paragraph number); 2) as true witnesses of Christ, the confirmed "are more strictly obliged to spread and defend the faith by word and deed" (CCC 1285) (LG 11); and 3) the sacrament of confirmation is conferred through the anointing with chrism on the forehead, the laying on of hands, and the words, "Be sealed with the gift of the Holy Spirit" (CCC 1320).

²⁰ *RCIA*, par. 215.

²¹ Cf. 2 Cor 2:15; Exod 30:22-25.

²² *RCIA*, General Introduction, par. 2.

²³ *Sermo* 227.1.

²⁴ *Sermo* 227. For an analysis of Augustine's approach in explaining the rites of Christian initiation, see W. Harmless, *Augustine and the Catechumenate* (Collegeville, MN: Liturgical Press, 1995), 316–24.

²⁵ Origen, *Commentary on Romans* 5:9, PG 14, 1047b.

²⁶ Tertuillian, *On baptism*, 18, 5.

²⁷ Augustine, Epistle 98, 5, PL 33, 362.

²⁸ It was in Augustine's dealings with the heresy of Pelagianism, a position that held that human beings are born with an absolute free will and are able to choose and turn to good as well as evil, that we see the development of the idea of original sin. Augustine argued that the human will is not free but sick, turned in upon itself and seeks only the gratification of its own self-oriented desires. Hence from the moment of birth human beings cannot choose, will, or do what is good but are in need of the medicine of divine grace in order to choose, will, or do good. The cause of this sickness is the sin of Adam. See Jaroslav Pelikan, *The Christian Tradition: A History of the Development of Doctrine*, vol. 1: *The Emergence of the Catholic Tradition (100–600)* (Chicago: University of Chicago Press, 1971), 278–331. As an illustration of how the Catholic Church is discussing the issue, see K. Stasiak, *Return to Grace: A Theology for Infant Baptism* (Collegeville, MN: Liturgical Press, 1996).

²⁹ *Rites of Baptism for Children*, Introduction, no. 1. The text is cited from the edition found in *The Rites of the Catholic Church as Revised by Decree of the Second Vatican Council and Published by Authority of Pope Paul VI*, The International Commission on English in the Liturgy, trans., vol. 1, study edition, Pueblo (Collegeville, MN: Liturgical Press, 1990).

³⁰ *Ibid.*, no. 3.

³¹ *Ibid.*, no. 9.

³² *Lumen Gentium*, 10.

Chapter 5

The Rite of Holy Baptism in the *Lutheran Book of Worship*

Jeffrey A. Truscott

BAPTISM IN THE LUTHERAN TRADITION

Baptism figured prominently in the spirituality and theology of Martin Luther (1483–1546).[1] For him baptism was a sacramental means of grace by which God delivered the person from sin, death, and the devil. Yet the efficacy of baptism resided not in the baptismal water itself, but in the fact that water was used by God's command and with his promise. Baptism was a comforting reminder of salvation in times of spiritual distress. At the same time, it brought about the daily crucifixion of the old sinful self and the resurrection of a new righteous self. Ultimately, baptism was a rehearsal for death, when one would be liberated from the power of sin.

Luther and the Lutheran confessions defended the baptism of infants. Luther used a number of arguments, for example, that infants were capable of faith and that the church's survival for many years with infant baptism was proof that God approved of the practice.[2] But the crucial point was that baptism depended on the word and command of God, not the faith of the recipient. "For my faith does not make baptism; rather, it receives baptism."[3] Indeed, the very faith that receives baptism is imparted through baptism, according to the Augsburg Confession, an important Lutheran confessional writing.[4] This document, which stressed the necessity of baptism for salvation,[5] likewise advocated the baptism of infants.[6] A willingness to baptize persons in peril of dying ("emergency" baptism or *die Nottaufe*) became a mark of orthodoxy for Lutherans in the sixteenth and seventeenth centuries. In such cases baptism could be administered even by laypersons.

Concerned that sponsors participate reverently and intelligently in the baptismal liturgy, especially during the intercessory prayers, Luther prepared a German baptismal rite. This 1523 *Taufbüchlein* ("little baptismal book")[7] was but a simplification of the medieval Latin rite.

The revised *Taufbüchlein* (1526) removed many of the accompanying ceremonies (giving of salt, anointing) in order that the washing itself could stand out as the central act.[8] Neither rite assumed the presence of a liturgical assembly or of preferred days for baptism (namely, the Easter Vigil or Pentecost).

Baptismal rites in the German Lutheran Church Orders tended to follow either of Luther's rites, although the 1526 rite was more influential. These church orders influenced baptismal rites used by American Lutherans into the late twentieth century.

THE RITE OF HOLY BAPTISM
IN THE *LUTHERAN BOOK OF WORSHIP*

The baptismal rite of the Evangelical Lutheran Church in America (ELCA), the Evangelical Lutheran Church in Canada (ELCC), and some congregations of The Lutheran Church–Missouri Synod is found in the *Lutheran Book of Worship* (LBW, 1978).[9] LBW provides one rite for candidates of all ages in order to avoid the perception that there are two different baptisms, one for infants and one for adults. The rite is modified when candidates are able to speak for themselves.

Holy Baptism begins with an address (section 2) that provides a theological interpretation of baptism. Through baptism, the person is sacramentally united with Jesus Christ in his death and resurrection. The effect of this union is that the person becomes a completely new creature in whom sin and death lose their power: the condemnation and guilt resulting from original sin are removed. The person is not only saved *from* sin and death, he or she is saved *for* faithful obedience to Jesus Christ, which is lived out in community with other Christians.

After the candidates are introduced (3), those who can answer for themselves (older children and adults) state their desire for baptism. Such an action is only natural, given that conversion and the request for baptism precede the baptismal act.[10]

Sponsorship (6–7) has an important role in baptism. Sponsors guide and accompany candidates (and the families of infant candidates) through the instructional process and baptism and help integrate the newly baptized into the life of the local congregation.[11] In doing these things, the sponsors act on behalf of the congregation. The promises of the sponsors are not understood as a precondition to God's action in baptism; rather, they reflect the presupposition that sponsors will provide for the Christian nurture of child candidates so that the latter can understand baptism and receive it in faith. Since this responsibility is presupposed, the promises are placed at the beginning of the rite; some writers, however, have argued that the sponsors' promises should be placed after the baptism proper so that they become a *response* to God's saving deed in baptism.[12]

When baptism is celebrated within the Sunday Communion service, the intercessory prayers for the day may be said during the baptismal rite (8). This arrangement enables the congregation to focus on the candidates and sponsors (and parents) as the objects of prayer.

A thanksgiving prayer (9), which begins like the eucharistic Great Thanksgiving, contains images that recall the role of water in salvation history. The implication is that each baptism is another saving act of God involving water. An epiclesis invokes the Holy Spirit upon the candidates for their attainment of new life; theologically, the epiclesis "is an acknowledgement that only the promised power of God can grant the gift of new life in Christ."[13]

The renunciation (10) shows that the baptismal union with Christ is concurrently a rejection of, or turning away from, the devil and evil. It is possible to have a threefold rejection—of all the forces of evil, the devil, and all his empty promises—that parallels the threefold creedal profession of faith that follows.

The phrase "the faith in which we baptize" indicates that baptism is an act of faith by the church. The church has no assurance that the baptized person, whether infant or adult, will receive the gift of baptism in faith and live as a committed Christian. So the church comes before the triune God in an attitude of prayer and in the fervent hope that the baptismal gift of the Holy Spirit will accomplish faith and obedience in the baptized person. In so doing the church does not baptize on the strength of its own faith but in response to God's command (Matt 28:19).[14]

The profession of faith (10) using the baptismal (Apostles') creed is made by the candidate and the liturgical assembly together. The joint confession expresses baptism as incorporation into the church, since the candidate is joining his or her faith to that of the church. Some Lutherans, however, might argue that the adult candidate alone should profess the faith as a way of underscoring his or her conversion.

The traditional triune baptismal formula (11) is used, but LBW also provides a passive baptismal formula, in the manner of Eastern Orthodox baptismal rites. The passive formula shows that baptism is a divine action accomplished through human agency—something that Luther himself emphasized.[15] The rubrics indicate that baptism may be administered by immersion "in one of its several forms" (by completely submerging the candidate, or by pouring water over a candidate who stands in a pool of water).[16] Notably, Luther advocated baptism by immersion (dipping an infant into the font) in order to portray baptism as a drowning.[17]

The washing is followed by rites that illustrate the meaning of baptism. The laying on of hands with prayer for the sevenfold gifts (13) and the marking of the sign of the cross (with optional use of oil) using the "seal of the Spirit" formula (14) together constitute a somewhat unique feature in Lutheranism. Indeed, at this point in many, if not most, Lutheran baptismal rites the minister lays hands on the neophyte while reciting a version of the traditional post-baptismal anointing formula, which Luther reworked to accompany the conferral of a baptismal garment.[18] Some Lutherans might argue that these two LBW post-baptismal rites—contrary to the Lutheran insistence that the Holy Spirit is received in the baptismal washing—constitute in fact a *separate* conferral of the Holy Spirit, and/or the addition of the Roman sacrament of confirmation.[19] But in fact the drafters of the LBW rite only intended to provide a fuller ritualization of the bestowal of the Holy Spirit in order to affirm that baptism constituted full Christian initiation.[20]

Two more explanatory rites follow. A lighted candle (16) is presented to the newly baptized as an expression of the ethical implications of baptism. There may also be a conferral of a white garment (cf. Gal 3:27) as a congregational representative says, "Put on this robe, for in baptism you have been clothed in the righteousness of Christ, who calls you to his great feast."[21] These two features constitute a restoration of the post-baptismal section of Luther's 1523 baptismal rite.[22]

When small children are baptized, the minister prays for their parents (17). The prayer reflects the Lutheran ideal that the home is a place of Christian instruction and faith formation. Realizing this ideal belongs to the baptismal vocation of parents.

Holy Baptism concludes with the congregation's welcome to the newly baptized (18), which reminds them that baptism constitutes their entrance into the church and their acceptance of its mission in the world. The assembled congregation is reminded of its responsibility to care for and nurture the faith of the newly baptized.

THE BROADER SIGNIFICANCE OF THE RITE

Four significant aspects of baptism as provided for in LBW are perhaps not obvious in the text itself. First, baptism is to be integrated into the ongoing cycle of congregational worship. The rubrics mention several preferred days for baptism: the Easter Vigil, The Day of Pentecost, All Saints' Day, and The Baptism of Our Lord (the First Sunday after Epiphany).[23] The goal is that the scriptural passages and preaching on these festival days will illumine the meaning of baptism. When baptism is celebrated on a Sunday in Ordinary Time, a special set of baptismal propers (lessons, collect, proper verse, eucharistic preface, and a post-communion prayer) may be used.[24]

Second, LBW gives attention to baptismal architecture. Specifically, it recommends "a font of ample proportions" located so as to make clear that baptism constitutes entrance into the church (for example, the font should be placed near an entrance to the liturgical space).[25] The rubrics also suggest a font that has continuously running water. This does not mean that LBW is undergirded by a theology that regards font size and the amount of water used as essential to the efficacy of the sacrament. Rather, these recommendations show an awareness of the symbolic dimension of the sacraments and the need to administer them in a way that accords with their theological and biblical meaning—as Luther himself advocated.

Third, LBW assumes that baptism constitutes admission to the Lord's Supper. According to the rubrics, baptism should be celebrated within the service of Holy Communion (following the sermon), so that newly baptized adults and older children can receive their first communion. Infants may be brought to the altar for a blessing during the distribution of communion.[26] The identification of preferred liturgical days for baptism and the connection to the eucharist together show that baptism is understood as a congregational act of worship rather than an "occasional service" for use in private.

Fourth, LBW recalls and draws out the baptismal implications of other rites. Notably, the pre-eucharistic penitential rite allows the entire congregation to make the sign of the cross "in remembrance of their baptism."[27] The funeral rite begins with a quotation of Romans 6:3 to accompany the draping of the pall over the casket, thereby pointing to death as the completion of one's baptismal journey.[28] Thus LBW is infused with the understanding that Christian life emerges from baptism and constantly returns to it.

The LBW rite of Holy Baptism represents new directions in baptismal thinking for Lutherans. More than just an occasional service involving only the minister, the candidate, and the sponsors, it is a congregational act of worship for Sundays and festivals. The assumed presence and involvement of the liturgical assembly is a reminder that

49

baptism is initiation into the church. While Lutherans have tended to focus on words in the liturgy, the rite makes significant use of gestures and actions such as the signing with oil, the conferral of a candle, and the clothing with a baptismal garment. Theologically, the eschatological aspect of baptism is brought out in the introductory address and the thanksgiving prayer. The traditional Lutheran emphasis on baptism as a remedy for original sin is subordinated to eschatology, ecclesiology, daily conversion, and the reception of the Holy Spirit.

DEVELOPMENTS AND CONTINUING ISSUES

Recognizing the need to evangelize, spiritually form, and baptize adults, North American Lutherans in the era after LBW have produced adaptations of the ancient catechumenal rites: *Living Witness* (1992)[29] by the ELCC and *Welcome to Christ* (1997)[30] by the ELCA. Both of these recognize four catechumenal times: 1) a period of inquiry; 2) the catechumenate, a time of in-depth exploration of the church's history and faith; 3) final baptismal preparation during Lent or Advent; and 4) baptismal living or "vocation in the world." Specific rites mark the entrance into the catechumenate, final preparation for baptism (that is, enrollment for baptism at the beginning of Lent), baptism (at the Easter Vigil), and affirmation of vocation in the world.

The use of the adult catechumenate, however, raises theological questions for Lutherans. It could be argued that the Lutheran doctrine of justification by grace alone is most aptly illustrated at the baptism of an infant, since it is then very apparent that God takes the initiative to save the person. An infant is completely passive and can only receive baptism in faith; but when the candidate is an adult, the conversion and conscious decision for baptism might appear to blunt the aspect of grace. There is also the danger that the catechumenate could be perceived as a process of fulfilling requirements—progressing through the stages or times of the catechumenate—until one finally achieves baptism as the "just reward" for one's efforts. Lutheran theology, however, could never accept such an understanding, precisely because it affirms that baptism is God's *gift* to us.

But these questions are easily addressed: to the first, it could be pointed out that divine grace and initiative are operative also for the adult baptismal candidate, since it is through the preaching of the gospel and the gracious work of the Holy Spirit that conversion and decision for baptism come about.[31] To the second, we need only remind ourselves of the early church's understanding that the catechumenate, far from being a way to merit salvation, is to be a school of spiritual formation that enables the catechumen to make the transition from worldly life to life as a member of the body of Christ.[32]

Another significant issue with initiatory implications has been the age of first communion. Lutherans have traditionally communed children old enough to understand the meaning of Holy Communion on a cognitive level. For both European and American Lutherans, a period of catechetical instruction and a rite both known as "confirmation" (German: *die Firmung*) became prerequisites for the reception of communion by adolescents aged twelve and (usually) older. The connection between confirmation and first communion was broken in 1970, when the largest Lutheran churches in North America officially eliminated confirmation as a prerequisite for communion and allowed children in the fifth school grade (at the age of ten) to receive communion following a period of instruction.[33] This policy change sought to overcome the perception that confirmation constituted the attainment of full membership status (communicant status) and thus marked the termination of Christian instruction and faith formation. There was also a theological concern that the conferral of communicant status enabled confirmation to overshadow baptism in theological and liturgical importance.

The move to an earlier, pre-confirmation communion was the beginning of an evolution in thought and practice. Eight years later, the LBW rubrics declared that communion "is the birthright of the baptized"[34]—a statement that hints of infant communion. But a 1978 joint communion practices statement of the ELCA's predecessor churches (The American Lutheran Church and Lutheran Church in America) ruled out the practice.[35] Discussion continued nevertheless, for the ELCA's *Use of the Means of Grace* (1997) gives official sanction to the communion of infants at the service of their baptism but stops short of endorsing the *regular* communing of infants thereafter.[36]

Finally, baptism has implications for something dear to the Lutheran heart: interdenominational eucharistic sharing.[37] Many Lutherans in North America agree with the statement of *Baptism, Eucharist and Ministry* that baptism is the "basic bond of Christian unity."[38] They therefore have difficulty understanding why the Roman Catholic Church (for example) will accept the validity of a baptism administered in a Lutheran church yet will decline to welcome Lutherans to Holy Communion. Lutherans would argue that the unity established through the biblically mandated sign of baptism supersedes any other unity that might be considered a prerequisite to eucharistic sharing.

CONCLUSION

Christian initiation in North American Lutheranism has undergone significant development in the last thirty years, as is evident from the LBW baptismal rite. Yet the changing pastoral situation in North America calls for continued reflection on the theology and practice of Christian initiation. For this task, we as Lutherans seek the guidance of the Holy Spirit and the help of those with whom we share a common baptism into Jesus Christ.

Notes

[1] See especially the sections on baptism in Luther's Small and Large Catechisms, both in Robert Kolb and Timothy J. Wengert, eds., *The Book of Concord* (Minneapolis: Fortress Press, 2000), 359–60 and 456–467 (hereafter *BC*); and "Holy and Blessed Sacrament of Baptism" (1519), in E. Theodore Bachmann and Helmut T. Lehmann, eds., *Luther's Works*, American Edition (Philadelphia: Muhlenberg Press, 1960), 29–43 (hereafter *LW*).

[2] *BC* 462.49.

[3] *BC* 463.53.

[4] Augsburg Confession, Article V, *BC* 40.2.

[5] Augsburg Confession, Article II, *BC* 36.1.

[6] Augsburg Confession, Article IX, *BC* 42.1.

[7] Martin Luther, *The Order of Baptism* (1523), *LW* 53, 96–101.

[8] Martin Luther, *The Order of Baptism Newly Revised* (1526), *LW* 53, 107–109.

[9] *Lutheran Book of Worship* (Minneapolis and Philadelphia: Augsburg and Board of Publication, Lutheran Church in America, 1978), 308–12; this and further citations refer to the *Ministers Edition* (hereafter *LBW*). A new baptismal rite largely based on the *LBW* rite appears in the ELCA's new *Evangelical Lutheran Worship* (Minneapolis: Augsburg/Fortress, 2006), 226–231.

[10] See Edmund Schlink, *The Doctrine of Baptism*, trans. Herbert J. A. Bouman (St. Louis: Concordia, 1972), 187.

[11] Evangelical Lutheran Church in America, *Use of the Means of Grace: A Statement on the Practice of Word and Sacrament* (Minneapolis: Augsburg, Fortress, 1997), 26 (Principle 20).

[12] See Bryan D. Spinks, "Luther's Timely Theology of Unilateral Baptism," *Lutheran Quarterly* 9 (Spring 1995): 40–42.

[13] *LBW* 31.

[14] Martin Luther, Large Catechism, *BC* 464.57.

[15] "To be baptized in God's name is to be baptized not by human beings but by God himself" (Large Catechism, *BC* 457.10).

[16] *LBW* 31.

[17] Martin Luther, "Holy and Blessed Sacrament of Baptism," *LW* 35, 29.

[18] The text of this formula is: "Almighty God, the Father of our Lord Jesus Christ, who hath begotten thee again of Water and the Holy Ghost, and hath forgiven thee all thy sin, strengthen thee with his grace to life everlasting" (*Service Book and Hymnal* [Minneapolis and Philadelphia: Augsburg and Board of Publication, Lutheran Church in America, 1958], 244.)

[19] See Maxwell E. Johnson, "The Shape of Christian Initiation in the Lutheran Churches: Liturgical Texts and Future Directions," *Studia Liturgica* 27 (1997): 36–44. Johnson notes that this post-baptismal unit was identified as theologically problematic by a report of the Lutheran Church–Missouri Synod, which ultimately rejected the *Lutheran Book of Worship* and published its own worship book, *Lutheran Worship*. See "Report and Recommendations of the Special Hymnal Review Committee" [n. d.], 27.

[20] See Eugene L. Brand, *Baptism: A Pastoral Perspective* (Minneapolis: Augsburg, 1975), 107. This and other issues regarding the development of the *LBW* baptismal rite are detailed in my book *The Reform of Baptism and Confirmation in American Lutheranism*, Drew University Studies in Liturgy, No. 11 (Lanham, MD and Oxford: Scarecrow Press, 2003).

[21] *LBW* 31.

[22] Martin Luther, *The Order of Baptism* (1523), *LW* 53, 101.

[23] *LBW* 30.

[24] Ibid.

[25] Ibid.

[26] Ibid.

[27] Ibid., 195.

[28] Ibid., 331.

[29] See *Living Witness: The Adult Catechumenate* (Evangelical Lutheran Church in Canada, 1992), which consists of two booklets: "Congregational Prayers to Accompany the Catechumenal Process," by Gordon W. Lathrop, and "Introduction: Preparing Adults for Baptism and Ministry in the Church," by Frederick P. Ludolph.

[30] *Welcome to Christ: A Lutheran Introduction to the Catechumenate/A Lutheran Catechetical Guide/Lutheran Rites for the Catechumenate* (Minneapolis: Augsburg/Fortress, 1997).

[31] Note the following statement by Luther: "I believe that by my own understanding or strength I cannot believe in Jesus Christ my Lord or come to him, but instead the Holy Spirit has called me through the gospel, enlightened me with his gifts, made me holy and kept me in the true faith . . ." (Small Catechism, *BC* 355.4).

[32] See "The Apostolic Tradition of Hippolytus," chs. 16–18 and 20, in E. C. Whitaker, *Documents of the Baptismal Liturgy*, 2nd ed. (London: SPCK, 1970), 3–4.

[33] Lutheran Church in America, Convention Minutes, Minneapolis, MN, June 25–July 2, 1970, 613–14; American Lutheran Church, Convention Minutes, San

Antonio, TX, October 21–27, 1970, 633–34. For a discussion of the rationale behind this change, see "A Report for Study from the Joint Commission on the Theology and Practice of Confirmation to the Honorable Presidents of The American Lutheran Church, Lutheran Church in America, and The Lutheran Church–Missouri Synod," in Frank W. Klos, *Confirmation and First Communion: A Study Book* (Minneapolis, Philadelphia, and St. Louis: Augsburg; Board of Publication, Lutheran Church in America; and Concordia, 1968), especially ch. IV, 199–211.

[34] *LBW*, 31.

[35] The American Lutheran Church and Lutheran Church in America, *Statement on Communion Practices* (n.p., 1978) II, A, 2, d.

[36] Evangelical Lutheran Church in America, *Use of the Means of Grace*, 42 (Application 37D).

[37] Evangelical Lutheran Church in America, *Use of the Means of Grace*, 53.

[38] World Council of Churches, *Baptism, Eucharist and Ministry*, Faith and Order Paper No. 111 (Geneva: World Council of Churches, 1982), "Baptism," par. 6, 3.

Chapter 6

Baptism in the Anglican Communion
Paul F. Bradshaw

CURRENT TRENDS

Provinces of the Anglican Communion throughout the world are free to order their baptismal rites in whatever way they deem appropriate, although the Fourth International Anglican Liturgical Consultation, meeting in Toronto, Canada, in 1991, did produce a Statement on Christian Initiation that included seven recommendations.[1] These held to the traditional Anglican view that baptism "is for people of all ages, both adults and infants," but cut through more than a century of debate by declaring that it "is complete sacramental initiation and leads to participation in the eucharist. Confirmation and other rites of affirmation have a continuing pastoral role in the renewal of faith among the baptized but are in no way to be seen as a completion of baptism or as necessary for admission to communion." They also added that "the pastoral rite of confirmation may be delegated by the bishop to a presbyter."

While such views have not yet achieved complete acceptance throughout the Communion, various steps in that direction can be seen. There has been a widespread movement away from separate baptismal rites for infant and adult candidates that were quite distinct from one another and toward a single rite that can be used for both with the minimum of variation (recommended in the Report of the Toronto Consultation, Section 4, 4). There has also been an increasing trend for the "normative" version of this service to include both the baptism and confirmation of adult candidates on the one occasion, rather than as separate rites. A few provinces (USA, Canada, and more recently Scotland) have moved much more decisively toward the understanding indicated in the Toronto Statement and prescribed as a post-baptismal ceremony for both infants and adults alike the formulary, "N., you are sealed by the Holy Spirit in Baptism . . . ," accompanied by the laying on of hands and/or anointing—a pneumatic emphasis more commonly associated with confirmation than baptism in Anglicanism. While these provinces continue to retain a separate rite of confirmation for those baptized as infants, it is no longer viewed as absolutely essential before they can be considered "full" Christians.

Another widespread feature of modern Anglican practice is the preference for baptism to take place within a service attended by the local congregation rather than one attended solely by the candidate's family and friends—as was often the case in the past—in order that the ecclesial dimension of the sacrament may receive a stronger liturgical expression. A number of provinces regard this as not merely desirable but normative and indicate the principal eucharistic celebration on a Sunday or holy day as the proper occasion for baptism (recommended in the Toronto Report, 4, 3) so that the intrinsic connection between baptism and eucharist may be made more visible. Some even recommend particular days or seasons of the liturgical year as the normal times for baptism.

Finally, in a significant departure from classic Anglican practice, many provincial rites include, in addition to the central water act, symbolic actions such as anointing, giving a lighted candle, and clothing with a white garment, although frequently as optional ceremonies. This reflects the growing recognition of the value of liturgical symbol within Anglican worship.

AN EXAMPLE

The rite reproduced with this article is from the Church of England and is fairly typical of modern baptism services within the Communion, though with some distinctive features of its own. It was originally authorized in 1998, the first of the *Common Worship* series of services to appear, though minor changes were made to it in 2000 in the light of experience. Several alternative arrangements of the rite are provided in order to cater to different situations—at the eucharistic rite or another service; baptism alone or accompanied by confirmation; etc. The one printed here is for a combined service of baptism and confirmation, over which the bishop presides, since confirmation in the Church of England must still be administered by a bishop and may not be delegated to a priest.

The Liturgy of Initiation begins with the presentation of the candidates to the congregation, a new feature of Anglican baptismal rites and something recommended in the Toronto Report (4, 4.1). Here the act of presentation has been made optional, but not the questions put to the candidates. On the occasion that children are among those to be baptized, questions from the version of the rite for children are put to their parents and godparents[2] about the support that they will give to the candidates. The opportunity for candidates to offer individual testimony to their faith is also without previous precedent in the Anglican tradition (though again encouraged in the Toronto Report, 4, 4.2) and marks the growing influence of the evangelical and charismatic renewal movements in the Church of England.

In line with modern rites in several other Anglican provinces, the section called here "The Decision" expands the traditional renunciation of evil with a parallel threefold act of adherence to Christ modeled on the ancient *apotaxis/syntaxis* pattern in baptismal rites of the Eastern traditions. The alternative form of decision mentioned here is a simpler one retained from the 1980 Church of England rite, and the "large candle" refers to the Easter candle used in some Anglican congregations.

The use of the sign of the cross at baptism has been consistently retained from medieval practice in Anglican rites from the Reformation onward, though meeting with opposition as being unscriptural from Puritans in the sixteenth and seventeenth centuries and with misunderstanding from some others in later centuries who saw it as constituting part of the essence of the sacrament because it was located immediately after the immersion in water. Although it may still take place as a post-baptismal ceremony in this rite, its preferred position is at this earlier point, partly in order to avoid such misunderstanding and partly reflective of the ancient practice at the making of a catechumen, when those being enrolled were signed with the cross to mark them as henceforth belonging to Christ. In another departure from earlier Anglican tradition but again restoring more ancient custom, the notes to the service allow the option of using for this purpose "pure olive oil, reflecting the practice of athletes preparing for a contest."

These preliminaries over, the action then moves to the baptismal font, where the bishop says a prayer over the water and then asks the congregation to say the Apostles' Creed in response to his questions (the alternative profession of faith referred to is a shorter threefold Trinitarian affirmation, again based on that in the 1980 rite). Thus, instead of the candidates alone professing their faith immediately before the immersion, which has been the traditional Western practice since early centuries, the candidates in this rite and in those of a number of other Anglican provinces, having already professed their own allegiance to Christ earlier in the service, join with the whole congregation in a statement of the church's collective belief, in which they will be baptized, a change that gives the act a somewhat different emphasis.

The immersion itself is traditional in form. However, as indicated earlier, the optional post-baptismal ceremony of clothing with a white garment, though an ancient Christian custom, is a recent innovation in Anglican rites, as is the provision for confirmation candidates to sign themselves or be sprinkled with the baptismal water as a reminder of their own baptism.

The confirmation of those old enough to profess their own faith follows. This conforms to the traditional Anglican model of prayer for the sevenfold gifts of the Holy Spirit and the laying on of hands by the bishop. The notes to the service again permit anointing to accompany the confirmation, this time recommending the use of oil mixed with fragrant spices (chrism), "expressing the blessings of the messianic era and the richness of the Holy Spirit."

The optional "commission" is a new feature in Anglican baptismal rites. It is in effect a responsive version of the older pattern of an exhortation addressed to those who were baptized, or their godparents in the case of infants, and is designed to spell out that baptism is not an end in itself but the beginning of a new pattern of living. The rite continues with a welcome by the congregation and the exchange of the peace—further liturgical expressions of the ecclesial dimension of baptism. The giving of a lighted candle can be found in most other modern Anglican rites as one of the post-baptismal ceremonies immediately after the immersion, but here it has been deferred until the very end of the service. This has been done partly to avoid the unintended symbolic implications of handing someone a representation of the light of Christ and then immediately having them blow it out while the service continues but, more important, as the Liturgical Commission's commentary accompanying the rites states, to indicate "that the primary symbolism is a summons to shine in the world, which is appropriate to the Sending Out of the whole people of God."[3]

RESIDUAL ISSUES

While the question of whether or not it is legitimate to baptize infants at all does not constitute a major area of disagreement within

Anglicanism, the actual theological basis for the practice still continues to provoke some debate. At issue is the question of the requisite faith. Some would want to view baptism as primarily a sign of God's prevenient grace and hence baptize all who are presented solely on the basis of the faith of the church; others would want to demand evidence of repentance and faith in the parents and/or godparents themselves as the justification for the baptism. Still others would continue to adhere to the position that it is the faith (or future faith) of the infants that is being articulated through the responses made in the rite by the godparents.

This results in some variety of practice in modern Anglican baptismal rites both as to exactly what parents and/or godparents are asked to renounce and affirm and also as to whether they do so on their own behalf or on that of the infants. For example, while the 1980 Church of England rites had asked parents and godparents to speak both "for themselves and for these children" in making the baptismal renunciations and profession of faith, the newer *Common Worship* rites reproduced here return to the classic form of a proxy decision spoken in the name of infant candidates. The Toronto Report adopted the view that "the context of the baptism of infants is the faith of the church as mediated by believing parents, other sponsors, and other Christians. . . . Hence, it is appropriate to baptize infants when there is a reasonable expectation that the child will in fact be nurtured within the community of faith. Ordinarily, therefore, the baptism of infants requires the support of a believing parent" (1, 7). While setting its face firmly against "indiscriminate" baptism (1, 8), it did not, however, spell out what liturgical provision ought to be made to embody its view of faith but merely laid out the various options (4, 7).

As the number of infant baptisms continues to drop both in England and in some other parts of the Anglican Communion, the proportion of Anglicans being baptized as adults increases. This raises the issue of the provision for a formal catechumenate with appropriate liturgical rites to mark stages on the way to baptism, along the lines of the Roman Catholic Rite of Christian Initiation of Adults (RCIA). Such rites have already been produced by a few provinces, and it is likely that others will follow suit in the near future. There has also been discussion in some provinces about the possibility of creating an adaptation of the catechumenate for the parents and godparents of infant candidates, or even the formation of a catechumenate for young children themselves.[4]

Since the role of the confirmation rites has long been a controversial issue within Anglicanism, and in spite of the Toronto Statement having come down firmly on the side of sacramental initiation being complete in baptism, variation in the meaning of confirmation still persists in modern rites. While (as was indicated earlier) there has been a growing preference to unite baptism and confirmation within a single rite for adult candidates, there is still a general expectation that those baptized in infancy will undergo a separate rite of confirmation at a later age.

What this rite is understood as effecting, however, appears to vary from province to province, implied both by where in service books it is to be found (that is, with initiation services or among other episcopal or pastoral rites) and by the differing forms of words used at the laying of hands. There are those who have stayed close to the classic Anglican formulary, "Defend, O Lord, this thy servant with thy heavenly grace, that he/she may continue thine for ever and daily increase in thy Holy Spirit . . . ," suggesting a nonsacramental view of the rite, with the emphasis falling instead on it providing an opportunity for a mature profession of faith to be made before the bishop. There are some who instead ask God to "strengthen" the candidate with the Holy Spirit, echoing—although perhaps unintentionally—the medieval interpretation of the sacrament of confirmation.[5] Still others, like the Church of England rite reproduced here, more ambiguously ask God to "confirm" the candidate with the Holy Spirit.

The 1998 Scottish rite is radically unambiguous, asking the Spirit to "rekindle" the gifts of grace in the candidate and "renew her/his life in Christ." There is also variation between provinces as to whether confirmation still functions in the traditional Anglican manner as the "gateway" to communicant status in the church, or whether the communion of all the baptized has become common practice. The latter in turn further distances the separate rite of confirmation from initiation as such, in the direction of either a sacramental or pastoral rite for Christians already well advanced in their spiritual journey.

Thus, baptismal rites in the Anglican Communion today reflect a church still in transition as regards its theology of baptism and confirmation, and not one that has reached a plateau on which it is likely to rest for long.

Notes

[1] "Walk in Newness of Life: The Findings of the International Anglican Liturgical Consultation, Toronto 1991," in David R. Holeton, ed., *Christian Initiation in the Anglican Communion*, Grove Worship Series No. 118 (Nottingham: Grove Books, 1991); and in David R. Holeton, ed., *Growing in Newness of Life: Christian Initiation in Anglicanism Today: Papers from the Fourth International Anglican Liturgical Consultation, Toronto 1991* (Toronto: Anglican Book Centre, 1993), 227–56.

[2] The Church of England rites use the term "godparent" for those who present children for baptism and "sponsor" for those "who agree to support in the journey of faith candidates (of any age) for baptism, confirmation or affirmation of baptismal faith."

[3] *Common Worship: Initiation Services* (London: Church House Publishing, 1998), 198.

[4] See Toronto Report, Section 2, 11–16.

[5] The American and Canadian books allow either of these two options to be used.

Chapter 7

Baptism in the Presbyterian and Reformed Tradition

Martha Moore-Keish

The baptismal liturgy presented with this article is from the *Book of Common Worship* of the Presbyterian Church (USA) published in 1993.[1] This liturgy was developed over many years, through denominational as well as ecumenical consultation. It is still in the process of being received by the churches of the Presbyterian Church (USA), who are encouraged but not required to use it in their baptismal practice. Following a concise presentation of the liturgy, I will examine variations in understanding and practice and then note central issues under discussion today both in the Presbyterian Church (USA) and ecumenically.

LITURGICAL FLOW OF THE BAPTISMAL SERVICE

1. *Presentation*

The baptismal liturgy follows the proclamation of the word. It begins with sentences of Scripture read by the minister, always including the Great Commission from Matthew (which serves as a "warrant" for the practice), followed by one or more of the options provided. After the scriptural sentences, an elder (an ordained member of the congregation with responsibility for leadership, government, and discipline) presents the candidates for baptism. The minister then asks the candidates (or their parents, in the case of infants) if they desire to be baptized. Parents, sponsors, and the congregation promise to nurture the baptized in the faith.

2. *Profession of Faith*

The baptismal candidates are asked to turn from evil and turn to Christ in the renunciations. Having done this, the candidates then join the entire congregation in the recitation of the Apostles' Creed, which may take the ancient question and answer form. After this corporate profession of faith, the minister turns again to the candidates and asks them to promise to be faithful members of the church. Depending on the form used, this may focus more on the local or more on the universal dimension of the church.

3. Thanksgiving over the Water

The baptismal prayer, like the eucharistic prayer, begins with the opening dialogue (but without the *sursum corda*). The minister then gives thanks over the water by praising God for God's faithfulness in the covenant, remembering God's reconciling acts that have particular baptismal imagery (such as the Creation, the Flood and Noah, the Exodus, Jesus' baptism in the Jordan, and Jesus' death and resurrection). Touching or gesturing toward the water, the minister then invokes the Holy Spirit to attend and empower the baptism, to make the water a water of redemption and rebirth, and to equip the church for faithfulness. The prayer concludes with an ascription of praise to the triune God.

4. The Baptism

The actual water bath may take place in a variety of ways depending on the setting and size of font: the minister may dip water with a hand from a basin and sprinkle it on each candidate's head; the candidates may kneel and water may be poured over their heads; or the candidates may be dipped under the water. In the vast majority of Presbyterian churches, the minister baptizes by pouring or sprinkling the water. The one invariable element is that the minister uses the baptismal formula: "(*name*), I baptize you in the name of the Father, and of the Son, and of the Holy Spirit."[2]

5. Laying On of Hands

Following the water bath, the minister lays hands on the head of the newly baptized and offers a brief prayer for the Holy Spirit to uphold those persons and guide them into increased holiness of life. The minister then marks the sign of the cross on the forehead of each newly baptized, using oil if desired, and telling the new Christians that they have been sealed in the Holy Spirit and marked as Christ's own.

6. Welcome

At this point, the newly baptized are welcomed by the congregation. This may consist of a formal welcome using printed words or a congregational song; it may also include more informal gestures of welcome such as handshakes or hugs by members of the congregation.

7. The Peace

The peace which is exchanged at this point is a particular opportunity to share Christ's peace with the newly baptized.

SIGNIFICANT VARIATIONS
IN BAPTISMAL UNDERSTANDING AND PRACTICE

The *Book of Common Worship* also contains an Alternative Service for the Sacrament of Baptism[3] prepared by the Consultation on Common Texts (CCT), an ecumenical forum for liturgical renewal among many of the major Christian denominations of North America. It is substantially the same as the first baptismal rite, except that the prayer over the water comes after the renunciations and creed in the first rite and before these actions in the Alternative Service. The latter emphasizes slightly more strongly the presence of salvific grace prior to promise making, while the first rite accents the nature of repentance and conversion as the spiritual posture called for in the presence of such grace. Also, the Alternative Service suggests the giving of a baptismal garment and a candle to the newly baptized after the laying on of hands and before the welcome. (Although offered as a suggestion, the giving of a baptismal garment is practiced only very rarely in Presbyterian churches in North America.)

Though these baptismal liturgies are contained in the *Book of Common Worship* of the Presbyterian Church (USA), many congregations actually use a form much shorter than this. This shorter form usually consists of the presentation of the one(s) to be baptized, questions to these baptismal candidates, a brief prayer, baptism, and act of welcoming the person(s) by the congregation. The renunciations are a relatively new introduction, still alien to many Presbyterians; and even the use of the Apostles' Creed at baptisms is not widely practiced. Many Reformed feel that use of the renunciations verges on semi-Pelagianism, implying that human actions precede—and even prompt—the action of God. In addition, the prayer over the water frequently does not follow the form outlined above (due to discomfort over its length and unfamiliarity with the form) but consists of a prayer for the one(s) being baptized, with a call on the Holy Spirit to work through the water to seal God's promises.

1. A Specific Variation

Some Presbyterian churches in the United States are discovering and including in the baptismal liturgy a declaration from the Order for Holy Baptism (of infants) in the Church of Scotland's *Book of Common Order* published in 1994. This declaration was adapted from an earlier liturgy of the French Reformed Church, and it displays the characteristic Reformed emphasis on God's grace that precedes our faith. When this declaration is used, it follows the prayer over the water and precedes the act of baptism. The minister addresses each child with these words:

> [Name],
> for you Jesus Christ came into the world;
> for you he lived and showed God's love;
> for you he suffered the darkness of Calvary
> and cried at the last, "It is accomplished";
> for you he triumphed over death
> and rose in newness of life;
> for you he ascended to reign at God's right hand.
> All this he did for you, [name],
> though you do not know it yet.
> And so the word of Scripture is fulfilled:
> "We love because God loved us first."[4]

2. Preparation

There is wide variation in baptismal preparation among Presbyterian and Reformed congregations. Some baptize with no preparation, while others require (or at least encourage) months of intentional preparation for baptism. Increasing numbers of Reformed and Presbyterian churches in the United States are turning to the ancient catechumenate as a model for preparing new adult disciples to receive baptism.

3. Infant Baptism

Although the Reformed heritage has a strong tradition of infant baptism, some Reformed are beginning to raise questions about this practice, and some parents choose to delay baptism until children come of age to make the decision for themselves. The Presbyterian Church (USA) *Book of Order* advises that parents have infants baptized without undue haste or undue delay. The former United Presbyterian Church in the USA (one of the denominations that united in 1983 to form the

Presbyterian Church [USA]) had, for a time, in their *Book of Order* a paragraph allowing parents to decide whether or not to have their children baptized as infants. This has led to some regional difference in practice, since the other uniting denomination (the Presbyterian Church in the United States, found mostly in the south of the country) never had this constitutional provision.

Because of their historically strong commitment to infant baptism, Presbyterian and Reformed churches face the issue of how to understand and practice baptism of babies: is baptism primarily a *familial* rite, the welcome of a baby by the biological family—or is it a fully *ecclesial* rite, the engrafting of a new Christian into the body of Christ?

4. Baptism and the Calendar

Is baptism reserved for certain days of the liturgical year, or can it be celebrated anytime? This is related to the issues raised by infant baptism: is it primarily a family rite or a rite of the church rooted in the liturgical calendar?

5. Baptism and Proclamation of the Word

Does baptism follow the order outlined above, in which baptism follows the preaching of the word and is expected to precede eucharist, or does it precede the proclamation of the word? This points to a variation in understanding baptism, that is, either as a response to the word or as a preliminary act before the word. It is also related to the debate about the unified rites of initiation. Those local churches that are trying to recover the link between baptism, confirmation, and eucharist will be more intentional about celebrating baptism following the proclamation of the word; churches that are less interested in, or less aware of, the historic connection of these rites may place baptism before the proclamation for practical reasons.

6. Ritual Embellishments of the Sign: Excessive Indulgence and Blind Rejection

Since the introduction of the baptismal rite outlined above, there have been extreme reactions at both ends of the spectrum to the richness of the suggested ritual action. Some Reformed have reacted immediately against symbols such as anointing with oil and giving the newly baptized a candle or garment, fearing that these detract from the central symbol of the water or that they are not "truly Reformed." Others have embraced the added symbolism with such enthusiasm that the basic act of baptism is lost. Both reactions fail to reflect adequately on the ways in which the added symbols amplify—but do not replace—the significance of the washing with water.

7. Local and Universal Dimensions of Baptism

Presbyterian and Reformed churches differ over whether baptism is predominantly a ritual of welcome into a local church or incorporation into the universal church, Christ's body. The former is, of course, a dimension of the latter, but the dimension of local welcome is often elevated to *the* meaning of baptism. Related to this is the common (mis-) understanding of baptism as the welcome into a particular denomination (it is not uncommon to hear someone claim, "I was baptized Methodist, but raised Presbyterian").

ISSUES IN CURRENT REFLECTION AND DISCUSSIONS

1. God's Grace and Human Response

The chief issue in Reformed baptismal discussion continues to be how to maintain our historic emphasis on baptism as God's gracious action while also attending to the human dimension of the sacrament. Faithful Reformed people disagree on how to manage this balance. This basic issue underlies many of the particular questions that arise in baptismal debates: for instance, when is it permissible to refuse to baptize someone? Is every such refusal a denial of the generosity of God's grace? How much should we require of those preparing for baptism? Should catechesis precede or follow the act of baptism?

Baptism is God's act of cleansing, redeeming, and renewing, and it is also the welcoming of a new Christian into community. Reformed theology always encourages attention first to God's action, but there is increased concern about how persons *receive* God's action: how God works not only in the act of baptism narrowly construed but also through the life of the community of faith to form new Christians in personal lives of gratitude. Some Reformed object to the language of "Christian initiation," claiming that such a term focuses too much on the human community into which one is initiated at baptism. This discomfort points to the debate in the Reformed tradition over how to maintain a focus on the radical priority of God's action while also attending to the shape of human living in response to that grace.

One form of this question is: what is the relationship between *baptism and faith*? Those who profess "believer baptism" expect faith to be present in the individual before baptism is received: it is that faith which receives God's action in the sacrament. Some Reformed persons share this understanding of baptism as the confirmation of a covenant already formed, diminishing the real sacramental view of the water bath itself. Most Reformed Christians, however, have emphasized the notion that baptism points to God's utter grace in choosing us before we have any ability to comprehend who or what God is. But this can make it difficult for Reformed Christians to describe adequately the relationship between baptism and faith. How can it be the case that faith receives the sacraments, as Calvin would have us believe, if there is no visible faith in the tiny baby dripping with water?

Some answer this difficulty by focusing on the faith of the community into which one is baptized. Parents and sponsors make promises on behalf of the child, because she/he cannot yet do so. Faith in this case is communal, not individual. Others talk about the faith of the baptized infant as "proleptic," suggesting that in baptism faith is present in an anticipatory fashion. Thus, in a variety of ways, baptism and justification by grace through faith remains a knotty relationship to be worked out.

A related question is the relationship between *baptism and faithful living*. How is baptism related to sanctification, the ongoing life of faith? The promises of nurture made by the congregation at an infant's baptism are necessary but not sufficient to answer this question. Some Reformed Christians are seeking to recover Calvin's emphasis on the link between baptism and "discipline," or the structure of the faithful life. This moves the discussion from the question of what constitutes valid baptism (which allows for minimalist celebration) to how baptism shapes a life of faithfulness (which focuses on a more expansive process of preparation for, and celebration of, baptism).

2. Baptism and Eucharist

Another important set of issues revolves around the relationship between baptism and eucharist. Some Presbyterian congregations are now admitting non-baptized persons to the table, arguing that to do otherwise contradicts Jesus' practice of hospitality. Among those who "open" the table in this way, there is little conversation about how the sacraments of baptism and eucharist are intertwined. A related question is the relationship of baptism and confirmation. More congregations are recovering the link between confirmation and baptism, but confirmation is still usually understood as a rite of passage at the time of adolescence. Presbyterian churches are largely unaware of, or indifferent to, the early church practice of the unified rites of initiation.

3. *The Norm for Baptismal Age*

Although Presbyterians continue to affirm infant baptism, more and more baptisms are of adults coming to faith for the first time. This situation, coupled with ecumenical conversation about baptism, is raising the question of what we understand to be the normative age for baptism. Is baptism primarily an adult rite into which we incorporate infants who are part of a believing family, or is baptism primarily an infant rite which we practice on adults who were not baptized in the ordinary way? Where does this leave the children who fall between these two poles? We still struggle with how to understand the baptism of those who are between the ages of four and twelve—old enough to desire baptism, but not old enough to make their own full profession of faith.

4. *The Status of Symbols Generally*

This is a persistent issue for Reformed Christians. Can material things really bear and convey the presence of God? There is deep tension in the Reformed tradition with regard to symbols. On the one hand, we profess faith in Christ's incarnation and God's accommodation to human capacity, but on the other hand we affirm the transcendence of God and are suspicious of anything that smacks of idolatry or seems to take the place of God.

5. *Baptism as Isolated Rite or as Way of Life?*

While most Presbyterian and Reformed Christians continue to think of baptism as the water bath alone, in recent years some Reformed have begun moving toward a broader understanding of baptism as the identifying mark of the Christian life as a whole. Exploration of the catechumenate has contributed to this shift in understanding. This serious attention to baptism as a primary source of Christian identity is helping Reformed churches to "receive" the ecumenical shift from a focus on communion ecclesiology to a rediscovery of, and renewed focus on, baptismal ecclesiology.

Notes

[1] Presbyterian Church (USA), *Book of Common Worship*, prepared by the Theology and Worship Ministry Unit for the Presbyterian Church (USA) and the Cumberland Presbyterian Church (Louisville, KY: Westminster/John Knox Press, 1993), 402–15.

[2] Ibid., 413.

[3] Ibid., 419–29.

[4] Church of Scotland, *Book of Common Order of the Church of Scotland* (Edinburgh: St. Andrew Press, 1994), 89.

Chapter 8

The Baptism of Believers
Paul Fiddes

There is no accepted liturgy for baptism among Baptist churches worldwide, in the sense of any full "script" of scriptural passages, declarations, promises, and prayers. However, there is a generally recognizable pattern that will be given appropriate content in particular contexts and cultures, so that Baptists sharing in the service in a country not their own will find it partly familiar and partly unfamiliar. This continues a Baptist tradition of balancing "the freedom of the Spirit" and "worship from the heart" with a concern that worship should be in "good order"; it also reflects a deeply rooted aversion to anything that might be regarded as an official prayer book imposed upon a local congregation.

Most Baptist Unions and Conventions will provide their churches with worship material and offer models for liturgy that they hope will bring into the local church some perspectives from the practice of the early church and the wider church today, while expecting them to be modified and adapted to meet the needs of a particular congregation. This is the case with the example given to accompany this article from a *Guidebook for Worship Leaders*[1] produced by the Baptist Union of Great Britain. This is widely used among Baptist ministers in Great Britain and has also been adopted by English-speaking ministers in other Unions and Conventions throughout the world.

In 2005 the Baptist Union of Great Britain produced an extensive new book of worship material, *Gathering for Worship. Patterns and Prayers for the Community of Disciples*.[2] This includes a revised liturgy for "baptizing disciples," but comments on the earlier liturgy in this article are still relevant, and the earlier version is probably still in wider use among Baptists worldwide.

THE SHAPE OF THE EVENT
The overall shape as presented in this order of service is:

1. ministry of the word
2. the act of baptism
3. laying on of hands
4. reception into membership
5. participation in the Lord's Supper.

This sequence of actions is shaped by the fact that the candidates for baptism are all "believers," in the sense that they can, and do, profess their own faith. In this flow of the event, those to be baptized first hear, together with others, the word of God through human words of Scripture and preaching, offering new life through the death and resurrection of Jesus and calling them to be his disciples. They respond to the grace of God in baptism, are commissioned for service through the laying on of hands, and are received into membership of the local church, which is the fellowship of those who are called to share in God's mission in the world; their covenant with God and with each other is then sealed in the covenant meal of the Lord's Supper.

In recent years, it has become a regular practice[3] to integrate these elements into one continuous event, though some churches will delay reception into church membership until the next regular celebration of the Lord's Supper. Laying on of hands is the one element that may not appear in some Baptist churches today, although it was a feature of early Baptist practice, especially among General Baptists in England.[4] Some may regard the reality that it signifies as being included both within the act of baptism itself and in the offering of the "hand of fellowship" at reception into membership.

The act of baptism is set in the context of a service of public worship and takes central place within it. It would be inconceivable among Baptists to have anything like a private baptism, partly due to the importance of the candidates' witness to their faith before others and partly due to the strong sense that this is an act for believers belonging to a fellowship *of* believers. This communal setting of the act helps to mitigate against the danger of its being regarded as a subjective, individualistic moment of "personal faith."

If we look in more detail at the flow of the liturgy, we see that a statement about the meaning of baptism is followed by prayer for the candidates, which includes some supplication for the work of the Holy Spirit in their lives both at this moment and in the future. It is characteristic of a Baptist approach not to tie the work of the Spirit closely to the element of the water in itself (there is, for instance, no prayer for blessing of the water) but to relate it to the whole action of the event and to the life of the candidates. There follows a declaration of the candidates' faith, and most Baptist congregations will include some kind of question, answer, and promise. Before this more formal dialogue, many Baptist churches would expect the candidates to "give their testimony" or bear witness to their faith in their own words. In some Baptist churches in Eastern Europe, however, this testimony before the church happens a few days earlier in a midweek meeting. It is traditional for candidates to be given a text of Scripture by the minister just before or after baptism; increasingly among Baptist churches, other members of the congregation will offer words of Scripture or a spontaneous word of encouragement (in more charismatic churches this may be called a "word of prophecy").

The baptism itself follows in the name of the triune God and by immersion in the water. In Southern Baptist churches of the USA, almost always the minister will accompany the act of immersion with the words: "You are buried with Christ in baptism and raised with him to new life." However, some Baptist churches today will offer an alternative mode of baptism, by pouring of water, for those who are prevented through physical disability from being immersed, and many will think that the belief of the candidate is more important than the mode.

Following baptism, the whole congregation is invited to make its own response to the word of God received through Scripture and in acted event. An opportunity is given for some to make a confession of faith for the first time or for some to request preparation for baptism. While an "appeal" is regularly made in Southern Baptist churches in the USA, in many Baptist churches elsewhere a baptismal service will be one of the few occasions when such an invitation is given. Other response to God is made in prayers, which will include intercession for the needs of the world, since sharing in God's mission in the world can begin with intercession. The offering belongs also to this time of response, providing opportunity for self-giving and dedication as well as gifts of money.

The laying on of hands and reception into membership are set in the context of the Lord's Supper, the covenant meal of the church. This underlines the fact that the candidate is being commissioned to serve *in* the community and to serve *with* the community in the world. For these reasons it is perhaps more accurate to regard baptism in Baptist churches in the European tradition as a "disciples' baptism," since it is administered at an age (usually not before adolescence) at which it is possible to think of commissioning Christian disciples to share in the ministry given to the whole church. In Southern Baptist churches of the USA, where the stress falls simply upon being a "believer," young children may be baptized from the age of seven or eight upward.

THE THEOLOGY OF BAPTISM, IN BAPTIST DIVERSITY

1. Sacramentality

A significant difference of understanding about the meaning of baptism among Baptists is represented by the two suggested introductory statements provided by the order of baptism accompanying this article. The first statement offers a more "sacramental" interpretation than the second, insofar as it makes clear that baptism is a means of grace as well as a profession of faith by the believer. The first statement expects God to act in a transformative way through the rite itself, so that the baptismal water is a place of meeting between grace and faith, divine gift and human response. The second statement places more emphasis on witness to what the grace of God *has* already achieved in the experience of those baptized and what *they expect* to receive from God in their lives in the future. Those who take the second approach have often preferred to use the term "ordinance" rather than "sacrament," laying stress on the fact that baptism has been instituted by the command of Christ. This distinction of language is, however, somewhat misleading and is a relatively modern innovation; an examination of early Baptist writings and confessions shows that the terms "sacrament" and "ordinance" were used interchangeably and often both in the same sentence.[5]

Those holding both viewpoints agree, of course, that baptism is an event only for those who have already repented of sin and can already profess their faith in Christ for themselves, and that it is an act of obedience to God following the command of the risen Christ. Both approaches also agree that baptism is a symbol that signifies the saving activity of God as expressed in a number of images, including union with Christ in his death and resurrection, cleansing from sin, deliverance from hostile powers, adoption as children of God, and immersion into the life of the Spirit. All these images find expression in the liturgy. The central, controlling picture is perhaps death and resurrection, symbolized by being plunged beneath the water and then rising from it—which accounts for the Baptist preference for the mode of immersion. The difference between the two approaches is that only the first understands God to give, in the very act of baptism, what is being signified by the symbol (though of course this gift does not come exclusively in this one event).

The sacramentality of the first statement reflects a good deal of Baptist writing on the subject during the last hundred years.[6] The phrase "in baptism [God's] grace is displayed" is not to be taken in the sense of a mere visual aid, as is underlined by the use of the Scripture text Galatians 3:27. There is also a sacramental content in *both* the pre-baptismal prayers, asking God that baptism may be for these candidates "union with Christ in his death and resurrection," a washing away of sin, the gift of new life, and an occasion for filling with the Spirit.

2. *Baptism and Membership of the Local Church*

The shape of the order for baptism clearly links baptism with entrance into membership of the local church, and this would be the understanding of many Baptist churches. Classes in preparation for baptism will usually also prepare candidates for the responsibilities and privileges of church membership. However, baptism and church membership may become disconnected in two ways. First, the act of baptism itself may not be followed by entrance into membership of a local fellowship for one of several reasons: emphasis may be laid on the meaning of baptism for the candidate as an individual, the person may already be attending a church of another denomination, or the person may be thought to be too young for the responsibilities of membership.

Among Southern Baptist churches of the Unites States, while baptism as a believer is generally required as a *qualification* for membership, actual admission into that membership by consent of the gathered congregation usually happens at the end of a church service, dislocated both from baptism and the Lord's Supper. In all these cases, baptism would still be regarded theologically as entrance into "the body of Christ" or the universal church of all true believers (1 Cor 12:13), but the implications for membership would strangely fail to be drawn at the place where the church is manifest on the local level.

A second way in which baptism and church membership can become dislocated is through "open membership." This policy, in which local churches do not make baptism as a believer a qualification for membership but require only a profession of faith, offers the greatest potential for ecumenical partnership. It is the majority practice among Baptist churches in England and widespread among Baptist churches elsewhere. Dating to the seventeenth century in English Baptist life, it developed as a means of offering church fellowship to those who had been baptized as infants in other Christian churches, thus rightly recognizing their membership in the body of Christ. However, since this practice was not generally accompanied by the creation of a theological framework in which infant baptism could be positively affirmed, in a secular age it has sometimes resulted in admission to membership of those who have not been baptized in *any* mode or at *any* age. Moreover, Baptists who cannot attribute significance to infant baptism will separate baptism, in their own minds, from church membership in the case of those baptized only as infants. Confusions have resulted that have begun to be addressed in some contemporary Baptist thought by laying stress on the complete process of initiation rather than the moment of baptism in isolation (see below).

CURRENT ISSUES IN ECUMENICAL DISCUSSION

The most intense problem in ecumenical relations, especially where congregations are shared between believer-Baptist and infant-Baptist members, is that of so-called "rebaptism." The overwhelming majority of Baptists agree with other Christian churches that baptism is unrepeatable, since it symbolizes the once-for-all act of redemption achieved by Christ in his death and resurrection. But many local Baptist churches will still administer baptism as a believer to some Christians who have been baptized as infants. "Closed membership" churches will *require* this, while many "open membership" churches will feel that they *cannot refuse* the request of believers already baptized as infants who themselves ask for baptism out of a firm conviction that Christ is calling them to obey him in this way. Churches that baptize such candidates—for either reason—will generally not regard this as *rebaptism*, since they only recognize the baptism of believing disciples as true baptism. They will also think that they are not "un-churching" those baptized only as infants, since they regard faith in Christ, and immersion into the life of the Spirit of God, as being the essential basis for membership in the body of Christ regardless of water baptism.

Some Baptist contributions to recent ecumenical discussions have suggested a way forward out of this impasse.[7] Rather than urging an equivalence of infant baptism with believer-baptism, it might be possible to recognize whole *patterns of initiation* as being equivalent.

Baptism, at whatever age, could be seen as only part of a journey of Christian beginnings, a journey with its starting point in the prevenient grace of God and its ending with an "owned" faith of a Christian disciple, a believer saying "yes" to God's "yes" to him or her and being commissioned for ministry in the world. Along the way there will be various kinds of opportunities for receiving children into the fellowship of the church (whether by baptism or by the blessing of infants) and for growth into faith in Christ. Baptism would stand as a focus for the whole journey of beginning the Christian life, whether it came earlier or later in the process as a whole.

The theological basis for this approach would be the understanding of salvation as a process rather than something occurring at a single point in time. Baptists who take a sacramental view of believers' baptism already, in fact, take this view: salvation must be a process ("being saved") if the act of immersion is actually a dying and rising with Christ, and yet it is a believer who is being baptized. The believer has *already* received the saving grace of God and been filled with the Spirit and yet, on this journey into life, can still have sins washed away and be united with Christ in baptism.

Baptists have been able to contribute this focus on the overall pattern of initiation, rather than the moment of baptism itself, to the ecumenical movement. Here it has found a strong echo among other churches, as reflected in recent work on baptism being done in the ecumenical context.[8]

Notes

[1] *Patterns and Prayers for Christian Worship: A Guidebook for Worship Leaders.* The Baptist Union of Great Britain (Oxford: Oxford University Press, 1991), 93–107.

[2] Christopher J. Ellis and Myra Blyth, eds., *Gathering for Worship. Patterns and Prayers for the Community of Disciples* (Norwich: Canterbury Press, 2005).

[3] Southern Baptist churches in the United States, however, present an exception here: see below.

[4] See, for example, "The Standard Confession" (1660), art. XII, in W. L. Lumpkin, *Baptist Confessions of Faith* (Philadelphia: The Judson Press, 1959), 229.

[5] For example, "A Short Confession of Faith" (Amsterdam, 1610), art. 23, in *Baptist Confessions*, 108; "The Orthodox Creed" (1678), art. xxvii, 317.

⁶ Notable examples are: H. Wheeler Robinson, *Life and Faith of the Baptists* (London: Kingsgate Press, 1946 [1927]); R. E. O. White, *The Biblical Doctrine of Initiation* (London: Hodder and Stoughton, 1960); and G. R. Beasley-Murray, *Baptism in the New Testament* (London: Macmillan, 1963).

⁷ For example: the response of the Baptist Union of Great Britain in Max Thurian, ed., *Churches Respond to BEM: Official responses to the "Baptism, Eucharist and Ministry" Text, Vol. 1* (Geneva: World Council of Churches, 1986), 70–71; *Believing and Being Baptized: Baptism, so-called re-baptism and children in the church* (London: Baptist Union, 1996), 28–33; Paul S. Fiddes, "Baptism and the Process of Christian Initiation," *The Ecumenical Review* 54, no. 1 (2002): 48–65. On the proposal that we should be looking for a "common pattern of initiation" rather than a common baptism, see especially two recent conversations between Baptists and the Anglican Church: *Conversations Around the World 2000–2005: The Report of the International Conversations between the Anglican Communion and the Baptist World Alliance* (London: The Anglican Consultative Council and the Baptist World Alliance, 2005), 44–51; *Pushing at the Boundaries of Unity. Anglicans and Baptists in Conversation* (London: Church House Publishing, 2005), 31–57.

⁸ See "Ecclesiological and Ecumenical Implications of a Common Baptism: A JWG Study," in *Eighth Report, 1999–2005: Joint Working Group Between the Roman Catholic Church and the World Council of Churches* (Geneva-Rome: WCC Publications, 2005), 45–72; and the Faith and Order study document-in-process: "One Baptism: Towards Mutual Recognition." This text-in-process, which is not yet an official text of the Faith and Order Commission, is available in "Minutes of the Standing Commission on Faith and Order, 12–19 June 2007, Crans-Montana, Switzerland," Faith and Order Paper No. 206 (Geneva: Faith and Order, 2007), Appendix V, 57–81, or directly from Faith and Order, WCC, 150, Rte. de Ferney, 1211 Geneva, Switzerland.

Chapter 9

Baptism and the Quaker Tradition

Janet Scott

> I have baptized you with water; but he will baptize you with the Holy Spirit. (Mark 1:8)

These words of John the Baptist provide a biblical basis for the Quaker position on baptism, which has historically been an emphasis on the activity of the Holy Spirit in a person's life and a rejection of water baptism. Thus it is difficult, if not impossible, to provide an example of a typical Quaker baptismal liturgy! Perhaps the nearest written material would be the minutes of a Monthly Meeting recording that someone had been accepted into membership. This paper therefore will look first at the process of becoming a member of the Religious Society of Friends, then at the membership of children; then it will explore the meaning for Quakers of baptism in the Holy Spirit; and finally it will discuss how Quakers might understand the use of water for baptism in other churches.

Initially, it should be remarked that many of the ecumenical issues surrounding the mutual recognition of baptism are of little or no interest to Quakers except as a matter of curiosity: whether or not someone has been baptized with water, how it was done and by whom, and what words were said are all irrelevant. What is important for us is the interior direction of people and how that is manifested in the way they live.

MEMBERSHIP

Most Quakers today formally enter the Society by applying for membership after a period of time as an attender (one who is recognized as regularly attending meetings for worship). The details of the process differ slightly between Yearly Meetings, but for each Yearly Meeting the process can be found in its book of Faith and Practice. The application is usually made to the Monthly Meeting, the business meeting that covers the area in which the applicant lives. In some parts of the world (such as Britain) the Monthly Meeting normally brings together members from more than one worshiping group or meeting: in others, such as parts of the United States, the Monthly Meeting has members from only one local meeting.

What happens next is a process of discernment. The meeting and the applicant are, in effect, seeking to determine whether the applicant is already spiritually a member of the Society, so that the membership can be recorded in the minutes of the Monthly Meeting. In most cases Friends (normally two) are appointed to visit the applicant and to report to the Meeting on their discussion. The meeting will normally make a decision straightaway, but it is at liberty to make further enquiries or to postpone consideration for a while. In some of the African Yearly Meetings there will be a period of probation, normally a year, during which the applicant is expected to show through his or her way of life an adherence to the principles of the Society.

When a Friend moves home, transfer of membership between Monthly Meetings, and between Yearly Meetings, can easily be arranged. A certificate confirming membership is sent to the new Monthly Meeting and the membership is actually transferred when the sending Monthly Meeting records in its minutes that the certificate has been accepted by the new Monthly Meeting. Isolated people who do not live within the compass of a Monthly Meeting are able to apply to the Friends World Committee for Consultation and can be placed on an international membership list.

Because the recording of membership is the recording of a commitment to the Society and its ways, it is possible to cease to be a member if that commitment wanes. The Friend can resign, or a Monthly Meeting can take steps to discontinue membership if it discerns that it no longer has any real meaning. Great care is taken over this. The "disownment," frequently used in the eighteenth and nineteenth centuries, is still possible though rarely used today. There is no problem about someone whose membership has ended applying again for membership if a sense of commitment is renewed.

CONVINCEMENT

Those who apply for membership as adults are referred to in Quaker terminology as "convinced Friends." Convincement is described in different language at different times, but at its heart it is an experience of the living God who is met in worship and who gives new life, new hope, and a new spirit. Robert Barclay (1648–1690) described it as ". . . when I came into the silent assemblies of God's people, I felt a secret power among them which touched my heart; and as I gave way unto it I found the evil weakening in me and the good raised up . . ."

Among early Friends there was no formal membership. Convincement led people to act according to Friends' principles, and since these were at odds with the surrounding society Friends suffered ridicule, imprisonment, distraint of goods, and even death. When it was illegal to attend a meeting for worship (as in Britain at various times before 1689) or to be a Quaker (as in Massachusetts in the late 1650s), those who were prepared to suffer for declaring themselves Quakers were clearly convinced.

Today, Friends are more likely to speak of "feeling at home" in a meeting and the process of convincement may be lengthy, continuing after entry into formal membership. One of the problems of having a noble history and strong principles is that many feel that they are "not good enough" to become a member: this can be accompanied by disillusionment when they realize that none of the members are "good enough" and that all continue to be "humble learners in the school of Christ."

Britain Yearly Meeting writes in its book of discipline (1994):

> People still become Friends through convincement, and like early Friends they wrestle and rejoice with that experience. Membership is still seen as a discipleship, a discipline within a broadly Christian perspective and our Quaker tradition, where the way we live is as important as the beliefs we affirm. Like all discipleships, membership has its elements of commitment and responsibility but it is also about joy and celebration. Membership is a way of saying to the meeting that you feel at home, and in the right place. Membership is also a way of saying to the meeting, and to the world, that you accept at least the fundamental elements of being a Quaker: the understanding of divine guidance, the manner of corporate worship and the ordering of the meeting's business, the practical expression of inward convictions and the equality of all before God. In asking to be admitted to the community of the meeting you are affirming what the meeting stands for and declaring your willingness to contribute to its life.[1]

Though other Yearly Meetings will phrase it differently, the essential elements of convincement are the inward personal experience of God that leads to a recognition of the truth in Quaker ways and testimonies, the living out of those convictions, and the willingness to be led into new ways of service. It is the discernment of this spiritual state which leads to membership.

Oddly, since many of those who are convinced and enter the Society come from other churches, many current members have been baptized with water as infants. However, in general the question of whether or not applicants have been so baptized is not asked, since it is seen as irrelevant to Quaker procedures and discernment. The Society could be open to challenge for not accepting people into membership on the basis of baptism into another church, and the question of whether membership could be transferred into or from another church would be a new issue for Friends to investigate.

THE MEMBERSHIP OF CHILDREN

Among the stories Quakers tell from their tradition are those of the times in the seventeenth century when the adult members of a meeting were imprisoned for being Quakers, and the public meetings for worship were kept going by the children. In Bristol in 1682, for example, eleven boys and four girls, aged mostly from ten to twelve, were sent overnight to prison and threatened with beatings unless they agreed to stop going to meetings. Besse in his *Book of Sufferings* says "they were unmoveable." For Quakers, therefore, it has always been clear that, whatever their formal status, children have a relationship with God and a membership of the meeting. Furthermore, Quaker worship conducted by children is as "valid" as that conducted by adults.

When adults and children worship together, children may (and sometimes do) contribute spoken ministry under the guidance of the Holy Spirit. They also have by their presence their own ministry, as reminders of the presence of Christ and the nature of the kingdom of God (Matt 18:3-5). They help us to remember that we do not have to be perfect or learned or wise—or even well-behaved—to be loved members of God's family and to be growing in grace.

How this fits into formal membership structures differs over time and place. Quakers try to express two principles that are not easily practiced simultaneously: first, that it is evident that children are members of the community; second, that membership requires personal commitment and convincement.

Quakers developed the concept of "birthright membership," where the children of Quaker parents became members as babies because they would be brought up within the ways of Quakers. This is still found in some Yearly Meetings, but others have abandoned it in favor of membership on application by the parents; this leads to far fewer children being in formal membership. In both cases there is generally an attempt, when the children reach an appropriate age, to encourage them to confirm their membership for themselves. Ideally, the child brought up in a Quaker family and meeting will feel a sense of membership and Quaker identity from a young age, will grow in a relationship with God, and will enter adult life as a convinced member, whether that membership comes through the parents or from a personal application. However, it is probably true to say, of Britain at least, that a high proportion of those whose membership is discontinued by Monthly Meetings are adults who were the children of Quakers and in whose lives membership has become a sentimental remembrance rather than a living reality.

Few ceremonies will mark this passage. When a baby is first brought to meeting, some words of welcome and encouragement, and perhaps prayer, will probably be part of the worship; when the birth of a child to a member is recorded in the minutes of the Monthly Meeting, one or two Friends will usually be appointed to visit the family and welcome the baby. At sixteen, a child may be given his or her own copy of the book of faith and practice; when membership is confirmed or entered into at the Monthly Meeting, there may be an announcement at a meeting for worship.

Within the Quaker tradition the emphasis on the individual is much more commonly found at the end of life, when it is possible at a funeral or memorial meeting to look back and see how God worked through the whole of a person's life. A memorial minute, or a "Testimony to the grace of God in the life of . . ." (a Friend), will record the spiritual journey, the struggles and the achievements of the person, and will help to illuminate for other Friends some of the meaning of the membership that they have undertaken.

BAPTISM IN THE SPIRIT

Such testimonies and minutes are perhaps the best way of finding what Quakers mean when they refer to "baptism in the Holy Spirit." They are rarely referring to one overwhelming experience, though there may be individuals for whom an experience of the presence of God in their lives provided a turning point. For most Quaker traditions the operation of the Holy Spirit is through the "still small voice" rather than the "rushing mighty wind," though this is not to deny the power of the Spirit which can be felt in a gathered meeting for worship or can be heard through spoken ministry that is truly inspired.

For Quakers, the baptism of the Spirit is a lifelong experience of transformation. It includes quiet listening to God's promptings of love and truth in the heart, an inward willingness to be obedient to God's leadings, and actions directed toward making God's love visible in the world. At its best, the action of the Holy Spirit in a willing soul is creative, fearless, and joyful. It evokes faithfulness, the persistence to pursue obediently the path to which one is called despite difficulties and failures, the mind to value the least and humblest task if it serves God's purposes, and the power to do extraordinary things whilst admitting "not I, but God in me."

There is a Quaker tradition of recording such experience in journals, as, for example, when John Woolman (1720–1772) recounts the event that made him see that he could no longer be involved in the buying and selling of slaves, or George Fox's account (1647) of how, when all his hopes were gone and there was none to help him: "[T]hen, Oh then, I heard a voice which said, 'There is one, even Christ Jesus, that can speak to thy condition', and when I heard it my heart did leap for joy."[2] These experiences help to set a direction, and the journals record the steps taken, the failures as well as the successes, the process of learning and the gaining of insight, and the spiritual discipline needed to subdue the self and to keep faithfully within one's guide. These stories are told to help others with their own path; they are a sharing of how God is known and followed that may be recognized in another heart and that may strengthen, comfort, and encourage another on the way.

Baptism in the Holy Spirit may also be described as the operation of the Light, the Light of Christ that enlightens everyone (John 1:8). In our experience, when there is a response to the Inward Light in the heart, it heals and cleanses as well as guides and empowers. Thomas Ellwood (1639–1713) described it thus: "I receive(d) a new law—an inward law superadded to the outward—the law of the spirit of life in Christ Jesus, which wrought in me against all evil . . . so that here began to be a way cast up for me to walk in. . . . and this way with respect to me I saw was that measure of divine light which was manifested in me."[3]

The way is closely connected with what Quakers call the "testimonies," ways of living that bear witness to the loving rule of God. Peace, equality, simplicity, and truth are, for Quakers, some of the major qualities of a life lived in the presence of God and are both a sign and a manifestation of God's kingdom in the individual, in the worshiping community, and in the world. Paul's description of the fruits of the Spirit as "love, joy, peace, patience, kindness, generosity, faithfulness, gentleness and self-control" (Gal 5:22-3) results for us not only from the action of the Spirit indwelling in the heart but also from the way of transformation. It is the eschatological reality which is with us now.

BAPTISM IN OTHER CHURCHES

For Quakers, therefore, the religious life is the inward life of the spirit. Its outward expression is in holy living, in doing the will of God (Matt 7:21); therefore, outward symbols such as baptism with water have traditionally been regarded as at best unnecessary and at worst as distracting and misleading, since they cannot bring about that which they symbolize.

Nevertheless, some Quakers have seen a value in a powerful symbol. For example, in a few of the more evangelical Friends' churches (most often in parts of the USA) there are pastors who will, on request, baptize a child with water or an adult who has come to believe—not because it is regarded as necessary but because it is felt to be helpful. One Quaker working as a chaplain in a hospital has reported baptizing a dying baby because the ritual symbolized the love of the parents for their child and their handing over of her into God's keeping.

Reflecting on the symbolic value of baptism with water, we can see two aspects that might have a strong appeal for Quakers. The first is the public nature of baptism, especially believers' baptism, as a declaration of faith and commitment. This enables a community to welcome and celebrate a new member and to be reminded of the faith and life that binds it together. It is a public witness to the nature of the Christian life lived as an individual disciple of Christ—and therefore inescapably as one of his community.

The second is that water baptism is a symbol of the equality of all Christians. It is the same for everyone: rich and poor, old and young, male and female, of whatever race, nationality, or time. All come equally into their own relationship with Christ, all become part of the body of Christ of which each is a necessary member and within which none can say of another, "You do not belong," nor of themselves, "I do not belong" (1 Cor 12:13-21).

The danger for this, as for any symbol or rite, is when the symbol comes to replace the reality, and the life of the church does not bear witness to the inclusive love of Christ, to the equality of all before God, or to faith made active in the world.

It is particularly saddening when what should be a symbol of Christian unity becomes a cause and a symbol of division within the body of Christ. We pray that all churches will be able to put first the command of Jesus that we love one another as he has loved us (John 13:34-35), and that we will be able to find ways to show that love to one another as a sign of our discipleship to him who first loved us, who humbly washed our feet, and who gave up his life for our sake.

Notes

[1] Britain Yearly Meeting (Society of Friends), *Quaker faith & practice : the book of Christian discipline of the Yearly Meeting of the Religious Society of Friends (Quakers) in Britain* (London: Yearly Meeting of the Religious Society of Friends, 1995).

[2] George Fox, *The Journal of George Fox: A Revised Edition by John L. Nichalls, with Epilogue by Henry J. Cadbury and an Introduction by Geoffrey Nuttall* (Cambridge, UK: Cambridge University Press, 1952), 11.

[3] Thomas Ellwood, *Thomas Ellwood, The History of the Life of Thomas Ellwood, written by Himself*, ed. and intro. Rosemary Moore (Walnut Creek, CA: Alta Mira Press, 2004), 18–19.

Chapter 10

Baptismal Practice among North American Mennonites[1]

Rebecca Slough

Baptism stands as one of the defining characteristics of the sixteenth-century Anabaptist movement. Unconvinced by biblical evidence for the practice of infant baptism, these "rebaptizers" forged a theology of believers' baptism now taken for granted by many Protestants. Throughout the Reformation era and well into the seventeenth century, Anabaptists were executed for holding biblically grounded beliefs that threatened church and state authority. The baptism of believers was one such threatening belief.

ANABAPTIST UNDERSTANDINGS OF BAPTISM

Seeking faithfulness to the testimony of Scripture, Anabaptist leaders questioned whether an infant or young child could respond to the movement of the Holy Spirit in its inner being. They saw that in the New Testament the majority of early Christians first believed in the gospel they heard, asked for baptism, then were baptized with water and the Holy Spirit (though not necessarily in that order). They did not believe that a young child could fulfill the joyful, though sometimes difficult, calling of being a disciple of Jesus Christ or being a responsible member in his Body, the church. They saw no evidence that God's gift of salvation, given to all moved to faith by the Holy Spirit, depended upon the water of baptism. Contrary to the doctrine of other churches, these leaders did not count baptism as a sacrament. They were most concerned that believers correctly understood the implications of baptism for a life of discipleship. Baptismal rites to regulate practice were of small consequence to them.

Baptism is an action commanded by Christ (Matt 28:19-20; Mark 16:15-16) and done in the name of the Father, the Son, and the Holy Spirit. It is a particular event within a larger process in which a person hears the gospel preached and taught, confesses, repents, is forgiven, is regenerated, requests baptism, is incorporated into the church, and remains a disciple. Article one of the Schleitheim Confession (1527), one of the first Anabaptist writings on church order, reads:

> Baptism shall be given to all those who have been *taught* repentance and the amendment of life and [who] *believe truly that their sins are taken away* through Christ, and to all those who *desire to walk* in the resurrection of Jesus Christ and be buried with Him in death, so that they might rise with Him; to all those who with such an understanding themselves *desire and request* it from us.[2]

In a context where baptism was administered to infants who did not know the meaning of the church's action on their behalf, the Anabaptists stressed the importance of the new believer's desiring and requesting baptism as an intentional act.

Based on scriptural testimony, the Anabaptists believed that God through the Holy Spirit initiates the process of salvation in human beings and guides them to respond in faith. For this reason, baptism cannot be coerced or demanded by church, state, or family. Covenant describes the vital relationship through Christ that God begins with each believer. While the regenerating relationship between God and the believer is well under way before baptism occurs, through the baptismal rite the believer publicly acknowledges the gift of salvation received, repentance of past sin, the presence of new life, and the intention to follow the way of Christ for the rest of life. Article 7 on Holy Baptism in the Dordrecht Confession (1632), a systematic outline of beliefs and practices drafted for Dutch Mennonites,[3] states:

> Regarding baptism, we confess that all *penitent believers*, who through *faith, the new birth and renewal of the Holy Ghost, have become united with God*, and whose names are recorded in heaven, must, on such scriptural *confession of their faith, and renewal of life*, according to the command and doctrine of Christ, and the example and custom of the apostles, be baptized with water *in the ever adorable name* of the Father, and of the Son, and of the Holy Ghost, to the burying of their sins, and thus to become *incorporated into* the communion of the saints; whereupon they must *learn to observe all things* whatever the Son of God taught, left on record, and commanded his followers to do.[4]

The covenant of baptism incorporates the believer as a member into the Body of Christ—the church, a sign of God's kingdom—where discipleship is nurtured through instruction, discernment, giving and receiving counsel, and worship.

The Anabaptists believed Christians undergo three baptisms (based on 1 John 5:7-8). The baptism of water is a sign of the forgiveness of sins. Water is poured over the believer's head and the baptismal words from Matthew 28:19 spoken. Few other details from early baptismal services are found in the sources. The baptism of the Holy Spirit released the spiritual gifts of the believer for building up the church. The Spirit guided the believer in deepening faith and enabled a life of discipleship. The baptism of blood acknowledged that living the way of Christ would entail suffering, hardship, and possibly death for the sake of the gospel. While Anabaptists and their Mennonite descendants have suffered for many reasons, commitment to Christ's example of love, including nonresistance in the face of danger or hostility and love for enemies, has given this baptism particular meaning across the generations.

CONTEMPORARY MENNONITE UNDERSTANDINGS

Many basic teachings and understandings of the Anabaptists on baptism still reverberate in the *Confession of Faith in a Mennonite Perspective* (1995)[5] and the baptismal order given in the *Minister's Manual* (1998). According to two paragraphs from Article 11 on baptism in the *Confession of Faith*:

> We believe that the baptism of believers with water is *a sign of their cleansing from sin*. Baptism is also a *pledge* before the church of their *covenant* with God *to walk in the way of Jesus Christ through the power of the Holy Spirit*. Believers are *baptized into Christ and his body* by the *Spirit, water, and blood*.
>
> Christian baptism is for those who *confess* their sins, *repent, accept* Jesus Christ as Savior and Lord, and *commit* themselves to follow Christ in obedience *as members of his body*, both giving and receiving care and counsel in the church. Baptism is for those who are of the *age of accountability* and who *freely request* baptism on the basis of *their response* to Jesus Christ in faith.[6]

Mennonites continue to reject the term "sacrament" applied to baptism. However, finding appropriate terms for understanding baptism as an action has proven difficult:[7] it is variously called an ordinance, a symbol, a representation, and a sign. The Commentary on Article 11 affirms:

> In this confession of faith these ceremonies [baptism and Lord's Supper] are called signs, a biblical term rich in meanings. Sign is, first of all, an act of God: signs and wonders in Egypt (Exod 10:1; Num 14:11), signs to prophets (Isa 7:14; 55:13), and Jesus' performance of signs (John 2:11; 12:37; 20:30). John 2:18-22 sees Jesus' death and resurrection as a sign. A sign is not only an act of God, but a human action as well: eating unleavened bread at Passover (Exod 13:9), binding of the commandments to oneself (Deut 6:8), keeping of the Sabbath (Exod 31:13; Ezek 20:20). Likewise, baptism is a sign, representing both God's action in delivering us from sin and death and the action of the one who is baptized, who pledges to God to follow Jesus Christ within the context of Christ's body, the church.[8]

Mennonite pastors, elders, or deacons are not required by ecclesial authority to follow the baptismal rite(s) outlined in minister's manuals. Manuals are offered as guides to ensure that the basic purpose of the rite is preserved without mandating detailed rubrics or prescribed words. Local adaptations abound. However, a survey of twentieth century minister's manuals demonstrates a number of recurring features.

1. Baptism follows a period of instruction, examination, and preparation and is not limited to particular times of the year or seasonal celebrations.
2. Baptism is normally part of a Sunday worship service, making it a public and corporate event.
3. The rite is introduced with an explanation or brief teaching on the nature and purpose of baptism.
4. New believers are asked a series of questions outlining essential tenets of Christian faith from a Mennonite perspective.
5. Before or after water is administered, a spoken prayer asks for the Holy Spirit's activity in the life of the believers.
6. The new believers kneel for baptism.
7. "I baptize you in the name of the Father, and of the Son, and of the Holy Spirit" is spoken while water is poured over the new believers' heads.
8. The right hand of fellowship is extended.

As the twentieth century unfolded, the minister's manuals offered more variations in the services. The manuals from 1950 and 1983 gave two different forms. Alternate prayers, questions to the new believers, and forms of the baptismal words were offered in the 1950, 1983, and 1998 manuals. This variety demonstrates changing congregational sensibilities and attempts to account for regional practices. It also reflects the sixteenth-century Anabaptist impulse to worry little about the fine points of the rite, focusing instead on proper understanding, confession of faith, and water administered in the words of Jesus. Unity in baptismal practice is not found in strictly following a common rite. It flows from the activity of the Holy Spirit.

COMMENTARY ON A SUGGESTED BAPTISMAL RITE

The baptismal service offered here as an example of Mennonite understanding and practice is taken from the *Minister's Manual* of 1998. A congregational worship service built around baptism is the ideal context for celebrating the baptismal rite. The congregation's praise, proclamation, prayer, and offering demonstrate God's saving work in Christ and believers' response to the gift of salvation. In the manual a variety of hymns and Scripture texts are suggested to aid worship planning. Prior to the rite itself the new believers received instruction in baptismal understanding, asked for baptism, were introduced to the congregation, and gave a public testimony of faith. Any number of new believers may be baptized in a service; time and logistical constraints dictate the appropriate limit.

The opening remarks summarize the warrant for baptism and basic Mennonite baptismal understandings. Of particular note: baptism is an act of God, the church, and the believer. *God* gives a good conscience, the seal of the Holy Spirit, and makes believers dead to sin and alive to Christ. The *church* vouches for the believer's faith and the work of grace in his/her life. The *individual* enacts the surrender of the old self and embraces the new.

The questions to the new believer serve as the public profession of faith.[9] The first question asks the believer to claim Jesus Christ as savior; the second calls for affirming faith in the members of the Trinity. The remaining questions focus on beliefs and practices that will shape the believer's life of discipleship. In answering them the believer claims an orientation for living.[10] The manual offers three additional sets of questions. Options (a) and (b) come from earlier minister's manuals. Selection of questions is left to pastoral discretion and/or local practice.

The pastor, another congregational leader, spiritual friend, or mentor, with whom the baptismal candidate has discussed issues of faith and life, offers a personal address to the new believer.

The new believer kneels. Pouring water over the believer's head remains the common mode of baptism, though some congregations choose sprinkling or immersion.[11] The pastor or leader of the rite places hands in open cup-like form on the believer's head. A church elder, deacon, pastoral leader, mentor, brother or sister in the faith, or family member pours water from a pitcher, cup, or dish into the open hands. While speaking the baptismal words, the pastor's hands separate, allowing water to run over the believer's head. Ideally, enough water is used for the new believer to get wet, but not drenched. In the case of sprinkling, the pastor or leader of the rite dips his/her fingers in a bowl of water and sprinkles the believer's head once while speaking the baptismal words or three times with each name of the Trinity. Congregations regularly practicing immersion will have a baptistery in the worship space. Where immersion is less frequent, other arrangements are made or locations chosen for the service.

A prayer over the believer immediately follows the water baptism.[12] It invokes the Holy Spirit to continue its regenerating work and to release the believer's spiritual gifts for ministry. A blessing addressed to the believer follows this brief prayer. Both the prayer and blessing affirm what God has done and direct the believer toward his or her new calling as a follower of Christ.

Throughout the prayer and blessing the believer kneels. At the reception, the pastor or leader of the rite offers a hand and helps the believer stand. Moving from kneeling to standing positions mirrors the words spoken by the pastor that affirm the new life in Christ the believer received. The words mark the believer's incorporation into Christ's church and into the local congregation.

New believers may be given a Scripture text to guide their living and as a memorial of the day. In some congregations a certificate of baptism is given to each new believer.

The final blessing acknowledges the believer's new relationship with Christ and offers a greeting of peace or the right hand of fellowship in Christ's name. At its conclusion, the believer is given some type of physical affirmation and welcome into the body of believers from congregational leaders, family, believing friends, mentors, or other new believers. In many congregations embraces have replaced the kiss of peace, though the kiss is still practiced.

The congregational response allows the witnessing body to voice its welcome of the new believer into its midst. It commits the members to share together in the ongoing life of discipleship. This particular response assumes a single believer is baptized. In the case of multiple baptisms a different form of response is required.

Celebration of the Lord's Supper is recommended at the conclusion of the baptismal rite, but this is not universal practice. Alternate questions, baptismal words (a controversial addition), and prayers are included with the rite in the *Minister's Manual*. They may substitute what is given or can expand the given service. These examples model fitting words or accent particular beliefs traditionally held by Mennonites.

CHALLENGES TO BAPTISMAL UNDERSTANDINGS AND PRACTICE

Until the closing decades of the twentieth century, people from other denominations seeking church membership in Mennonite congregations had to be rebaptized. As more Mennonites married spouses from other church traditions and as non-Mennonites sought church membership, the issue of rebaptism focused sharply. Believers new to Mennonite teaching did not believe their first baptism was invalid and declined rebaptism. The 1998 *Minister's Manual* provides a rite for transferring membership predicated on the completion of instruction in the essentials of faith from a Mennonite perspective, a confession of faith, and evidence of a vital relationship with Christ. Believers baptized as infants and later confirmed are invited to be rebaptized but are not required. The confession of faith and life witness of the believer in his or her first denomination are deemed more significant than the act of baptism.[13] This approach is practiced in various locations, though it has not been adopted officially.[14]

Most new believers baptized in Mennonite congregations are youth and young adults. Many are known and loved in their congregations. Such familiarity helps new believers grow in faith and find their place in the church. However, sometimes the baptismal rite becomes so focused on "what the youth want" that God's active presence and the congregation's role in the rite are obscured. Baptism belongs to the congregation as much as it belongs to the new believers, but the primary focus is on God's saving work in all the church's believers.

Too often the rite of baptism is "tacked on" to a service of worship. Rather than being an integral part of the service, the rite seems like a disconnected appendage. When this happens the congregation misses opportunities to hear the purposes of baptism proclaimed and to claim again its identity as a baptismal community. Religious seekers, children, or youth miss the vital connections between worship and baptism, worship and discipleship, and the gathered community as a place for practicing the good news.

During the period of instruction prior to baptism, new believers explore suffering as a potential, even likely outcome of being Christ's disciple. But, the absence of any reference to suffering in the 1998 rite, particularly in the prayers and blessings for the Spirit's ongoing work, is odd. Perhaps one of the biggest challenges facing contemporary Mennonites in their baptismal practice is finding appropriate means to celebrate the joy of salvation and rebirth, knowing full well that faithfulness to Christ's gospel can bring suffering or even death. Contemporary North Americans, including Mennonites, are not prepared to embrace this fundamental wisdom about Christian discipleship. It is a threatening and dangerous truth.

BIBLIOGRAPHY

Armour, Rollin S. *Anabaptist Baptism: A Representative Study*. Scottdale, PA: Herald Press, 1966.
Bender, H. S. "Baptism." *Mennonite Encyclopedia*. Vol. 1. Scottdale, PA: Mennonite Publishing House, 1955.
Confession of Faith and Minister's Manual. Comp. John S. Coffman and John F. Funk. Scottdale, PA: Mennonite Publishing House, 1890. Fourteenth Printing, 1979.
Confession of Faith in a Mennonite Perspective. Scottdale, PA: Herald Press, 1995.
Confession of Faith: Commentary and Pastoral Application. Winnipeg, Manitoba, and Hillsboro, KS: Board of Faith and Life and Kindred Productions, 2000.
Forms of Service for the Use of Ministers. Berne, IN: Mennonite Book Concern, 1908.
Janzen, Heinz and Dorothea, eds. *Minister's Manual*. Newton, KS, and Scottdale, PA: Faith and Life Press and Mennonite Publishing House, 1983.
Loewen, Howard John. *One Lord, One Church, One Hope, and One God: Confessions of Faith in North America*. Elkhart, IN: Institute of Mennonite Studies, 1985.
The Minister's Manual. Newton, KS: General Conference of the Mennonite Church of North America Board of Publications, 1950.
Rempel, John, ed. *Minister's Manual*. Scottdale, PA: Herald Press, 1998.

Notes

[1] This essay examines the order for baptism printed in the *Minister's Manual*, ed. John Rempel (Scottdale, PA: Herald Press, 1998), used by most congregations of Mennonite Church Canada and Mennonite Church USA. These two

denominational bodies include congregations that were formerly part of the Mennonite Church and the General Conference Mennonite Church in North America. Reference is made to baptismal understandings among the Mennonite Brethren, but this work does not explore specific orders for that group or of smaller church groups with ancestors among the sixteenth-century Anabaptists.

[2] Howard Loewen, *One Lord, One Church, One Hope, and One God: Mennonite Confessions of Faith in North America* (Elkhart, IN: Institute of Mennonite Studies, 1985), 79, emphasis added.

[3] In Holland followers of the Anabaptist leader Menno Simons were called Mennists, an appellation that evolved into the name Mennonite. In North America the name Mennonite has been universal. "Anabaptist" is finding increasing use in certain regions of the North American church.

[4] Loewen, *One Lord, One Church*, 65.

[5] This confession was drafted and accepted as normative for faith and practice by the Mennonite Church of North America and the General Conference Mennonite Church. Subsequently, these two bodies completed an integration and reorganization process that created Mennonite Church Canada and Mennonite Church USA.

[6] *Confession of Faith in a Mennonite Perspective* (Scottdale, PA: Herald Press, 1995), 46–47.

[7] The problem of terminology has increased with the renewal of sacramental theology since Vatican II and changing understandings of symbol, sign, image, and metaphor in linguistics and philosophy.

[8] *Confession of Faith in a Mennonite Perspective*, 47.

[9] In various manuals these questions are called vows or promises.

[10] "It is of utmost importance that the nature of God's initiative and our responce be made clear to baptismal candidates. . . . Baptism is not the end but the beginning of a Christian's walk with God and the church. It is offered to sinners whose hearts are set on Christ. It is not reserved for people who have arrived at maturity of faith; it is intended for people who have come to Christ and want to live for him. By ourselves we cannot live a life of love. God works it in us through the indwelling of the Spirit, and through the biblically based counsel which sisters and brothers give one another. The obedience of faith is a lifelong process sustained by corporate and individual prayer, Bible study, and engagement with the world" (Commentary on the rite, *Minister's Manual*, 40–41).

[11] Mennonite Brethren churches and several smaller Anabaptist-related groups practice immersion. According to H. S. Bender, this mode of water baptism was likely borrowed from Baptists who preached revival in the Mennonite colonies of Russia during the 1860s. See H. S. Bender, "Baptism," *Mennonite Encyclopedia*, vol. 1 (Scottdale, PA: Mennonite Publishing House, 1955), 227.

[12] This is the first minister's manual in the twentieth century to place such a prayer here.

[13] *Minister's Manual*, 57.

[14] Mennonite Brethren now accept baptized believers who have not been immersed, but they require rebaptism upon confession of faith for those baptized as infants. See *Confession of Faith: Commentary and Pastoral Applications* (Winnipeg, Manitoba and Hillsboro, KS: Board of Faith and Life and Kindred Productions, 2000), 88.

Chapter 11

The Initiatory Rites of the United Methodist Church

Karen B. Westerfield Tucker

BACKGROUND

World Methodism, of which the United Methodist Church is a part, traces its roots to the Church of England. The eighteenth-century Anglican priest John Wesley is acknowledged as the founder of Methodism; his lifelong intention was not to separate from the Church of England but to reform it along evangelical lines. From the 1730s to the 1780s Methodism existed as one among several "societies" within the Church of England, with the single requirement for membership being a "desire to flee from the wrath to come" (Matt 3:7; Luke 3:7; 1 Thess 1:10). Methodist preaching services in England and in the English colonies were held outside of "church hours," since members of the Methodist societies were expected to participate in the life and sacramental ministries of their local parish.

Only after relations broke down between Anglicans and the Methodist societies in the United States following the American Revolution did Wesley, in 1784, make the irregular move to ordain ministers in order to provide services and sacraments. Later that same year, the Methodist Episcopal Church in America was constituted. Although for political and ecclesiastical reasons Methodism in England was slower to establish itself as a separate entity, by the early nineteenth century it had done so—and in several different denominational configurations.

Because he considered the 1662 *Book of Common Prayer* to be the best liturgy in the world—though not flawless—John Wesley in 1784 abridged the Prayer Book to provide liturgical texts for Methodist people. Among the rites provided in *The Sunday Service of the Methodists with other Occasional Services* were one for the baptism of infants and another for the baptism of those of "riper years." The Prayer Book contained a text for the "Ministration of Private Baptism of Children in

99

Houses," but Wesley did not include it, thereby signaling his expectation that baptism would be a public event. He also did not print a confirmation rite, since in his day it was little used and he found no warrant for it in primitive Christian practice. Besides, because Wesley saw no need for a Methodist episcopacy, it was unnecessary to publish a rite whose administration, as he understood it, was restricted to the bishop.

When Methodists accepted Wesley's version of the Prayer Book baptismal texts, they received his interpretation of those rites. Wesley deleted references to godparents, preferring instead the active participation of parents or candidate. He did not claim any particular mode as necessary for the efficacy of the sacrament (he listed, by rubric, dipping [immersion] and sprinkling for infants, dipping and pouring for older persons), but he insisted upon application of the water in the name of the Father, Son, and Holy Ghost. There is some question whether he expected the signation of newly baptized infants; a rubric for signation appears in some copies of the 1784 *Sunday Service*, but not in later editions.

Perhaps the most significant of Wesley's emendations—at least for the developing Methodist theology of baptism—was his deletion of post-baptismal references to regeneration, though he did retain the Prayer Book's pre-baptismal testimony to spiritual birth and the washing away of sin. Nevertheless, Wesley's editorial change, seen alongside his sermons on the "new birth," has raised questions about his adherence to a theology of baptismal regeneration. Wesley never doubted that infants were "born anew" in baptism. Adults might be regenerated at baptism, or possibly before or after the rite. Yet according to Wesley, persons baptized as infants, who later through sin lost the "principle of grace," needed to be born anew a second time by a conscious experience of saving grace. Thus two new births were necessary for most persons, one sacramental and objective, the other experiential and subjective. Unfortunately, Wesley did not thoroughly delineate the connection between these two, or identify the second new birth as a recovery of what was granted in the first.

The consequence for Methodists has been generally the absence of a strong understanding of baptismal regeneration in infants, since emphasis came to be placed on the profession of personal assurance. Compounding this were other theological and social factors present in the American and European environments of the nineteenth century, such as a stress on the individual and his or her personal liberty, and a positive view of human nature, ability, and achievement (and with it a questioning of original sin). The language of regeneration was further reduced or eliminated from some Methodist baptismal rites, while baptism as a sign of adoption and an act of initiation was accentuated. Thus baptized infants became members of the "universal church" in what was often perceived as a dedication service; rites were developed (later popularly called "confirmation" in some Methodist denominations) that granted membership in the local congregation following public profession.

In effect, the sacramental action of divine grace took second place to human decision (though Methodists were usually quick to defend the sacramentality of infant baptism in controversies with believer baptists). Thus Methodists from around the globe in the twenty-first century have inherited confusion and disagreement about what it means to call baptism a "sacrament," what baptism actually "does," and how baptism stands in relation to the fullness of Christian life. Closer adherence to the texts received from Wesley (for example, in the historic African-American Methodist or Holiness denominations) does not necessarily eliminate this confusion.

DEVELOPMENT OF THE BAPTISMAL COVENANT SERVICE

With the creation in 1968 of the United Methodist Church from the union of the Methodist Church with the Evangelical United Brethren Church, it was determined that new rites were needed for the new church. Like the Methodists (as set out in their *Discipline* and in their 1964 *Book of Worship*), the Evangelical United Brethren practiced both infant and adult baptism; but they also brought to the union a rite of infant dedication which, it was agreed, would not be continued. (The elimination of the text did not, however, discourage the practice.)

Inspiration for the new rites was to come from several sources: the interpretation of Scripture; the practices and theology of apostolic Christianity, favored by Wesley and also by advocates of twentieth-century liturgical renewal; the Wesleyan/Methodist sacramental and evangelical heritage located within the wider church; ecumenical conversations (in particular, the WCC Faith and Order statement on baptism produced in the 1970s[1]); recently produced liturgical texts (especially *An Order for the Celebration of Holy Baptism* published in 1973 by the Consultation on Church Union[2]); and the cultural and spiritual realities of modern life. It was expected that the rites would address the perennial issues of rebaptism; the connection between baptism, "confirmation," and eucharist; the relationship between infant and adult baptism; and church membership.

The revision committee agreed that two principles recovered from early Christian praxis, and widely accepted ecumenically, would direct their work. Theologically, the paschal character of baptism and baptism's centrality for Christian life were to be expressed in and through the ritual text (to that end, newly revised rites of marriage and burial would incorporate baptismal referents). Liturgically, the rite was to take the shape of a comprehensive and unified rite of Christian initiation drawn from ancient models of adult (professing) initiation, and consisting of the baptismal water bath, laying on of hands and anointing ("confirmation"), and eucharist. The revisers were aware that both fundamental principles represented significant departures from then-current United Methodist assumptions and practices.

A wide range of views existed within the denomination on the meaning and purpose of baptism (necessitating in 1988 a denominational study on baptism, yielding the document *By Water & the Spirit* in 1996[3]). Some evangelicals, in particular, worried that the revision might emphasize God's activity and baptismal regeneration to the degree that the personal response of faith would be unduly diminished. Elimination of a distinct and separate rite of confirmation also proved to be difficult, even though a specifically named and officially approved Order for Confirmation and Reception into the Church had appeared for the first time in the Methodist Church only in 1964 (the Evangelical United Brethren Church had no "confirmation" text).

The 1964 rite had been quickly accepted and widely used—both for those baptized as infants and now making public profession and for those who professed at their baptism—in part because other mainline Protestant denominations, such as the liturgically respected Lutherans and Episcopalians, employed it as an integral part of their initiatory process. The 1964 Order had included a denominational loyalty statement ("Will you be loyal to The Methodist Church, and uphold it by your prayers, your presence, your gifts, and your service?") which several members of the revising committee regarded as inappropriate but found impossible to extricate from the rite.

In dealing with the matter of confirmation, the committee proposed a unitive rite, with laying on of hands following the water bath (anointing was not mentioned in the ritual text, since it was believed to be alien to the experience of most United Methodists). In addition, they allowed for a separate act of confirmation redefined as an opportunity for the "renewal of the baptismal covenant" occasioned by growth in faith. The language of "covenant renewal" came directly from the church's Wesleyan heritage: drawing upon biblical foundations, in 1780 John Wesley printed *Directions for Renewing Our Covenant with God*; generations of Methodists, often annually at the new year, have renewed their covenant using some form of Wesley's text.

The revision committee also desired to reintroduce Wesleyan and Methodist baptismal practices previously abandoned, some of which had apostolic roots. Among these were the renunciation of sin, confession of faith using the Apostles' Creed (in the interrogative form), prayer over the water, and the public character of the initiatory rites. There was some nervousness, both inside and outside the committee, about the first two points: that the renunciation would evoke concerns about demonology and that use of the historic symbol of faith would, in effect, make United Methodism a "creedal" denomination. Nevertheless, both of these components found a place in the new rite.

The work of the committee was introduced to the denomination in 1976 as *A Service of Baptism, Confirmation, and Renewal: An Alternate Text*.[4] An introduction to the new service, the basic text of the service, an extended commentary on the text, and general instructions were published together; the basic text, in pamphlet form, was also issued separately for placement in the pews. This was an experimental text, lacking the official authorization of the denomination's General Conference, yet it circulated widely. As a unified text it was deemed useful for several occasions: the baptism of infants and children, the baptism of youth and adults, confirmation, individual baptismal renewal (the advised solution to requests for rebaptism), and congregational renewal.

Surprisingly, the ritual text did not mention participation in the Eucharist after baptism or confirmation; the general instructions, however, encouraged inclusion of the Supper. A rubric that more formally linked the Table in the sequence of events appeared in the next published revision of the text (the booklet *We Gather Together*, 1980[5]) that set out the initiation service and others approved by the denomination for trial use. Four years later, after another revision, the General Conference authorized the service under the new general title "The Baptismal Covenant." The service appeared (again revised) in the *United Methodist Hymnal* (1989)[6] and with expanded rubrics in the *United Methodist Book of Worship* (1992)[7]; at this writing, these two books contain the official liturgical texts of the United Methodist Church.

COMMENTARY ON
THE "SERVICES OF THE BAPTISMAL COVENANT"

The *United Methodist Book of Worship* contains six services related to baptism. "Baptismal Covenant I," the direct descendant of the 1976 rite, is a comprehensive text for baptism, confirmation, reaffirmation of faith, and reception of members. Three rites for the baptism of children fall under the general heading of "Baptismal Covenant II": a full baptismal order drawn from Covenant I; a brief order that uses material from Covenant I (designated "II-A"); and a service that conflates the baptismal texts for those unable to answer for themselves from the former Methodist Church and the former Evangelical United Brethren Church ("II-B"). A similarly conflated text, but for the baptism, confirmation, reaffirmation of faith, and reception into membership of youth and adults, is labeled "Baptismal Covenant III." Using selected portions of Covenant I, "Baptismal Covenant IV" supplies a congregational affirmation of the baptismal covenant. Rubrics recommend that all services of baptismal covenant be placed after the reading and exposition of Scripture, so as to connect explicitly word and sacrament.

Baptismal Covenant I is included with this article as illustrating the understanding and practice of baptism within the United Methodist Church.[8] As a unified service, Baptismal Covenant I establishes a theological connection between baptism and the other actions related to it and is practically useful because it avoids repetitions when multiple actions are performed. The service is divided into numbered sections to aid the pastor and congregation in the progression of the rite and to provide reference points when certain actions are omitted. The additional rubrics provided with the text in the *Book of Worship* suggest variations on the rite and alternate practices.

Sections 1 and 2 of Baptismal Covenant I comprise the introduction to the service and give a pithy summary of the purposes of baptism, confirmation, and reaffirmation. There was hesitation to be precise about the moment at which the new birth occurs; nevertheless, it is declared that "through the Sacrament of Baptism we are initiated into Christ's holy Church" and "we are incorporated into God's mighty acts of salvation and given new birth through water and the Spirit." Confirmation and the reaffirmation of baptismal vows are recognized as essentially the same thing and can be repeated throughout a lifetime, though confirmands also commit themselves to the denomination (section 14) and are received into the local congregation (15). The distinctions between membership through baptism in the "universal" church, in the denomination, and in the local congregation raise significant theological and ecclesiological questions that have been left unresolved.

Candidates are presented not by the pastor but by a representative of the congregation (3), thereby bearing witness to the ministry of all the baptized and the baptismal character of all Christian ministry. The renunciation of sin and the profession of faith then follow (4), signaling that entrance to the baptismal covenant requires a turning away from sin and a turning toward life in Christ (Eph 4:22-24). In bold and demanding language, the candidate or parent(s) (and sponsors) renounce the cosmic "spiritual forces of wickedness"; accept God's power to "resist evil, injustice, and oppression"; and promise "to serve Jesus Christ as Lord." The church, and the Christians who constitute it, are here pictured (ideally) as a community notably different from the rest of the world. Sections 5 through 8 are peculiar to the baptismal action, and address specific questions of intention and commitment to the parents (and sponsors) of those who cannot answer for themselves, to a professing candidate and to his or her sponsor(s), and to the whole congregation.

Because baptism is a congregational as well as personal event, the congregation actively reaffirms its commitment to Jesus Christ and promises to nurture those coming to the font. Then all join in a rehearsal of the Apostles' Creed (9) in the form of three questions and three responses. While it is preferred that the entire creed be used, the text as printed in the *United Methodist Hymnal* brackets the majority of the second and third articles in recognition that denominational membership is contingent only upon profession of faith "in God, the Father Almighty, maker of heaven and earth; in Jesus Christ his only Son, and in the Holy Spirit" (2000 *Discipline*, par. 216).

Thanksgiving over the water is then made (10) in a prayer that is rich in biblical allusion and similar in construction to the denomination's standard eucharistic prayer. Congregational responses throughout (these can either be said or sung) help to indicate that this is the people's prayer. The candidate is then baptized (11) using the active formulation ("*Name*, I baptize you in the name of the Father, and of the Son, and of the Holy Spirit"); no specific mode of baptism is identified. Immediately following, hands are laid on the candidate, with a declarative invocation of the Holy Spirit in order that he or she may be equipped for faithful discipleship ("The Holy Spirit work within you, that being born through water and the Spirit, you may be a faithful disciple of Jesus Christ"). Again in recognition of the ministry of all the baptized, the imposition of hands is not restricted to the ordained pastor. At this point, rubrics in the *Book of Worship* allow for practices previously unknown—at least officially—to United Methodists: signation, anointing, vesting in white garments, and presentation of a lighted candle. The congregation then welcomes the newly baptized.

With confirmations or reaffirmations of faith (12), water may be used as a way to "remember your baptism and be thankful," but only in a manner that cannot be interpreted as baptism. Hands may be laid on these candidates, and almost the same formulation as at baptism is given: instead of "being born through water and the Spirit, you may be a faithful disciple," the formulation is "having been born through water and the Spirit, you may live as a faithful disciple." With this subtle shift in wording, baptism's centrality is made clear, as is the necessity of ongoing growth in Christian faith and life.

Those who have professed their faith are then received as members of the United Methodist Church (14) and of the local congregation (15); in the question in each section, a fragment of the 1964 loyalty statement is used. The pastor commends to the congregation those who have been baptized and/or confirmed, who have reaffirmed their faith and/or been received as members of the denomination and local church (16). The congregation gives another welcome, and the pastor offers a blessing. A rubric then declares that "it is most fitting that the service continue with Holy Communion." Answering the question about the communication of children, the rubric continues: "The new members, including children, may receive first."

Although many United Methodists have faulted their baptismal services for being too long, the new texts take seriously recent findings in liturgical scholarship as well as denominational particularities. A wide range of perspectives on baptism still exists, with pastors and congregations typically "editing" the standard text in accordance with their views. Nevertheless, the authorized rite represents for United Methodists a normative statement on baptism by which they can enter into conversation and dialogue with other ecclesiastical communities also on the road to unity.

BIBLIOGRAPHY

Felton, Gayle Carlton. *This Gift of Water: The Practice and Theology of Baptism among Methodists in America*. Nashville: Abingdon, 1992.

Peiffer, Robert Brian, *How Contemporary Liturgies Evolve: The Revisions of United Methodist Liturgical Texts*. PhD diss., University of Notre Dame, 1993.

Westerfield Tucker, Karen B. "The Rites of Christian Initiation." In Karen B. Westerfield Tucker, ed., *American Methodist Worship*. New York: Oxford University Press, 2001, 82–117.

Notes

[1] "Baptism," in *One Baptism, One Eucharist and a Mutually Recognized Ministry: Three Agreed Statements*, Faith and Order Paper No. 73 (Geneva: World Council of Churches, 1975), 9–17.

[2] The Commission on Worship of the Consultation on Church Union, *An Order for the Celebration of Holy Baptism* (Cincinnati: Forward Movement Publications, 1973).

[3] *By Water & the Spirit: A United Methodist Understanding of Baptism* (Nashville: Discipleship Resources, 1996).

[4] *A Service of Baptism, Confirmation, and Renewal: An Alternate Text* (Nashville: United Methodist Publishing House, 1976).

[5] *We Gather Together* (Nashville: United Methodist Publishing House, 1980).

[6] *United Methodist Hymnal* (Nashville: United Methodist Publishing House, 1989).

[7] *United Methodist Book of Worship* (Nashville: United Methodist Publishing House, 1992).

[8] *United Methodist Book of Worship*, 87–94; also in the *United Methodist Hymnal*, 33–39.

Chapter 12

Baptismal Understanding and Practice in the Christian Church (Disciples of Christ)

Keith Watkins

Liturgical practice within the Christian Church (Disciples of Christ) is determined by each congregation. Although there is considerable variation in order and text, most congregations conduct their worship, including baptism, within a framework that has been observed and affirmed by Disciples throughout their two hundred-year history.

DISCIPLES' BAPTISMAL PRACTICE

Disciples base their practice upon New Testament texts that describe conversion and baptism and interpret the theological meaning of Christian initiatory rites. Perhaps the most important of these texts is Acts 2:38, in which Peter instructs the multitude on Pentecost that they should "repent, and be baptized every one of you in the name of Jesus Christ so that your sins may be forgiven; and you will receive the gift of the Holy Spirit." Another is Romans 6:6-10 in which Paul describes baptism as burial into death with Christ and resurrection with him to eternal life. Disciples have also made extensive use of Acts 16:25-34, in which the writer describes the episode in the jail in Philippi when Paul preached to the jailer, converted him to the gospel, and, in the same hour of the night, baptized him and his entire family.

Despite the reference in Acts 16 to the baptism of the entire family, which many scholars assume to have included small children as well as adults, Disciples have understood New Testament baptism to be a rite performed only upon people old enough to answer the questions of faith on their own behalf. They have also believed that the mode of baptism in the New Testament was total submersion of candidates in water. These understandings of the earliest rites of Christian initiation continue to shape Disciples baptismal rites.

Although many Disciples now use the word "sacrament" to describe baptism, "ordinance" was the word that Disciples favored in previous generations. Repentant sinners come to be baptized in obedience to Christ's command. In baptism, God acts to forgive us our sins, enroll us in the church, and empower us with the gift of the Holy Spirit. Something happens in baptism that is initiated by God and embodied in the conscious act of obedience by those who are called by God to this change of life.

Historically, the most common liturgical pattern used by Disciples has consisted of two parts which ordinarily take place on different occasions, usually during the congregation's Sunday services of worship.

The Confession of Faith is the focus of the first occasion. Following the sermon, the pastor invites persons to come to the front of the church during the singing of a hymn, in order to confess their faith in Christ in preparation for baptism or to transfer membership to this congregation. The persons who respond to the invitation are asked to affirm the Christian faith, usually in words adapted from Peter's confession in Matthew 16:16: "Do you believe that Jesus is the Christ, the son of the living God?" After the candidate's response, the pastor offers a brief commendation or blessing. At the close of the service, congregants greet the persons who have come forward.

The baptism ordinarily takes place the following Sunday in the church. In most church buildings, this facility—a pool for immersion of adults—is located within sight of the worshiping congregation. While the pastor and baptismal candidates clothe themselves (in dressing rooms set aside for this purpose) for the baptism, another leader of worship reads Scripture texts about baptism and the congregation sings a hymn. The pastor enters the baptistery, followed by a candidate. While reciting the baptismal formula, the pastor leans the candidate backward into the water until he or she is fully immersed, and then brings the person back to an upright position. Later in the service, when all have dressed again, the newly baptized are welcomed into membership in the congregation.

A DEVELOPING BAPTISMAL PRACTICE

Due to a pastoral interest in strengthening traditional Disciples practice, and in response to their participation in the ecumenical discussions about baptism, Disciples of Christ have recently published baptismal liturgies that extend their traditional practices.[1] Included with the present article as a representative Disciples baptismal liturgy is the recent text that most closely follows normal Disciples custom.[2]

Several parts of this rite require comment. First, these actions usually take place in the regular Sunday service of worship, which among Disciples always includes preaching and the Lord's Supper. It is possible, however, for these initiatory rites to take place in other settings, including other stated times of worship, services for evangelism and renewal, special services focused upon baptism, and vigil services, such as those related to Easter. Frequently, the people who "come forward," to use traditional language, have already participated in classes of instruction and their action has been anticipated by the pastor. Disciples custom, however, includes the readiness to receive people who come spontaneously, without prior preparation or notice.

Second, the invitation to Christian discipleship usually is addressed to three groups of people: those who are making their confession of faith in preparation for baptism, others who are renewing their baptismal vows or their dedication to the Christian life, and still others who are moving their membership from one congregation to another.

A third observation concerns the blessing of the water. Disciples, along with most others in the historic Protestant churches, have not been accustomed to using such a prayer. Most of the baptismal liturgies developed by these churches during the liturgical reforms of the latter part of the twentieth century, however, have included a prayer that parallels in form and function the Great Thanksgiving Prayer at the Eucharist. The baptismal prayer is explicit in its petition, "Send now your Holy Spirit upon this water, that it may bathe your children clean of sin and death, and satisfy all who thirst for your righteousness." If the pronoun "it" refers to the Holy Spirit, most Disciples could use this prayer without difficulty; if the word refers to water, however, some Disciples would be uneasy.

Fourth, the questions asked of candidates prior to their immersion—if they renounce all manner of evil and turn to Jesus Christ—are insertions also influenced by baptismal liturgies developed in recent decades. Although these actions have been implied in Disciples practice, they have not been accustomed to asking candidates to turn from their sin, renounce evil, and turn to Jesus Christ.

A fifth observation is that this rite is consistent with Disciples custom in that it does not include an anointing with oil or marking with the sign of the cross, or invocation of the Holy Spirit following the immersion. Disciples have understood that immersion in the name of the triune God is in itself the action by which the gift of the Holy Spirit is transmitted, and they have not followed the immersion with an invoking of the Holy Spirit. This rite, however, does include an abridged invocation. A more extended prayer for the Holy Spirit can be seen in another contemporary Disciples liturgy that directs that "immediately after the administration of the water, as hands are placed on the head of each person, the celebrant says to each: The Holy Spirit abide with you, the Spirit of wisdom and understanding; the Spirit of counsel and inward strength; the Spirit of knowledge and true godliness; the Spirit of joy and hope."[3]

The sixth observation is that this rite directs the service to conclude with a welcome into membership and reception of the newly baptized at the communion table. It does not, however, offer texts or ceremonies to use in this concluding portion of the liturgy.

Although Disciples of Christ do not baptize infants or small children, even those from families within the church, they do conduct services of thanksgiving, blessing, and sometimes naming. These liturgies usually take place during Sunday worship. Parents bring their child to the front of the congregation where a minister greets them, reads a brief Scripture text, and leads the family in a litany of thanksgiving and covenant. Ordinarily these liturgies include promises by the congregation to sustain families and their children in Christian nurture. Prayers on behalf of the child and family conclude the liturgy.[4]

ECUMENICAL ISSUES AND IMPLICATIONS

Perhaps the most important topic for discussion within the Christian Church (Disciples of Christ) is the significance of ecumenical witnesses concerning rites of Christian initiation. Although Disciples began as a movement for Christian unity, based on the ecclesial practices described in the New Testament and affirmed by the church in all times and places, they quickly institutionalized specific practices that distinguished them from most other churches. The Disciples theology of baptism is consistent with classical understandings, but their baptismal practice separates them from the historic Protestant churches with which they are, in many respects, most closely allied.

Most of the recent publications on this topic within the Christian Church (Disciples of Christ) recommend that Disciples revise their baptismal rites so that they conform more closely to the emerging ecumenical consensus. Ordinary practice in congregations, however, remains largely unchanged.

Disciples continue to discuss a second topic, the reception into membership of persons who have been baptized in infancy or by affusion rather than immersion. Until midway through the twentieth century, a majority of Disciples congregations restricted formal church membership to people who had been baptized by immersion as believers. (Even if they were not members of the congregation, persons from other ecclesial traditions were welcomed into most aspects of the congregation's life—including regular participation in the Lord's Supper.) By the late twentieth century, however, most Disciples congregations were accepting into full membership persons who have been baptized in other churches regardless of mode or time of life.

A third topic for discussion among Disciples is the relationship of baptism and participation in the Lord's Supper, which is celebrated weekly in the principal services of worship. Throughout their history, Disciples have maintained the classic assumption that baptism is required as the prerequisite to admission to the table. In recent years, however, there has been an increasing tendency for children within the worshiping community to be welcomed to the table prior to their baptism. This trend has been shaped, in part, by the presence in the congregation of young children who had received baptism as infants, when their families had been members of a church practicing infant baptism. If former Methodist or Presbyterian children of tender years are admitted to the table, how can the children of Disciples parents be kept away?

The sequence of baptism followed by communion is also being challenged because of factors related to the evangelism of youth and adults. Some Disciples are persuaded by the argument that an open table is the sacrament of hospitality and God's gracious favor, and that therefore the Lord's Supper is the doorway into the church. Baptism, according to this point of view, is the sign of mature incorporation into the family of God.

Until the beginning of the twentieth century, most Disciples baptisms took place outside in running water. Early in the new century, churches installed baptisteries inside their buildings so that adult immersions could be done throughout the year and in the presence of the congregation. Despite the fact that nearly all Disciples church buildings include baptisteries, they have been given only modest architectural attention. Among the baptisteries of unusual interest are those in North Christian Church, Columbus, Indiana, and Sweeney Chapel at Christian Theological Seminary in Indianapolis. Both facilities are dominated by large pools, and each has places where congregants can sit or stand during the baptismal liturgy. The Columbus baptistery is separated from the major worship room, whereas the space in Sweeney Chapel is a side extension of the principal place of worship.

Disciples' baptismal understanding and practice will continue to develop in dialogue with both the historical heritage of the church and its growing experience within the ecumenical movement.

Notes

[1] A liturgy that closely parallels recent liturgies in other historic Protestant churches was published in "A Word to the Churches on Baptism: Report of the Commission on Theology, 1987." It can be found in several places, including in Keith Watkins, ed., *Baptism and Belonging* (St. Louis: Chalice Press, 1991), 42–49; and (in condensed form) in Paul A. Crow, Jr., and James O. Duke, eds., *The Church for Disciples of Christ: Seeking to be Truly Church Today* (St. Louis: Christian Board of Publication, 1998), 132–34. Another liturgy that has been significantly influenced by the Faith and Order convergence text *Baptism, Eucharist and Ministry*, Faith and Order Paper No. 111 (Geneva: World Council of Churches, 1982) was published in Colbert S. Cartwright and O. I. Cricket Harrison, eds. and comp., *Chalice Worship* (St. Louis: Chalice Press, 1997), 26–32.

[2] See Watkins, ed., *Baptism and Belonging*, 25–30. This resource was prepared for use in the Christian Church (Disciples of Christ) by its Division of Homeland Ministries.

[3] Cartwright and Harrison, *Chalice Worship*, 30.

[4] An example of liturgies at the birth of a child is found in ibid., 22–25.

Chapter 13

The Baptismal Liturgy of the Mar Thoma Syrian Church of Malabar

George Mathew

INTRODUCTION

The Mar Thoma Syrian Church is a part of the ancient Church of Kerala, the southernmost state of India. The church is traditionally believed to have been founded by St. Thomas, the Apostle of India, during the first century CE. It underwent a certain degree of reformation during the nineteenth century through the influence of Anglican Missionaries. The Mar Thoma Syrian Church follows the West Syrian liturgical tradition, and is Eastern in the nature of its worship and ethos. It is in relationships of full communion with the Anglican Communion, the Church of South India, and the Church of North India.

Baptism is a sacrament associated with the ministry, death, and resurrection of Jesus Christ. It has been understood as the "great commissioning," given by Jesus Christ to the church through the apostles, to preach and baptize all peoples (Matt 28:17-20). The practice of baptism existed in the early church, as we see in the New Testament and in the writings of the church fathers. Baptism is thus a command of our risen Lord. Through baptism we participate in the suffering, death, and resurrection of Jesus Christ; we are incorporated into the body of Christ. Conversion, pardoning, and cleansing also take place through this sacrament. We are initiated into the gift of the Holy Spirit to bear witness to the risen Lord. These are the theological and ecclesiological realities of baptism; the practice and expression of faith given in baptism varies from one liturgical tradition to another.

THE MAR THOMA BAPTISMAL TEXT

The Mar Thoma baptismal text is of West Syrian origin, and in the prayers and practices there are many elements which are common to other churches that follow the same tradition (such as the Syrian

Orthodox Church, the Malabar Independent Syrian Church, and the Syrian Malankara Catholic Church). However, due to the reformation in the Syrian Church, certain adaptations and revisions were made to the original text. At present the Mar Thoma Church is using a revised baptismal liturgy; the text has been translated from Syriac by Malpan Maliakkal Zachariah, with the first official English translation published in 1988.[1] This text is a true version of the original Malayalam text. The Mar Thoma text is identified below as "MT."

The West Syrian baptismal liturgy has been attributed to Severus of Antioch (512–518). In the thirteenth century, Gregoris Bar Hebraeus (1284) revised and shortened this text; later this was published in Pampakuda.[2] This text is in use in the Orthodox and the Malankara Catholic Churches of Kerala. The principal text taken for this study is that of the Pampakuda Text, identified below as "P," which is given in Matthew Elenjikal's *Baptism in the Malankara Church*.[3] I am indebted to the author for the commentary on the baptismal text.

Before analyzing the text in detail, we must consider the major events which occur in baptism and the sequence of the liturgical text. The next section will review each prayer and elucidate its theological and ecclesiological significance. Major differences from other texts will also be noted for comparison. This study will end with the challenges and problems faced by the church in the Indian context.

MAJOR EVENTS IN THE BAPTISMAL SERVICE

In our church the major events of the baptismal service are: an initial prayer, readings from the Scriptures, exorcism, renunciation, affirming the faith, anointing with olive oil, blessing of the water, baptism (symbolic immersion), chrismation, crowning, exhortation, and dismissal. We will look at each of these in some detail.

1. Initial Prayer

The service begins with the Trisagion ("Holy, Holy, Holy") and doxology. The initial prayer can be divided into two parts. First, the celebrant beseeches God to make him worthy to administer the holy sacrament of baptism. This may be considered the prayer of preparation, similar to the *Thooyaba* (service of preparation) in the eucharistic rite. This is considered a spiritual service, one entrusted to the apostles of the church through their "great commissioning" by the Lord Jesus Christ (Matt 28:17-20). It is an ecclesial act, with the authority to baptize being given to a priest through the church. The second part of the prayer is an intercession for the baptismal candidate. This prayer explains the nature, institution, and effects of baptism.

2. Kuklyon

Psalm 23 is given in MT. In P there is a separate Psalm (45:10-13). Psalm 23 refers to the Lord as our shepherd, leading to the waters which represent baptism; it speaks of anointing the head with oil, referring to the chrismation. These baptismal images taken from the psalms point toward the actual baptismal act. By baptism one will dwell in the house of God: that is, he or she is incorporated into the body of Christ (cf. again Ps 23). This again is an ecclesial act, and by baptism the candidate becomes a member of the church.

3. Ekba

This text is very significant in respect of the theology of baptism, it being considered a seal of grace. Baptism is compared to the blood sprinkled on the doorposts and lintels of the Hebrew people (Exod 12:1-13), the only mark by which they might be saved from the destroyer. The candidate is initiated into the process of salvation through Christ, the unfading light of the Trinity.

4. Prayer

This is a prayer for the candidate, that he or she may be blessed by God. Through baptism one is incorporated into the holy church, and here it is stated that baptism is the outward sign of one's membership in the church. The celebrant beseeches God to enlighten the candidate so that he or she will renounce all the works of death, will see the vanity of this world, and will praise the glory of the Trinity.

5. Promion

Here the Lord is addressed as one who instituted holy baptism for the spiritual flock and who is the true and indescribable light. He is worthy of praise, honor, and adoration at the time of baptism and all the days of our life.

6. Sedra

The first part of this prayer is the recalling of the salvific work of Christ. The narration is soteriological in nature, focusing on Christ as guiding us away from sin, inviting us to observe his holy commandments, admitting us to the spiritual fold, calling us to the stream of salvation (baptism) and the fountain of eternal life, and cleansing us from defilement (cf. Jer 4:14).

The second part of the prayer is a petition for the effect of baptism and refers to what is "actually happening" through the event. Baptism is considered the seal of life. "Sealing" refers to the candidate's belonging to God; through baptism candidates are adopted as sons and daughters of God (Eph 1:15; Rom 8:15, 9:4; Gal 4:5). The baptized becomes a member of the household of God (Eph 2:19), one become fully grown into Christ's likeness (Eph 4:13). Through baptism the candidate puts off the old person and puts on the new person in Christ (1 Tim 2:2; Eph 4:22-24). He or she will be made a new creature, created after the likeness of God. Putting on the imperishable prefigures the imperishable robe, the robe of immortality, the garment of salvation, the imperishable inheritance, as expressed in the biblical images (Isa 61:10; Rom 2:7; 1 Cor 15:33; 2 Tim 1:10; 1 Pet 1:4; 3:4). Baptism leads to that holy, quiet, and peaceful living which leads to everlasting life.

7. Chant

This is a supplication for the candidate, recalling the promise of John the Baptist about the advent of the Messiah (John 3:5-6). In the following prayer, the celebrant prays for the candidate that he or she may be sealed for eternal life, become an heir in God's household, be bound by the holy commandments of God, and offer praise and thanksgiving to the true God.

8. The Readings

The ministry of the word is an important part of the baptismal service. It is the word of God that gives authority for any sacrament, therefore in the Eastern Church the reading from the Scripture is done with great devotion and solemnity. The psalms, Pauline epistle, and gospel are read and the congregation is asked to listen to the proclamation of the living word of God with reverence. The theology of baptism is well explained through the biblical readings, as indicated below.

The words in Psalm 42:1, "As the deer longs for flowing streams, so my soul longs for you, O God," are interpreted as the desire of the candidate for baptism being prefigured in the Old Testament. The water and the spirit represent the baptismal act as mentioned in the gospel (John 3:5, 6).

The epistle reading of Romans 5:20, 6:8 emphasizes the act of baptism as an expression of God's grace to sinful humanity and the candidate's identification with the death, burial, and resurrection of Christ. Christian baptism effects the Christian's separation from sin and entry into new life through Jesus Christ, incorporating the candidate into the body of Christ through participation in his death and resurrection.

On the gospel readings of Luke 3:15-16 and John 3:5-6, M. Elenjikal comments:

> [T]he central theme of the passage from Luke is to explain the efficacy of the sacrament of Baptism by drawing a comparison between the Baptism of John and the Baptism of the New Testament. Though there are some similarities between the two, the former is only (purely symbolical) baptism of water, where as the latter is with the Holy Spirit and fire. However John's Baptism prepared those who submitted themselves to it to face the coming day of the Lord, confident that those who repented would be forgiven and granted a place in the future Messianic community.[4]

The role of the Holy Spirit in this rebirth is developed in John 3:5, 6, with its themes of confessing the new life, being born again from the Spirit in a birth that is other than fleshly, and into eternal life. Other gospel passages referring to baptism (Matt 28:18, Mark 16:16) are not used as they do not convey the real nature of sacraments as does John's gospel.

9. The Enrollment of the Candidate

P includes a ceremony of registering the name of the candidate and sponsors (godparents) with a special prayer.[5] The priest prays that the name of the candidate should be written in the book of life; the idea of heavenly tablets on which the name of the elect one is inserted is taken from the Old Testament (Exod 32:32f.), and similar expressions can be found in the New Testament (Luke 10:20, Rev 3:5). Through the writing of the name, the candidate is enrolled as a member of the worshiping community, and it is made clear that the candidate no longer belongs to Satan but to God, who made the candidate in his own image. By enlightenment and sanctification, the candidate becomes the possession of God by sealing. The cross of Jesus Christ is a protection for the candidate (Eph 2:5-8; John 8:12; 1 Thess 5:5).

In the Mar Thoma Church the inscription of the name of the candidate, parents, godparents, and sponsors is done in the baptismal register before the beginning of the baptismal service proper. There is no liturgical prayer for the inscription of names. This may not be a deliberate omission, since the symbolism is very biblical in nature. Baby Varghese is of the opinion that this rite seems to have been associated with the catechumenate, especially the inscription of names.[6]

In the second part of this prayer, the priest breathes three times in the form of the cross on the candidate's face and says: "Give him your divine breath that your only begotten son breathed on his Holy disciples, prepare him for the reception of your Holy Spirit and drive out all remnants of idolatry from his mind."[7] The breath of God is the symbol of the Holy Spirit that God sent forth to make everything new (Gen 1:2; 2:7). John says that baptism is the birth by water and the Spirit (3:5). The Holy Spirit is the agent of creation and re-creation, and breathing is the symbolic expression of that reality.

The wording is that used by Jesus Christ himself after his resurrection, when he breathed on the Apostles and asked them to receive the Holy Spirit (John 20:22). In the Mar Thoma liturgy the prayer mentioned above is not given. This may not be a deliberate omission, since a similar breathing on the candidate is found in the text of the ordination rite,[8] accompanied by the reading of John 20:22.

10. Consignation (Without Oil)

The priest makes the sign of the cross with his thumb on the forehead of those to be baptized, saying: "*Name* is sealed in the name of the Father + and of the Son + and of the Holy Spirit +."

According to Elenjikal, "different terms are frequently used in the text to describe the 'seal or sign.' The entire baptismal rite may be called a seal of grace, seal of Christ, seal of Spirit."[9] There are mainly three signings: the first, without oil; the second, with olive oil (*Syth*); and the third, with Holy Muron after the baptism.

As noted above, when a person is marked in the name of God, he or she becomes the property of God. The sign of the cross is the mark of our protection, acknowledging that we belong to Christ and are under his ownership. During the signing, the name of the candidate—which represents their personality and identity—is announced for the first time by the priest, showing that he or she is a new person in Christ and begins to become a member of the church.

11. Exorcism

By "exorcism" we mean liberation from Satan; it is a casting out from the person of all evil powers. The prayer of exorcism is very elaborate in the Eastern liturgies. In P there is a rubric about the "stripping" of the candidate, denoting putting off through baptism the old person, our corrupted nature, and sin. There are prayers in inclination and aloud. In MT this prayer is shorter and the stripping is done just before baptism in front of the baptismal font.

The wording of the prayer shows that there are two elements in the rite of exorcism. Negatively, it is intended to free the person from the power of the evil one, thus purifying the mind and heart of the candidate. Positively, it prepares the candidate to be a worthy dwelling place for the Holy Spirit.[10]

12. Renouncing Satan

In the rubric of MT we read: "Then one of the Godparents (the Godfather in the case of a boy, the Godmother in the case of a girl) holding the left hand of the child with his/her left hand, repeats thrice the words of renunciation after the priest." If the candidate is an infant, the godfather or godmother repeats the following: "I, who am being baptised, renounce Satan—all his angels—all his hosts—all his worship—and all his deceits."

Here the candidates (or sponsor, if the candidate is an infant) declare their renunciation of Satan and pronounce a sincere and wholehearted profession of allegiance to Christ. In Greek this rite is known as *apotaxis*, meaning "to renounce," "to give up," "to part from." The profession of allegiance is known as *syntaxis*, meaning "to put in order together," "to draw-up."[11] The renunciation and profession are the formal liturgical expression of the candidate's conversion from sin and service of Satan to the loyal service of Christ.

13. Adhesion to Christ (Professing Christ, Syntaxis)

The rubric indicates: "Then holding the right hand of the child with his/her right hand the Godparents repeat thrice: I, who am being baptised, believe and accept Jesus Christ and all the divine teachings —entrusted to our holy fathers—through the apostles and prophets." At this point the candidate faces toward the east while professing faith in Christ.

This statement of faith is significant as the formal profession of faith in Christ and allegiance to him. At this point the candidate (or sponsor, on his or her behalf) accepts faith in Christ and all the divine teachings entrusted through the Old Testament (the prophets), the New Testament (the apostles), and the traditions of the church (the holy fathers). These three authorities are the source of the faith of the church, and through this adhesion the candidate (or sponsor, on his or her behalf) acknowledges this reality. This has been further affirmed by the recital of the Nicene Creed, the universal creed of the church. The symbolic act of facing east while adhering to Christ means that the candidate is turning to Christ, the sun of righteousness (Mal 4:2) and the light of the world (John 8:12).

14. The Confession of Faith (the Nicene Creed)

According to Elenjikal, reciting the Creed is not only an expression of one's faith but also the ritual manifestation of taking upon oneself the service of God after renouncing the service of the evil one. The confession of God's greatness in the Creed clearly expresses several aspects of Divine Salvation, including the faithful community's faith in Christ and loyalty to the church.[12]

15. Prayer before Unction with Olive Oil

This prayer contains the central baptismal themes of rebirth and sanctification. The fact of creation, and the role of the Holy Spirit in birth and rebirth, are mentioned here, and the prayer expresses well the notion of re-creation through baptism. The celebrant prays: "O Lord! Build him upon the foundation of your holy apostles. Plant him/her to grow and flourish in your church," reflecting the Pauline image of church as a building or temple of God. The prayer shows the intimate relationship of the members of the church with God through the Holy Spirit (Eph 2:20). This prayer has great ecclesiological significance, since it points toward the relationship between the church and the baptized. Concluding with "make him/her open to the mystery of the anointing of the Holy Spirit," it stresses the significance of the candidate's anointing.

16. Anointing with Olive Oil

The rubric specifies that "The priest anoints the forehead of the candidate with Syth," and notes that "As a token of being born anew as a child of God, (name) is sealed with Holy oil in the name of the Father and of The Son and the Holy Spirit." The number and place of anointings vary in different texts of the Syrian baptismal rite.[13] S. P. Brock has elaborated the place of signing and anointing in his study on the Syrian Baptismal text.[14]

Olive oil is specified for the anointing. This is no accident, for the Bible includes several significant references to the olive: the dove returning to Noah (Gen 8:1); the believer like an olive tree flourishing in the house of God (Ps 52:8); the people of God like an olive tree, onto which God has grafted the Gentiles (Rom 11:17, 24). St. Ephrem considered the "tree of life" to have been an olive tree (Gen 3:22-24).[15]

Anointing with olive oil (signing) also symbolizes the healing that Christ gives to the believer. This is the inner healing worked by grace, of strengthening and protection, and effecting sanctification, rebirth, and the adoption of the baptismal candidate as a son or daughter of God.[16]

17. Stripping

Before leading the candidate for baptism, the child's clothes are removed or stripped. In MT there is no rubric about this, but it is practiced if the candidate is an infant.

18. Mixing and Blessing of the Water

In several of our liturgical texts this has been given as a separate section, or as a second part. In MT, where there is no such distinction, one can still identify it as a separate section. The rubric indicates that "the priest mixing hot and cold water in the font, blessed the water"; this prayer varies slightly from the MT to other texts, such as P and the Malankara Text.

In MT the prayer of the mixing of the water carries less symbolism and is simple and direct. The priest prays for the sanctification of the water through the operation of the Holy Spirit: Jesus has given the fountain that truly cleanses the candidate from the defilement of sin; Jesus Christ is the one who saves, cleanses by washing (e.g., through baptism), and gives all good gifts. In P the celebrant asks God to mix the water with the power of the Holy Spirit, so that it may become a spiritual womb and a refining pot, or furnace, that forms incorruptibility (e.g., immortality). In MT, a similar prayer is given at a later stage while blessing and signing the baptismal water.

Different interpretations have been given for the mixing of cold and hot water. For some it is a symbol of two springs which flow into the river Jordan where Jesus was baptized; to the Armenians, it represents the flood and the water which flowed from the pierced side of Jesus Christ. It is also regarded as a symbolic expression of the fire and water by which one is baptized according to the gospels (Luke 3:15-16; John 3:5-6).

19. Kukaya-Chant

In this chant, the baptism of Jesus in the river Jordan is recalled as a sign of the fountain of life sanctified by the Father, Son, and Holy Spirit.

It affirms that every baptism follows the pattern of Jesus' baptism in the river Jordan, and that the Father proclaims every child as his beloved son or daughter. Through baptism we become the adopted children of God.

20. *The Rite of Insufflation (Breathing) on the Water*

This special prayer is given in P and other West Syrian texts (but not in MT): "Thou hast given us, O Lord, through the intercession of us, sinners, the breath which thy only begotten Son has breathed on the candidate."[17] It is followed by breathing thrice on the baptismal water.

In these texts the baptismal water is considered as a true spring of purification, one purified from all stains and marks of sin. According to Moses Bar Kepha,

> The priest breathes upon the water for these reasons. Firstly, as God breathed on Adam the breath of life (Gen 2:7) when He created him and as baptism too is a fashioning anew, it is right that the priest should breathe on the water as if it were first fashioning. Secondly, the priest breathes on the water as in the passage, our Lord breathed on His disciples and said "Receive ye the Holy Spirit" (John 20:22).[18]

Here the breathing symbolizes the presence of the Holy Spirit in the baptismal water. A similar breathing on the candidate can be seen in the ordination rite of the Mar Thoma Church.

21. *Epiclesis*

MT includes another prayer for the sanctification of the water: "We beseech you, O Lord. Sanctify this water by your mercy and abundant grace. Grant that those who are baptized in the water may put off the defiling lust of the old person and put on the new person that recreates them into the image of the Creator (Col 3:9-10)." This is followed by the response, "Answer unto us, O Lord!" (3x). In the West Syrian liturgy this is a response to the epicletic prayer.

22. *The Invocation of the Holy Spirit*

The main theme of this prayer is the acclamation of the deacon, and the invocation by the priest, to send the Holy Spirit upon the water and the people. A similar prayer is found in the eucharistic text of the Eastern churches.[19] This prayer is not found in the baptismal liturgy of the MT; Philip Tovey notes that "unlike in the Eucharitic rite, the Epiclesis in MT is rather vague or soft and the work of the Holy Spirit is not fully acknowledged." According to Tovey, some of the early texts also omit this prayer,[20] and S. P. Brock has noted the variety of forms of epicleses in the West Syrian Baptismal liturgy.[21] The prayer of consignation on the water (in MT there is a long prayer at this point, with the rubric: "The priest makes the sign of the cross three times on the water") reveals the effects of baptism, which are the following: cleansing from defilement, freedom from bondage, the remission of sins, forgiveness of trespasses, entering into a holy inheritance, donning imperishable garments, entering into the newness of the Holy Spirit, and identification with the death and resurrection of the only begotten Son.

23. The Infusion of Muron (Holy Oil) upon the Water

The priest holds up the container of Muron and says, "Glory be to the Father, Son and the Holy Spirit. We pour the Holy oil upon this water in the name of the Father and the Son and the Holy Spirit." Muron is the symbol of the working of the Holy Spirit, which "broods" upon the waters (Gen 1:2) and denotes the regenerative aspect of salvation, the fact that in baptism we are born of the Spirit. As water and spirit are united in Jesus' teachings (John 3:5-6), so in the Syrian baptism water and Muron (chrism) are united in two ways: by the infusion of Muron in the baptismal water and by anointing the candidate with Muron after baptism.

After pouring out Muron on the waters, the priest says a prayer for the candidate. Significantly, the working of the Holy Spirit is mentioned not at a particular moment of the baptismal service, but rather throughout the service. This emphasizes that baptism is the work of the Holy Spirit.

24. Baptism

The rubric indicates that: "The candidate is placed in the water facing east and water is poured thrice over his/her head by the priest: (name) is baptised in the hope of the remission of sins and eternal life. In the name of the Father, the Son and the Holy Spirit." This indicates that baptism is a divine washing for regeneration, offering the hope of eternal life (John 3:5, 16; 4:14, 10:28; Rom 2:7; 5:21; 6:2). In the Eastern baptismal liturgies, the passive voice is used: "(name) is baptised," stressing that baptism is the work of the Holy Spirit rather than the priest or any human agent. According to Elenjikal, "The Trinitarian aspect of the baptismal formula is very significant. Having been baptised in the name of three divine persons, the baptised person is assimilated not only to Christ but also into the church, the body of Christ. He/she has joined into the community of sons and daughters of God."[22]

Before the anointing with the Holy Muron, as the sign of the Holy Spirit, there is a chant and an exhortation to the newly baptized. In the chant, the celebrant seeks the blessing of God for the baptized and asks God to grant him or her the Holy Spirit, so that he or she may do God's will and praise God's name. In the exhortation, the celebrant expresses the wish that "by baptism, they are the light of the world and are strong by the Holy Spirit"; he or she bears witness to the Word of God by the strength of the Holy Spirit and seeks to strive toward eternal life.

25. Anointing with Holy Muron (Chrismation)

The priest anoints the baptized person with Muron and says, "(name) is anointed with Holy Oil as a sign of the gift of the Holy Spirit given to true believers. In the name of the Father and of the Son and of the Holy Spirit." The text given in P is slightly different: "With Holy Muron which is the sweet odour of Christ, the sign and mark of true faith and the perfection of the gift of the Holy Spirit given to true believers."

The Holy Muron is the "odour" of Christ, symbolizing the gift and reception of the Holy Spirit and of the true faith by the true believers. This also represents the sacrifice of Christ as a fragrant offering to God (Eph 5:2). The new Christian has been baptized in the Holy Spirit, and now he or she is perfected and confirmed through the gift of the Holy Spirit. This is a sacramental perfection; not only the head but all the spiritual senses are anointed to mark their awakening.

26. Crowning

In MT there is no rubric or practice of crowning, but a prayer gives the effect of this act: "The priest prays to adorn the baptised with the crown of radiance. The life of the candidate reflects the Glory of God. May he show forth the Grace of Sonship and be adorned by the crown of glory." A chant referring to the crowning is also sung.

In the Malankara Catholic Church, the Orthodox Church, and in P, the *urorion* or *zende* is placed on the head of the baptized person. In some churches a physical crown is placed;[23] in any case the crowning of the baptized is mentioned in all the baptismal texts. There is no need to think of this practice as unbiblical, as it is rooted in Scripture. Several meanings can be attributed to the act of crowning. It refers to kingship (Eccl 47:7; Isa 28:5; 62:3; Jer 13:18; Ps 21:4) and shows glory or victory (Jas 1:2; 1 Pet 5:4; 1 Cor 9:25; 2 Tim 4:8; Rev 2:10; 3:11; 4:4; 9:7). The crowning also points toward the unfading crown which believers will receive during the *eschaton* or end time. Interestingly, a similar crowning is also practiced in the matrimonial rite of the Syrian churches.

In all texts except MT, the Reception of the Holy Eucharist by the newly baptized takes place toward the end of this service. In the Mar Thoma Church the Eucharist is given to the baptized only at a later "age of understanding," which is at present understood to be twelve and above (see further, below). In all other Eastern churches baptism qualifies one to receive the Holy Eucharist immediately. However, in churches from the time of the Reformation, such as Anglicans, Lutherans, and the Church of South India and the Church of North India, infant communion is not practiced.

27. Exhortation

The exhortation is given to the parents and godparents before the final blessing of holy baptism. The parents and godparents are reminded of their Christian responsibility to bring up the child within the Christian faith: they must be an example to the child in all respects; it is their responsibility to train the child in such a way that the child will make his or her own declaration of faith when he or she grows up. This exhortation, which is a later addition and is found only in MT, offers a significant reminder of the important vote of sponsors in bringing up the child within the Christian faith.

28. The Final Blessing

The baptismal service and chrismation ends with the final blessing given by the priest. This is again a commissioning of the believers to their work for the glory of God.

THEOLOGY AND UNDERSTANDINGS OF BAPTISM

In the understanding of the Mar Thoma Church, baptism is a sacrament which admits a person, whether an adult or an infant, into the membership of the church. Infant baptism is the accepted practice, as a rite which testifies to the reality of God's presence and grace in the child as a member of his body. Water is the outward and the visible sign of the grace of God that bestows upon us the new life in Christ.[24] In *Some Important Documents about the Faith and Practice of the Mar Thoma Church* the theology of baptism is well explained as follows:

> We, as a church, believe in infant baptism. It is the practice from the apostolic period. No magical blessing is given in baptism. In the sacrament of baptism, we commend the children into [the] Lord's hands and

pray. The Lord accepts those children and blesses them. It is the sign of dying to sin with the Lord and rising in new life with the Lord (Rom 6:3-6). It is also a service of accepting the child into the membership of the church. In this service, the Lord blesses the child. The baptism becomes meaningful when the children are brought up in that experience. The parent and the church have a great responsibility in this matter.[25]

This does not mean, of course, that the Mar Thoma Church baptizes only infants. Those who have been born into a Christian family have been so baptized, but "believers' baptism" is administered to those who respond, by faith, to the proclamation of the gospel through the evangelistic work of the church. The emphasis of the church is that baptism occurs only once: those born of Christian parents are baptized at infancy; believers coming to faith are baptized as adults.

In the Eastern church all the sacraments, especially baptism and Eucharist, are considered a mystery, something that cannot be explained. Thus there have not been many attempts to "explain" the sacrament of baptism; it has just been accepted as a norm of faith. However, the church tries to teach its believers about its faith, and several studies have been initiated by the theological commission of the church. In one study on baptism, the following interpretation has been given:

> In conversation with Nichodemos, Jesus says "No one can enter the Kingdom of God without being born by water and the spirit. What is born of the flesh is flesh and what is born of the Spirit is spirit" (John 3:5-6). Born anew, born by water and Spirit, born of the Spirit, all these expressions reveal the same aspect. The Greek word "Anathon" means born-again, born from above, etc. The birth is beyond human understanding and rationale. God makes it possible.
>
> Water, fire, dove, etc. are the sign of the Holy Spirit (John 7:38-39; Luke 3:22; Acts 2:1-4). Born by water and by Spirit are not different activities at two different times. It is a sacrament where water and Spirit works together. Water works visibly and Spirit works invisibly (Gen 1:2). Thus, God makes the rebirth possible and [the] candidate receives the Holy Spirit. Anointing the Muron (Chrism) is the sign of this. Rebirth is the work of the Spirit of God. By the physical birth, one enters into the world and in the rebirth, one initiates into the Kingdom of God and God makes it possible. Both births are only the beginning and need further growth. Growth in Christian life reveals [to] us that knowledge. It is a process by which those who are born anew grow into the full stature of Christ. This perfection becomes possible by our active participation in Christian life.[26]

The Mar Thoma Church, with other churches, agrees that baptism (whether administered in childhood or adulthood) is incorporation into the body of Christ. This is to take place within the context of the community of believers. The church upholds the link between the baptism and the gift of the Holy Spirit, both aspects understood as requiring growth and leading to fulfillment. The Mar Thoma Church believes that baptism involves growing; it is not a static and momentary experience.[27] It is unrepeatable and is, in fact, the ordination by which every believer is incorporated into the corporate, priestly ministry of the church.[28]

ISSUES FOR THE CHURCH TO ADDRESS

We seek now to look into the real issues in baptismal theology and practice in the church—to look into the link between the liturgical text and the actual faith and practice of the church today. In addition, we will consider how far baptismal theology is drawn from the liturgical text and functions as an expression of faith for today.

1. A Lack of Proper Teaching about the Theology of Baptism

As noted, infant baptism is the norm of the church for children born of Christian parents; this has been emphasized and practiced over centuries. But Anabaptists and other free churches influence our believers to receive baptism again. The church should be serious in its teaching about baptism; it should make clear that it will accept neither any scripturally unwarranted baptismal practice nor a "magical" view of baptism that denies the importance of personal commitment to the faith.

2. Barring Communion to Infants

Theologically, a person can be qualified to receive Holy Communion after baptism and chrismation—indeed, that was the practice of the early church. As a Reformed church, we currently follow the practice of not giving communion to children, preferring to postpone communion to an "age of understanding" (now twelve years of age), as in other Protestant churches. We recognize that this practice needs to be addressed further and considered ecumenically.

3. The Need to Emphasize the Role of Sponsors

The urbanization and breakdown of the extended family, the development of individualistic values, and other factors have paved the way for a situation in which we are not inculcating, educating, training, and nurturing Christian values among the faithful. There is an exhortation, but the godparents need further motivation and training. Many godparents, and even parents, take on this responsibility without being serious about it. Both infant and believers' baptism take place within the church as the community of faith; in the absence of this, baptism will become a private affair between the believer and God or degenerate into a "magical" view of the sacrament. The communal celebration reminds us of the responsibility of the church toward the baptized infant, who is initiated into baptismal grace through the faith of the community and its desire to nurture infants within that community.[29]

4. A Loss of Symbolism in Liturgy

Our baptismal liturgy also needs attention in regard to its symbolism. As a Reformed church, we experience reflexive reactions seeking to remove some symbols from our liturgical life—even symbols taken directly from biblical imagery (for example, the breathing on the candidate, the baptismal water symbolizing the economy of the Holy Spirit, or the practice of crowning). As an Eastern church we should give more prominence to symbolism, which is common in the churches standing in the same tradition.

5. Is Baptism Necessary for Faith in Christ?

This question has been asked by Indian theologians since the early 1950s. It needs to be addressed within an ecclesiological-missiological context: confessing Christ publicly, and the notion of baptism as a sign of that confession, are potentially sensitive in the present sociopolitical context of India. This is an ecumenical issue, one that needs to be addressed collectively in order to find a viable answer to the problems facing us today.

6. No Separate Rite of Baptism for Adults

Although theologically there is no difference between infant baptism and adult baptism, for practical purposes the church needs a distinctive rite for baptizing adults. After all, adults can follow the service by participating in it in a more meaningful way. This must be considered as a pastoral need of the church.

7. The Link between the Liturgical Text and Our Actual Theological Teaching

The question here is whether or not the church's baptismal liturgy actually expresses its theology of baptism. For example, in infant baptism the chrismation (Muron) as a sign of the Holy Spirit is very well reflected in the baptismal liturgy. However, at least some members of the church interpret the Bible literally in such a way that they are ready to receive baptism for a second time. A wrong notion about the reception of the Holy Spirit reduces the rite from its full biblical implications and from the understanding which has flourished since the apostolic tradition of the early church. We need to undertake a rediscovery of the lost significance of our liturgical text as a source of theology and as an expression of faith.

* * *

GLOSSARY OF SYRIAC TERMS

Ekba: A short one-verse anthem.

Kolo (or Qolo): A short anthem of several verses, sometimes modeled on the Psalms.

Kuklyon: Literally, "cycle." Several items arranged in a standard pattern, usually beginning with a Psalm and Ekba and leading into a Promion and Sedra.

Kukaya: Technical terms for various songs, canticles, and chants.

Muron: Olive oil mixed with various spices, prepared and consecrated by the Metropolitan together with the other bishops. Used mainly for the final anointing at baptism (chrismation) and for the consecration of a church.

Syth: Blessed olive oil; used for various anointings.

Promion: An introductory prayer introduced by a dialogue.

Sedra: A long prayer in prose or verse, usually dealing with the main subject of the service.

Notes

[1] Mar Thoma Syrian Church, *Order of Services, Baptism, Matrimony, Prayer for Sick, House Dedication and Funeral* (Tiruvalla: The MarThoma Sabha book Depot, 1988), 9–23.

[2] B. Varghese, *Baptism and Chrismation in the Syriac Tradition*, SCC, 8 (Changanassery: St. Ephrem Ecumenical Research Institute, ca. 1989), 26–27.

[3] M. Elenjikal, *Baptism in the Malankara Church* (Bangalore: Dhamaram College, 1974).

[4] Ibid., 94.

[5] Ibid., 61–62.

[6] Varghese, *Baptism and Chrismation*, 31.

[7] Quoted from ibid., 31; cf. Elenjikal, *Baptism*, 63.

[8] G. Mathew, "An Investigation into the Rite and Doctrine of the Ordination of the Priest in the Mar Thoma Syrian Church," M. Phil. Thesis (Bristol, unpublished, 1990), 108.

[9] Elenjikal, *Baptism*, 101.

[10] Ibid., 106.

[11] Ibid., 103.

[12] Ibid., 119.

[13] For further discussion on this, see: G. Winkler, "The original meaning and implications of the pre-baptismal anointing," *Worship* (1978): 24–38.

[14] S. P. Brock, *The Holy Spirit in the Syrian Baptismal Tradition*, The Syrian Church Series, vol. 9 (Poona: Anita Press, 1979), 11–19, 37–44, 95–106.

[15] R. Murray, *Symbols of Church and Kingdom. A Study in Early Syriac Tradition* (London and New York: Cambridge University Press, 1975), 129.

[16] P. Tovey, *Spiritual and Celestial Mysteries* (Kunnamkulam: St. Thomas Press, 1993), 21–24.

[17] Text No. 27, in Elenjikal, *Baptism*, 134.

[18] Quoted from Varghese, *Baptism and Chrismation*, 42–43.

[19] For the epiclesis in the Eucharist in the Mar Thoma Church see G. Mathew, *Eucharist, the Celebration of the Economy of Salvation* (Vadavathoor: Oriental Institute of Religious Studies, India, 1999), 118–122.

[20] P. Tovey, *Essays in West Syrian Liturgy* (Vadavathoor: Oriental Institute of Religious Studies, India, 1997), 92.

[21] Brock, *The Holy Spirit*, 70.

[22] Elenjikal, *Baptism*, 151.

[23] Ibid., 164.

[24] K. K. Kuruvilla, *History of the Mar Thoma Church and its Doctrine* (Tiruvilla: CLS, 1951), 36.

[25] *Some Important Documents about the Faith and Practice of the Mar Thoma Church* (Tiruvilla: n.p., 1965), 35f.

[26] A. Kuruvilla and C. Thomas, *A Study of Holy Baptism and Holy Communion* (Tiruvilla: Mar Thoma Sabha Council, 1995), 28–36.

[27] For the view of the Mar Thoma Church on Baptism, see Max Thurian, ed., *Churches Respond to BEM: Official responses to the "Baptism, Eucharist and Ministry" Text, Vol. IV*, Faith and Order Paper No. 137 (Geneva: World Council of Churches, 1987), 7–13.

[28] For further discussion on this, see "Priesthood of the Baptised," in Brock, *The Holy Spirit*, 58–62.

[29] Thurian, *Churches Respond to BEM*, 7–13.

Chapter 14

Baptism in the Uniting Church in Australia: The Liturgy, with Commentary and Reflections

Robert Gribben

INTRODUCTION

Following an introduction to The Uniting Church in Australia, I will give and then comment on the successive sections of the church's baptismal liturgy. Thus, unlike many of the texts in this collection, this baptismal liturgy is included within the present explanatory essay.

The Uniting Church in Australia was formed in 1977 by a union of three churches of Congregational, Methodist, and Presbyterian origins. It thus inherited the theology and liturgical practice of these churches, initially in the forms of the late nineteenth century. For some years after union, the authorized service books and hymnbooks of the uniting denominations remained in use, but (after a period of experiment) the church's first liturgical resource, *Uniting in Worship*, was published in 1988[1] and authorized for use by the national assembly. (A new resource, *Uniting in Worship – 2*, was published after this essay was written. Since it does not change the church's theology or practice in any substantial way, changes will be referred to largely by footnotes.) "Authorization" means the church regards these services as normative, as indicating a standard, without requiring them to be used word-for-word. Ministers may use other resources or their own words, provided these conform to Uniting Church doctrine.

All three churches shared the custom of baptizing candidates of any age (though until recently adult baptisms were rare). The received liturgies reflected the emphasis on infant baptism. Comparatively few babies born in Australia are now brought to the churches for baptism. Some have realized that this means that, if the church's evangelization is effective in this generation, most candidates for baptism will be adults. The implications of this change for baptismal liturgy and practice has only begun to be popularly perceived.

There is a large section in *Uniting in Worship* (1988) titled "Baptism and related services."[2] This contains two baptismal liturgies: "Baptism and the Reaffirmation of Baptism called Confirmation" and "Baptism of a Child."[3] There was no intention to suggest that there are "two baptisms"; the Commission on Liturgy was of a mind to combine the two into a single liturgical form, but there were a number of difficulties, including the page design.[4] The 1988 ordering of the two services may suggest that in some sense the Commission saw the baptism of adults and families as the norm, and the baptism of children born "within the covenant" (that is, to a Christian family) as derivative. There is no implied move to deny baptism to infants—indeed, the national Assembly made it clear that individual ministers (chiefly responding to neoevangelical or charismatic influences in their congregations) may *not* refuse to baptize babies who fulfill the usual criteria. These criteria include a "founded hope" that the child will be raised in the Christian faith. There is an authorized service of Thanksgiving and Blessing of children which is an alternative to baptism.[5]

The other change from the denominational past in the 1988 services is in the understanding of confirmation. Historically, neither the Reformed nor the Methodist tradition used the word "confirmation" until the late twentieth century. The Reformation heritage meant that there were largely didactic criteria for admission to communion, it not being regarded as a sacrament. Methodists were received into what was (strangely) called "full membership" years after their baptism. However, the age of ecumenical borrowing in which the Uniting Church was born meant that confirmation was adopted as a title for the rite, though what it meant was less clear: is the candidate confirming for him- or herself what was received in baptism, or is the Church (or God) confirming those promises afresh in some significant way? (Comment is made on this below.) Following the general scholarly consensus, in 1988 the Uniting Church endorsed the definition: "the Reaffirmation of Baptism, also called Confirmation."

THE SERVICE OF BAPTISM AND THE REAFFIRMATION OF BAPTISM CALLED CONFIRMATION (1988)

The Notes for leaders place this service after the preaching of the word and indicate that it ought normally to take place during a regular Sunday service. There is a strong emphasis on the responsibility of the church's (lay) elders in the decision to baptize and in the preparation and pastoral care of the candidate or their family. An elder introduces the candidate to the congregation at the service. Since the main biblical readings of the day have already been proclaimed, one or two verses are read at this point as a kind of "warrant," always including Matthew 28:18-20 and/or Romans 6:3-4; there are further brief readings to choose from if the preacher wishes to speak of baptism rather than follow the lectionary.

The minister (understood to be an ordained presbyter or deacon[6]) then gives this summary of the meaning of baptism and confirmation:

> Obeying the word of the Lord Jesus,
> and confident of his promises,
> the church baptizes those whom he has called.
>
> Baptism is the sign of new life in Christ Jesus.
> By water and the Holy Spirit
> we are brought into union with Christ
> in his death and resurrection.
> In baptism we are sealed with the Holy Spirit,
> made members of the body of Christ,
> and called to his ministry in the world.
>
> In confirmation we acknowledge what God is doing for us;
> we renew in faith the covenant declared in our baptism;
> and we are commissioned for our ministry in the world.[7]

The next section is titled "Renunciation and Affirmation," and when adults are involved, reads:

> *The minister says to all the candidates:*
> Through baptism
> we enter the covenant which God has established;
> and in confirmation
> we affirm that we belong to God's covenant people.
> In the light of the gospel we proclaim,
> I ask you now:
>
> *The minister addresses each candidate in turn:*
> N [= the person's name], do you repent of your sins?
> **I repent of my sins.**
>
> Do you turn to Jesus Christ,
> who has defeated the power of sin and death
> and brought us new life?
> **I turn to Christ.**

> Do you pledge yourself to God,
> trusting in Jesus Christ as Saviour and Lord
> and in the Holy Spirit as Counsellor and Guide?
> **I pledge myself to God.**
>
> *The minister may touch each candidate's ears and mouth, saying:*
> N, may the Lord open your ears to receive his word,
> and your mouth to proclaim his praise.[8]

The whole congregation is invited to "confess the faith into which we are baptised" in the Apostles' Creed, which is then recited in an interrogative form. At this point, candidates for confirmation only return to their places. An elder pours water into a font which the Notes indicate should be visible during all services, and of such size that "a generous quantity of water may be poured into it." Note viii reads:

> Baptism is administered by totally immersing the candidate in water or by pouring water on the head of the candidate. Sprinkling water on the head of the candidate has also been recognised and practised by the church through many centuries. Because sprinkling is a less adequate use of the sign of water, its practice in the Uniting Church is discouraged. Sprinkling is regarded as valid baptism in the Uniting Church, but it should be noted that some other denominations no longer permit baptism to be administered by this mode.

The minister now offers a "Prayer of Thanksgiving" over the water similar to that over bread and wine at the Lord's Supper, and opening with the same dialogue ("Lift up your hearts," etc.). There are two possibilities, both in the style of Luther's "Flood prayer."[9] The first will be given here:

> Eternal God,
> we thank you for the gift of water:
> in the beginning you moved over the waters
> to bring order out of chaos;
> from the great flood in the days of Noah
> you saved those on the ark;
> through the Red Sea you led your people to freedom
> from slavery in Egypt;
> across the river Jordan you led Israel
> to the land you promised;
> in the waters of the Jordan
> our Lord was baptised by John
> and anointed by the Spirit.

By the power of the Holy Spirit, bless this water
and those/this person who are/is baptised in it;
that they/he/she may be born anew
of water and the Spirit,
be raised to new life in Christ,
and continue to be his faithful disciple(s);
through Jesus Christ our Lord,
to whom with you and the Holy Spirit
be all honour and glory, now and for ever.
Amen.

Baptism now takes place according to one of the modes described above, with these instructions:

The people remain standing for the act of baptism.

If the mode of immersion is used, the candidate is dipped in water three times, once at each name of the Trinity.

If the mode of pouring is used, the candidate bows his/her head over the font. The minister pours water visibly and generously on the candidate's head three times, once at each name of the Trinity.

In baptising, the minister shall use the following words:
NN, I baptise you
in the name of the Father,
and of the Son,
and of the Holy Spirit.

The people respond:
Amen.

This further symbolic action usually follows.

The minister marks the sign of the cross on the forehead of the newly-baptised person, and may say:
NN, from this day on
the sign of the cross is upon you.

And then

The minister presents the baptised member to the congregation saying:
N is now received into the holy catholic Church
according to Christ's command.

Those to be confirmed now come forward to join the newly baptized during the singing of a hymn. The rubrics suggest it may be a hymn to the Holy Spirit or one based on the theme of commitment to discipleship. The laying on of hands is accompanied by this exhortation and followed by prayer and a blessing sung (usually) by the church:

The minister says to the candidates:
Always remember you are baptised,
and be thankful.

The candidates kneel.

Elders and other members appointed by the council of elders to lay on hands come forward and stand around the candidates.

The minister calls the people to silent prayer, after which one or more people may offer free prayer.

The minister, with both hands extended over the candidates, offers this prayer:
By the Holy Spirit, Lord,
strengthen these your servants,
and set their hearts on fire with love for you.
Increase in them your gifts of grace:
the spirit of wisdom and understanding,
the spirit of counsel and might,
the spirit of knowledge and wonder in your presence,
the spirit of joy and delight in your service,
now and for ever.
Amen. *Based on Isaiah 11:2*

The minister, elders and any others appointed lay hands on the head of each candidate in turn, and the minister says:
N, by the power of the Holy Spirit,
be a faithful witness to Christ
all the days of your life.

The candidates and the people respond each time this is said:
Amen.

The baptismal promises now follow. It is the understanding of the Uniting Church in Australia that baptism is an act of grace; all that is required is to turn to Christ (see the Renunciation and Affirmation, above). These undertakings are therefore a response to that grace (the section is headed "Responses").

The newly-confirmed members answer together these questions:
Do you promise to follow Christ
in your daily life?
With God's help,
I will seek to love and obey Christ,
and to grow in my relationship with God
through prayer and study of the Bible.
Do you promise to be a faithful member
of the Christian community?
With God's help,
I will share in the worship of the church,
and support its work
with my time, talents and money.
Do you promise to participate
in God's mission to the world?
With God's help,
I will witness to Christ in word and deed,
and look for the coming of his kingdom.

It has been remarked that these particular responses seem more appropriate to younger adults. They are replaced in *Uniting in Worship–2* by a set of questions on faith and mission such as are found in the Congregational Reaffirmation of Baptism,[10] based on the *Book of Common Prayer*, 1979, of the Episcopal Church in the USA. In the case of a child, the parents make promises to bring up the child in the way of Christ.[11]

The congregation also renews its promises to be a baptized community:

The minister addresses the people:
I charge you,
the people of this congregation,
to love, encourage and support
these brothers and sisters in faith,
that they may continue to grow
in the grace of the Lord Jesus Christ
and the knowledge and love of God.

The people respond, saying:
With God's help,
we will live out our baptism
as a loving community in Christ:
nurturing one another in faith,
upholding one another in prayer,

and encouraging one another in service,
until Christ comes. [from the text of 2005].

Certificates may now be presented, an offering taken, and notices given, leading to the "Prayers of the People." Some prayers for the newly baptized and confirmed are offered, but the prayers will also include general intercessions.[12] It is usual in this service for the sacrament of the Lord's Supper to follow.

The Uniting Church in Australia has made a significant modification to ecumenical practice in that it has moved the giving of the baptismal candle from immediately after baptism to the dismissal rite. This was partly because of early fears that the introduction of a candle after the baptism was likely to overshadow the symbol of water itself; but more strongly, the candle was seen as a symbol of mission, of carrying the light of Christ into the world. It therefore belongs in The Sending Forth of the People of God.

The newly-confirmed members and their elders may gather at the front of the church.

The elder of each person, both those previously baptised and those newly baptised, may take a white candle, light it from the Easter candle standing near the font and present it, saying:
N, you belong to Christ,
the light of the world.

When all have received a lighted candle, the minister says:
Let your light so shine before the world
that all may see your good works
and give glory to our Father who is in heaven.   Matthew 5:16

A final exhortation (or word of mission) and general blessing follows, then the new members, holding their lighted candles, process with the leaders out of the church.

THE BAPTISM OF A CHILD (1988)

This baptismal service follows exactly the same pattern, with modifications in the words as appropriate.

At the Renunciation, it is the parents who are asked and who respond:

Do you believe that the gospel
enables us to turn from the darkness of evil
and to walk in the light of Christ?
We do.

The intention is to seek a degree of belief in the parents—or in one parent at least—that faith in God does make a difference to the direction of life.[13] The Apostles' Creed follows as before, said by the whole church. The Uniting Church has declared that it "will baptise those who profess the Christian faith, and children who are presented for baptism and for whose instruction and nourishment in the faith the Church takes responsibility."[14]

Immediately prior to the act of baptism (in both the texts of 1988 and of 2005), the following address is read or recited to the child. It is adapted from a French Reformed source and is intended as a statement of a theology of grace in the baptism of those too young to answer for themselves:

> *Addressing the child, the minister may say:*
> Little child,[15]
> for you Jesus Christ has come,
> has lived, has suffered;
> for you, he has endured the agony of Gethsemane
> and the darkness of Calvary;
> for you, he has uttered the cry, "It is accomplished!"
> For you, he has triumphed over death;
> for you, he prays at God's right hand;
> all for you, little child,
> even though you do not know it.
> In baptism,
> the word of the apostle is fulfilled:
> "We love, because God first loved us." *1 John 4:19*

It is possible that where there are children old enough to speak for themselves some modification of the responses, as suited to the children's ability, might be suggested by the minister.

ISSUES FOR THE CHURCH TO ADDRESS

Some aspects of these rites signify debates in the Uniting Church in the early decades of its life. Its ecumenical commitment is affirmed in the declaration that baptism is into the "holy catholic Church" and not merely into the Uniting Church in Australia. The church has entered into a number of relationships with other churches in which there is mutual acceptance of baptism. It participates with some other churches in the use of a Common Baptismal Certificate (see "Australia's Common Baptismal Certificate: Its History and Significance" in section III of this book).

The redefining of modes of baptism also indicates a response to ecumenical discussion (including, particularly, *Baptism, Eucharist and Ministry*), for example, in the encouragement of a more generous use of water.

It should be noted that the precise words at the act of baptism are mandatory. This is by decision of the national Assembly in 1988.[16] There is a strong desire in some places to find a formula which does not use "Father/Son" language, but at the present stage of that search the Uniting Church believes that ecumenically acceptable and historic baptismal practice should prevail.

The number of provisions for "re-affirmation of baptism" (Confirmation, Personal and Congregational services, and the Covenant Service) was, in part, a response to rebaptisms that were occurring under charismatic influences in the 1980s. It became clear that baptism as the church had practiced it, especially in the case of infants, was not seen as meaningful or memorable. The Assembly moved strongly to rule out anything that seemed like rebaptism; it therefore supplied material for occasions to celebrate and reclaim the promises under which Christians live.

There is some confusion over the practice of confirmation, in that newly baptized adults are immediately confirmed. This arises from the requirements of church government rather than from theological or liturgical necessity. Only *confirmed* members are eligible for certain offices in councils of the church. By an earlier decision, the Assembly authorized the admission of children on the basis of their baptism. There seems some need to distinguish between children—who are now seen as full members of the church by their baptism, to which nothing can be added—and those who can legitimately (by maturity and experience?) take part in the governance of a congregation. Confirmation is, then, one of several ways in which one's baptism may be reaffirmed as life takes its course, but the way it is distinguished from other reaffirmations remains unclear.

The sign of the cross is a secondary symbol of baptism, new to the Uniting Churches and drawn from ecumenical experience. It has been welcomed for its core meaning and is not derived from historic practice (namely, an exorcism or a post-baptismal anointing). Some are now calling for the use of oil at this point as a further symbolic elaboration of the meaning of baptism (chrismation), and this is provided for in *Uniting in Worship–2*.[17]

Notes

[1] *Uniting in Worship* (1988) was published in two volumes, a *People's Book* and a *Leader's Book*. The latter contains a full provision of alternative prayers and other resources. The 2005 resource is a single volume.

[2] The section also contains baptismal reaffirmation services for individuals and for congregations (this latter somewhat akin to Roman Catholic and other churches' practice, especially at Easter), and a modern form of the Covenant Service from the Methodist tradition. The 2005 book adds material for a catechumenate, under the title *Becoming Disciples*.

[3] The change of title from "Infant" to "a Child" indicates that a significant number of children now come to baptism after infancy. This sometimes reflects a change of attitude within a particular family as to the appropriate age of baptism. It may also reflect uneven pastoral practice.

[4] *Uniting in Worship–2*, published in 2005, has produced a single liturgy for use with either or both children and older candidates. It remains to be seen whether ministers can find their way through the alternatives (designated A for "adults and families" and B for children throughout). This unitive liturgy has resolved some of the questions mentioned above.

[5] In 1988, this was a "Service of Thanksgiving for the Gift of a Child," intended either for parents who did not believe in paedo-baptism, or for those unwilling to commit themselves to the required promises. In 2005, the service was titled "A Service of Thanksgiving for and a Blessing of a Child" and provides an explicit blessing of the child (in which head, hands, and feet may be touched, without anointing). This was intended to resolve the issue raised by members who believed the Uniting Church should have a "service of dedication," parallel to that held by some Baptist churches. The solution offered here is that the child be *blessed* by God through the church's minister (but not baptized); any dedication involved is of the *parents to their vocation as parents*, not of the child.

[6] The Uniting Church has two distinct ordained ministries, the Minister of the Word (equivalent to presbyter in other traditions—the usual congregational pastor) and the Deacon. The latter's work is not distinguished by liturgical or sacramental function but by context: the deacon is called to work on the frontier of church and world and may be involved with worshiping groups in workplaces, hospitals, and so on, beyond formal congregational boundaries. There are pastoral situations in which the Uniting Church may also authorize lay persons to preside at both sacraments.

[7] The "Meaning of Baptism" section was expanded in *Uniting in Worship–2* (2005) and omitted the reference to confirmation. This gave rise to some questions from ministers when they had candidates for confirmation but none for baptism; the Working Group on Worship reaffirmed the baptismal context of confirmation and suggested some adaptation of the liturgy on such occasions.

⁸ In 2005, the heading was changed to "The Confession of Faith" (again with reference to confirmation omitted); adults were asked the questions as above, with some minor changes; in both books, the parents answer for *themselves* if the candidate was a child. To deal with the lack of reference to confirmation, the Working Group suggested the following alternative if only confirmands were present:

[Minister:] N, what do you ask of God's Church?

[Candidate:] I come that the Church may confirm God's promises in Jesus Christ declared at my baptism, that I may live as a faithful disciple.

[Minister:] N has been called by the Holy Spirit to claim the faith of Jesus Christ as his/her own and, through baptism, to die to sin and rise to newness of life through a new birth by water and the Spirit.

Note the carefully nuanced statement on who is confirming what.

⁹ In 2005, the second prayer was replaced by a newly composed one which takes up the baptismal image of rebirth: "God of life, through the breaking of waters, and the coming of the Spirit, you bring us new birth . . ." and at the epiclesis, "bless this water, and those to be baptised in it, that they may be born anew . . . and come to share your likeness . . ." The metaphors of quenching thirst and washing are also included.

¹⁰ I ask you now to pledge yourselves to Christ's ministry in the world:

Will you continue in the community of faith, the apostles' teaching, the breaking of bread and the prayers?

With God's help, we will.

Will you proclaim by word and example the good news of God in Christ?

With God's help, we will.

Will you seek Christ in all people, and love your neighbour as yourself?

With God's help, we will.

Will you strive for justice and peace, and respect the dignity of every human being?

With God's help, we will.

May the God of grace, who has given us new birth by water and the Holy Spirit, keep us steadfast in the faith, and bring us to eternal life; through Jesus Christ our Lord. Amen.

¹¹ The Uniting Church makes no provision for godparents; when by family custom such are asked for, they usually answer with the parents.

¹² In the 2005 revision the possibility is offered of a congregational Recollection of Baptism, including the sprinkling of water toward the congregation, the opportunity for individuals to sign themselves at the font, or to immerse themselves as appropriate. The rubric warns against actions which suggest rebaptism.

¹³ This address is omitted in 2005; the parents are expected to profess the Christian faith.

¹⁴ The Uniting Church in Australia's *Basis of Union*, par. 7, and n. iii.

[15] In the 2005 text: "N and N/for you, Jesus Christ has come," adapting the exhortation for use with adults.

[16] "That all ministers of the Word and others authorised to administer the sacrament of baptism be required to use the following words as the baptismal formula, without variation or exception: 'NN, I baptize you in the name of the Father, and of the Son, and of the Holy Spirit,'" Assembly Minute 88.24.3 (*The Trinitarian formula at baptism*). See also n. 15 in *Uniting in Worship–2* (2005).

[17] A Note (18) before the service gives this explanation: "The sign of the cross after baptism symbolises the 'sealing' of God's promises; from this moment, we live in and for Christ (Rom 6:8-11). It is appropriate for oil to be used when the sign of the cross is given after baptism. The Greek New Testament word for oil, *chrisma*, carries important meanings, e.g., 'Christ' (the anointed One; see Luke 4:18-21). 'Chrismation' (anointing) contains a number of meanings including healing, protection and commissioning. Ordinary olive oil is used. It is important to remember that the fundamental symbol in baptism is water, generously used; secondary symbols such as oil and candle are used to indicate some further significant meanings of the primary action."

Chapter 15

Witness in the Waters: Baptism and Pentecostal Spirituality

Daniel Albrecht

INTRODUCTION TO PENTECOSTAL BAPTISMAL RITES

1. Variety and Commonality: Pentecostal Liturgy and Spirituality

The Pentecostal tradition represents broad and varied theological and liturgical currents. Pentecostal diversity results, in part, from its worldwide expressions rooted in a variety of cultures, ecclesiologies, and pastoral traditions. No denomination or ecclesiastical organization can claim Pentecostal spirituality as its own. The tradition—or the *movement*, as Pentecostals prefer to call it—moves in and through a host of networks, groups of fellowships, and even independent churches locally and globally. Consequently, Pentecostal liturgies, including baptismal rites, can differ from group to group, region to region, and culture to culture. However, while variety marks the Pentecostal movement, several common emphases, traits, and values support and animate Pentecostal spiritualities and its liturgies, and it is these features which enable us to speak of "Pentecostal" baptismal rites.

2. Rites Shaped by Orality and Other Values

Generally, Pentecostals avoid written liturgy. This reveals one of their traits or values that they hold in common: orality. Pentecostal liturgies, and their spirituality in general, are kin to oral culture. The virtual absence of written rubrics does not mean that Pentecostals do not have liturgy or rites (though they often fail to recognize, or name, their practices as "rites"). This means that their rites and liturgies are shaped, performed, and transmitted orally. In fact, scholars of Pentecostalism locate orality at the core of Pentecostal worship, its tradition and spirituality. Orality as a value supports and complements other fundamental Pentecostal liturgical values, including personal experience of God and a certain amount of spontaneity and improvisation in worship services.[1]

While *experience* emerges as a central value within Pentecostal spirituality, a Pentecostal theological understanding insists that liturgical experiences be rooted in the Bible—love for Scripture and biblical authority are also chief among Pentecostal values. Pentecostal spirituality is particularly keen on the early church narratives in Scripture (notably the Acts of the Apostles). This propensity for biblical narrative gives rise to other primary Pentecostal values and traits, not the least of which is personal testimony and witness. As we consider the forms and meanings of baptism below, Pentecostal values will come into play.[2]

3. Common Type: (Basic) Beliefs and Practices

Before we consider a processual structure for Pentecostal baptismal rites, it would be good to identify a few key beliefs (traits) and practices common to Pentecostal water baptism.[3] The majority of Pentecostals practice believers' baptism, following in this the Anabaptist and Baptist traditions. Water baptism typically represents an "act of obedience" (to something seen as a command of Christ). Generally, Pentecostals view baptism as an outward sign of an inward change; they believe the change represented in conversion should normally precede the baptism. In addition, in many places Pentecostals expect, and look for, outward changes in lifestyle prior to baptism. These outward expressions symbolize the person's conversion and the seriousness of his or her commitment to Christian discipleship. Such strong expectations are not universal among Pentecostals; in many places, baptism is encouraged almost immediately following conversion. In nearly all cases, however, water baptism is seen as a public testimony of identification with Christ, his universal Church, and a local assembly of believers.

The central theme of testimony in baptism coincides with the key Pentecostal values of narrative and orality. For Pentecostals, baptism is a rite of testimony or witness. As such, it focuses more on the grace of salvation as initiated in conversion—conversion as both initial in the past and an ongoing dynamic that proceeds into the future. As a rite of testimony, the act of water baptism is viewed more as a step of obedience that gives witness to the grace of God than a sacrament through which grace flows. Pentecostal understanding acknowledges little salvific meaning in the actual rite itself. In fact, some early Pentecostals minimized the role of baptism; today, on the other hand, most encourage baptism—but still do not recognize the rite as an experience necessary for salvation. It is conversion, not baptism, that holds the central place in Pentecostal theologies and spiritualities of salvific grace.

4. Fundamental Structure of a Baptismal Rite

A Pentecostal baptismal service or liturgy may occur as a "stand alone" rite with a brief introduction and conclusion. However, the baptismal rite is frequently part of a larger liturgy, and the baptismal rite then fits within the greater liturgical frame of the public worship service. We note here the basic outline of the service, which is structured symmetrically.

Pastoral Introduction (or Transition): Pastoral Words

Part ("Act") I: INTO THE WATERS

    1. Entry into the waters

        2. Candidate's Narrative Testimony

            2a. Pastoral Questions (or interview)

            2b. Extemporary Testimony

            3. Pastoral address and pronouncement

                3a. Address and prayer

                3b. Formulaic pronouncement

                4. Plunged into the waters

                    Baptizo, **The Nexus: Witness in the Waters**

Part ("Act") II: OUT OF THE WATERS

                4' **Raised up out of the Waters**

            3' **Signs of the Spirit: The Spirit Testifies**

        2' **Congregational response and affirmation**

    1' **Exit from the waters**

Pastoral Closing: Pastoral Words

As this exposition makes clear, a Pentecostal baptismal rite may be thought of as a twofold rite, the parts being "Into the Waters" and "Out of the Waters." Within these fundamental parts of the baptismal rite, four phases can be identified. A chiastic structure may emerge as the rite proceeds. If the rite occurs independently of a larger worship, the twofold rite opens and closes with pastoral words. However, if a complete worship liturgy enfolds the baptismal rite, then the pastoral words prior to and subsequent to the rite function as transitional words, which move the liturgical flow into, and then out of, the baptismal service. We will give a fuller explanation of the baptismal liturgy after making some inquiries into the function of baptism and its type as a Pentecostal rite.

BAPTISMAL RITES AND SPIRITUALITY: A DESCRIPTIVE PENTECOSTAL UNDERSTANDING

1. *The Rite: Types and Functions*

A. Rite of Passage

Baptism is a *rite of passage*. The candidate and congregation both recognize the passage that is taking place. For Pentecostals, baptism is as much a rite of passage with psychological overtones as it is a sacramental rite. As one Pentecostal pastor explains to candidates, "baptism helps to 'cinch down' your salvation experience." It assists the candidate in solidifying the commitment to Christ and it makes visible that commitment to congregation and the public.

Rites of passage proceed as three-stage rituals—the past state or status of the individual, the future status, and the status "betwixt and between" the past and the future.[4] As a Pentecostal rite of passage, baptism marks the moment that ritually ends a past life while declaring a dedication to a new, future life-time. Many Pentecostals have expressed their intention of commitment from within the waters of baptism, saying, "I want to go all the way with Him!"[5] This testifies to an initial conversion that expects to deepen in an ongoing way as it looks into the future, indeed as far as the "telos" of the kingdom.

The "betwixt and between" state can be thought of as post-conversion and pre-baptism. It culminates in a moment from the midst of the waters as a testimony, prior to the actual immersion, which declares a resolution to identify with Christ and the Church for all time. In short, baptism as a rite of passage functions for the individual candidate as a change of status, a transformation, from a pre-Christian to a Christian status, and from outsider to insider within the Christian congregation.

Another function of baptism involves not only the effect on the candidate but also the role it plays in the life of the congregation. The congregation witnesses this witness; it discerns the candidate's decision and dedication; it affirms the intention. And it receives a fellow believer into a Pentecostal congregation of witnesses, as well as into the Church universal. In short the congregation sees, confirms, and adjusts to the changing status of the candidate.

A third function of the baptismal rite of passage for Pentecostals is that of public testimony—"public" being understood as broader than the believing community. Pentecostals look for opportunities to express their faith within the larger society. Almost any event has evangelistic potential, and baptism is no exception. Many Pentecostals seek venues for baptism that afford evangelical possibilities; rivers, beaches, and lakes can be consciously chosen in order to share the good news through a Christian rite of passage, a rite that for Pentecostals is at its core a "testimonial rite."

B. Rite of Testimony

For Pentecostals, baptism dramatizes becoming a Christian. In baptism the candidate testifies to conversion and ritually enters the congregation and becomes a witness. To be a witness, a living testimony is a particularly important role in Pentecostal spirituality. Ritually, the first testimony of a convert is from the baptismal font. For Pentecostals, baptism is not only a rite of passage but also a rite of testimony. As such, it incorporates the new baptized witness into a body of believers that sees itself as living witnesses—congregationally and individually—of Jesus Christ in the World.

Because baptism is experienced as a dramatized liturgy of testimony—in word and act—it is seldom a private event. Baptismal rites are "social" events and, as such, have an interactive dimension. Baptismal rites are testimonial expressions, including both narrative and action; they are rites of witness both heard and seen. The symbolic-expressive rite unfolds interactively. The pastor and candidate speak and act; the congregation (and possibly the attending public) listens and sees. But the body of believers is not composed of passive observers; they confirm, and affirm, the rite dispositionally and orally. Ultimately, however, for Pentecostals the rite is an interactive testimony with God. In the rite the candidate proclaims commitment unto God, and God is expected to affirm the testimony through the congregation and possibly through other signs. In a phrase, a Pentecostal baptismal service is an *interactive narrative-drama*.

2. *Processual Structure: The Baptismal Rite as a Narrative Drama*

Since little is prescribed concerning the Pentecostal baptismal rite and very little has been written about it, the following seeks to produce a descriptive interpretation of the rite as we have observed, experienced, and understood it through Pentecostal eyes. We outlined above the fundamental structure of the rite. Here we will discuss the processual structure as a narrative, which unfolds dramatically in two "acts" and eight "scenes."

A. Setting/Space

The baptism can occur in a variety of places. Often natural settings are sought: rivers, lakes, or the ocean suffice; even swimming pools can be used. At least two kinds of rationale motivate the choice of venue. A pragmatic reason often dominates. The Pentecostal church building, or rented space for congregational meetings, may lack a baptismal font (or what Pentecostals might call a baptismal "tank"). The second reason, as noted above, flows from the inherent value of evangelism, and the nature of Pentecostal spirituality with its propensity for oral/narrative and kinesthetic means to express the gospel. A public venue gives vent to these intrinsic values. Even when the location of the rite finds its way into a sanctuary baptismal tank, testimony and evangelism suffuse the service. So, while to some extent the setting shapes the service, the Pentecostal ethos holds sway.

B. Pastoral Introduction (or Transition): Pastoral Words

When the baptismal rite is nearly ready to begin, the pastor will walk into the waist-deep waters of the river or baptistery. If the baptismal rite occurs in the midst of a larger liturgy, the transition may be made with congregational singing—usually an upbeat chorus—typically a song of testimony. After the pastor positions her- or himself in the baptismal waters, the rite begins.

The singing ceases and the pastor speaks. The pastoral words seek to complete the transition into the rite, and to set the context and meaning of the rite. Often a brief explanation of baptism and its significance focus the rite to follow. This introduction moves the mode of sensibility from a celebrative sense in the singing to a didactic, more formal sensibility that coincides with the instructional function. But this congregational disposition is short-lived. It soon gives way to a more ceremonial mode of sensibility as the actual rite begins.[6]

The following commentary develops the outline of the rite given on page 149 above. As indicated, the rite can be understood in two Acts (parts): "Into the Waters" and "Out of the Waters." Each of these two Acts has four scenes (or phases), and each of the four scenes (phases) in Part I in some way "mirrors" a corresponding scene (phase) in Act II. For example, the "Candidate's testimony" in Act I, scene two, mirrors the "Congregation's response and affirmation" in Act II, scene seven. Hence, the scenes of Acts I and II create together a mirror effect throughout the liturgy, forming a loose and mutable chiastic structure. It must be said that, as with any Pentecostal rite, baptism is not fixed. The procedure is open to changes, whether premeditated or spontaneous. The following represents an idealized type; as with any type, rarely does its typical form and procedure conform completely to the ideal.

3. A Two-Part Rite: Two Acts in Eight "Scenes"

"ACT" I – INTO THE WATERS
from the World into the Waters . . .

1. Entry into the Waters: Exiting the World (Scene one)

The opening scene commences as the candidate enters, walking into the deepening waters to stand near the waiting pastor. When the baptism takes place in a church baptistery, the candidate descends the stairs into the pool of water. When the rite occurs in a river, lake, or ocean, the candidate leaves the shore and moves out to deeper water, where the pastor reaches out to take the candidate's hand, leading the candidate from the "world" and into the waters of both death and life.

2. The Candidate's Testimony: A Narrative of Salvation (Scene two)

When the candidate has walked into the water and is positioned next to the pastor, together they turn to face the congregation and to give the "Candidate's testimony."

2a. Pastoral Questioning

The first part of the Candidate's testimony is the more structured. After the pastor has introduced the candidate by name, a few questions follow the pastor's address to the candidate. This scene formalizes what has already been discerned by the pastor and the congregation. The questions function as a review of the candidate's personal experience of conversion and of the beginnings of discipleship. A certain form of this period within the service can be discerned, but it lacks the more formal "examination of the candidate" typical of many communions. The questions do, however, give candidates the opportunity to affirm publicly their initial faith, their conversion, as well as their intention and commitment to an ongoing faith and life in Christ.

2b. Extemporaneous Testimony:
Opportunity for and Expectation of Testimony

This confession of faith and commitment proceeds from the pastoral questions to a more extemporaneous genre of testimony. Several subtle shifts occur. There is a shift of attention. The direct engagement between the pastor as questioner and the candidate as respondent changes; the candidate is encouraged now to turn his or her attention to the congregation. He or she is expected to give a testimony in his or her own words to a very attentive congregation. The mode of sensibility also shifts. It moves momentarily from a ceremonial sense to a more improvisational sensibility. The form of speech changes as well. A "Pentecostal," more or less spontaneous, style emerges as the candidate takes the opportunity to construct a narrative of the changes that God has brought about in his or her life.

3. *Pastoral Address and Pronouncement: Sanctioning the Testimony (Scene three)*

As the candidate finishes the extemporaneous testimony a new scene emerges, and attention moves back to the pastor. The tone changes as well, moving back to a more ceremonial one.

3a. Pastoral Address: Charge and Prayer

The pastor briefly addresses the congregation and then turns to the candidate. The body positions change, and the most formal part of the rite begins. The pastoral language takes the form of a charge. Prayer by the pastor can occur prior or subsequent to the charge.

3b. Formulaic Pronouncement or Initial Statement

The pronouncement and formula, while not completely standardized among Pentecostal congregations, often resembles this: 1) "Upon your profession of faith in Jesus Christ as your personal Savior . . . 2) I now baptize you in the name of the Father and Son and Holy Spirit." In part, the pastoral address and pronouncement serve as sanction to the profession of faith, an endorsement to the authenticity of the testimony.[7]

4. *Plunged into the Waters (Scene four)*

With these words scene three concludes and a new, very brief scene rushes in. The pastor immediately immerses the candidate. It is normally a quick action, a plunging into water with the accompanying sounds and sights of splashing waters. The candidate has probably been instructed how to yield to the pastor's touch and allow him- or herself to be laid down into waters completely, to be symbolically "buried with Christ."

Baptizo, *the Nexus: Witness within the Waters*

In the instant between the plunging into and rising up out of the waters, a transformation occurs. Ritually, this moment signifies the nexus—

the center and climax—of the dramatic narrative. In this moment, in this betwixt and between, suspended moment, the waters themselves give witness, as it were, to the metamorphosing taking place—the candidate becoming the baptized, and the candidate, who was entombed with Christ, identifying with the Crucified. The waters also witness, signifying a womb ready to issue forth a new life. Act II of the rite begins.

"Act" II – Out of the Waters:
from the Waters into the World (in Newness of Life)

4' "Raised" up out of the Waters (Scene five)

As with scene four, scene five too is brief. The solemn moment breaks into a celebratory mode as the candidate is raised by the pastor, breaking through the waters that covered him or her into the open air and the Spirit in the awaiting congregation. The church celebrates!

3' Signs of the Spirit: The Spirit Testifies (Scene six)

As described thus far, baptism favors the Pauline imagery of being buried with Christ and dead to sin, then being raised to walk in newness of life (cf. Rom 6:1-11). This Pauline paradigm represents one of the primary New Testament models of Christian baptism.

The gospel narratives focus on Jesus' baptism. The importance of these narratives, and the image of Jesus' baptism as a model for Christian baptism, is attested to by many early church fathers. For them Jesus' baptism in the Jordan stands as a paradigm alongside the Pauline imagery. Whereas Paul's paradigm images regeneration, Jesus' baptism in the Jordan sees baptism as the sign of the Spirit coming, as a dove descends, and points to the Father's pleasure, God's affirmation of the Son as beloved.

In this sixth scene, Pentecostal congregations draw more upon the gospels' model of Jesus' baptism than the Pauline. Pentecostals are open to signs of the Spirit. In some cases a congregation anticipates this moment with a heightened expectancy: How will the Spirit testify? Will the Spirit manifest with a sign? Although the gospel accounts of the baptism of Jesus influence a Pentecostal understanding of baptism directly, they seem also to have intuitively picked up on the ancient church traditions.[8] Drawing from a gospel paradigm, many of the fathers of the first eight centuries taught and expected signs of the Spirit—often spiritual charisms—to accompany Christian baptism.

Pentecostal groups vary in their anticipation of charisms during the baptismal rite. Many Pentecostals, both candidate and congregant, have witnessed that they have experienced physical or emotional healing, or another blessing, in the midst of the baptism. Pentecostal congregations with a lesser expectation of charisms during Christian initiation, still anticipate at least a subtle "sign" of the Spirit. Raised hands, audible praises on the lips of the baptized one, a glow on the faces, excitement in demeanor, or perhaps an "inner witness" in and among the congregants, is discerned as a testimony of the Spirit, confirming the coming of the Spirit.[9] Scene six, in which the Spirit confirms and testifies after the baptism, links back to scene three in which the pastor sanctions the pre-baptism testimony of the candidate.

2' Congregational Response and Affirmation (Scene seven)

Scene seven occasions an exuberant congregation responding, affirming, welcoming, and receiving. The Pentecostal congregants are not passive bystanders—the baptismal rite, as most Pentecostal liturgies, is a participatory rite. As the congregation witnesses the baptism and discerns the signs of the Spirit, members of the observing and participating congregation express their involvement in a chorus of response, affirmation and praise (that is, shouts of joy, expletives of praise, sounds of singing, gestures of gladness, raising of hands, applause, and other kinesthetic and auditory exclamations that tell of their sharing in the moment). It is a charismatic moment, pointing to baptism itself as a charismatic event.[10]

This congregational response and affirmation parallels the "testimony of the candidate" in scene two prior to the baptism. This phase of the rite functions as praise to God for his salvific work on the one hand, and on the other as an affirmation of the work of God in the person who has just been baptized. It is the congregation's affirmation (or testimony) of the candidate's testimony in word and in water. The congregational response also symbolizes a "welcome" into the Body of Christ. It is a ritualization of the beginning of fellowship as the congregation reaches out to include the newly baptized Christian into its ranks. In their words and actions, the congregation testifies to itself, the candidate, the world at large, and to God of their understanding and experience of salvation, and of the joy that emerges in that experience.

Pentecostals also believe that the sign of the Spirit (in scene six), the affirmation of the congregation, and the rite in general is a call to the unbeliever to follow Jesus. Therefore the baptismal rite is seen as a moment in which an unbeliever may respond in repentance and faith, experiencing a conversion within the baptismal liturgy. Pentecostals see the whole service as a testimony to the unbeliever. It is a service open to the public, an evangelistic event that hopes for new converts to join with the congregation in a chorus of testimony.

1' Exit from the Waters: Reentering the World (Scene eight)

The final scene in Act II mirrors the first scene in Act I. The newly baptized Christian now exits from the waters of baptism to reenter the world. Whether ascending the stairs of the baptistery, or striding to the shores of a stream, the baptized one, still dripping with the waters of testimony, makes his or her exit. But this action progresses toward both the exit and the entrance—exiting the rite and entering new "worlds": the congregation, the Church universal, and the greater society.

As the newly baptized exits the waters she or he formally, and literally, enters the waiting congregation. Pentecostals look to baptism as the symbol of entrance into the Church universal, as well as the local congregation as the Body of Christ. The particular congregation represents the Church at large and the fellowship of believers into which the newly baptized now moves. Pentecostals understand the fellowship of believers to be fellowship of witnesses: again the theme of testimony emerges.

Pentecostals understand the neophyte's exit from the baptismal water as a reentry *into the world*. Candidates are baptized, in the words of the Lukan Jesus, "to be my witness." While Pentecostal congregations often form a tight bond of fellowship, they foster and expect believers to live and speak as witnesses living in the world, witnessing to their life and faith in Christ. So the new Christian moves from the baptismal water, dripping and testifying, to extend the testimony from the baptismal rite into a life in the world. In the first scene we observed the candidate entering into the waters, thereby exiting the world; in this final scene the frame is complete. Exiting the waters means reentry into the world—reentry as a new creature.

VARIATIONS IN BAPTISMAL UNDERSTANDING AND PRACTICE

We have portrayed Pentecostal water baptism as it is transmitted and administered within a tradition that is largely oral. We have admitted that the Pentecostal movement incorporated a wide range of practices and experiences. Yet, we have maintained that the rites do reflect important identifying ritual patterns and practice. Here we note significant variations within the Pentecostal movement as examples of distinct differences, rather than as slight variations in practices or beliefs.

1. *Variation in Types and Modes*

While the great majority of Pentecostals practice believers' baptism, there are some who do not. Pentecostal groups in Chile, Africa, and Germany, to name a few, practice infant baptism. Also, some denominations of Pentecostals—including some in the United States—have, in the past, drawn from their Methodist heritage to suggest or allow infant baptism. In these and some other cases, the preferred mode is sprinkling or pouring the baptismal water upon the candidate.

However, a large majority of Pentecostals practice baptism by fully immersing a believing, adult candidate (or a pre-adult conscious of conversion). In this type and mode, the Pauline imagery dominates. Some Pentecostals do not consider a believer to have been baptized if she or he has not yet received baptism by immersion. For these groups, immersion is inseparable from "adult" believer baptism.

But baptism is not seen as salvific by most Pentecostals. It seems a bit curious, then, that such great stress would be placed on immersion, since no type of baptism is acknowledged to impact salvation. Such adamancy is also interesting in light of the fact that many early Pentecostals (near the turn of the twentieth century) seem not to have stressed water baptism at all. No doubt the strong Pentecostal orientation to immersion and believers' baptism has been drawn from the traditions of their Anabaptist and Baptist cousins who have, in their histories, rebaptized.

For the most part, the Pentecostals who insist on immersion and/or believers' baptism do not think of themselves as "rebaptizers" when a new adult convert comes into their fellowship. Instead, they see the baptism that they teach and practice as biblical in its type. In addition, they believe that baptism—ritualizing the converting faith—should be a conscious, informed decision of an individual to follow Christ and participate in his or her church. Yet the practice serves as a challenge to ecumenical dialogue.

2. *Baptism in Jesus' Name, Oneness*

The most significant variations within Pentecostal understandings and practices of baptism come from the branch of *Oneness* (or "Apostolic" or "Jesus Only") Pentecostals. The variations center around at least three issues: the baptismal formula, the Trinity, and salvific initiation. Oneness Pentecostals represent a minority group within Pentecostalism that originally split with the Assemblies of God in 1914 over the issue of the correct baptismal formula. This group of Pentecostals came to believe that candidates should receive baptism in the "Name of Jesus," in accord with Acts 2:38. Subsequently, they opposed the Trinitarian formulas (Matt 28:19). In part, this shift emerged from a special reverence for the name of Jesus among early Pentecostals, rooted again in their reading of Lukan narratives in Acts. Also, the shift represents the "perennial possibility for latent themes and concepts in Scripture to be rediscovered and adapted to a new context."[11]

The result of the move to another baptismal formula was a theological variation in the understanding of Trinity. In some ways this understanding rejects the theology of the early Christian creeds; it asserts a radical oneness in the nature of God, rejecting the doctrine of three distinct persons. Oneness Pentecostals believe this assertion to be consistent with the apostolic understanding of God. Thus, some prefer to be called "*Apostolic* Pentecostals."

Another variation in Pentecostal understanding implies a certain salvific comprehension of Christian initiation. While all Pentecostals teach a doctrine of baptism in the Spirit, and most see a distinction between water baptism and Spirit baptism, Oneness Pentecostals see a tight relationship between conversion, water baptism, and Spirit baptism. In some ways, Oneness Pentecostals have a sacramental understanding of the nature of baptism. Baptism plays a much more central role in salvation for the Oneness than for the Trinitarian Pentecostals. Baptism is integral to regeneration. In their baptismal understanding initial conversion, water baptism in the name of Jesus, and the baptism in the Holy Spirit are seen as one "complex event of initiation to Christ and the life of the Spirit."[12] Using Acts 2:38 as a paradigm for Christian initiation, Oneness Pentecostals posit a "unique three-stage soteriology that blends a conversionist theology, the Pentecostal doctrine of Spirit baptism, and the Oneness teaching of the name of Jesus."[13]

INTERNAL AND ECUMENICAL ISSUES

We will now consider a few issues that are internal to Pentecostals and also some that have broader, ecumenical dimensions.

1. Internal Issue: Oneness

One might suspect that an ongoing issue within the Pentecostal tradition is the relation between Trinitarian and non-Trinitarian

(Oneness) Pentecostals. Decades of disagreement between the two groups have, at times, become severely antagonistic. However, calls for and attempts at fellowship seem recently to be on the increase. In typical Pentecostal style, many have sought to bridge the gaps by not focusing on the differing doctrinal statements, baptismal formulas, or particular variations in hermeneutics, but rather by affirming one another's experience of God and by seeking to understand the other not as heretical, but as descriptively different (for example, as describing the reality of the Godhead differently).

2. *Internal Pastoral Issues*

Another set of issues might be thought of as "pastoral," relating in particular to the readiness of a baptismal candidate. Since Pentecostals generally practice believers' baptism, and assume a conscious conversion and the subsequent life graced in faith prior to baptism, discerning the appropriate time for baptism is a pastoral responsibility of the church as well as reflecting the individual's sense of call to baptism.

A. THE AGE OF A CHILD

This can become an issue for one who was born into a Christian family, grew up in the fellowship of the Church, and professes faith as a child. When is the child old enough to be baptized? While Pentecostals agree that the child must be able consciously and personally to make a confession of faith, they differ on how early such a profession is possible. When can a child responsibly make a personal decision?

B. CHRISTIAN MATURITY AND READINESS

A similar pastoral issue of readiness emerges for adult converts. Here it is not a question of age but of Christian maturity. Some Pentecostals believe that baptism should occur as soon after conversion as possible. Of course, *metanoia* within a Pentecostal context is expected soon to produce a personal testimony of faith. To the Pentecostal perspective that seeks to baptize as soon as possible, the testimony should be ritualized in baptism immediately if it is discerned to be authentic. At the other end of the spectrum, some Pentecostals may require a rather stringent set of requirements prior to an adult baptism. This more rigorous orientation often emerges in a missional context. Here post-conversion lifestyle changes are both expected and looked for. A level of Christian maturity will need to be discerned by the congregational leadership, and some kind of catechesis or instruction will typically be employed. Accomplishing such criteria may take months, or even years, following an initial profession of faith. These two Pentecostal practices represent two poles of readiness for baptism; there is, naturally, a range of beliefs and practices between the two extremes.

3. "Rebaptism": An Internal and Ecumenical Issue

The issue of rebaptism affects both internal Pentecostal reflections and their broader ecumenical interactions. With the exception of Oneness Pentecostals these churches do not, for the most part, believe in "rebaptism." However, converts who have come to Christian faith as adults, and who do not recognize or remember a (that is, an infant) baptism, may be encouraged to receive a believers' baptism. For the Pentecostals who embrace this practice it is, strictly speaking, not seen as *rebaptism*.

Other Pentecostal groups teach that if one has had a "Christian baptism" in a Christian church this must be recognized, and no baptism in a Pentecostal church is needed. Of course for these groups the question arises, what is a Christian church? The answer may vary considerably from group to group. Many Pentecostal churches do not, as congregations, determine the answer but rather leave it to individual church members. In these cases, the form of baptism is not a requirement for church membership.

While the issue of "rebaptism" is a pastoral problem among Pentecostals, it can be an ecumenical stumbling block beyond Pentecostal boundaries—for whether Pentecostals call it "rebaptism" or not, it appears as such to Christian communions who practice infant baptism. This issue requires more extensive pastoral and theological reflection among Pentecostals as well as honest ecumenical dialogue.

We turn now to some current issues of baptism that reflect fewer internal disagreements or concerns among Pentecostals but are potentially issues that have significant ecumenical implications.

4. Baby Dedication: An Ecumenical Possibility

Pentecostals rarely baptize infants; they do, however, practice "baby dedication." In some ways the baby dedication parallels the baptism of infants, though dedication is not seen as sacramental. In a baby dedication the parents or guardians present the baby in the church to the Lord and to the congregation, and then dedicate the baby to the Lord. This act of dedication is linked to Hannah's dedication of Samuel to the Lord (1 Sam 1–2) as well as to the words of Jesus, "Let the little children come to me" (Mark 10:14). The parents are exhorted and charged, as is the congregation, to bring the child up in faith so that they will continue in that faith and make a personal commitment to Jesus Christ as Savior when they come of age. The parents (and sometimes the congregation) take simple vows responding to the pastoral charge. The baby and the parents are then prayed for.

Because the rite of baby dedication has some functional, pastoral, and liturgical similarities with the baptism of babies, the rite may provide a door for ecumenical dialogue. This may be true in part because both Pentecostals and Christians who practice infant baptism recognize that the gift of God's grace precedes, and makes possible, a person's response to grace. In other words, both groups teach that God's grace is active prior to the individual's conscious awareness of God's active grace.[14]

5. Metanoia *and* Ordo Salutis: *Topics for Discussion*

A discussion of *metanoia*, or conversion, could also bring into ecumenical dialogue possibilities for greater understanding and Christian unity. While Pentecostal doctrine views God's graces as prior to human consciousness, and therefore prior to the possibility for a conscious faith commitment, Pentecostals insist on the role of *metanoia* (repentance and conversion) in a Pentecostal conceptualization of *Ordo Salutis*, the order of salvation.

Clearly, the understanding of the order of salvific events and rites varies between those who practice infant baptism and Pentecostals who baptize believers only. As Pentecostals consider the New Testament writings, they find several items involved in Christian initiation, including proclamation of the gospel, faith and repentance (*metanoia*), baptism in water, and the receiving of the Spirit. Most likely, there is little disagreement with such a reading. The disagreements emerge in the understanding of the relationship and the order among the items. Generally, Pentecostals believe that the order in the New Testament is normative for succeeding generations of Christians rather than unique to the "missionary situation" of the earliest Church.

Amid the apparent disagreements, however, conversion or *metanoia* remains a common element (though conceived variously)—in Pentecostal parlance, "getting saved."[15] For Pentecostals *metanoia* is fundamental; it forms the basis for baptism and is at the core of Pentecostal spirituality. Within Pentecostal spirituality *metanoia* involves repentance and conversion; it is a call to change of heart and life. Conversion is connected to the remission of sins, receiving the grace of God and Jesus as personal Savior. It represents a "new birth." *Metanoia* marks a change of consciousness, recognition of sin and a sorrow for it. It is a rejection of sin on the one hand and, on the other, a submission to God with a movement toward God. It is an act of faith in and response to God, God's word, and God's grace.

How do other Christian groups conceive of conversion (*metanoia*) and its role in the *Ordo Salutis*? This question could function within an ecumenical dialogue. Doubtless, the aspects of *metanoia* and their order and configuration vary among Christian theologies; still, reflection on the role of *metanoia* in salvation, and in the follow-up to baptism, would be worthwhile, informative, and potentially productive ecumenically.[16]

6. Christian Initiation and the Giving of the Spirit

The general topic of Christian initiation and the giving of the Holy Spirit is a topic that warrants ecumenical discussion between Pentecostals and other Christians. There are several subtopics that cluster around the general subject, each of which is related to baptism.

A. Christian Initiation and Baptism with Water

Christian traditions of initiation include a number of rites rooted in Scripture and Christian history. Baptism in or with water, of course, is central to rites of initiation. As discussed above, conversion (*metanoia*) is a key initial moment, an initiation, recognized within Pentecostal spirituality. We noted that baptism in water is the ritual expression of the conversion. These two moments of initiation are bound together; one testifies to the other.[17]

B. Life in the Spirit: Conversion and Spirit Baptism

With few exceptions, Pentecostals believe that the receiving of the Spirit occurs at the new birth (*metanoia*). Consequently, reception of the Spirit is ritualized, testified to, in the rite of water baptism. This is implicit in the rite that signifies regeneration.[18] The Holy Spirit is seen by Pentecostals as an agent of regeneration given in the moment of initial conversion. It is the Spirit who unites the convert and places her or him in a personal and sanctifying relationship with God. This initial conversion is expected to deepen as the Spirit sanctifies and gifts. The Christian life is to be a life in the Spirit—a spirituality marked by *openness* to the sanctifying and transforming power of the Spirit. The Holy Spirit sovereignly expresses the Spirit's freedom to gift whenever and whomever God wills.

The believer's role in Pentecostal spirituality is to orient toward God, to practice seeking after God, and to pursue the life of holiness.

Pentecostals believe that while it is the Spirit who sanctifies and sovereignly gifts, it is the responsibility of the Christian believer, with the Spirit's help, to seek to grow in Christ (Eph 4:15-16), remaining faithful to God and responsive to the promptings of the Holy Spirit (Gal 6:7-9; 1 John 3:24). This is part of the life in the Spirit, the normal Christian life.

Consequently, Pentecostals teach that the Holy Spirit is active in both the initial conversion and in the life of holiness that deepens the initial conversion in an ongoing way, that is, in the process of sanctification. Both dynamics are represented in water baptism. The baptismal rite looks back to the Holy Spirit's work in initial conversion, and looks forward upon the role of the Spirit in ongoing conversion.

c. Spirit Baptism: Role and Understanding[19]

When Pentecostals look at the earliest churches, they look primarily through Lukan eyes (the Acts of the Apostles) and they see there "another" baptism—a baptism in the Spirit. As we have just said, the life in the Spirit includes regeneration and the process of sanctification; but in Pentecostal spirituality the Christian life can also include Spirit baptism as a baptism subsequent to water baptism. According to most Pentecostals, Spirit baptism occurs within the larger process of sanctification. Though a part of the process, Pentecostals expect baptism in the Spirit to ensue as a decisive experience—an identifiable baptism—distinct from initial conversion and from water baptism. It is a baptism not in water but in the Holy Spirit.

Spirit baptism neither makes one a Christian nor, in itself, sanctifies. Pentecostal spirituality experiences baptism in the Holy Spirit as an empowerment for the believer to live the life of a disciple—one who, in the waters of baptism, has been plunged into the Body of Christ. Thus, empowerment through Spirit baptism does cooperate with the process begun in justification and continued in the dynamic of sanctification. It does assist the Christian to increase in the life of the Spirit.

Normally, Spirit baptism transpires as an event but continues to impact the believer in ongoing ways. In Pentecostal spirituality, Spirit baptism marks a kind of awakening within the Christian's life—often experienced as a change, or deepening of awareness, of the Spirit's presence. Baptism in the Holy Spirit points toward transformation—anticipated in Pentecostal spirituality—of the person baptized in water. The Spirit animates and guides the believer's personal devotion, worship, and edification.

Pentecostals testify that Spirit baptism deepens their openness toward gifts of the Spirit (including the Pauline charisms given in 1 Cor 12), gifts which operate for the good, for the edification, of the Body of Christ. They believe also that it is a baptism that intensifies and empowers the life in the Spirit—which is the normal life of a follower of Jesus!—toward charismatic ministry. Within Pentecostal spirituality, empowerment for charismatic ministry has been "democratized," it is for everyone. Such ministry depends upon the Holy Spirit and the baptizer, Jesus Christ, to empower for service and witness to the world. It foments a Spirit-baptized empowerment and gifting, to assist in the building up of the Church.

Some ecumenical dialogue participants have agreed that the difference between a committed Christian without Pentecostal baptism, and a committed Christian living out her or his Pentecostal spirituality, may not be mainly about theological focus (or, we would add, about holiness or even about service). Rather it may be more about a potentially expanded openness and expectancy with regard to the Holy Spirit and the Spirit's gifts and ministry in the Spirit.[20] The role of the Holy Spirit, including Spirit baptism in the life and ministries of those baptized in water, and the connections between water baptism and Spirit baptism, could continue to be the basis of a fruitful ecumenical discussion.

BIBLIOGRAPHY

Albrecht, Daniel E. "Variations on Themes in Worship: Pentecostal Rites and Improvisations." *Worship Today: Understanding, Practice, Ecumenical Implications*. Ed. Thomas F. Best and Dagmar Heller. Faith and Order Paper No. 194. Geneva: WCC Publications, 2004.

———. *Rites in the Spirit*. Sheffield, UK: Sheffield Academic Press, 1999.

Bernard, David K. *The New Birth*. Studies in Pentecostal Theology, vol. 2. Hazelwood, MO: Word Aflame Press, 1984.

Blumhofer, Edith. *Restoring the Faith*. Chicago: University of Illinois Press, 1993.

———. *The Assemblies of God*, vol. 1. Springfield, MO: Gospel Publishing House, 1989.

Burgess, Stanley, ed. *The New International Dictionary of Pentecostal and Charismatic Movements*. Revised and expanded edition. Grand Rapids, MI: Zondervan, 2002.

Cox, Harvey. *Fire from Heaven*. New York: Addison-Wesley, 1995.

Hocken, Peter. "Charismatic Movement." In Burgess, *The New International Dictionary*, 477–519.

Hollenweger, Walter. "Pentecostals and the Charismatic Movement." In *The Study of Spirituality*. Eds. Cheslyn Jones, Geoffrey Wainwright, and Edward Yarnold, SJ. New York: Oxford University Press, 1986, 549–54.

———. *The Pentecostals*. Reprint. Peabody, MA: Hendrickson Publishers, 1988.
Hunter, Harold. "Ordinances, Pentecostal." In Burgess, *The New International Dictionary*, 947–99.
Land, Steven. *Pentecostal Spirituality*. Journal of Pentecostal Theology, Supplement Series. Sheffield, UK: Sheffield Academic Press, 1993.
Larere, Phillippe. *Baptism in Water and Baptism in the Spirit: A Biblical, Liturgical and Theological Exposition*. Collegeville, MN: Liturgical Press, 1993.
Macchia, Frank D. "Baptism, Pentecostal." In *The New Westminster Dictionary of Liturgy and Worship*. Edited by Paul Bradshaw. Louisville, KY: Westminster John Knox Press, 2002.
McDonnell, Kilian, and George Montague. *Christian Initiation and Baptism in the Holy Spirit: Evidence from the First Eight Centuries*. Collegeville, MN: Liturgical Press, 1991.
Pentecostal–Roman Catholic Dialogue. "Final Report of the Dialogue between the Secretariat for Promoting Christian Unity of the Roman Catholic Church and Leaders of Some Pentecostal Churches and the Charismatic Movement within Protestant and Anglican Churches, 1976." In Harding Meyer and Lukas Visher, eds., *Growth in Agreement I: Reports and Agreed Statements of Ecumenical Conversations on a World Level, 1972–1982*. Faith and Order Paper No. 108. Geneva: World Council of Churches, 2007 [reprint of original publication by Paulist Press, 1984], 422–31.
Reid, David. "Oneness Pentecostals." In Burgess, *The New International Dictionary*, 936–44.
Spittler, Russell. "Spirituality, Pentecostal and Charismatic." In Burgess, *The New International Dictionary*, 1096–1102.
Turner, Victor. "Betwixt and Between: The Liminal Period in *Rites de Passage*." In *The Forest of Symbols: Aspects of Ndembu Ritual*. Ithaca, NY: Cornell University Press, 1967.
———. Turner, Victor. *The Ritual Process: Structure and Anti-structure*. Ithaca, NY: Cornell University Press, 1969 [1977].
Yun, Koo Dong. "Water Baptism and Spirit Baptism: Pentecostals and Lutherans in Dialogue." *Dialog: A Journal of Theology* 43, no. 4 (Winter 2004): 344–51.

Notes

[1] See Walter Hollenweger, "Pentecostals and the Charismatic Movement," in *The Study of Spirituality*, eds. Cheslyn Jones, Geoffrey Wainwright, and Edward Yarnold, SJ (New York: Oxford University Press, 1986), 549–54; also Russell Spittler, "Spirituality, Pentecostal and Charismatic," in Stanley Burgess, ed., *The New International Dictionary of Pentecostal and Charismatic Movements*, Revised and expanded edition (Grand Rapids, MI: Zondervan, 2002), 1096–1102.

[2] For values and traits see Daniel E. Allbrecht, *Rites in the Spirit* (Sheffield: Sheffield Academic Press, 1999); Peter Hocken, "Charismatic Movement," in Burgess, *The New International Dictionary*, 477–519; Hollenweger, "Pentecostals and the Charismatic Movement"; Spittler, "Spirituality, Pentecostal and Charismatic."

[3] "Water baptism" is a term that is less common among non-Pentecostal groups. Pentecostals, however, when speaking of "baptism" commonly distinguish between water baptism and Spirit baptism.

[4] For Pentecostal rites and ritual see Albrecht, *Rites in the Spirit*; also Albrecht, "Variations on Themes in Worship: Pentecostal Rites and Improvisations," in Thomas F. Best and Dagmar Heller, eds., *Worship Today: Understanding, Practice, Ecumenical Implications*, Faith and Order Paper No. 194 (Geneva: WCC Publications, 2004); and anthropologist Victor Turner for "betwixt and between."

[5] The waters of baptism surround the candidate as he or she stands in the midst of a baptistery, river, lake, ocean, or nearly any other body of water deep enough for the candidate to be baptized by immersion.

[6] For Pentecostal sensibilities see Albrecht, *Rites in the Spirit*.

[7] Below we consider the Oneness Pentecostal variation of water baptism and the variant "formula," "in the name of Jesus," which draws upon Acts 2:38 and not Matthew 28:19.

[8] Killian McDonnell and George T. Montague have demonstrated that for key church fathers from the first eight centuries of the Church the paradigm of Jesus' baptism maintained a primary place in the teachings of the Church and the practice of baptismal rites: *Christian Intitiation and Baptism in the Holy Spirit* (Collegeville, MN: Liturgical Press, 1994). See also Koo D. Yun, "Water Baptism and Spirit Baptism: Pentecostals and Lutherans in Dialogue," in *Dialog: A Journal of Theology* 43, no. 4 (Winter 2004): 344–51, on a comparison of Pauline and Lukan forms of baptism.

[9] See Frank D. Macchia, "Baptism, Pentecostal," in Paul Bradshaw, ed., *The New Westminster Dictionary of Liturgy and Worship* (Louisville, KY: Westminster John Knox Press, 2002).

[10] Macchia considers the entire rite as a charismatic event that may include in the congregational response speaking in tongues, prophesying, healing, and other things.

[11] David Reid, "Oneness Pentecostals," in Burgess, ed., *The New International Dictionary*, 940. For other explanations of Oneness Pentecostalism see David K. Bernard, *The New Birth*. Studies in Pentecostal Theology, vol. 2 (Hazelwood, MO: Word Aflame Press, 1984); Edith Blumhofer, *Restoring the Faith* (Chicago: University of Illinois Press, 1993); Edith Blumhofer, *The Assemblies of God*, vol. 1 (Springfield, MO: Gospel Publishing House, 1989).

[12] Macchia, "Baptism, Pentecostal," 51.

[13] Reid, "Oneness Pentecostals," 931.

[14] Phillippe Larere, OP, *Baptism in Water and Baptism in the Spirit: A Biblical, Liturgical and Theological Exposition*, trans. Patrick Madigan, OSB (Collegeville, MN: The Liturgical Press, 1993), 49, 58–64.

[15] "Getting saved" or the term "salvation" used in a personal, nontechnical way can denote all the aspects of *metanoia*, conversion, and all or most of the elements of *Ordo Salutis* for the Pentecostal lay person.

[16] See, from the Pentecostal–Roman Catholic bilateral dialogue: "Final Report of the Dialogue between the Secretariat for Promoting Christian Unity of the Roman Catholic Church and Leaders of Some Pentecostal Churches and the Charismatic Movement within Protestant and Anglican Churches, 1976," in Harding Meyer and Lukas Visher, eds., *Growth in Agreement I: Reports and Agreed Statements of Ecumenical Conversations on a World Level, 1972–1982*. Faith and Order Paper No. 108 (Geneva: World Council of Churches, 2007) [reprint of original publication by Paulist Press, 1984], 422–31; also Larere, *Baptism in Water and Baptism in the Spirit*, 60–62.

[17] Another initiation tradition known and practiced in Christian history is the laying on of hands as a symbol of request for, or actual reception of, the Holy Spirit (see "Final Report of the Dialogue," par. 16, 425). Although this rite has been practiced at various liturgical moments within different understandings of *Ordo Salutis*, it signifies the prayer for and/or impartation of the Holy Spirit. Pentecostals practice the laying of hands as a part of numerous rites, e.g., prayers for healing, ordination, commissioning to forms of lay service, as well as in prayer for Spirit baptism.

Our main topic here, however, is not that of the rite of laying of hands, it is the receiving of the Holy Spirit in Christian initiation. Thus as a part of this explanation the topic of Spirit baptism and its relationship to Christian initiation, water baptism, and the reception of the Spirit in Pentecostal spirituality emerges.

[18] "Final Report of the Dialogue," par. 18, 425–26.

[19] Larere, *Baptism in Water and Baptism in the Spirit*, 76–81.

[20] "Final Report of the Dialogue."

Chapter 16

Christian Baptism: A Seventh-day Adventist Appraisal

Bert Beach and George Reid

In harmony with other Christians, Seventh-day Adventists recognize baptism as an essential element in the practice of the Christian faith. On this basis, all persons who enter the church receive baptism.

PURPOSE

Briefly stated, baptism serves three primary purposes. First, it is an initiatory rite marking the beginning of Christian experience. Second, it is a public testimony to one's faith in Christ. And third, it becomes a symbol of the renunciation of the old life and adoption of a new life in Christ. All these carry a theological significance which influences the manner in which we understand the meaning as well as the practice of baptism.

BAPTISM'S BIBLICAL BASIS

Baptism appears at the beginning of the Christian movement, as manifested in the Christian adoption and transformation of ceremonial washings as practiced by the Jewish community. Hence its origins appear to be traceable to the Mosaic ordinances. The beginning of Christ's ministry came at a time when the earlier work of John the baptizer was approaching its fullest influence. At that time Jesus came requesting baptism, which was administered with an endorsement by divine manifestations that marked the beginning of Jesus' own ministry.

From this beginning Jesus emphasized the importance of baptism, underscoring this especially in his conversation with Nicodemus (John 3). Although not frequently reported in the gospels, Jesus' disciples apparently regularly baptized those who became followers of Jesus and his teachings.

Some hold that the baptism within households reported in the book of Acts supports infant baptism. This is an argument from silence, for there is no explicit biblical precedent for the suggestion. Historically, the baptism of infants first appears in Christian practice toward the end of the second century and has, in our understanding, no genuinely biblical precedent.

THEOLOGICAL SIGNIFICANCE

The fullest theological development of baptism is found in Paul's epistle to the Romans, where in the sixth chapter he draws strong parallels between the believer's experience in baptism and the death and resurrection of Christ. The old, unregenerate character of the unbeliever dies and is buried, followed by a beginning of new life symbolized in the believer's emerging from the water. The memorial element, or existential echo, between the experience of Christ and the new believer is inescapable.

The Swiss reformer Zwingli stressed the memorial quality of baptism, while challenging the prevailing sacramental interpretation of its meaning. Adventists follow much of his general understanding. For Adventists, baptism marks the believer's break with the old life and entrance to a new life of trust in and obedience to Christ. Following this approach, faith comes as a gift of God made possible as the person, by intentional choice, surrenders his or her will to Christ.

Paul teaches that baptism into Christ means that the believer "puts on Christ" (Gal 3:27), resulting in transformed values and lifestyle choices that follow (Rom 6:4; 13:14). Baptism, then, takes on a continuing significance, becoming the initiatory marker of a dedicated life. Biblically it is a seal unto salvation. From the biblical perspective, Adventists do not understand baptism as conveying salvific merit, but as representing a profound symbolism that fulfills the three foundational purposes—as an initiatory rite, a public testimony, and renunciation of the old life and adoption of a new life—mentioned above.

PRACTICAL CONSIDERATIONS

With baptism as the marker of a person's deliberate choice to follow Christ, several practical elements emerge. The baptized person is received into the church, the corporate body of Christ, demonstrating a commitment to the values and will of God as revealed in the Scriptures. Well beyond being simply an initiatory ceremony, it involves lasting repentance, faith, and surrender to Christ as Lord.

Believers' baptism requires sufficient maturity to grasp the teachings of Christian faith and an ability to make lasting choices. The New Testament passages on initiation assume this principle, with decisions required of candidates that call for the intentional renunciation of sin and idols, and the holding of a personal faith in Christ. In Adventist practice, the qualifying norms relate more to maturity and depth of commitment than to the simple achievement of chronological age. Generally these criteria are reached by early adolescence.

Adventists acknowledge the validity of baptisms meeting these biblical criteria when performed in other Christian communions. Therefore such persons applying for Adventist membership need not be baptized again, except by their own request.

The New Testament reports Paul's rebaptism of believers who had received the baptism of John (Acts 19:1-7). Following this pattern, Adventists allow for rebaptism in cases where a major advance in understanding and living out the gospel has occurred.

LITURGY

The Adventist approach to baptism is neither sacerdotal nor sacramental; however, the church respects Paul's counsel that all things be done decently and in order. Several elements unite in the baptismal service: the candidate him- or herself, a recognized prior preparation of the candidate, the candidate's testimony of faith, the baptismal formula, and a simple but specific format which is followed in the service.

Baptisms are performed by an elder chosen as leader of the church; this is generally the pastor but on occasion may be an ordained lay elder. In preparation for baptism, the candidate will have participated in an extended series of studies to review all the major elements of Christian faith and life.

On the day of the baptism itself, ordinarily the candidate is interviewed in the presence of the congregation, which serves as witness to his or her confession of faith. The candidate then joins the pastor or presiding elder in the baptismal pool where, in a brief service using a Trinitarian formula, the candidate is immersed once into the water, then lifted up.

Following baptism, the congregation affirms the newly baptized candidate with a welcome to the body of Christ and a vote bringing the candidate into membership of the local church. Apart from the use of the biblical Trinitarian formula, elements of the service may be modified so that its structure will respond to practical needs.

In many places baptisms are conducted outdoors in bodies of water, with members of the congregation gathering on the shore to witness the rite and welcome the new members. Whether inside a church or outdoors, baptisms frequently are accompanied by singing and extemporary prayers. Following the service, newly baptized members are greeted informally with affection by the members of the church.

CONCLUSION

The major passages in the Scriptures relating to baptism stress confession, repentance, cleansing, death to sin, and rising to a new life. All these point to profound commitment to Jesus as well as to forgiveness and cleansing; baptism symbolizes the cleansing from sin made possible through faith in him.

The believer is baptized into Christ and into fellowship with the church, hence the experience is both personal and collective. Those in Christ are in intimate communion with him and enjoy as well a special relationship with the other members of the church. In this manner baptism brings assurance to the believer, both of identification with Christ and of participation in his spiritual body on earth.

Chapter 17

A Salvation Army Perspective on Baptism: Theological Understanding and Liturgical Practice

Earl Robinson

BAPTISMAL LITURGY IN THE SALVATION ARMY

The Salvation Army accepts the description, which is indeed generally accepted among churches, of a sacrament as "an outward and visible sign of an inward and invisible grace." It further recognizes that the majority of Christians find value in the ritual celebrations of baptism and the eucharist and has no difficulty accepting those whose understanding of God's word leads them to these forms of worship. Since 1883 those two rituals have not been required in Salvation Army practice but, as indicated in the World Council of Churches (WCC) Faith and Order book *Ecumenical Perspectives on Baptism, Eucharist and Ministry*, this does not mean that The Salvation Army can be termed completely "nonsacramental" inasmuch as it does observe a number of "outward signs of inward grace."[1] None of those "outward signs" is, however, considered necessary to inward grace or salvation. The Army's beliefs that no "particular" outward observance is necessary to inward grace, and that God's grace is freely and readily accessible to all people at all times and in all places, were reaffirmed in its 1998 *International Spiritual Life Commission Report*.[2]

Two outward signs observed in The Salvation Army have some parallel to baptismal liturgies in other churches in terms of their underlying meaning. These were referred to in the Army's response to the WCC Faith and Order text *Baptism, Eucharist and Ministry*.[3]

First, we see our "enrollment" or "swearing-in" procedure for Salvation Army membership as having equivalence to the symbolic act of water baptism in being a human response to what God offers as the gift of being baptized into the one body of Christ by his Holy Spirit. In that ceremony, the human response is in the form of a covenant in which the applicants swear to the following:

They testify that:
> They worship God as Father, Son and Holy Spirit.
> They have accepted Jesus Christ as Saviour and Lord.
> They desire to fulfill their membership of his Church on earth as a soldier of The Salvation Army.
> They affirm their belief in the Bible as the word of God and their acceptance of The Salvation Army's articles of faith.

They declare that:
> They will be responsive to the Holy Spirit and seek to grow in grace.
> They will make the values of the Kingdom of God the standard for their lives, showing Christian integrity in their deeds, maintaining Christian ideals in their relationships, and upholding the sanctity of marriage and family life.
> They will be faithful stewards of all they have and are.
> They will abstain from the use of all enslaving substances and harmful activities.
> They will be active in God's work both in sharing the gospel and in serving the needy, and will contribute financially to its support.
> They will be true to the principles of The Salvation Army.

They witness that they freely enter into this covenant, convinced that the love of Christ requires the devotion of their lives to his service for the salvation of the whole world.

And they declare their determination, by God's help, to be true soldiers of The Salvation Army.[4]

The above swearing-in ceremony, for persons over fourteen years of age desiring to become soldiers in the Army, marks their acceptance as a member of The Salvation Army church. For the believer, it is a public confession of Christ as Lord and Savior. For the Church, it is a sign, in the setting of the Christian community, that the believer is received and welcomed into Christian fellowship. Salvationists so received would attest to the same sense of incorporation into the family of God and the life and service of Jesus Christ, with the beginnings of the inner working of the Holy Spirit, as do baptized believers in other Christian churches.

Second, The Salvation Army, in common with some other churches, responds to the example of Jesus who himself was dedicated in the temple and called young children to him, blessing them by laying his hands on them. The Army's infant dedication ceremony takes place within congregational worship and is a commitment by the parents and the local congregation to bring up the child in the nurture and admonition of the Lord. In the infant dedication ceremony, the commitment is on the part of the parents as they accept the following pledge:

> In the dedication of this child you desire to give him/her fully to God. You wish to thank God for entrusting this precious life into your hands, and you want him/her to be nurtured in all that is pure, lovely and honest. To this end you promise that you will keep from him/her, so far as you are able, everything which is likely to harm him/her in body, mind or spirit.
> You also promise that, as he/she grows in wisdom and stature, you will teach him/her the truths of the gospel, encourage him/her to seek Christ as Saviour, and support him/her in the commitment of his/her life to the service of God. You must be to him/her an example of a true Christian.
> If you are willing to make these promises, I will receive the child in the name of God, and on behalf of The Salvation Army.[5]

Unlike the implications of infant baptism in some churches, this act does not mean that the infant becomes a Christian by being dedicated. The encouragement of family worship and the family altar for prayer and Bible study are implicit in the dedication service—in the hope, however, that children will share their parents' faith with growing perception. Salvationists believe that children are, in this way, at the beginning stage of spiritual formation, to be nurtured and cared for by parents and the Church until faith is awakened. Salvationists believe in the ability of children of even tender years of understanding to come to the personal acceptance of Jesus Christ as Savior. Then, after instruction, children coming to that faith can be accepted as "junior" soldiers in The Salvation Army through a ceremony similar to that of the senior soldier noted above.

LITURGICAL, THEOLOGICAL, AND ECCLESIAL UNDERSTANDINGS

1. Liturgical Flow

While the above liturgies are often followed closely by persons conducting the swearing-in and dedication ceremonies, variations in liturgical flow are permitted. What is of primary importance is that the content of the covenants and pledges being agreed to must be agreed to by the persons involved in the ceremonies. The focus, in other words, is not on the liturgy or on its flow but on the commitments made. This has to do with The Salvation Army's understanding of a freedom in Christ which is encouraged by Scripture. The setting of fixed forms of words or acts is not part of Salvationist tradition, though the value placed upon them by some other denominations is recognized.

2. Theological Meaning

The theological meaning behind our position that no "particular" outward observance is necessary to inward grace is that we believe that Jesus Christ is the one who alone reveals God to us and conveys his grace to our hearts. He is the one, true, original sacrament of God (Col 2:2); he is God's outward and visible sign, the one "we have heard . . . we have seen with our eyes . . . we have looked at and touched with our hands" (1 John 1:1).

Jesus, who was fully human, nevertheless conveyed fully in his person the extraordinary grace of God (John 1:17). In his ministry on earth he communicated grace by his presence, his words, and touch. Above all, his self-offering on the cross was a visible outpouring of the love and grace of God for all humanity. Through the resurrection, this outpouring of grace became available for all time. Sacraments of the Church derive from Christ, the one, true, original sacrament, and bear witness to him; he is the sacrament that all Christians share. By our faith in Jesus Christ, the one, true, original sacrament, we receive grace from him, the giver of all grace. As in the ministry of Jesus on earth, that grace may be communicated through a variety of signs, or sacraments, or ceremonies of words and touch and public witness. We understand that water baptism is one of those ceremonies, as is the swearing-in of a Salvation Army soldier.

Such ceremonies witness to and confirm a life-changing encounter with Christ that has already happened. That moment of encounter may happen at any time and in any place, as the Holy Spirit's gracious action meets a response of faith in the life of the believer. The ceremony itself is not the encounter and should not be confused with the act of becoming a Christian. The ceremony, however, does confirm and give tangible expression to that personal encounter. It provides for the practical outworking of the encounter, which includes membership in the Church of Christ and commitment to a life of discipleship.

1 Corinthians 12:13 says: "For in the one Spirit we were all baptized into one body . . . and we were all made to drink of one Spirit." The

reference to being baptized by one Spirit into one body has to do with regeneration, being born again of the Spirit, the life of the Holy Spirit imparted to us whereby we are incorporated into the body of Christ as members of his Church. All who are born again of the Spirit can claim such incorporation into the body of Christ, his Church, whether they are officially accepted as members of a particular church through a ceremony such as water baptism or being sworn in as soldiers of The Salvation Army.

3. Ecclesiological Meaning

The following points outline The Salvation Army's understanding of, and approach to, the relationship between our soldier enrollment and water baptism. These points were formulated by the International Spiritual Life Commission and approved by the international leadership of The Salvation Army in 1998.

   a. Only those who confess Jesus Christ as Saviour and Lord may be considered for soldiership in The Salvation Army.
   b. Such a confession is confirmed by the gracious presence of God the Holy Spirit in the life of the believer and includes the call to discipleship.
   c. In accepting the call to discipleship Salvationists promise to continue to be responsive to the Holy Spirit and to seek to grow in grace.
   d. They also express publicly their desire to fulfil membership of Christ's Church on earth as soldiers of The Salvation Army.
   e. The Salvation Army rejoices in the truth that all who are in Christ are baptised into the one body by the Holy Spirit (1 Corinthians 12:13).
   f. It believes, in accordance with Scripture, that "there is one body and one Spirit . . . one Lord, one faith, one baptism; one God and Father of all, who is over all and through all and in all" (Ephesians 4:5-6).
   g. The swearing-in of a soldier of The Salvation Army beneath the trinitarian sign of the Army's flag acknowledges this truth.
   h. It is a public response and witness to a life-changing encounter with Christ which has already taken place, as is the water baptism practised by some other Christians.

i. The Salvation Army acknowledges that there are many worthy ways of publicly witnessing to having been baptised into Christ's body by the Holy Spirit and expressing a desire to be his disciple.

j. The swearing-in of a soldier should be followed by a lifetime of continued obedient faith in Christ.[6]

VARIATIONS IN UNDERSTANDING AND PRACTICE

The Salvation Army began as a Christian Mission in 1865 and took on its present name in 1878. Throughout that period and until 1883, christening in the form of infant water baptism was practiced. Since 1883, this has not been part of Salvationist practice. One of the primary reasons for the change was the belief that the all-important baptism enjoined in the New Testament was the baptism of God the Holy Spirit. In the place of christening, the Army adopted the infant dedication service noted above. The swearing-in of soldiers as the church membership ceremony had already been introduced by 1882.

The relationship between the swearing-in of soldiers and believers' water baptism had arisen in earlier Salvation Army discussion and writings. That relationship was further developed and clarified, as noted above, in the International Spiritual Life Commission report of 1998.

CENTRAL ISSUES IN CURRENT REFLECTION AND DISCUSSIONS

Internally, there is ongoing discussion concerning elements of a sacramental theology for The Salvation Army with the possibility of further detailed theological development in that regard. Deliberations related to such theological discussion have caused the Army to admit more readily that it is a sacramental community, even though it does not require the observance of the traditional sacraments of water baptism and the eucharist. Its handbook of doctrine, for example, says:

> As his sacramental people, we find him living and at work in our own life-experiences. We celebrate the presence, the gift, the healing, the reconciliation, the joy in our own story by connecting it with the story of Jesus. We are a sacramental community because our life, our work, and our celebrations centre on Christ, the one true Sacrament. Our life together is sacramental because we live by faith in him and our everyday lives keep stumbling onto unexpected grace, his undeserved gift, again and again.[7]

Terminology is also undergoing change in that the document used in the swearing-in ceremony is now often referred to as the "Soldiers' Covenant" rather than "Articles of War." There is therefore some discussion as to whether the swearing-in ceremony should be referred to as the "Soldiers Covenant Ceremony." In keeping with articles 5 to 9 of the International Spiritual Life Commission's "Statement on Baptism," in which it outlines The Salvation Army's understanding of the relationship between its soldier enrollment ceremony and water baptism, there is also some reflection on incorporating into the swearing-in of soldiers ceremony reference to the truth that all who are in Christ are baptized into the one body by the Holy Spirit.[8]

Ecumenically, we continue to respect and accept the worthy ways in which other churches differ from us in the observance and meaning given to water baptism. We look forward to better understanding and acceptance of such differences in a mutual way as, since 2003, we begin to engage in bilateral theological dialogues with other Christian World Communions.[9]

Notes

[1] Max Thurian, ed., *Ecumenical Perspectives on Baptism, Eucharist and Ministry*, Faith and Order Paper No. 116 (Geneva: World Council of Churches, 1983), 162.

[2] Robert Street, *Called to be God's People, The International Spiritual Life Commission – Its report, implications and challenges*, articles 1 and 2 (London: The Salvation Army International Headquarters, 1999), 89.

[3] Faith and Order Paper No. 111 (Geneva: World Council of Churches, 1982). For the Army's Response see Max Thurian, ed., *Churches Respond to BEM: Official responses to the "Baptism, Eucharist and Ministry" Text, Vol. IV*, Faith and Order Paper No. 137 (Geneva: World Council of Churches, 1987), 238–240.

[4] By Authority of the General, *Salvation Army Ceremonies* (London: The Salvation Army International Headquarters, 1989), 4–5.

[5] Ibid., 10–11.

[6] Street, *Called to be God's People*, 105.

[7] *Salvation Story* (London: The Salvation Army International Headquarters, 1998), 114.

[8] Street, *Called to be God's People*, 105. The articles referred to are quoted in full above under "3. Ecclesiological Meaning," points e–i.

[9] Two such bilateral theological dialogues took place between The Salvation Army and the World Methodist Council in June 2003 and January 2005, and three dialogues were held with the Conference of Seventh-day Adventists in

January 2004, March 2005, and February 2008. Published texts on the World Methodist Council dialogues are available in the November 2005 and May 2006 issues of *Word & Deed, A Journal of Salvation Army Theology and Ministry*, available through the circulation manager at Salvation Army National Publications, PO Box 269, 615 Slaters Lane, Alexandria, VA 22314, USA, telephone 1-800-725-2769.

Chapter 18

Water Baptism in African Independent Churches: The Paradigm of Christ Holy Church International

Thomas Oduro

INTRODUCTION

The emergence of African Instituted Churches (sometimes known as AICs) on the continent of Africa has posed many challenges for missiologists, theologians, and scholars. These challenges have emerged due to the distinct nature of the doctrines and ethos of many African Independent Churches, and attempting to define these churches only makes the situation more difficult. As a result, scholars have given these churches different names such as "African Instituted Churches," "African Initiated Churches," "African Indigenous Churches," "African Independent Churches," "African Reformation," and others. Some scholars have also attempted to categorize African Independent Churches into types. As a result, some are called "Ethiopian," "Prophet/healing," and/or "Spiritual" churches.[1] Though none of these descriptive names and types is adequate, each of them aptly describes either a particular historical aspect or a specific doctrinal inclination of African Independent Churches.

Harold Turner describes an African Independent Church as ". . . a church which has been founded in Africa, by Africans, and primarily for Africans."[2] Philip Jenkins similarly defines African Independent Churches as ". . . African churches with African leaders for African people."[3] In my view, defining African Independent Churches as churches founded for Africans is equivalent to perceiving the Methodist Church, for example, as a church founded for Europeans. Admittedly there could be some truth in this definition at a certain point in the life of the African Independent Churches, but many leaders of these churches did not perceive their calling as being exclusively for Africans. Agnes Okoh, the woman through whom Christ Holy Church International was founded in Nigeria, had the evangelization of the entire world as her focus. The following song was, as a result, composed after Agnes had challenged her followers not to be satisfied with spreading the gospel in Nigeria only:

> *Ayi ga'bu kwasi ndi ama—ndi ama Chukwu* (2x)
> *Nime Nigeria, Nime Ghana, rue ebe nine nke Africa*
> *Rue Jerusalem, rue Samaria, rue ebe nine uwa soturu*
> (We shall be witnesses—witnesses of God (2x)
> In Nigeria, in Ghana, up to all parts of Africa
> To Jerusalem, to Samaria, unto the end of the earth.)[4]

The missiological activities, the spread of AICs beyond Africa, and the racial composition of their membership in the West render the above definition inadequate. Pobee and Ositelu have, for instance, observed:

> The thriving reality of AICs in the Netherlands is especially significant. At least 20 AIC congregations are found in Amsterdam alone. This is noteworthy in a country which has been described as the most secular in Western Europe. True, quite a few of the members are Africans who have made their way to Holland fleeing expulsions, economic hardship and warfare in their own countries. But these churches have been attracting Dutch members as well.[5]

Thus the complexity of the ethos and faith of African Independent Churches, their attempts to integrate culture into their religious life, and the many facets of African culture enlarge the challenge of writing about them and particularly of defining them. Recognizing the breadth of their membership, African Independent Churches have nevertheless been defined as "congregations and or denominations planted, led, administered, supported, propagated, motivated, and funded by Africans for the purpose of proclaiming the Gospel of Jesus Christ and worshiping the triune God in the context and worldview of Africa and Africans."[6]

BAPTISM AND AFRICAN INDEPENDENT CHURCHES

Baptism in African Independent Churches forms part of the challenge of their self-definition and identity. There are similarities as well as differences compared to other churches. These will be discussed briefly, with the concept and practice of baptism in the Christ Holy Church International cited as a paradigm.

Many African Independent Churches are not sacramentally inclined; indeed the word "sacrament" is scarcely heard from their lips. They nevertheless believe that baptism was instituted by God—in a rite which Jesus voluntarily underwent—thus making it obligatory for every Christian. There are some in the church who claim to have been called to baptize.[7] Being exegetically handicapped in many respects, African Independent Churches do not use the Greek language to argue which form of baptism is "biblical." They cite the immersion of Jesus Christ in a flowing river, in his adult age, as their paradigm. Baptizing adults by immersion in a flowing river, or in some cases in the ocean, is therefore normative to many African Independent Churches.[8] Where proximity to a running river or the ocean is a problem, many African Independent Churches travel to the nearest flowing river.

Infant baptism is rarely practiced by these churches. The importance of baptism among them is seen in their insistence on rebaptizing those who were baptized as infants, or later on by sprinkling. Andrew Walls is thus not far from right in observing some stark similarities between African Independent Churches and the Anabaptists in Western Church history (albeit in a different context).[9]

African Independent Churches regard baptism as a rite symbolizing the death and resurrection of Jesus Christ. When one is baptized, one is reminded that the significance of the death of Jesus Christ must be practically and personally experienced through the rite. In baptism one dies and is buried with Christ, and then resurrected with Christ when brought out of the river. This signifies newness in life. Three students of the Good News Theological College and Seminary in Accra, Ghana, representing three African Independent Churches, shed more light on the significance of baptism in their respective denominations. Baptism, according to Emmanuel Kpakpo of the Muzama Disco Christo Church (M.D.C.C.), brings one from darkness to light. The act of burial and resurrection makes one experience the difference between darkness and light in a pragmatic manner; it makes one appreciate the essence of light and the need to live in the light.[10] In the Evangelical Mission Church, baptism is a public acknowledgement of one's acceptance of Christ.[11] To the Twelve Apostles Church, baptism is seen as a constant reminder that one must never go back to one's pre-baptismal sins. It also assures the baptized of their integration into a new family—a Christian family.[12] Among members of the Zion Christian Church, baptism is a time when demons are exorcised.[13]

Zionist and Apostolic churches in South Africa regard baptism "as symbolizing the washing away of sins."[14] Thus, baptism among African Independent Churches serves as a definitive event in a Christian's onward journey toward Christlikeness—an event that can be cited as a reference point in one's life.

Many of these churches take baptismal candidates through a series of pre-baptismal studies and rites. The period of instruction varies,[15] but the candidates are taught the fundamental doctrines of Christianity: the birth, death, and resurrection of Jesus Christ, sin, repentance, salvation, prayer, fasting, love for one another, and so on. As part of pre-baptismal preparations in some African Independent Churches in South Africa, Allan Anderson observes that: "In many Zionist and Apostolic churches, before baptism takes place there must be a full confession of sins in the presence of the minister."[16] In some AICs one is baptized after one has taken all the prescribed lessons; a limited number of abstentions from these lessons disqualifies one from being baptized.

In addition to the period of instruction, candidates in the Twelve Apostles Church, for instance, are required to fast and pray for three days prior to the day of baptism. The candidates are also required to spend twenty-four hours of each of those days at the place of worship, also known as the Garden, so that leaders of the church can supervise their fasting and prayers, particularly their night prayers. Prophets and prophetesses in charge of Twelve Apostles Gardens pray for baptismal candidates every six hours during their pre-baptismal days of prayer and fasting. The candidates confess their sins, ask God for forgiveness of sins, and ask for the divine ability to resist temptations in their post-baptismal Christian journey.

Days set aside for baptism differ from one African Independent Church to another.[17] Baptismal services are usually joyous occasions for both candidates and noncandidates. Given that the candidates have been told of the benefits of the sacrament—that their sins would be washed away and their membership in the church legitimized, that they would be eligible to become members of a vibrant Christian family that promises to be more caring, that demons worrying them would be exorcised, and many other things—and given that it has taken some time to prepare them, the candidates' expectations become so high that worship on the day of baptism is nothing but a time of celebration. Some of these churches hold baptismal services at the banks of rivers, while others hold their worship at the usual place before going to the riverside for the baptism.

Many African Independent Churches are noted to endorse the priesthood of women without any reservations on biblical or societal grounds.[18] They are known to have ". . . changed the face of Christianity in Africa by their enlarging of religious space for women."[19] In spite of this, some African Independent Churches prohibit women from baptizing candidates. The prohibition, in some of these churches, is not based on any doctrinal grounds but rather on their physical frailty—once they are immersed in the water many candidates behave as if they were possessed, and controlling such candidates becomes difficult, a situation that could result in drowning.[20] To avert disasters during baptisms many AICs, as a matter of rule, insist on more than one pastor administering the sacrament.

While most African Independent Churches baptize in the name of the Father, Son, and the Holy Spirit, in compliance with Jesus' Great Commission,[21] there is disagreement on how many times a candidate should be immersed in the water of baptism. Some of these churches immerse a candidate each time one of the three persons of the Trinity is mentioned. Others immerse the candidate once after mentioning all the names of the triune persons.[22] The churches that immerse candidates thrice emphasize the individuality of the triune persons, while those that immerse candidates once stress their unity.

Making theological confessions just before baptism is the norm in many African Independent Churches. Before being immersed, baptismal candidates in the Twelve Apostles Church make a confession by answering the following questions: "Do you understand what is going to be done?" "Do you accept Jesus Christ as your Lord and Savior?" "Do you agree that Jesus should judge you on his return, based on your new creaturehood?"[23] Unlike the practice in the early church,[24] African Independent Churches do not dip the candidates in baptismal rivers after they have answered each question.

AN EXAMPLE: WATER BAPTISM
IN CHRIST HOLY CHURCH INTERNATIONAL

To understand the identity and ethos of this church it is necessary to know the story of its origin. The church was founded through the efforts of Agnes Okoh, an Igbo woman who could hardly read and write any language. Agnes developed a severe migraine after the death of her husband and only daughter. After many unsuccessful attempts to receive healing from Western medical centers and traditional healers, she was directed to see a prophetess, who was able to heal her in a very short time; Agnes began worshiping with the prophetess. In 1945, while returning from a market, she heard a voice telling her "Matthew 10" several times. Rushing to the home of a friend she asked, "What is Matthew 10?" whereupon this chapter of Matthew's gospel was read to her from an Igbo Bible. When news about her religious experience reached the prophetess through whom Agnes had been healed, she interpreted the incident as a divine call for Agnes to begin an itinerant evangelistic ministry. Agnes, who later became known as "Holy Prophetess," reluctantly began an evangelistic campaign in eastern Nigeria in 1947. Though illiterate, she was able to touch the hearts of many by quoting the Bible profusely, exercising unflinching faith in God, and using her spiritual gifts—notably healing and prophetic utterances—until she died at the age of ninety on March 10, 1995. Christ Holy Church International now has over eight hundred fifty congregations in Nigeria, ten in Ghana, and one in the Republic of Togo.[25]

The Church's Statement of Faith regarding baptism is stated thus: "We believe in the sacrament of baptism by immersion in the name of the Father, Son and Holy Spirit."[26] Marius Okoh, Agnes's son and later a leader of the church, defines baptism as "to immerse or dip."[27] He describes the symbolism of baptism as "burying the old and sinful nature in the water in the name of the Father, Son, and the Holy Ghost and rising again in the newness of life unto the glory of the Father; accepting *only* Jesus Christ (and none other) as the Saviour."[28] According to Nicholas Udemba, the General Secretary and Assistant Superintendent of the church, baptism symbolizes one's submission to the Lord Jesus Christ.[29]

In addition to his definition of baptism, Marius uses the famous classical story of Achilles' heel to illustrate the need for one to be immersed during baptism:

> When Achilles was young, the mother thought of making the body of her son invulnerable in order to fortify him from wounds of enemies; perhaps he was the only son. One day she took the child to the Styx (one of the rivers of Hades) and dipped him therein; holding tight the heal [heel] whereon the mother held him. The child grew up as a hero and could not be wounded on the body by any human weapon. Achilles felt that he was completely invulnerable until one day when he was mortally wounded during the encounter with Paris, the son of the King of Troy. Therefore, till today, the vulnerable heel of Achilles remains a parable or metaphorical expression. This Greek hero would have lived longer if no part of his body was left undipped in the Styx. So is any type of baptism besides *immersion*.[30]

The church does not baptize infants. After giving elaborate exegeses on the texts Matthew 3:2; 3; Mark 1:15, 16; Acts 2:38; 8:37, Marius states:

> The scriptures made it clear *that teaching Christ, believing in Him, and repentance from sin* precede baptism. But a baby cannot be taught Christ: for it has no sense of comprehension and as it cannot comprehend the teaching of Christ, it can neither believe in Him nor repent from a sin it knows not. The baby therefore cannot be baptized. Likewise, any child below the age of accountability needs no baptism; rather they are been dedicated [*sic*]. Luke 2:22. Logically, the Bible rules out infant baptism.[31]

The age of accountability in the church is twelve; such persons are considered old enough to make intelligible confessions and be responsible for their confessions. Thus only those who have repented and confessed their sins are baptized. Christ Holy Church International, similarly, rules out bringing godparents or godfathers into baptismal practice. Marius rejects such practice by teaching:

> . . . we have learnt from this [*sic*] portions [of Scripture] that neither Jesus nor the Ethiopian eunuch was asked to bring sureties or God-Parents before having the baptism . . . Therefore it would be counted sordid heresy and unruly for any one to appear and stand a surety for another in the question of belief or confession when one is to be baptized.[32]

Leaders of the church do not take into consideration the Christian maturity, experience, and position of those who have not had the experience of adult baptism by immersion prior to becoming either a Christian or a member of the church; such people are rebaptized. The church, then, is thoroughly Anabaptist in its baptismal teaching and practice.

Christ Holy Church International makes a distinction between two groups of persons who have not been baptized. *Converts* are those who have believed in Jesus Christ as their Lord and Savior and are willing to be baptized at any time; like the Ethiopian Eunuch, the *converts* do not even need to be a member of the church to be baptized. *Candidates*, on the other hand, are those who are in the church but, for some reason unknown to its leaders, are not ready to be baptized. Since there are no special benefits of baptism in the church, a candidate need not hurry or be persuaded to be baptized. Baptismal candidates are allowed to continue participating in Bible studies until they express their readiness to be baptized.

No special day is set aside for baptism, though a baptismal service precedes the sacrament. The service is not different from others—it involves singing, dancing, clapping, jumping, shouting "Halleluiahs," and preaching. The sermon explains the significance, need, and value of baptism. Those to be baptized are at liberty to invite friends and relatives to witness their baptism, albeit this is not mandatory. Except in the case of an emergency request, baptism is usually done between nine o'clock and midday.

In spite of its belief in adult baptism by immersion, the church does not baptize in ponds but insists on baptizing in flowing rivers. Rivers abound in Nigeria, so members of the church do not usually have to travel long distances to experience baptism. Members of the church sing merrily on their way to the riverside no matter how far it may be.

A pastor of the church goes to the river two days before a baptism to measure the depth of the river to be used for the rite. He does so again on the day of baptism. Baptism takes place where the river is knee-deep and not swampy and stony; all these measures are undertaken to avert any baptismal catastrophe.

At the riverside, the officiating minister blesses the river and asks God to rid it of all evil forces and dangerous elements, thus making it holy and fitting for the sacrament. Two booths are provided for men and women to change their clothing. The officiating minister is the first to change; he wears a white T-shirt and shorts, as this color is understood to symbolize purity. Men precede women in the river, as was done in the order of creation. The person to be baptized is made to sit in the river—a posture, according to Udemba, that makes the convert relaxed. The sitting posture enables the officiating minister to control the body of the convert, whatever their relative sizes may be.[33] The officiating minister then asks the convert: "Do you believe in Jesus Christ? Do you believe that Jesus is your Savior? Have you rejected Satan and all his works?" After the one to be baptized has answered all questions in the affirmative, the minister asks the person, "What is your name?" The minister repeats the name and says, "Because of your confession of faith I baptize you in the name of the Father, Son, and Holy Spirit." The candidate is then immersed once, while the pastor mentions the name of the triune God.[34]

The process of water baptism in Christ Holy Church International does not end after the immersion of converts in the river. All newly baptized persons go back to the worship center (if this is not far from the baptismal site); the officiating minister immediately teaches them about the baptism of the Holy Spirit. After this the pastor lays his hands on one or two persons, and other persons are then asked to lay their hands on others. The pastor prays for the infilling of the Holy Spirit and in the course of the prayer some begin to speak in tongues, while others begin to shake their bodies, a gesture indicating possession by the Holy Spirit. The occasion ends with the issuance of baptismal certificates to those who have been baptized.

CONCLUSION

Water baptism, from all indications, is a sacrament that is dear to the hearts of African Independent Churches. It is also a sacrament that is well understood. AICs see it as a sacrament that requires full preparation before participation. Leaders of AICs see the preparation of candidates as a leadership obligation that must be done meticulously so as to avoid any blame (divine or human) should candidates backslide in their post-baptismal lives. The importance they attach to baptism leads to some theological contributions they have made.

In addition to the traditional explications of the significance of water baptism, the concept of baptism in terms of family is a significant theological contribution of African Independent Churches to the understanding and significance of water baptism. Africans are known to be family oriented. They know the importance of a family no matter its extent. (They also know the shortcomings of human family networks.) Likening baptism to a rite that introduces one to a Christian family—a family where Jesus Christ is the head—is a practical method of teaching candidates the need to live a life befitting their identity as a new creature, as belonging to the body of Christ, without having to expound the meaning of various Greek words.

Another important theological contribution of African Independent Churches to the understanding of water baptism is the vivid, picturesque example of *darkness* in connection with being buried, and *light* when being raised. The newness of life after baptism, therefore, becomes more real through being empirically encountered in the waters of baptism.

African Independent Churches are handicapped in formalized theological education, but the importance they attach to water baptism and their contributions to the theology of baptism show that they are working within their context, making independent theological decisions with the aim of making the gospel more meaningful and relevant to their constituencies.

Notes

[1] For a full discussion of the classification and types of AICs, see Allan Anderson, *African Reformation* (Asmara: Africa World Press, 2001), 10–20.

[2] Harold Turner, *Religious Innovations in Africa* (Boston: G. K. Hall & Co., 1979), 92.

[3] Philip Jenkins, *The Next Christendom: The Calling of Global Christianity* (Oxford: Oxford University Press, 2002), 52.

[4] The song was composed in 1963 when the church was sixteen years old, with no congregation outside of Nigeria.

[5] John S. Pobee and Gabriel Ositelu II, *African Initiatives in Christianity* (Geneva: WCC Publications, 1998), 52.

[6] Thomas Oduro, *Christ Holy Church International: The Story of an African Independent Church* (Minneapolis: Lutheran University Press, 2007), 17.

[7] Anderson, *African Reformation*, 116. Johane Marange, founder of African Apostolic Church of Johane Marange (AACJM), is an example of AIC leaders who claim to have been called to baptize.

[8] A prominent exception to the norm of using water to baptize is The Church of Jesus Christ on Earth through the Prophet Simon Kimbangu (also known as the EJCSK). This church practices laying of hands instead of using water, as their form of baptism. The African Holy Ghost Christian Church and other Roho churches in Kenya likewise do not use water to baptize; a threefold shaking of hands and laying of hands is their form of baptism. See Anderson, *African Reformation*, 129 and 159.

[9] Andrew Walls, *The Missionary Movement in Christian History* (Maryknoll, NY: Orbis Books, 1996), 116.

[10] Interview with Emmanuel Kpakpo, a final-year diploma student of the Good News Theological College and Seminary, Accra, December 5, 2005.

[11] Interview with Euphemia Adobea, a second-year diploma student of the Good News Theological College and Seminary, Accra, December 5, 2005.

[12] Interview with Theresa Appah, a third-year diploma student of the Good News Theological College and Seminary, Accra, December 5, 2005.

[13] Greg Cuthbertson and others, eds., *Frontiers in African Christianity: Essays in honour of Inus Daneel* (Pretoria: UNISA, 2003), 144.

[14] Allan Anderson, *Zion and Pentecost* (Pretoria: UNISA, 2000), 159.

[15] The period of instruction for the Twelve Apostles and the Evangelical Mission, for instance, is six months.

[16] Anderson, *Zion and Pentecost*, 159.

[17] Baptismal candidates in the Musama Disco Christo Church are baptized on Sundays. In the Twelve Apostles church, baptism takes place on Saturdays.

[18] For a detailed account of the role of women in AICs see Philomena Njeri Mwaura, "Gender and Power in African Christianity: African Instituted Churches and Pentecostal Churches," in Ogbu Kalu, ed., *African Christianity: an African Story* (Pretoria: University of Pretoria, 2005), 410–45.

[19] Ibid., 416.

[20] Some AIC leaders have encountered disasters during baptism by immersion. Prominent among them is Tomo Nyirenda of the Watch Tower Society in Malawi, who was hanged in 1926 for drowning twenty-two suspected witches during baptism by immersion. See Anderson, *African Reformation*, 134.

[21] Matthew 28:18-20.

[22] The Twelve Apostles Church and Musama Disco Christo Church, for instance, immerse candidates three times.

[23] Interview with Theresa Appah, Accra, December 5, 2005.

[24] Michael Smith, "Worship and the Christian Year," in Tim Dowley, ed., *The History of Christianity* (Herts: Lion Publishing, 1977), 10–12.

[25] For a detailed account of the history, growth, and challenges of Christ Holy Church International see Oduro, *Christ Holy Church International*.

[26] Ibid., 311.

[27] Marius Okoh, "Immersion Baptism," in *Good Tidings*, 3rd issue, Onitsha, n.d., 14.

[28] Ibid., 14 (capitalization in original).

[29] Interview with Nicholas Udemba, Accra, December 5, 2005.

[30] Okoh, "Immersion Baptism," 16–17 (capitalization in original).

[31] Ibid., 15 (capitalization in original).

[32] Ibid., 17.

[33] Interview with Nicholas Udemba, Accra, December 5, 2005.

[34] Oduro, *Christ Holy Church International*, 233.

Part II

Survey Articles

Chapter 1

Toward Mutual Recognition of Baptism

Paul Meyendorff

The second half of the twentieth century saw a number of remarkable changes in the understanding and practice of baptism across the whole Christian spectrum. First, the liturgical movement helped to uncover the rich baptismal traditions of the early centuries of the undivided Church. The liturgical reforms in the Roman Catholic Church following Vatican II, particularly the renewed Rite of Christian Initiation of Adults (RCIA), were inspired by the findings of the liturgical movement and set the stage for further reflection on baptism in that tradition and beyond. The Faith and Order study *Baptism, Eucharist and Ministry* (BEM)[1] placed the issues relating to baptism squarely in the center of the ecumenical table.

During the years immediately following the publication of BEM, however, the focus was largely on the eucharist, on eucharistic ecclesiology, and on *koinonia*. This discussion was certainly fruitful, and it facilitated several significant "full communion" agreements among mainline Protestant churches. But this approach had its limitations, particularly for those churches, including Orthodox and Roman Catholic, which saw "full communion" as possible only after theological agreement on the most significant dividing issues had been achieved.

In recent years, Faith and Order has increasingly turned its attention to baptism and baptismal ecclesiology. Negatively, this happened because baptism remained one of the stumbling blocks to Christian unity, due to the variety of baptismal practices and understandings among the churches today. Positively, it happened because baptism offered various possibilities for churches to recognize one another as being Christian, short of having achieved full communion. Though this development could be interpreted as a step back, as a compromise, in fact it is an important, positive step in the common recognition of the absolute centrality of baptism—for Christian anthropology, for soteriology, and for ecclesiology.

In the present volume, representatives of the various Christian communions describe how members are initiated—usually, but not always, through water baptism—and how these rites of initiation are understood. My task is to offer an overview, to point out areas of consensus as well as those that still cause dissension, and to make some suggestions for further reflection. I will do this speaking out of my own tradition, Eastern Orthodox, though not in any official capacity. The challenges I raise, however, face all Christians equally, including those from my own communion.

Even a quick glance at the rites included in this volume immediately reveals the extent to which, over the last few decades, the work of liturgical scholars, as well as progress in the ecumenical movement (particularly through BEM), has contributed to the development of practices that increasingly resemble one another. This tendency can be seen in the overall shape of the rites as well as individual elements within them.

All Christian traditions have a process for admitting new members. This typically includes formation and catechesis, a rite welcoming members into the community (typically, but not always, including baptism), followed by ongoing life in the community. It is possible to discern this fundamental pattern in each of the traditions represented in this volume, even if these stages are not always made explicit in the rites themselves. In those traditions that eschew elaborate rituals, such as the Quakers, there is a careful, at times prolonged, process to determine the readiness ("convincement") of a candidate to assume membership. Subsequently, the new member is expected to participate fully in the life of the community, with the risk of "disownment" should the commitment wane. Though the Quakers do speak of "baptism of the Spirit," the term refers not to a water rite or to a momentary event, but to lifelong growth in the Spirit within the church.

In those traditions with elaborate baptismal rites, this same pattern is evident. The Orthodox baptismal rites, for example, contain nearly all the elements that can be found in the fourth century—generally considered the "classical period" of Christian initiation.[2] These ancient rites developed at a time when Christianity was shifting from being a persecuted minority to becoming the established religion of the Roman Empire. Faced with a huge influx of new members, the Church developed a highly elaborate and structured system for receiving converts. This included years of preparation and catechesis and moral formation (the "catechumenate"), repeated exorcisms, pre- and post-baptismal anointings, integration into the eucharistic community, and post-baptismal instruction on the mysteries of baptism and the eucharist (known as "mystagogical catechesis"), followed by lifelong growth into Christ within the community of the Church.

It was a long process indeed, spanning many years and involving the entire community to ensure both that the conversion was authentic and that new members continued to be nurtured by and in the community following their climactic entrance into the Church at the Paschal Vigil. The Roman Catholic RCIA has in recent years restored this classical pattern for adult converts, and a number of Protestant traditions have, in recent years, moved to expand their own rites along these lines as well.

Characteristic of the ancient rites was a richness of symbolic and ritual imagery: pre- and post-baptismal anointings, breathing, spitting, exorcisms, blessing of water, candles, white garments, and more. In recent years, among the Western traditions one senses much less hostility toward these secondary baptismal symbols than in the past. Some (including, for example, the Lutheran, Presbyterian, and Methodist churches) have incorporated some of these practices in their rites. Many traditions now call for more abundant use of water, if not outright immersion. The Lutheran, Presbyterian, and Reformed traditions now include a thanksgiving over the water, even if they avoid using the term "blessing" in this context. Consistently, one finds rites and actions intended to make explicit the role of the Holy Spirit in baptism, whether through prayer, the laying on of hands, or a specific anointing akin to Eastern chrismation. Even the Quaker tradition, though it remains highly uncomfortable with symbols and does not practice water baptism, nevertheless recognizes their value as long as they do not replace the reality of the thing being symbolized.

This brings us to a key hermeneutical point, one critical for mutual recognition among Christians—the understanding and value of symbols and their role in ritual activity. This is an issue which has caused great misunderstanding, and which explains, at least partly, why (despite the significant advance of BEM) greater progress toward mutual recognition has not been achieved. The fact remains that all Christians do not share the same understanding of symbol.

In the world of late antiquity in which the Church developed, symbol and reality were neither distinct nor opposed to one another. The whole cosmos, all creation, was understood to be symbolic and to participate in the reality which it symbolized. Underlying this was a cosmology that saw the world as created by God, and therefore as good and transparent to God. Although affected by the fall of Adam, material creation nevertheless retained this potential ability to communicate divine reality, and this potential was restored through the incarnation, death, and resurrection of Christ—which had implications not just for humanity but for the entire cosmos. This is vividly expressed in the Byzantine prayer for blessing the baptismal water:

> . . . All creation sang your praise when you appeared. For you, our God, were seen on earth and lived among mortals. You also sanctified the streams of Jordan by sending down on them from heaven your all-holy Spirit, and you crushed the heads of the dragons that lurked there. Therefore, O King, lover of mankind, be present now too, through the visitation of your Holy Spirit, and sanctify this water. Give it the grace of redemption, the blessing of Jordan. Make it a source of incorruption, a gift of sanctification, a deliverance from sin, a destruction of demons. . . .
>
> But do you, Master of all things, declare this water to be water of redemption, water of sanctification, cleansing of flesh and spirit, untying of bonds, forgiveness of offenses, enlightenment of soul, washing of rebirth, renewal of spirit, gift of adoption, garment of incorruption, source of life. For it was you, Lord, who said, "Wash and be made clean, and put away evil from your souls." It is you who have given us the grace of rebirth from on high through water and Spirit. Manifest yourself, Lord, in this water, and grant that the one being baptized in it may be transformed for the putting off of the old self that is corrupted after the desires of deception, and may put on the new that is renewed after the image of the One who created him/her. So that, planted in the likeness of your death through baptism, he/she may also become a partaker in your resurrection, and having guarded the gift of the Holy Spirit and increased the deposit of grace, may receive the prize of his/her high calling and be numbered with the firstborn, whose names are inscribed in heaven, in you our God and Lord, Jesus Christ. . . .[3]

In this prayer we see an elaborate baptismal theology fully integrated within a holistic soteriology and cosmology. God uses material creation for the economy of salvation—whether in the incarnation itself (which serves as the model) or in the liturgical, sacramental life of the Church. For the Eastern churches, underlying this approach is the classical understanding of the symbolic value of creation. Eastern Christians thus find it difficult to understand the reluctance of Western

Christians to ascribe full importance, value, and, indeed, power to material symbols and symbolic acts.

Among Western Christians, probably around the eleventh century, this cosmic, symbolic view changed to a more Aristotelian perspective, in which symbols and reality came to be understood as distinct, indeed, as mutually opposed.[4] One of the unfortunate results of this development was the gradual separation of symbols and symbolic (ritual) actions from the reality they were trying to re-present (that is, to make real and present). From this developed the later Scholastic approach to the sacraments, which distinguished "form" from "essence." This, in turn, gradually led to a significant reduction of ritual symbolism in Western liturgy, a reduction even more strongly emphasized among the Reformers of the sixteenth century and later, as they took this (philosophical) approach to its logical conclusion. One can still hear the strong resonance of this view in a number of the explanations offered in this volume.

Connected to this Aristotelian perspective is a type of dualism which disparages the material in favor of a primarily spiritual reality—again positing the two as mutually opposed. The authors of many of the interpretive articles in this volume repeatedly stress that what is important is the spiritual reality, and that the "symbols" (water, oil, candles . . .) and ritual acts are "merely illustrative," having little or no value in themselves. To this, Eastern Christians would unabashedly say that God does indeed act through material creation, through these symbols, because in Christ all creation is redeemed, restored, and thus a means of communion with God.[5]

Thus while Eastern Christians welcome the increased openness to material symbols among the Western churches, they would also like to see further reflection on the significance of this development. Does the greater acceptance of symbol and ritual reflect, in fact, a more positive approach to creation? Or is it simply making the rites more colorful, less stark and boring?

At the same time, all Christian communities need to take seriously the challenge of connecting the material symbols and ritual actions with spiritual reality. There is always the risk that the symbols and rituals become disconnected from the spiritual reality—then indeed the rituals can become magic, and symbols can become idols. The baptismal rite, performed in isolation from the story of the death and resurrection of Christ, becomes an empty ritual. The rite performed in the absence of faith has no power. The rite performed in the absence of a faith community into which the candidate is introduced, and which will nurture him or her in the Christian life, is ineffective. For it is in baptism that we are incorporated into Christ, that we die and rise with him into new life in the Spirit, which is life in the Church. Yet it is a fact that, all too often, baptism is experienced on the level of folk religion, as the occasion for an elaborate party, with little or no understanding of its tremendous significance.

This becomes a problem particularly with the baptism of infants, which remains the practice among a majority of Christians worldwide. It is not possible here to review the historical arguments on both sides of the "infant/adult" baptism issue. The New Testament evidence is inconclusive, and the arguments are based on divergent historical practices—and especially on divergent theological positions—which color the way the biblical and historical data are interpreted.

On this issue, however, I detect a perceptible shift from the fixed, often polemical, arguments in the centuries following the Reformation. While the Anabaptist churches, for example, have not abandoned their fundamental position or practice, there has been a significant softening in their position. This has been made possible, as Paul Fiddes's paper points out, by focusing not simply on the baptismal rite itself but on the broader pattern of initiation of which baptism is only a part. Thus, while baptism proper might take place either in infancy or upon a proclamation of the individual's faith later on, it is possible to discern a larger pattern of growth and formation in faith and integration into the life of the Church. This, from the perspective of this particular tradition, may very well make it possible to recognize as authentic (and therefore unrepeatable) even the baptism of children performed in other churches.

A further shift has been the perception that baptism means more than a confession of mature faith but is also incorporation into a living community, into the body of Christ at a particular time and in a particular place. Combined with a deeper understanding of child development, churches today have come to accept that children, even at a very young age, can truly belong in the Church and can participate fully in its life to the limit of their abilities. Within a caring, nurturing community, they can grow into mature faith and eventually claim it boldly as their own. In other words, baptism in its broader sense is more than a single moment or event; rather it is part of a lifelong process of growth into Christ. Here again, discerning this process, both within one's own tradition and in others, should help all the churches move toward greater acceptance of the initiatory processes in other traditions, particularly those that practice infant baptism.

With regard to infant baptism, several other issues are significant for different reasons. First is the obvious question about the limited, or nonexistent, ability of infants to proclaim their faith. Here it is important to affirm that *all churches* stress the vital importance of faith in the baptismal or initiatory process. Usually, though not always, this is expressed in the form of a creed, typically the Nicene-Constantinopolitan in the East, often the Apostles' Creed in the West. It is important to note here that the liturgical use of creeds originates precisely in the baptismal liturgies of the early centuries—hence the use of the first-person singular, "I believe. . . ."[6] In churches that do not use creeds, a personal profession of faith replaces the more formal creeds, but even this profession must be consonant with the beliefs of the community.

The important thing to note, first of all, is that this faith is corporate, held in common with the gathered church. The faith of each individual, each "I," is called into conformity with the faith of the corporate "We," the Body of Christ, the Church, into which the baptized are entering. Thus, whether in the case of a child or of an adult, in each case the faith of the gathered community is primary, and the newly baptized are expected to make that faith their own to the extent that they are able. Obviously, in the case of a child, the responsibility of the community is even greater. Historically, this was the primary duty of sponsors ("godparents"), an institution that developed originally not for infant baptism but for adult candidates for baptism. Sponsors had to vouch for the good character of candidates seeking entrance into the Church. They participated in their pre-baptismal formation and were responsible for post-baptismal follow-up as well.[7]

To those churches that do not baptize infants or small children, this poses the challenge of dealing with those who are unable fully to profess their own faith. Can they be members of the Church? And what about those who, though not children, are mentally ill or suffering from senility that inhibits their ability to express their faith? To those churches that do baptize infants, this poses the challenge of taking seriously their responsibility to nurture the continued growth into Christ of those who may not even remember their own baptism.

Second, baptism is not only for forgiveness of sins and for the affirmation of faith but also for incorporation into the family of the Church where, by our incorporation into Christ, we all become members of one another, brothers and sisters in the Lord. In this familial analogy, children are every bit as much members of the family as are the adult members. This has always been self-evident for churches that practice infant baptism,[8] but even those churches that do not have this practice are now seeking to find more formal ways to include children in the life of the community. In the Society of Friends, for example, children of adult members are generally considered members of the community and may participate fully in its worship.[9]

Third, and closely related to the second point, is the question of whether the baptism of infants implies their full membership in the Church. We face here a historical development in the West that has greatly confused the issue. In the early centuries, the undivided Church had a unitary baptismal process. Baptism was immediately accompanied by the bestowal of the Spirit, either through the laying on of hands or by anointing (chrismation), and then by a procession into the church where the newly baptized were greeted with the kiss of peace and participated in the eucharist, thus affirming their membership in the Church, local and universal.[10] So important were these rites of initiation in the early Church that some parts were reserved for the bishop—typically, this involved the laying on of hands or chrismation. And here is where the paths began to diverge.

In the liturgically more conservative West, the laying on of hands was a gesture reserved for the bishop. At a time when Christianity was still largely urban and the bishop of the city was readily available, this worked well. During the medieval period, as Christianity spread to the countryside and north into missionary territories, the situation changed, and bishops were not readily available every time baptisms were celebrated. As a result, the part reserved for the bishop became separated, often by many years, from the rest of the baptismal rites—and the Western rite of confirmation appeared. Baptized infants did not have hands laid on them until the bishop could come and do this, and they were not permitted to receive communion until after they had been confirmed. This practice, which originated for very practical reasons, was wanting a theological rationale, which was provided with the notion of "the age of reason." Eventually, the order was changed in Roman Catholic practice, and children would be baptized in infancy, admitted to the eucharist around the age of seven, and confirmed around the age of twelve.[11] This was the situation inherited as well by the churches issuing from the Reformation.

Among the Eastern churches, the rite maintained its unitary character. The connection with the bishop was maintained by requiring that chrism be blessed by the bishop, but his presence at each baptism was no longer required. However, in contemporary Eastern practice, while infants are communed, the actual rite of baptism is most often done apart from the eucharistic liturgy, and often as a private ceremony with only a priest and close family and friends in attendance.[12]

In recent years, many Christian communions have moved toward a more unitary celebration of the rites of initiation. In doing so, they have been challenged by the question of whether baptism confers full membership in the Church. For the historical reasons mentioned above, the question is complicated. While practices remain diverse, there has in recent years been much greater openness to discussing these issues and to listening to the various positions, as well as a gradual shift toward the fuller integration of children into the life of the Church. In the years to come, the various churches will continue to struggle with this issue.

* * *

It is evident that significant progress has been made in recent decades. Largely through the work of Faith and Order, the churches have reflected together on baptism and its implications, first in the BEM process, and more recently on the question of mutual recognition of baptism. As a result, a number of communions have significantly renovated their baptismal rites, consciously or unconsciously bringing them closer to ancient patterns of initiation. In doing so, they looked not only at the structure and content of the rites themselves but also at the overall pattern of initiation, recognizing that the liturgy of baptism was the visible expression of a lifelong process of initiation and growth into Christ within the context of an ecclesial community.

It is particularly the common recognition of this larger pattern that allows the various churches to discern it in other communions and thus to recognize their baptism. And this implies not merely the recognition of a particular ritual, but *de facto* the recognition of ecclesial reality in the other. Though short of full communion, this recognition is nevertheless a significant ecumenical advance, an important step toward the full communion we all seek.

It must be stated, however, that the progress in mutual recognition of baptism is more often implicit than explicit. The various communions have typically not made official declarations recognizing the baptism of other churches. More often than not, the issue arises when a person baptized in one church seeks entrance into another. While in recent decades the trend has been toward greater acceptance of a baptism performed in another church, the responses are not consistent, even within each communion. Some Baptists, for example, will baptize persons baptized elsewhere as infants, while others will not. Many churches leave the decision up to the individual candidate for membership—a solution that one finds quite often among both Eastern and Western communions. Among the Eastern churches, a majority will accept the baptism of persons baptized in the name of the Trinity,[13] but there is a (very vocal) minority that rejects the validity of any baptism outside the canonical limits of the Orthodox Church, on the basis of a strict Cyprianic[14] ecclesiology.

In speaking of mutual recognition of baptism, then, we are ultimately dealing with questions of ecclesiology. To the extent that churches can recognize marks of the Church in other communions, they are able to recognize their baptism. This is why the emphasis on the lifelong process of initiation is so helpful, because what we are presented with is nothing less than the essence of the Church, which exists to lead all into God's kingdom. Here the individual person, the community that gathers, faith, the Church, and its liturgical and sacramental life are all bound up together in a process that begins when we are born and ends beyond the grave. Discerning this larger pattern will allow us to overcome the many differences in practice that will inevitably remain—it will allow us to see the forest for the trees.

The mutual recognition of baptism is therefore a positive step toward the greater unity that we seek. Short of full communion, it nevertheless marks a degree of recognition of one another as churches. But it does not simply "paper over" the significant issues that continue to divide Christians from one another, and which we must continue seeking to resolve in mutual love. I see this as more honest than entering into full communion while remaining fundamentally divided. Yet, by recognizing one another's baptisms, we cannot but be reminded of the call to unity. Then, each repenting of our own sins, and in mutual love, we can continue the dialogue that, with the help of the Holy Spirit (whom we receive in baptism!), will lead to ever-greater unity among those who, in Christ (whom we put on in baptism!), call themselves children of the Father.

Notes

[1] *Baptism, Eucharist and Ministry*, Faith and Order Paper No. 111, 25th anniversary printing with added intro. (Geneva: World Council of Churches, [1982] 2007).

[2] Among the "Orthodox" I include not just those who follow the Byzantine tradition ("Eastern Orthodox") but also the Armenian and Malankara Orthodox Syrian Church ("Oriental Orthodox").

[3] This prayer, in the style of a classical, Antiochene anaphora, is usually ascribed to Proclus of Constantinople (fifth century).

[4] "What is symbolic is not real," became the cry of those who argued for the "real presence" of Christ in the eucharistic elements.

[5] This has great implications also for our Christian responsibility for the environment. The created world is perceived to be good, because it is willed by God, and we have the responsibility for it as God's stewards.

[6] At the councils which first defined the creeds, the first-person plural was used in the *acta*, but this was changed to the first-person singular for liturgical use in baptism. Later, in the sixth century, a creed was added to the eucharistic liturgy as well, precisely to ensure the unity of faith in each assembly.

[7] The spiritual relationship between godparent and godchild was taken very seriously in ancient Christianity. For example, such relationships were considered to be as close as biological relationships in laws governing marriage.

[8] However, in the Western churches, this has generally been implicit rather than explicit. The more frequently articulated justification had more to do with the need for the forgiveness of original sin, based on the Augustinian (and later Calvinist) view that we are born guilty of Adam's sin. This led in the West to speculation about the fate of children who die unbaptized and who enter into a condition of "limbo" (neither heaven nor hell). This view has recently been formally repudiated by the Roman Catholic Church, though the underlying question about original sin remains open. Among the Eastern churches, original sin is generally viewed not as inherited guilt but as the mortality and tendency to personal sin that we inherit as a result of the fall.

[9] Children of members are either so *de facto*, through "birthright membership," or because the parents apply for membership on their behalf.

[10] This is a pattern we observe, for example, in the fourth-century commentaries on baptism by John Chrystostom, Cyril of Jerusalem, Ambrose of Milan, and Theodore of Mopsuestia.

[11] See Aidan Kavanagh, *The Shape of Baptism: The Rite of Christian Initiation* (New York: Pueblo, 1978), and particularly his *Confirmation: Origins and Reform* (New York: Pueblo, 1988). He argues for a return to the primitive practice of celebrating all the rites of initiation, up to and including the eucharist, all at once.

¹² For a strong critique of these practices and an appeal for a more ecclesial and eucharistic rite, see Alexander Schmemann, *Of Water and the Spirit* (Crestwood, NY: St. Vladimir's Seminary Press, 1974).

¹³ On the question of Trinitarian language, many Eastern Christians are disturbed by a recent tendency in some quarters to avoid using the biblically revealed names: Father, Son, and Holy Spirit. They interpret this as erosion in the Trinitarian faith of historical Christianity, thus making recognition of baptism highly problematic.

¹⁴ Cyprian of Carthage was a third-century bishop, who, in the midst of severe persecution, expressed a very exclusive ecclesiology that allowed for no salvation outside the canonical limits of the church. This view was revived in some Orthodox circles in the seventeenth century in the context of polemics with Western churches, which at the time also shared that approach.

Chapter 2

Unity in Diversity: Convergence in the Churches' Baptismal Practices

James F. Puglisi, SA

"Unity presupposes the many": we make this affirmation so often in our ecumenical discussions. But we must ask whether or not we really believe this—or is it an excuse to continue hiding radical divisions between the churches without having the will to overcome them?

In any kind of theoretical work one needs to verify the facts, so as to confirm the truth of the thesis. Far too often in ecumenical discussions, I believe, we are caught up in the "theory" and never step back to verify whether the theory is actually seen in the "praxis." Dialogues among churches have helped to clarify this issue, but when confronted with the actual *practice* of the churches we often see greater convergence, if not consensus, than the theory would suggest. In another difficult area, that of ministry, my thesis is that there is greater convergence on the level of what the churches *do* than on what they *say* they do.[1] One must be careful not to make a "language game" out of this, but rather to do something that the Church has done almost from the outset—namely, to see liturgy as a *locus theologicus* for its reflection on faith.[2]

It is interesting to observe how churches interacted in the first centuries of their existence. In spite of their liturgical diversity, they continually affirmed each other as living out the apostolic faith as it was confessed in its liturgical expression and then confirmed in conciliar creeds. We know that one of the earliest expressions of the faith in creedal form derives from the baptismal liturgical form. For this reason the work of the Faith and Order Commission of the World Council of Churches, collecting in this book a variety of baptismal liturgies together with commentaries, offers us an inestimable resource for theological reflection using the liturgy as a *"locus."*

Thanks to the liturgical, biblical, and patristic movements and renewal that began in the mid-1800s and are still going on today, the churches in dialogue were able to make a common statement on the understanding of baptism in the "Lima document" *Baptism, Eucharist and Ministry*.[3] This convergence text has given rise to further revisions of the churches' liturgical practices, as well as to greater discussion on important theological issues. Throughout this process the churches continue to reflect on the faith that their liturgies express and, through their liturgies, try to state that faith in a fresh way. Thus liturgy is seen as a living, organic reality, a powerful and deep way of proclaiming, celebrating, and living the Word of God.

Here I shall draw attention to some areas of convergence in the liturgical expression of the churches, areas that articulate the same apostolic faith in diverse forms. Too many liturgies are presented to consider all of them closely. Their great diversity represents a broad spectrum ranging from Orthodoxy to traditions often tagged as "non-liturgical." However, in spite of this great diversity, one may see that there is indeed a deep convergence.

BAPTISM AS A RITE OF PASSAGE—
ANTHROPOLOGICAL FOUNDATIONS

All the baptismal liturgies gathered here include a common element that may be described as the understanding of baptism as "a rite of passage." This passage is sometimes expressed by a twofold movement: "into the waters/out of the waters" as in a Pentecostal ritual; or it may be expressed as part of a continuum within the catechumenal process ending in water baptism and chrismation, as it does in churches such as the Oriental, Catholic, Anglican, Lutheran, and Methodist. Whatever form this rite takes, what is important is that the anthropological dimension is foundational. This rite of passage is a liminal process whereby the individual passes from a former way of living/being to a new way of living/being, in and through death with Christ. Whether this happens solely through one ritual action, or whether it involves a more complex nexus of rituals indicating a growing conversion, the water rite of baptism marks the moment that ritually ends a past life, while declaring a dedication to a new and future life.

From an analysis of who the key actors are in this process, one may quickly affirm a convergence in understanding as to what is actually *happening* in baptism: the roles carried out in this liturgy are that of the individual who is being baptized, the congregation or the *ecclesia*, and the Holy Spirit. The role of witness is portrayed by both the individual and the assembly of the faithful. The latter attests to the fact that the *electus*, or chosen one, has indeed been marked by a change in life.

(In the case of infant baptisms the assembly attests to the faith of the church into which the individual is baptized, as well as the willingness of the church to accompany the baptized in his or her faith development as the child grows to maturity both physically and spiritually.)

A variety of rites may accompany this as happens during the catechumenate with the "scrutinies," or by individuals witnessing as happens during the first part of the Pentecostal baptismal liturgy. The individual likewise attests to the change or conversion that has taken place—sometimes with a ritual declaration (the renunciation of evil and sin) and sometimes with a more spontaneous testimony as found in the Baptist, Anabaptist, and Pentecostal traditions.

The key actor in the process of conversion is seen to be the Holy Spirit. It is the Holy Spirit who enables the individual to accept Christ, renounce a life of sin, and turn toward the God who offers salvation in Jesus Christ. All the baptismal liturgies presented here witness to the fact that the Spirit works both through the Scriptures and through the assembly of the faithful, who have both a discerning and an affirming role to play. In addition, in a good number of the liturgies there is also a link tying the gifts given by the Spirit to the water rite, in addition to some further rite. (That is, in certain cases either the laying on of hands or an anointing, or both, are linked to the water rite). Again this aspect of the baptismal rites may be seen in formal texts and prescribed ritual actions, or in more extemporaneous expressions offered by the individual, the minister, and/or the congregation.

It is true that there is a great diversity in the ways in which the passage from a life of sin to a life of grace is expressed or carried out. The important fact is that all the liturgies express this fundamental reality as part of the respective church's practice of baptism. Herein lies the *convergence in practice* that points to a *common understanding* of baptism as an initiation into a new way of being, as a son or daughter of the God who saves. This is achieved through the use of natural symbols and the language of birth, or coming to life, and/or the image of dying and transformation. This use of symbols and language is *anthropological* in the sense that it is rooted in, and expresses, certain basic realities about what it means to be a human being.

It is clear that the point of reference for this is found in the Scriptures, with the biblical metaphors being employed in the actual liturgies of baptism. From the various commentaries that accompany the liturgical rites, one may discern significant convergence on the theological level as well.

INTEGRATION INTO A BODY OF BELIEVERS

In all the baptismal liturgies presented, the individual being baptized is integrated into a group of other believers. We may conclude from this that even though the individual confesses his or her own faith in the saving Lord, that person becomes one with a multitude of believers. In some of the liturgies this is illustrated by the image of being grafted into the living vine which is Christ; elsewhere it is expressed through the imagery of being united to Christ in death, so that one may be raised with Christ in resurrection. In all cases an understanding of discipleship and mission is in some way expressed.

One is never a believer by oneself. Christian belief also implies that one takes up the very mission of Christ to bring the good news of salvation to all people. The *sequela Christi* is seen as an essential part of baptismal commitment; this continues the process begun in one's own personal conversion of dying to sin so that grace and life may abound. On a daily basis it involves assuming the cross of Christ and dying to self, following Christ from death to new life.

Some liturgies place more emphasis on the personal initiative in this process, while others underscore both the personal *and* the communal dimension of the faith being confessed. In addition to the belief that salvation comes through the personal confession of faith in Jesus Christ, who saves the individual, one may also find the Old Testament understanding that salvation comes through belonging to the *qahal*, the praying community. This communal dimension must not be seen in contradistinction to the individual or personal dimension, but rather as the context within which a personal confession of faith is made. In many baptismal liturgies we find the community engaged, nurturing the individual's faith and supporting persons in their journey together to fulfill the mission of the Church. The dimension of baptism as a grafting into Christ's body is seen in more and more liturgies. This may take the form of a question put to the congregation, or it may be expressed through the active participation of the believers in a renewal of their baptismal commitment, or otherwise through a prayer or response.

BAPTISM AND THE HOLY SPIRIT

In all the baptismal rites given in this volume there is a close link between baptism and the gifting of the Holy Spirit. Sometimes the link is made directly by the act of baptism, the water rite and conferral of the Spirit. In other cases there is a special rite that confers or invokes the Holy Spirit; this may include a gesture such as the imposition of hands, as well as anointing or even the sign of the cross. Several invocations of the Spirit are to be found as a formal *epiclesis* in the liturgy, for example, in the blessing of the baptismal water. In other instances the invocation of the Spirit may take place through the use of blessed, fragrant oil known as *muron,* or through chrism and an anointing. Finally, in other cases it is done through a prayer following the baptism itself.

The important issue here is that baptism is conceived as a trinitarian act whereby God, through the action of Christ and his Spirit, breathes life into the individual and makes him or her an adoptive child of God. Various biblical images are used to convey this reality: being adoptive sons or daughters of God, being children of light, being a new creation, and so on. The variety of biblical possibilities abound here; some churches use Pauline theological language to describe what happens in baptism, while others use Johannine images. But where the churches converge is on the trinitarian significance revealed through the diverse ritual practice.

CONCLUSION

Since the beginning of the liturgical movement in the nineteenth century, many churches have gradually recovered the liturgy as a *locus theologicus*. The baptismal rites and rituals collected and commented on in this book illustrate the degree of convergence which exists in the churches' baptismal practice.[4] This convergence represents not only a mutual sharing of liturgical experience but also a discovery of the biblical, theological, and patristic sources of baptism.

In the end what comes to the fore is that the churches, in spite of their differing ways of celebrating baptism, realize that even as they baptize they are indeed expressing the same apostolic faith. Thus what is important in a study of the liturgies of baptism is that the diversity of practices does not preclude discerning and receiving the same faith. This has emerged through the Faith and Order movement's work on the issue of baptism. From *Baptism, Eucharist and Ministry* as issued at Lima in 1982 to the current study document-in-process, "One Baptism: Towards Mutual Recognition,"[5] the work of Faith and Order has helped the churches to revise their liturgies in order to express more fully the faith of the Church as lived throughout the ages and articulated afresh in each generation.

Notes

[1] See the work I have done confronting the theology of ministry with the practice of the churches. I believe my work shows that there is much more convergence in the meaning of ministry, as seen in the various churches' liturgies of ordination, than is expressed in the various theologies of the churches: J. F. Puglisi, *The Process of Admission to Ordained Ministry: A Comparative Study*, 3 vols. (Collegeville, MN: Liturgical Press, 2001). The method I used in this work was again verified in a specific geographic area, namely, Scandinavia. See the published results from the research project of the Nordic countries in H.-R. Iversen, ed., *Rites of Ordination and Commitment in the Churches of the Nordic Churches* (Copenhagen: Museum Tusculanum Press, 2006).

[2] On this methodology for liturgical theologians see K. W. Irwin, *Context and Text: Method in Liturgical Theology* (Collegeville, MN: Liturgical Press, 1994).

[3] *Baptism, Eucharist and Ministry*, Faith and Order Paper No. 111, 25th anniversary printing with added intro. (Geneva: World Council of Churches, [1982] 2007).

[4] Much scholarly research has been done on the liturgical evolution of the rituals of baptism. Here we cite two examples: B. D. Spinks, *Early and Medieval Rituals and Theologies of Baptism: From the New Testament to the Council of Trent*, Liturgy, Worship and Society Series (Aldershot: Ashgate, 2006); and Spinks, *Reformation and Modern Rituals and Theologies of Baptism: From Luther to Contemporary Practices*, Liturgy, Worship and Society Series (Aldershot: Ashgate, 2006).

[5] As of this writing the text "One Baptism: Towards Mutual Recognition," which is not yet an official Faith and Order text, is given in *Minutes of the Standing Commission on Faith and Order Meeting in Crans-Montana, Switzerland, 2007*, Faith and Order Paper No. 206 (Geneva: Commission on Faith and Order, World Council of Churches, 2007), Appendix V, 57–81. The latest version of the text may be obtained from Faith and Order, WCC, 150, Rte. de Ferney, 1211 Geneva, Switzerland.

Chapter 3

Convergence and Divergence: Baptism Today
Karen B. Westerfield Tucker

> Go therefore and make disciples of all nations, baptizing them in the name of the Father and of the Son and of the Holy Spirit, and teaching them to obey everything that I have commanded you. (Matt 28:19-20)

This single sentence from Matthew's gospel is considered by many churches to be both the warrant and the instruction for carrying out Christian baptism. Yet as is clear from the survey of theologies, traditions, and practices represented in this collection of essays, Christian communities are not of a single mind in interpreting the passage. Are disciples to be made prior to baptism (as may be indicated by the sequence of verbs in the text), or does baptism itself make disciples? What material sign(s), action(s), and mode(s) stand behind the word "baptism" (*baptizo*)? Is it necessary to use water, and if so, in what quantity? Must the baptism be done in the name of the Father, Son, and Holy Spirit, or is another formulation, such as baptism in the name of Jesus (e.g., Acts 2:38; 10:48), appropriate also? Is teaching (catechesis) to be done after baptism, or should there be pre-baptismal instruction, or perhaps both? Who is to administer this baptism in the present age, since in this text Jesus is reportedly speaking only to the eleven remaining disciples? Thus, in the dialogues between and within Christian communions, reference to this commonly held Scripture may contribute to—rather than resolve—differences.

Despite the variety of understandings and practices that emerge from the interpretation of these two verses, basic commonalities can be recognized: baptism and evangelization are linked; baptism is done in the name of the One in whom faith is professed; and there is an ongoing baptismal life that includes formation and learning for the sake of obedience to the Gospel. Indeed, these three points could be viewed in sequence as a type of common *ordo* or pattern for Christian initiation. Acknowledging these similarities, even in the face of continuing differences, can be a step toward fulfilling both Jesus' prayer that "they may be one" (John 17:11) and the Pauline affirmation that there is "one Lord, one faith, one baptism" (Eph 4:5).

BAPTISM AND EVANGELIZATION

The acceleration of church growth in parts of Africa and Asia, the emerging mission fields of North America and Western Europe, and the retrieval (and adoption) of early Christian practices—thanks in part to the twentieth-century liturgical movement—have contributed to a greater consensus across the churches in favor of the theological and liturgical normativity of baptism upon profession of faith. In Faith and Order's convergence document *Baptism, Eucharist and Ministry* (BEM), it was observed that "baptism upon personal profession of faith is the most clearly attested pattern in the New Testament documents."[1] The baptismal study emerging more recently from the Joint Working Group between the Roman Catholic Church and the World Council of Churches recognizes "a paradigmatic and normative quality of baptism performed upon personal profession of faith, illustrated in the New Testament and practised by all churches, as the most explicit sign of the character of baptism."[2]

In fact many churches that encourage Christian parents to baptize their infants have, in the last fifty years, revised their infant and adult rites to reflect this recovery of the biblical and apostolic paradigm, reinterpreting the infant rite as a variant of believer baptism and (ideally) providing mechanisms for the evangelization of the child as he or she grows. This shift for paedo-baptists has supplied a common ground for conversations with the exclusively believer-baptist denominations, and both groups have increasingly recognized the need for pre-baptismal formation and catechesis. The introduction by the Roman Catholic Church of *Ordo Initiationis Christianae Adultorum* (the Rite of Christian Initiation of Adults) in 1972 inspired the production of Protestant texts as well as accompanying catechumenal processes of formation and learning (processes that have varied in the degree of their reception). A bold step to proclaim the common Christian confession to a post-modern world would be for churches to work together in the pre-baptismal catechetical enterprise: in the training of catechists and sponsors, in the formation of new adult believers (including participation in ministries of service and witness), and in the preparation of parents to raise their baptized children in the Christian faith.

Baptism identifies two new relationships: the communion established between followers of Jesus Christ and the triune God through the power of the Holy Spirit; and admission into the fellowship of disciples, the Body of Christ. As noted in BEM, baptism "is incorporation into Christ, who is the crucified and risen Lord; it is entry into the New Covenant between God and God's people."[3] However, the range of meanings relative to the dynamics represented by that "incorporation" and "entry" and "new covenant" varies among the churches. For Quakers (Society of Friends), baptism in the Spirit (Mark 1:8) is understood as a lifelong process in which the Spirit comes to dwell as the inward light of Christ in the heart. Within a Baptist baptismal service might be heard a prayer for the baptismal candidates that "they may know the fullness of your love and the filling of your Spirit as in baptism they signify their desire to follow your Son. May this important step on their lives' journeys wash away the fears and sins of the past."[4] A minister of the Uniting Church in Australia says in the introduction to their baptismal rite: "Baptism is the sign of new life in Christ Jesus. By water and the Holy Spirit we are brought into union with Christ in his death and resurrection. In baptism we are sealed with the Holy Spirit, made members of the body of Christ, and called to his ministry in the world."[5] A *sedra* from the liturgy of the Mar Thoma Syrian Church of Malabar asks:

> O' Lord Jesus Christ! You have gathered us from straying in sin. You have invited us to observe Your Holy Commandment and admitted us to your spiritual fold. You have called us to the streams of salvation and the fountain of eternal life, and with your life-giving voice have offered to cleanse us from our heart's defilement. Lord, bless this your servant who has come to receive the seal of life. Accept him/her into your fold. Number him/her among your sheep. May your countenance shine on him/her. Make him/her worthy of regeneration to become a child of your Father. Enable him/her to put off the old man and to put on the imperishable new man. . . .[6]

All four of the communities represented in the illustrations above take up some of the meanings of baptism found in the New Testament and identified in BEM: "participation in Christ's death and resurrection; a washing away of sin; a new birth; an enlightenment by Christ; a reclothing in Christ; a renewal by the Spirit; the experience of salvation from the flood; and a liberation into a new humanity." These images in sum "express the riches of Christ and the gifts of his salvation."[7] The question must then be raised: does the recognition of apostolicity—seeing in another church a continuity and consistency with the faith, life, witness, and ministry of the apostolic community chosen and sent by Christ[8]—depend upon which of these biblical meanings and images are highlighted in the practices and theological interpretations of a given ecclesiastical community?

Might a strong emphasis upon the pneumatological aspect of baptism—as is the case with the Society of Friends—be sufficient for recognition by a community in which baptism as participation in the paschal mystery is stressed as the central meaning? The complexity of this matter is heightened as some Protestant churches in the West (due to suspicion regarding a theology of original sin) shift away from historic denominational accents upon the regenerative aspect of baptism and toward a greater emphasis on the covenantal aspect. This complication is intensified for the process of mutual recognition when individual pastors and local congregations make such adjustments unilaterally. The decline in a baptismal theology of regeneration has, in some communities, eroded the connections between baptism and God's gift of salvation, though a number of groups have historically found problematic the claim that baptism is necessary for salvation.[9] A related subject is whether or not it is possible to recognize communities that define themselves as Christian, but do not include baptism (conceptually or ritually) among their practices.

Baptism is the nexus of new relationships between God, God's people the Church, and the individual person. Yet another relational aspect is operative in the case of infant baptism: the introduction of a new life into family and society. In certain contexts—such as a state church, an ecclesiastical community with close ethnic ties or local congregations of uniform ethnicity, and churches in a historically Christian nation—the familial and the social factors may appear to outweigh the ecclesial dimension of baptism. The "conversation in modern Sweden" imagined by Bo Larsson makes this point explicitly. Baptism, in some places, has come to double as a societal rite of passage marking the viability of human life and the creation of new relationships within the human family, thus potentially supplanting the life-transforming aspects of participation in Christ. Whether it is admitted or not, this is a problem for many Orthodox, Catholic, and Protestant communities. In order to maintain baptism's strong connection with evangelization, it may be incumbent upon Christian communities in their own locales—and also, perhaps, in ecumenical engagement—

to develop other rites or recognitions that focus upon the welcoming of new human life, especially if no such practices are currently available or can be found in the wider society and "Christianized." These new rites, such as a rite of thanksgiving for the birth of a child, should be so formulated as to avoid language reminiscent of baptism, and making a clear distinction between what may be a simple blessing or thanksgiving and a sacrament or ordinance.

BAPTISM IN THE NAME OF THE ONE IN WHOM FAITH IS PROFESSED

While a few communities today baptize using what they believe to be the older biblical formulation of "in the name of Jesus,"[10] the majority use the triune name revealed in Matthew 28 and documented in early church orders. "Father, Son, and Holy Spirit" is no "magical" formula; it names the Three-One God in whom faith is professed, and it is a shorthand, a summary of the faith more fully articulated in Scripture, in the historic baptismal profession known as the Apostles' Creed, in other ecumenical creeds, and in hymns and songs. By grace (Eph 2:5) and through the power and gift of the Holy Spirit (1 Cor 12:13), the baptized participate in that Trinitarian reality: they are incorporated into Christ and clothed with him (Gal 3:27), adopted as children and heirs of the Father (Rom 8:15-17), and remade as the dwelling place of the Holy Spirit (1 Cor 3:16-17). Thus the baptismal formula speaks simultaneously to the faith offered by God as a gift (*fides qua creditur*) and to the faith received and professed by the baptismal candidate (*fides quae creditur*). Changes made to the biblical formulation or the introduction of a new formula, for example, due to concern for "gendered" language, risk entering a candidate into something other than the scriptural and traditional faith of the Church. Again, much is at stake in terms of recognition when adjustments are made at the local level, or when a denomination sanctions variety in the baptismal formula out of a hermeneutic of diversity or inclusivity.

Uniform use of the baptismal formula is a means of joining the personal faith expressed by a candidate with the faith of the Church throughout the ages. God's gift of faith combined with formation in the company of the Christian community enables the "we believe" to become the "I believe" of personal commitment.[11] The "we" comprehends the local company of believers as well as the Church of all places, times, and peoples. Thus an individual's profession of belief and reception of baptism bring about a union with the entire people of God, past, present, and future. The understanding that personal faith is set into the context of the Church's faith may provide a challenge to post-modern values of individualism and unlimited freedom of expression. As James Puglisi observes, "No one can proclaim himself or herself a Christian. Only the Church can do this, since it is the Church which asks the baptized not for their 'opinions about God,' but whether they enter into the Trinitarian faith that has been received from the Apostles."[12]

The local and universal dimensions of baptism remain a point of confusion and tension within and among Christian communities. Martha Moore-Keish notes, in regard to Presbyterian and Reformed churches, that they "differ over whether baptism is predominantly a ritual of welcome into a local church or incorporation into the universal church, Christ's body."[13] Other denominations claim that their baptized infants are incorporated into the universal Church but not the local congregation, since they have yet to profess membership vows personally—this despite the fact that the children will be brought up in a particular confessional context that will shape their Christian identity. An affirmation that baptism initiates a person into both the local church and the universal Church creates a sad irony: while baptism incorporates a person into the unity of the body of Christ (1 Cor 12:12), the location of baptism in a given congregation links the person with a particular confessional identity—and hence disunity with other confessions.

On the matter of the ritual shape of Christian baptism, many communities in the last fifty years have rediscovered and reclaimed from the early Church a single complex rite and have come to understand what may be broadly termed "Christian initiation" as a comprehensive process. They understand this as a process that, after a life of ongoing post-baptismal formation into Christ, ends only with physical death and the hope of resurrection—the recapitulation of the baptismal act itself. While many of the components in this complex rite are shared in different communities, they may take place at different times in the life of the individual and the congregation (e.g., first communion) or come in a slightly different sequence, yet are understood to be part of the initiatory process.

Following a period of evangelization and of formation in Christian life and teaching, a candidate comes to baptism. Baptismal rites across Christian communities generally include these elements: "the proclamation of the scriptures referring to baptism; an invocation of the Holy Spirit; a renunciation of evil; a profession of faith in Christ and the Holy Trinity; the use of water; a declaration that the persons baptized have acquired a new identity as sons and daughters of God, and as members of the Church, called to be witnesses of the Gospel."[14] Then, as BEM notes, "some churches consider that Christian initiation is not complete without the sealing of the baptized with the gift of the Holy Spirit and participation in holy communion." Regular reception of holy communion (the repeatable part of the initiation process) and active involvement in Christian fellowship enable lifelong growth into Christ. In this comprehensive process—one that can accommodate persons who can answer for themselves and those who cannot, which can include believer baptists and paedo-baptists, Roman Catholics and Orthodox and Protestants—there is offered a common ground for theological conversation.

Even so, there remain distinctions in theology and ritual practice which may or may not be obstacles to mutual recognition; these may be signs of diversity within the one body, or they may be perceived as divergences that threaten *koinonia*. Several of these differences arise in respect of the use of water. As previously observed, there are some communities, identifiably Christian in witness and service, that use no material sign, while others employ a sign other than water. Several of the African Instituted Churches, for example, substitute laying on of hands or a threefold shaking of hands for water.[15] The quantity of water and the mode of its application may still divide Christians, even though in recent years traditions that poured or sprinkled are opting for more abundant amounts to convey the cleansing, death-dealing, and life-giving qualities of water, and to that end have constructed immersion pools in new church buildings or architectural renovations.[16] The association of the Holy Spirit with water has been affirmed by recently composed epicletic prayers of thanksgiving over the font in some denominations, while others remain hesitant about overtly connecting the two. The range of views on this topic is evident in these essays and liturgical texts: compare Paul Fiddes's comment that Baptists do not "tie the work of the Spirit closely to the element of the water in itself . . . but . . . relate it to the whole action of the event and to the life of the candidates"[17] with the practice in some Orthodox churches of pouring *muron* (chrism) into the font, thereby linking (by spoken or sung text) water and the "brooding" Holy Spirit.

Different understandings of the role and nature of confirmation in relation to water baptism exist within traditions[18] and between communities, but all do see it to be connected with the overall process of making Christians. Some churches see confirmation as a completion of baptism; others regard it as an opportunity for the public profession of persons baptized in infancy; still others employ it as a presbyteral post-baptismal laying on of hands and/or anointing. In other words, is confirmation the bestowal of a divine grace, a human response to God's initiatives, or both? A point of disagreement is whether or not confirmation is to be understood as a pneumatological event, especially since for some it appears to question the activity and the longevity of the gift of the Spirit in baptism. Nevertheless, most communities agree that Christian initiation involves in some way both water and Spirit (cf. John 3:5).

Another potential sticking point in mutual recognition pertains to the minister of baptism. While few would claim that the validity of a baptism done with water in the name of the Father, Son, and Holy Spirit is jeopardized by the character of the person administering the rite, questions could be raised if the administrator lacks ordination. Some Christian communities allow for lay administration under normal (nonemergency) circumstances; these persons may serve as unordained pastors of a local congregation or may simply be lay leaders within a local church and are acting in accord with the official protocols of their community. An additional complexity for some may arise with female administrators, ordained or not.

In discussions of baptismal practices, as is the case with the essays presented here, reference is usually made to official texts, normative patterns, or common customs. Certainly such documentation facilitates dialogue within and among groups. Yet it should be remembered that these sources present an incomplete picture of the practices of a given denomination or, more broadly, of an ecclesiastical family or world communion. Official rites and interpretations may not be—and likely are not—the same as local practices and understandings. Liturgies are living events, not just words on a page. Local communities may have the legitimate option within their denominational polity to depart completely from an authorized rite; others may not stray so far but still may localize or inculturate aspects of the standard text, especially when they are encouraged to examine how elements of the ambient culture may express richly and creatively the meanings of baptism. Such variability makes ecumenical conversation and the prospect of mutual recognition more challenging. But perhaps the word of the apostle Paul about spiritual gifts is pertinent here: "Now there are varieties of gifts, but the same Spirit; and there are varieties of services, but the same Lord; and there are varieties of activities, but it is the same God who activates all of them in everyone" (1 Cor 12:4-6).

ONGOING BAPTISMAL LIFE

Baptism is a single, unrepeatable event, set in the broader framework of the process of Christian initiation. Yet, as BEM states, "baptism is related not only to momentary experience, but to life-long growth into Christ. Those baptized are called upon to reflect the glory of the Lord as they are transformed by the power of the Holy Spirit, into his likeness, with ever increasing splendour" (2 Cor. 3:18).[19] In recent years many communities have striven to be more intentional about cultivating the baptismal life among their members, young and old. The directive in the ecumenical baptismal document produced by the Massachusetts (USA) Commission on Christian Unity speaks to such intentionality: "Christian formation depends upon ongoing instruction in Scripture and doctrine, ongoing discipleship and ongoing encouragement from the members of that community. Each tradition has its own way of accomplishing this. In any situation, it must not be taken for granted."[20]

Frequent participation in the repeatable part of Christian initiation, the eucharist, is key to the cultivation of the Christian life and is itself a reminder of baptism. Communities that previously celebrated the rite of the Lord's Supper three or four times a year have, in recent decades, come to recognize the importance of regular table fellowship with Christ and with the neighbor and now observe the Supper more frequently. Churches that historically celebrated the Supper every Lord's Day have begun to connect the holy meal more explicitly with the baptismal life. These mutually shared connections of eucharist and the baptismal life may become an avenue to greater *koinonia* between the churches. However, this progress may be compromised when the unbaptized (children and adults) are intentionally and routinely invited to join in the Supper. The scriptural witness is clear that there is a qualitative distinction between Jesus' last meal with his disciples and his table fellowship with tax collectors and sinners.

The ongoing baptismal life was nurtured in the early Church by regular instruction and formation, and many communities today have striven to imitate and encourage these practices. Formation for all ages may encompass cultivation of private prayer, engagement in corporate and family worship, study of the Scriptures, participation in structured Christian education, and appropriation of spiritual and ethical dimensions of the Christian life which yield fruit in the care for neighbor and the world. Some of this work of post-baptismal formation could be done ecumenically, thus giving witness to the "royal, priestly, and prophetic" people of God in service to Church and world even when full communion still may not be possible.

Most communities agree that baptism is not repeatable. Yet the personal and corporate faith professed in baptism can be regularly renewed by the rehearsal of the baptismal (Apostles') creed and by a formal reaffirmation of baptism. The celebration of baptism in a community is an invitation for all the baptized to remember their own baptism, and special liturgies of baptismal renewal or reaffirmation of the baptismal covenant have been created in some denominations that may be scheduled for those Sundays with baptismal connections such as Easter, Pentecost, Epiphany/Theophany. Christian communities that do not yet engage in eucharistic sharing may nevertheless be able to reaffirm their baptisms together and so take a further step toward mutual recognition.

In the last part of Matthew 28:20, Jesus tells the eleven: "I am with you always, to the end of the age." The journey into the fellowship of the triune God that begins with baptism takes the community of the baptized toward the completion of all things when "at the name of Jesus every knee should bend, in heaven and on earth and under the earth, and every tongue should confess that Jesus Christ is Lord, to the glory of God the Father" (Phil 2:10-11). During this pilgrimage they grow in faith, hope, and love, and into the likeness of Christ as disciples and as children of God. This movement forward in time brings with it hope for the ecumenical task, for as the people of God seek to reconcile their differences and find unity in faith and witness, the risen and exalted Christ provides the assurance of his presence on the way.

Notes
[1] *Baptism, Eucharist and Ministry*, Faith and Order Paper No. 111 (Geneva: WCC Publications, 1982), "Baptism" section, par. 11, 4.
[2] "Ecclesiological and Ecumenical Implications of a Common Baptism: A JWG Study," in *Joint Working Group between the Roman Catholic Church and the*

World Council of Churches: Eighth Report 1999–2005: Geneva-Rome 2005 (Geneva: WCC Publications, 2005), 45–72, par. 53, 57.

[3] *Baptism, Eucharist and Ministry*, "Baptism," par. 1, 2.

[4] See below, Fiddes, "The Baptism of Believers," 395.

[5] See above, Gribben, "Baptism in the Uniting Church in Australia: The Liturgy, with Commentary and Reflections," 135.

[6] See below, Mar Thoma Syrian Church, "Order of Holy Baptism and Chrismation," 424.

[7] *Baptism, Eucharist and Ministry*, "Baptism," par. 2, 2.

[8] See *Confessing the One Faith: An Ecumenical Explication of the Apostolic Faith as it is Confessed in the Nicene-Constantinopolitan Creed (381)*, Faith and Order Paper No. 153 (Geneva: World Council of Churches, 1991), par. 241, 89–90.

[9] See above, for example, Scott, "Baptism and the Quaker Tradition," 81–88; Beach and Reid, "Christian Baptism: A Seventh-day Adventist Appraisal," 169–72; Robinson, "A Salvation Army Perspective on Baptism: Theological Understanding and Liturgical Practice," 173–80.

[10] See above, Albrecht, "Witness in the Waters: Baptism and Pentecostal Spirituality," 147–68.

[11] This theme (as well as an emphasis on baptism within the process of lifelong growth into Christ) is developed in the Faith and Order text-in-process "One Baptism: Towards Mutual Recognition." This document, which is not yet an official text of the Faith and Order Commission, is available in "Minutes of the Standing Commission on Faith and Order, 12–19 June 2007, Crans-Montana, Switzerland," Faith and Order Paper No. 206 (Geneva: Faith and Order, 2007), appendix V, 57–81, or directly from Faith and Order, WCC, 150, Rte. de Ferney, 1211 Geneva, Switzerland.

[12] See above, Puglisi, "Rite[s] of Baptism in the Catholic Church: A Theological-Pastoral Commentary," 35.

[13] See above, Moore-Keish, "Baptism in the Presbyterian and Reformed Tradition," 68.

[14] *Baptism, Eucharist and Ministry*, "Baptism," par. 20, 6.

[15] See above, Oduro, "Water Baptism in African Independent Churches: The Paradigm of Christ Holy Church International," Note 8, 190.

[16] On the quantity of water, *BEM*, "Baptism," par. 18, states: "In the celebration of baptism the symbolic dimension of water should be taken seriously and not minimalized. The act of immersion can vividly express the reality that in baptism the Christian participates in the death, burial and resurrection of Christ." The commentary on "Baptism," par. 18, 7, further develops the meaning of the baptismal waters: "As seen in some theological traditions, the use of water, with all its positive associations with life and blessing, signifies the continuity between the old and the new creation, thus revealing the significance of baptism not only for human beings but also for the whole cosmos. At the same time, the use of water represents a

purification of creation, a dying to that which is negative and destructive in the world: those who are baptized into the body of Christ are made partakers of a renewed existence."

[17] See above, Fiddes, "The Baptism of Believers," 74–75.

[18] See above, related comments in Bradshaw, "Baptism in the Anglican Communion," 55–61.

[19] *Baptism, Eucharist and Ministry*, "Baptism," par. 9, 4.

[20] See below, Massachusetts Commission on Christian Unity, "Baptism: Baptismal Practice in an Ecumenical Context," 239.

Part III

Signs of Recognition

Chapter 1

Mutual Recognition of Baptism Agreement: Germany

INTRODUCTION[1]

Thomas F. Best

For thirty years now, in some regions in Germany formal agreements establishing the mutual recognition of baptism have existed between member churches of the Evangelical Church of Germany (EKD) and dioceses of the Roman Catholic Church. No agreement, however, was in place at the national level between the EKD as a whole and the Conference of Roman Catholic bishops in Germany.

Initiatives undertaken in 2002 led to a working group being formed to develop such a national-level agreement; the group included representatives not only of the EKD and the Roman Catholic Church but also of the Orthodox Churches, the Methodist Church (also representing other Free Churches), and the Old Catholic Church (also representing the Anglican Church).

The text was signed during an ecumenical worship service held in the cathedral in Magdeburg, Germany, on April 29, 2007. This cathedral has what is thought to be the oldest baptismal font in continuous use in Germany; some one thousand years old, it predates not only the divisions at the time of the Reformation but also the division between Eastern and Western Christianity.

The text was signed by the following eleven churches:

The Ethiopian Orthodox Church in Germany

The Council of Anglican Episcopal Churches in Germany

The Armenian Apostolic Orthodox Church in Germany

The Evangelical Old-Reformed Church in Lower Saxony

The European Continental Province of the Moravian Church

The Evangelical Church in Germany

The Evangelical Methodist Church

The Catholic Diocese of the Old-Catholics in Germany

The Orthodox Church in Germany

The Roman Catholic Church

The Independent Evangelical-Lutheran Church

* * *

CHRISTIAN BAPTISM[2]

Jesus Christ is our salvation. Through him sinners have been reconciled to God (Rom 5:10), in order that we might be his sons and daughters. In enabling us to share in the mystery of Christ's death and resurrection Baptism achieves for us new birth in Jesus Christ. Whoever receives this sacrament and affirms through faith God's love becomes one with Christ and at the same time with his people at all times and in all places. As a sign of the unity of all Christians baptism binds us together with Jesus Christ who is the foundation of this unity. Despite differences in the understanding of what it is to be the Church, there exists between us a basic common understanding of Baptism.

Accordingly we recognise every baptism which has been carried out according to the commission of Jesus in the name of the Father and the Son and the Holy Spirit through the symbolic act of immersion in water or through the pouring of water over the person to be baptised. We rejoice over every person who is baptised. This mutual recognition of baptism is an expression of the bond of unity which is based on Jesus Christ (Eph 4:4-6). A baptism which has been performed in this way is unique and unrepeatable.

We confess together with the Lima Document: Our one baptism in Christ is "a call to the churches to overcome their divisions and visibly manifest their fellowship" (WCC Faith and Order convergence text *Baptism, Eucharist and Ministry*, "Baptism," par. 6).

29th April 2005

Notes

[1] Developed from a press release of April 23, 2007, issued simultaneously by the Evangelical Church in Germany (EKD) and the German [Roman Catholic] Bishops' Conference, and from a news report by Ecumenical News International (ENI) of April 25, 2007.

[2] Translation provided by the Council of Churches in Germany (ACK) and the Evangelical Church in Germany (EKD), with contributions by Colin Williams.

Chapter 2

Common Baptismal Certificate: Australia

AUSTRALIA'S COMMON BAPTISMAL CERTIFICATE:
ITS HISTORY AND SIGNIFICANCE

Robert Gribben

The idea of composing the text for a Common Baptismal Certificate first appeared in the minutes of the Australian Consultation on Liturgy (ACOL) in June 1979.[1] Theological dialogues between the Roman Catholic Church and the Anglican, Methodist, and Presbyterian Churches provided some background as to how baptism should be defined: that baptism was in the name of the Trinity, with water.[2] In terms of practice, water had to be used in a sufficient amount, so that it "flowed" on the candidate. The Churches of Christ and the Baptist Church were represented on the Consultation, so there was an immediate recognition that there would be a limit to what could be affirmed and accepted in "common." The present wording was sent out for approval by each participating church in 1983, and this was duly received.

The introduction to the list of participating churches was also carefully devised. The phrase "in this form" was intended to assure the reader that the named churches' practice of baptism was invariably with (sufficient) water, in the name of the Trinity in the precise form of words "in the name of the Father and of the Son and of the Holy Spirit."

It was understood from the beginning that each church may wish to design its own printing of the certificate, using these words, but allowing for additional information and such seals, stamps, or graphics as may be preferred. The form illustrated here is that of the Uniting Church in Australia.

Traditions that insist that the candidate must be a believer—in the sense that they are able to articulate Christian faith—were understood to introduce a further criterion for authentic baptism. This meant that their church authorities, being shown such a certificate, would not be able to accept that Christian baptism as they understood it had taken place.

This ecumenical conversation also challenged some churches to enrich their ritual practice of baptism by recovering a more generous use of water. Some also explicitly insisted that the certificate's stated baptismal formula—the name of God—not be altered or added to.[3] Such variations would break the trust between the cooperating churches.

The early list included Anglican, Lutheran, Presbyterian (that is, those who did not join the Uniting Church in Australia in 1977), Roman Catholic, Uniting, and Greek Orthodox churches. In more recent times the list has been extended through the "covenant" proposed by the National Council of Churches in Australia whereby other churches have agreed to accept each other's baptism in this form—thus the Antiochian Orthodox, Romanian Orthodox, Armenian Apostolic, and the Congregational Federation of Australia, now potentially use the certificate.

In fact the certificate is one aspect of the actual mutual acceptance between the churches. Some churches, especially Eastern, continue to use their traditional certificates (which have uses beyond baptism), but take note of the Common Certificate in the case of, for example, intermarriage. In these instances, the pastoral effect is palpable and has (in my experience) reconciled families who have been otherwise divided—and thus has taught people the real gains of the ecumenical dialogue in general, and the mutual recognition of baptism in particular.

Notes

[1] ACOL was formed to respond to the then-recent proposals of the ecumenical International Consultation on English texts (ICET), and it later became part of the international ecumenical liturgical network, the English Language Liturgical Consultation (ELLC).

[2] It should be noted that the water rite only was involved in the definition; nothing was said of the catechumenate, chrismation, confirmation, or admission to the Eucharist.

[3] So the Uniting Church: this formula is to be used "without variation or exception," Fifth Assembly, 1988, ref. 88.24.03, and *Uniting in Worship-2* (2005), #15, 65.

Certificate of Baptism

....

was baptised with water

in the name of the Father
and of the Son
and of the Holy Spirit

on ....

at ....

by .... (name)

.... (signature)

The following churches have agreed that a certificate used by them in this form is evidence of Christian Baptism:

The Anglican Church of Australia
The Catholic Church in Australia
The Antiochian Orthodox Archdiocese of Australia and New Zealand
The Armenian Apostolic Church
The Congregational Federation of Australia and New Zealand
The Greek Orthodox Archdiocese of Australia
The Lutheran Church of Australia
The Presbyterian Church of Australia
The Romanian Orthodox Church
The Uniting Church in Australia

Text © 1988, Australian Consultation on Liturgy.
Illustration © 1988, The Joint Board of Christian Education.

Certificate of Baptism

Chapter 3

"Baptismal Practice in an Ecumenical Context" Document: Massachusetts, USA

THE GENESIS OF AN ECUMENICAL TEXT

Gordon White

The Massachusetts Commission on Christian Unity felt the need for this document because, as pastors, we have become increasingly aware that at a celebration of a baptism the accompanying party often includes relatives and friends who are other than Christian—or of no faith foundation or orientation. Thus we faced the question: how can one recognize their presence and include them in the liturgical celebration?

In the process of preparing the document "Baptismal Practice in an Ecumenical Context," we discovered that the term "witness" is used in a variety of ways even within a specific tradition. Nevertheless, to "witness" is what one does when present at a baptism: whether one is Christian or not, one becomes a witness by virtue of one's presence. Thus, hopefully, this is one term which can be used at any baptism, rather than the more specific term of "sponsor."

Our process was one that had been used in preparing our Marriage Guidelines, which were published in the 1970s and revised in 1990.

A task force of five individuals (Greek Orthodox, Roman Catholic, Anglican, United Church of Christ, and Christian Unitarian) met regularly over a three-year period to discuss how we would format such a document. We arrived at an outline by defining as narrowly as possible what we saw baptism, in an ecumenical context, to be. For example, we decided that our document could not give guidelines *per se*, because each Christian tradition has so many diverse practices in the preparation of candidates, as well as in the form and intention of the rite (and sometimes there are legitimate diversities *within* specific traditions).

Therefore, in our document we refer to "Points [or Directives] of Baptismal Practice." Each "Point" defines who the participants in the rite are; the context of the Christian community in which the rite occurs; and the basic requirements of the use of water in the specific naming of the triune God (Father, Son, and Holy Spirit). As we worked each member of the task force checked with his or her own Christian tradition to ensure that what was said conformed to that tradition's teaching and practice.

As one might suspect, the use of language—especially the naming of the triune God—became one of our most-discussed issues, with the more "liberal" Reformed traditions wanting an alternative to the traditional language. To keep all members at the ecumenical table, it was agreed that the traditional language *must* be used at the moment of baptism; other language *may* be used at other places but never substituted at the moment of baptism itself.

Because this is an ecumenical document, and because we wanted to honor the superb work already done in this area by the World Council of Churches' Faith and Order Commission in its document *Baptism, Eucharist and Ministry,* we decided to quote extensively from that text to give the theological foundation for our work.

The final step in our process was having the entire document reviewed by the entire Massachusetts Commission on Christian Unity, which consists of about twenty members. Even the graphic symbol on the cover (of the original brochure) became an issue and needed to be narrowed down to two alternatives so that a choice could be made! The final text was approved at the May, 2001, meeting of the Massachusetts Commission on Christian Unity, and the text was published in June, 2001.

BAPTISM: BAPTISMAL PRACTICE IN AN ECUMENICAL CONTEXT

PREFACE

This document supports the rite of Christian Baptism celebrated and observed in an ecumenical context. It is the fruit of dialogue among the present members of the Massachusetts Commission on Christian Unity (MCCU), a body representative of Christian Orthodox, Roman Catholic, Anglican, Protestant and Reformed traditions with jurisdictions in this State and Commonwealth.

Our member churches, their congregations and pastors are increasingly dealing with the reality of witnesses to a public baptism coming from diverse Christian traditions. Moreover, friends may attend who are not Christian or any other faith.

It is the intention of this document to suggest ways in which the person being baptized can be supported in one's life-long Christian pilgrimage, specifically by those already baptized and committed, and more generally, by those who come from other faith communities.

As MCCU, we have drawn from the "Baptism" portion of *Baptism, Eucharist, and Ministry* (BEM), Faith and Order Paper No. 111, Geneva, Switzerland, World Council of Churches, 1982. We discovered this particular explication provides not only the theological base to support our endeavor, but also an easily understood common language based on that Gospel mandate that we be One for the sake of the world.

(For further definitions from BEM, note those contained in this document's Appendix.)

INTRODUCTION

First of all, BEM states the historical basis for the Institution of Baptism: "Christian baptism is rooted in the ministry of Jesus of Nazareth, in his death and in his resurrection. It is incorporation into Christ, who is the crucified and risen Lord; it is entry into the New Covenant between God and God's people" (BEM, page 2, paragraph 1). We assume this understanding and orientation.

"Baptism is a gift of God, and is administered in the name of the Father, the Son, and the Holy Spirit. Saint Matthew records that the risen Lord, when sending his disciples into the world, commanded them to baptize (Matthew 28:18-20)." (BEM, page 2, paragraph 1)

In the pursuit of appropriate language for describing the deity within the context of recent Biblical studies and interpretation, some Christian churches and congregations are experimenting with the Trinitarian formula in non-traditional terms (i.e., other than "Father, Son & Holy Spirit.") However laudable it may be to find dynamic equivalents that express God's love and God's relationship to all creation, this formula, the traditional Trinitarian formula, has been agreed upon as ecumenically acceptable and has been used historically by the churches of the East and of the West for almost 2,000 years. With respect to recognizing each tradition's baptism, it is imperative that this traditional Trinitarian formula, along with the use of water, be maintained. According to local usage, other language may be used throughout the rite, but not at the moment of baptism. At that time, other descriptive words may be added to the Trinitarian formula, but not substituted for it.

If a person expresses a desire for "re-baptism" with the implication that an earlier ritual action was in some way flawed, it would be advisable to offer an appropriate pastoral alternative to correspond to a particular personal need (e.g., a rite of entrance into the life of a particular church and congregation and/or a statement of recognition of the person's previous baptism.) What is known as Conditional Baptism is appropriate and expected when no record of baptism exists.

We recognize there are communities that baptize at any age and others who insist upon baptizing only those able to make a profession of faith themselves. Dialogue on this issue within and among churches and congregations of various traditions concerning these practices enriches the lives of all parties toward deeper discipleship.

Some churches presently represented in the Massachusetts Commission on Christian Unity encourage their congregations to be open in finding ways to celebrate this rite of initiation together with other Christian congregations in their locality and to use the following as guidelines in such preparation.

We recognize a host church may be welcoming those who come from increasingly complex populations within our churches. We offer these Points of Baptismal Practice. They are designed to support the candidate, the sponsors and all who witness this act of commitment.

POINTS OF BAPTISMAL PRACTICE

A person to be baptized is presented to a local Christian community by parent/s and sponsor/s from an inter-church or possibly inter-faith background in which all parties intend to sustain the candidate in the Christian faith.

1. Person to be baptized:

The person who is to be baptized may be an infant, a child or an adult.

If one is an adult, or an older child, there is normally a period of instruction and preparation of a duration set by the leadership of a local congregation. Both adult and child are normally accompanied by a sponsor, a godparent who testifies not only to the intent of the candidate for baptism but also to the person's knowledge and commitment within a faith community. In the case of an infant, the consent of the sponsor or godparent testifies to this intent and instruction is relegated, by necessity, to an age of maturity or understanding.

2. *Local Christian Community:*

Each candidate for baptism must be engrafted (incorporated) in a visible community of faith which has a structure to provide the new member with the necessary elements for one's life in Christ.

Christian formation depends upon ongoing instruction in Scripture and doctrine, ongoing discipleship and ongoing encouragement from the members of that community. Each tradition has its own way of accomplishing this. In any situation, it must not be taken for granted.

3. *Christian Nurture:*

It is expected that there will be a family environment which is faith nurturing and linked to a local Christian community for ongoing support.

Baptism is a corporate event in the life of an individual. Both the church community and the individual's baptismal party commit themselves to support and sustain the newly baptized. It makes no sense to baptize if such conditions are not likely to be honored. Neither baptismal party nor congregation should promise to support the candidate if such an intention is not present. The degree of preparation for sponsors or godparents by the congregation's pastoral leadership can ascertain the level of commitment.

4. *Congregation's Preparation and Reception of Candidate:*

Each Christian tradition and their congregations develop their own particular way for preparing an individual and the baptismal party for the rite of baptism.

Such preparation includes the following components:

- Instruction in the meaning and purpose of baptism.
- Instruction in the meaning of the Christian faith in relation to baptism.
- The explanation of responsibilities for the sponsors and parents if an infant is to be baptized.
- The explanation of responsibilities expected from within the congregation of the new member.

- A sharing of faith by parent(s), sponsors and candidate (if of age) according to the rite or in one's own words. In some traditions, this is a crucial part of Reception.
- A sharing of what this new life in Christ is meant to be for those baptized.
- An examination of the rite, even in the "free church" tradition.
- A plan and/or process for ongoing Christian education.

5. Baptismal Sponsors:
A sponsor or godparent holds a crucial role in the practice of baptism; each is obligated to sustain the newly baptized in the faith.

- The sponsor or godparent is to attest to the seriousness of the individual's commitment.
- The role of sponsor or godparent carries with it the obligation to advocate for the baptized.

Although it is a privileged moment of one's life, it bears the ongoing awesome responsibility to accompany the baptized on their faith journey.

Note: In some Christian traditions, the use of the term "witness" differs from that of sponsor or godparent. The "witness" does not assume the same obligations. As defined by a local Christian community, a "witness" may be a friend or other relative who may be from a tradition other than Christian. In any case, it is expected that such a "witness" would not object to the candidate's initiation into the Christian faith and would honor the commitment of the sponsors or godparents.

6. Baptism in the Christian Faith

The blessing over the water should remind those present of the history of the people of God from the beginning: giving thanks for the Spirit moving over the waters, Noah's flood, crossing the Jordan River and the birth of Jesus from the waters of the womb. In the life of Jesus himself, we will recall his own baptism, Jesus offering living water to the Samaritan woman, washing his disciples' feet and sending them forth to baptize by water and the Spirit.

The significance of water and the symbolism of immersion in baptism is central to our understanding of Christian servanthood and discipleship.

Unfortunately, in most churches in the west, we have reduced baptism by immersion to pouring water over the candidate. However, with liturgical reform, baptismal pools with running water are being introduced in renovated or new buildings, in place of stationary fonts.

In addition, a personal response is called for on the part of those who participate in a baptism. In part, their response is an expression of faith expressed in the form of a creed, statement of faith or covenant. Another part of the response to Baptism is an expectation of growth into Christian maturity exhibited in a life of worship, nurture and service.

7. Emergency Baptism

In instances of dire emergency, it is permitted for persons who are not ordained to administer the ordinance or sacrament of baptism.

Most churches recognize that there are occasions in which a baptism is to be performed when there is no time to receive baptism from an ordained person.

One such time is when a person is facing the possibility of death and expresses a desire to be baptized. In the case of a child, a parent may request.

It would be helpful to ask one's pastor what are the occasions and conditions under which emergency baptisms have been performed and recognized.

If the person so baptized should recover, it would be expected that a public ceremony would occur, at which time all the regular parts of the baptismal liturgy would be performed except for repeating the actual baptism by water and in the name of the Trinity.

An emergency baptism should be part of the patient's or recipient's official record.

When the person is dead or stillborn, baptism is not necessary. It is then appropriate to offer a prayer of blessing, naming the person as part of the Body of Christ forever, marking the forehead of the person with the sign of the cross, sheltered and received by God forever.

8. Certificate of Baptism

A record needs to be kept in the Christian Community in which the ordinance or sacrament took place.

This is especially important for the sake of those moving from one tradition to another, or for other sacramental participation for which the baptismal record may be required.

There is in use among some of our churches an "Ecumenical Certificate of Baptism" which records the event of a baptism in a particular congregation; it expresses the acceptance of that baptism by the wider church, includes references to the traditional Trinitarian words, the use of water and the signatures of the clergy authorized. Individual congregations may also issue and record a certificate of their particular Christian community.

". . . the issuance of a common Certificate of Baptism to each person baptized in any of our churches . . . would witness to this unity for which we work and pray—in response to Christ's prayer 'that they may all be one . . . so that the world may believe. . . .' (John 17:20-21, NRSV)" (Christian Conference of Connecticut, BEM Task Force of Faith and Order Commission, Report on Ministry Section, May 3, 1991, pages 4 & 5).

For safety, a copy of the record or certificate of baptism should be kept in a secure place (such as a safe-deposit box) by the individual candidate or responsible person.

In some instances, the baptismal record can attest to a person's birth.

BEM APPENDIX

In 1982 the Faith and Order Commission of the World Council of Churches meeting at Lima, Peru presented Faith and Order Paper No. 111 document to the churches.[1] Being entitled *Baptism, Eucharist and Ministry*, the booklet became known as "BEM." This document presented in a few pages major areas of convergence on these three topics. BEM represented one way for Christians to talk about baptism, Eucharist and ministry. The MCCU in preparing this paper has found it both helpful and informative.

The section of BEM having to do with Baptism is presented in five sections.

    I.   The Institution of Baptism

    II. The Meaning of Baptism

    III. Baptism and Faith

    IV. Baptismal Practice

    V. The Celebration of Baptism.

[Of these five sections]

    I. Is quoted in our opening paragraph

II. Presents Baptism as:
Participating in Christ's Death and Resurrection,
Conversion, Pardoning and Cleansing,
The Gift of the Spirit,
Incorporation into the Body of Christ,
The Sign of the Kingdom.

III. Describes the dynamics of growing in the Christian life.

IV. Lists three elements of the rite:
Believer and infant baptism,
Baptism, chrismation, and confirmation,
The mutual recognition of baptism.

V. Notes some of the liturgical units in a baptismal service including the form and elements of water and spirit.

Six of BEM's twenty-three paragraphs [on baptism] are accompanied by a short commentary. However, the real commentary on BEM came from the churches whose responses world wide filled six volumes under the title *Churches Respond to BEM*[2] and a report *Baptism, Eucharist, and Ministry 1982–1990*.[3] As a way of enjoying the fruits of the ecumenical movement you may want to see what your church said about baptism in *Baptism, Eucharist and Ministry*.

Notes

[1] *Baptism, Eucharist and Ministry*, Faith and Order Paper No. 111 (Geneva: World Council of Churches, 1982), see "Baptism," paras. 1–23, 2–7. [Ed. note]

[2] Max Thurian, ed., *Churches Respond to BEM: Official Responses to the "Baptism, Eucharist and Ministry" Text*, vols. I–VI, Faith and Order Papers Nos. 129, 132, 135, 137, 143, 144 respectively (Geneva: World Council of Churches, 1986–1988). [Ed. note]

[3] *Baptism, Eucharist & Ministry 1982–1990: Report on the Process and Responses*, Faith and Order Paper No. 149 (Geneva: WCC Publications, 1990). Additional related WCC Faith and Order texts include Max Thurian, ed., *Ecumenical Perspectives on Baptism, Eucharist and Ministry*, Faith and Order Paper No. 116 (Geneva: World Council of Churches, 1983), and Max Thurian and Geoffrey Wainwright, eds., *Baptism and Eucharist: Ecumenical Convergence in Celebration*, Faith and Order Paper. No. 117 (Geneva and Grand Rapids: World Council of Churches and Wm. B. Eerdmans, 1983), see "1. Liturgies of Baptism," 1–96. [Ed. note]

Part IV

Special Issues

Chapter 1

Baptism in a Post-"State Church" Situation: The Case of the Church of Sweden

Bo Larsson

A CONVERSATION IN MODERN SWEDEN

In Sweden today, when a couple with a newborn baby sits talking with each other about baptizing the child, the conversation might well run as follows:

> The mother: "I would like to take our daughter to the church to have her baptized!"
>
> The father: "Never. Why should we go to the church as hypocrites—I really don't believe, and you don't either!"
>
> The mother: "Yes, that's true, but I would like to do this anyway. It can't hurt."
>
> The father: "Who knows? The minister will examine us, ask if we visit the church regularly, if we say our prayers and . . ."
>
> The mother: "Don't be foolish! The baptism is not an examination of our faith. It is something else, a kind of symbol."
>
> The father: "A symbol? For what?"
>
> The mother: "Well, for affinity and kinship between God and humankind—if God exists, of course . . ."
>
> The father: "That's just where I have my doubts. Sometimes I do feel that God might exist and that there is a deeper meaning in life, but I definitely don't believe in the church and all its talk about Christ, salvation, and eternal life."
>
> The mother: "I have my doubts too about the church, but I want our daughter to be baptized. I want to give her everything good in the world, including all the things that we can't give her on our own. I

want to give her the possibility of having a connection to God, even though I'm not sure about God's existence."

The parents, as is typical in our society today, do not know very much about baptism. They don't know whether God exists or not. But even though they are critical of both church dogmas and of how the church lives and works, somewhere deep down they feel that baptism means something important. They are uncertain but still open to the possibility that there might be a God, a God who cares about a newborn baby.

After fifteen years as a parish minister in a large city of Sweden, my experience is that people often believe, but they believe in their own way. They respect baptism, but they don't have any theological knowledge (and are not interested in theological discussions) to help them understand the baptism that the church proclaims. As noted, they often dislike the church as an old and conservative institution but are still open to the possibility that God might exist. In short, I would characterize the situation with these words: God? Yes—maybe. Christ? Who is he?

Thus, although knowledge about Christian faith is decreasing, there still exists for many people an openness to something transcendent and holy, even though Sweden is seen as one of the most secularized countries in the world. Still: over 70 percent of the children are baptized and even though the percentage was higher thirty years ago (about 80 percent), baptism is still an important part of family life in our country. When all is said and done, most people still want their children to be baptized, and that fact hasn't changed much over the last decades. My impression is also that the discussions within the church about membership regulations and relations between the state and the church have not affected the way people think about baptism. Even if they don't know (and don't care) much about how the church is organized, they still believe that baptism is an important part of life.

BAPTISM IN THE CONTEXT OF THE CHURCH IN SWEDEN TODAY

Summarizing the discussions within the church during the last decades, we see a tension between, on the one hand, baptism as a gift from God, a gift of grace; and on the other, baptism as a rite of initiation that must be received in faith. These discussions culminated in 1996, when it was decided that one can no longer become a church member automatically at birth. The normal way to become a church member now is to be baptized. You can, however, still be a member of the church without being baptized; then you are seen as someone on the way to being baptized (this includes both members who were not baptized in 1996 and persons born after that year). Such persons can continue to be members without being baptized if they announce their status to the local parish, but only baptized persons can take positions of responsibility in the church.

The new regulations can be characterized as a very open compromise. They state that baptism, not birth, is the natural way to become a church member in Sweden as in other churches, but it is also possible to remain in the church without being baptized. The new relationship between the state and the church established in 2000 has not changed this, and, as noted above, my impression is that the status of the Church of Sweden today as a free church has not really affected people's way of thinking about baptism.

However, although most people still want to baptize their children, the situation could change rapidly during the coming years. One interesting question is: what will the picture look like in 2014, when people born after 1996 reach the age of eighteen? It is a very open question how they will then view their relation to the church, and one researcher maintains that the Church of Sweden will lose 10 percent of its members by that time.[1]

Another interesting question is, of course, how people view baptism and how this relates to the understanding of baptism proclaimed by the church. Obviously—as my fictional story above shows—there is a gap between the thoughts of ordinary people and the way the church wants to describe the theological significance of baptism.

An interesting dissertation on this issue was published in 1995 by Eva Reimers.[2] She examines, among other things, how parents and ministers look upon baptism, and she finds a rich variety of views. Most parents look upon infant baptism as a life cycle rite, a *rite-de-passage*, in the sense that it brings about, and confirms, a fundamental change in status— a family is established; a man and a woman become a father and a mother, and their parents become grandparents: "According to the interviews the prime function of infant baptism is the integration of the child into the history and communion of the family and into the greater community of the culture and society at large."[3]

When parents and ministers talk about the upcoming baptismal service, this view is confronted by the view of the minister. Eva Reimers finds a tension between some ministers who insist that for a baptism to be valid there must be a confession and a correct intellectual understanding of both the rite of baptism and the Christian faith, and others who believe that God acts in baptism through God's word whether people believe it or not. Reimers writes about the two aspects of the Church of Sweden: as carrier of both cult and culture, of both Christian faith and fundamental social values and practices. From this she concludes:

> Secularisation in Sweden seems to pose more possibilities than threats to the Christian faith. People are liberated from bondage to the religious institution but still partake in common religious practices. This is the case because the Church of Sweden is a carrier of both cult and culture. If the Church continues to integrate these two aspects, it will be possible for it to continue to carry and confirm the faith and trust of the people. But if the Church of Sweden separates these aspects and makes the cultic aspect into a subjective and intellectual endeavour, it will be marginalized, and the people of Sweden will not identify themselves, and their basic trust, with Christian faith.[4]

Eva Reimer's study shows that the crucial question for the Church of Sweden in the future concerns both its self-understanding and its ability to communicate this understanding to its members. The same point is made by Professor Anders Bäckström. In examining the relation between the church and its members, he has identified four major expectations: members expect the church to take care of basic human needs (and not only in crises but also in ordinary life); to deliver service such as baptisms, weddings, and funerals; to contribute to building a coherent culture and creating cultural affinity; and to promote feelings of security as symbolized by the church buildings and the services held there.

The challenge for the church, according to Anders Bäckström, lies in its ability to relate to peoples' expectations in a way that is both true to the church's own self-understanding and capable of being understood. People now look upon themselves as consumers, and the church has to meet this fact in a sensitive way so that people are willing to be more engaged and to take more responsibility without being harassed or pushed into it.

THEOLOGICAL REFLECTIONS ON BAPTISM WITHIN THE CHURCH AND THE CULTURE

The famous Swedish poet Tomas Tranströmer writes in one of his poems: "Every abstract view of the world is as impossible as the blueprint of a storm." His words remind us of the difficulty of analyzing and understanding a contemporary situation such as ours. But as a starting point for understanding our ongoing theological reflection, I would like to take another comment by Eva Reimers:

> The Church of Sweden regards the high rate of infant baptism not only as a positive sign of people's confidence in the Church but also as a problem. There are apprehensions that people baptise for reasons that are not compatible with the understanding of baptism that the Church wants to proclaim, and that the Church is simply being utilized to add lustre to a special occasion in the history of the family. In order to safeguard against profanation of the ritual of infant baptism, the Church of Sweden has elaborated the ritual so as to eliminate any misconceptions that the rite is a name-giving ceremony. In the ritual that was endorsed [in] 1986, a question was incorporated that asks whether or not the parents are willing to take on the responsibility of bringing up their child in the fellowship of the Church. This question, the baptismal question, is also used as one basic reason for conducting baptismal conversations in preparation for the ceremony. In these conversations, the priest is supposed to explain the fundamental theological content as well as practical issues regarding infant baptism.[5]

The "baptismal question" was itself very much questioned when it was formulated; the critical question was whether it demanded too much from the parents. The discussions led to a decision that the minister was not obliged to use it, but my impression today is that ministers use the question and do so without problems. The main question does not seem to be whether baptism is a rite of initiation that must be received in faith, or a gift of grace by God—it is obviously both a gift from God and a sacrament that needs interpretation and some kind of response from the individual. But what *kind* of response?

Here is the most important contemporary challenge to the church: to reflect upon, and communicate, a way of describing baptism as something important for how ordinary people interpret their daily lives. Baptism proclaims the reality of God in our lives—not a judgmental God, but the God who has created every human being in God's image: not only "religious" people, not only baptized people, but everyone, both those who long for God and those who despise God. From the first moment of our lives there is a relation to God, and baptism both lifts that connection up and deepens it. We affirm that there is an affinity between every human being and God, and baptism is, first of all, a sign of that affinity. But it is also more than that, since it gives us a share in the life, death, and resurrection of Christ. Baptism interprets our lives in the light of the Christ-event, and perhaps the most important thing is to provide opportunities for people to sit together and talk about what that means, to listen to the interpretations of others and to share one's own views.

Recently the Swedish people were characterized as "belonging without believing." One reason for this statement was the fact that you could be a church member simply by virtue of your birth; another reason was that only 6–8 percent of the Swedish people regularly attended worship services. Today we might be on our way to a new situation of "believing without belonging." Members are slowly leaving the church, and between 1995 and 2000 the church lost 240,000 members. A realistic prognosis is that people will continue to leave the church; but there is also another trend. A recent survey shows that even though people are leaving, there is an increasing confidence in the church: 96 percent of the Swedish people know about the church and 53 percent of those believe that the church is important or very important. One year ago this figure was 45 percent, which means that confidence in the church is increasing.

What this really means and what it will lead to is an open question, but obviously the church has many things to reflect upon. One of these is the need to work on the issue of communication and how to offer possibilities for people to talk about life and faith—and their doubts—in as many contexts as possible. Theology seems more and more to be a question of communication than a question of what to prescribe or require, and the great challenge for the Church of Sweden is to be able to talk about baptism as an essential part of life, one that people don't want to be without.

Conversations about baptism are, of course, crucial for the future. One of the most important things for the Church of Sweden is to be even more open, to give opportunities for people to formulate their own faith understanding and view of life—and then to connect their thoughts to baptism as both cult and culture.

Notes

[1] Ingegerd Sjölin, in a recently published article in *Religion och Sociologi* (Religion and Sociology) (Göteborg: Religio Böcker, 2002).

[2] Eva Reimers, *Dopet som kult och kultur (Infant baptism as cult and culture: Images of infant baptism in baptismal conversations and interviews)* (Stockholm: Verbum, 1995). Translation of quotations from this source by Bo Larsson.

[3] Ibid., 296.

[4] Ibid., 302.

[5] Ibid., 292.

Chapter 2

Interrogating Christian Practices: Popular Religiosity across the Ocean

J. Jayakiran Sebastian

> The destiny of human life is linked to the destiny of natural life. Once we reach our "ocean," who can say that we are not the essence or life of the ocean? More simply: we participate in the destiny of the water of the entire universe. Man, the World and the Divine share a common destiny and they are linked by a fundamental *religio*, the constitutive *dharma* of the universe.[1]

INTRODUCTION: THE INDIAN MEDITERRANEAN?

Baptismal water, the "water of the entire universe," is in a constant state of flux and movement, movement across time, peoples, cultures and situations. In this paper I would like to examine two differing contexts: Dalit Christian communities in India and, in a limited manner, African Instituted Churches, especially in regard to certain practices and patterns of response, and to ask whether these can help us in understanding baptismal issues and themes.

The distinguished French historian, Fernand Braudel, concludes his epic history of the Mediterranean with the observation:

> The Christian religion did not become the state religion without coming to some arrangement with the politics, society and even the civilization of Rome. The civilization of the Roman Mediterranean was taken over by the young forces of Christianity. As a result, it had to accept many compromises, fundamental and structural ones. And it is in this shape, and carrying this mixed message, that the civilization of antiquity has come down to us.[2] The intricate interrelationship between the Mediterranean versions of Christianity intertwined with the reality of Rome, especially after the "conversion" of the Roman emperor Constantine at the beginning of the fourth century, has been extensively documented and analysed.[3]

When it comes to India, one can say—recognizing the risk of overgeneralization—that Christianity came to India in three ways: the ancient Malankara form of "Syrian" Christianity, the later Catholic coastal missions, and the still later Protestant mission enterprise, which started three hundred years ago in 1706.[4] Christianity in India has evolved in many diverse ways and forms, and today, under the four main Christian "families" (Orthodox, Catholic, Protestant, and Pentecostal), we have a variety and range of Christian practices and beliefs uneasily coexisting and interacting under a rather tattered umbrella. Even within each of these families, one has the impression that labels sometimes are used as a matter of convenience rather than as an accurate description of the common features that link their members.

Leaving aside the consideration of "Syrian" Orthodox Christianity, it is true that the Catholic coastal missions and the Protestant missionary movements were directly and indirectly reflecting Mediterranean forms of Christianity. However, when these forms of Christianity came to interface with local religious customs and practices, there were several ways—some known to the missionaries and others quite unknown—in which the missionary versions of Christianity were appropriated, subverted, utilized, adapted, and transformed. This reality has raised a host of questions regarding religion, culture, mission, and conversion.[5]

It is the question of reception and subversion which is of interest here, and for this it is instructive to turn from the Mediterranean to the Indian Ocean, and to look at how the Dalit Christians in India, and the adherents of the thousands of African Instituted Churches, have transformed received forms of Christianity through cultural negotiations, transactions, and creative subversive interactions. This effort to reclaim indigenous Christian expressions is all the more pressing, given the increasing impact of Western materialism (or their Western-oriented Indian clones) on fundamentalist television programs and channels such as the "GOD channel." These yell out the gospel of material prosperity and immediate healing, and bring mega-events starring "evangelists" like Benny Hinn and Reinhold Bonnke; they are organized on the lines of great rock concerts in major Indian and African cities, with the attendant paraphernalia of high-tech communication equipment, business opportunities for "born-again caterers," and fawning politicians.

POPULAR DALIT RELIGION, THE BIBLE, AND QUESTIONS REGARDING BAPTISM

Dalit studies are now firmly established as an indispensable aspect of all attempts to understand and analyze the complexities of Indian society. For far too long, there seemed to be an almost embarrassed silence—or rather a conspiracy of silence?—when it came to fleshing out the harsh experiences of Dalit communities in independent India. The resurgence of Dalit pride and the increasing recognition of the vital role played by Dalit communities in the political landscape of India have resulted in the flourishing of studies dealing with the variety and range of the Dalit experience.[6]

Given the numbers, it is surprising that Indian Christian theology has also ignored Dalit hopes, fears, aspirations, and modes of theologizing for so long. The emergence of Dalit theology, and the growing literature on various phenomenological aspects of the Christian Dalit experience, is a welcome corrective to traditional modes of discourse.[7]

Homi Bhabha, in his programmatic essay "Signs Taken for Wonders," has offered us a very interesting reading of a particular incident regarding missionaries, Indian Christians, and the Bible. In this he commented that when "the words of the master become the site of hybridity—the warlike, subaltern sign of the native—then we may not only read between the lines but even seek to change the often coercive reality that they so lucidly contain." He concluded by quoting a "much-tried missionary" who wonders angrily why the "natives" would want to receive a Bible and exclaims that it may be for curiosity value, to sell for a pittance, as an object for barter, or to "use it for waste paper."[8] Such questions and attitudes recur with telling familiarity two hundred years later.

I would like to offer four examples from my pastoral ministry, the first three coming from my time as a pastor in the rural, predominantly Dalit, Gauribidanur congregation of the Karnataka Central Diocese of the Church of South India. During my many pastoral visits, I rarely took my own Bible with me; after the usual preliminaries I asked for their Bible so that I could read a passage before prayer. In one case, the family proudly pulled out a steel trunk which was under the rolled-up mattresses in the small house, took out several layers of folded clothing, took out a clean white towel in which a pristine Bible, with many of its pages uncut, lay wrapped; in another, the family pointed to the open Bible which had been placed on a small shelf on the wall, decorated with colored flashing lights, but when I gingerly took it off the shelf, I discovered not only a thick layer of dust but also the remains of a number of flying insects.

In a third case, I was given the Bible from among a pile of magazines, only to discover on opening it that it was serving as a store for the cutout pictures of film actors and actresses that were preserved among its pages. The fourth example comes from the time when I was a pastor in the urban Hudson Memorial Kannada congregation in Bangalore, where (among many other things) I had to bless unusual objects, including in this case a machine that converted old paper into pulp and then into egg trays. The owner told me that he employed a number of "rag pickers" to bring him paper of suitable quality for this purpose and discovered that there were a large number of New Testaments and Bibles (most probably those distributed gratis by organizations like the Gideons) in the material which had been brought in. He told me that at first he had tried to "rescue" the Bibles from the pile, but when he realized how many there were, he had just let them continue their journey of reincarnation into egg trays.

The question of the fetishization of objects is an old issue in religious studies, and the interaction between religious objects precious to one tradition in the encounter and acceptance of another is also an important area of research.[9] Does fetishization describe this reverence to the object rather than the Word which it preserves? What is intriguing in these examples is the complex interlinkage between the reality of commitment to a faith-praxis and the instrumentalization of the orienting symbols of that faith. The Bible, in these cases, has been seen as something so precious that it needs to be carefully stored away and, although out of sight, is unlikely to be out of mind. It is something to be illuminated externally; something adding value and providing security to that which offers enrichment to one's life; something whose worth would not be erased even when the "black marks on white paper" were no longer legible.

We need to investigate the relationship between the way in which the local has interacted with what was thought to be a given. Clarke, in his analysis of the religion of the Paraiyar community where he looks at the use of the drum in countering a word-centered religion, talks about subaltern religion making use of:

> . . . all and sundry in its religious construction. Bits and pieces are collected from various sources through numerous ways: some religious resources are discarded as irrelevant, many others are useful pieces annexed conveniently from the dominant communities' framework, while some are discovered from years of their own collective life experience.[10]

In recent years the Mylapore Institute for Indigenous Studies, Chennai, India, has sought to identify, explore, and research the growth of indigenous forms of Christianity in India. This work also involves analyzing the phenomenon of "unbaptized believers,"[11] and one of the most important pieces of research on this area is the work by Herbert E. Hoefer, originally published in 1991 and recently reprinted.[12] Some of the questions raised in relation to baptism when one examines Dalit religious practices, the growth of indigenous Christ-oriented communities, and attitudes to the Bible include questions about how baptism is understood as a physical phenomenon: Is the water seen as something that physically functions to achieve something during the baptismal sacrament? Is water understood metaphorically? How is the water used during baptism seen in relation to water in daily life, especially in a context where Dalit communities are marked by boundaries of purity and pollution, and denied access to common wells and sources of water by the so-called "upper caste"?

If, as Bradshaw notes, "in our fallenness, brokenness and confusion there is no place for rejection and lack of care for those intending discipleship . . . the baptismal imperative challenges all cold judgmentalism,"[13] then what about those who have been judged and denied access to possibilities of a fuller life through no fault of their own? If it is a fact that many of the "unbaptized believers" come from a Dalit background, how can there be growth and nurture of such persons in a context in which they decide to remain in their present position and not openly identify with a Christian church?[14]

One must also note that the role of the Bible and Christian practices have come under increasing scrutiny in recent years, especially by those who have benefited from the challenges set forth by postcolonial thinking. R. S. Sugirtharajah, in a series of writings,[15] has challenged the way in which the Bible was used to create and foster "colonizing monotheistic tendencies." He has reminded us of the need to recollect "the many-layered polytheistic context out of which it emerged."[16] For Sugirtharajah such recollecting is not a passive activity but something that has to be done with a sense of urgency, given the explosive way in which adherents of different religious strands deal with each other. Focusing on the exponentially burgeoning strategies being used to market the Bible to all kinds of interest groups in the West, and the transformation of the Bible into a kind of "indulgence," he wryly notes:

> The Bible is introduced into various sub-cultures and a niche carved out for it. The Bible, which was hailed as a universal word, transferable to all cultures irrespective of time and space without contaminating the purity of its message, is now being marketed tarnished with traces

of the very cultures it once abhorred. Now it is presented as an easily consumable commercial object—a postmodern fate for an artifact which emerged as a shining example of modernity.[17]

Although his primary examples are drawn from marketing strategies and the identification of niche groups in the West, issues and themes emerge that are of interest to those who want to learn from religious practices of Dalit communities and the rituals of the African Instituted Churches to which we now turn.

AFRICAN INSTITUTED CHURCHES AND CHRISTIAN PRACTICES

Phillip Mazambara has opened up for me this perspective on the acceptance and transformation of an alien, external, religious tradition by Africans in Africa.[18] Although the older research tends to characterize these churches as African "independent" churches, the current terminology of "instituted" is more apt. One observer points out that these churches, "being largely but not exclusively nonliterate, and largely the 'poor' of society . . . are not so beholden to the methods of the North and West, especially to the Enlightenment style of reflecting on faith."[19] One documented example is that of the Musama Disco Christo Church of Ghana. Although Ghana borders the North Atlantic Ocean, and even though it is methodologically improper to "extrapolate from one church to a general statement,"[20] nevertheless certain significant features do emerge.

This church was founded in 1922 by a Methodist teacher and catechist who had been expelled from the parent church for prioritizing visions and prophecies.[21] "This new movement subsequently embarked on a vigorous policy of blending its Christian heritage with elements of Akan culture." Among these was the assumption by the founder of the role of "paramount chieftaincy," with all the paraphernalia, including a royal title, "court elders, drummers, linguists and other functionaries/regalia befitting an important Akan chief."[22]

What is also of interest is the role of the prophet-priest, who blends practices in the traditional Akan religion with the transcreation of priestly functions recorded in the Hebrew Scriptures. In addition this church and the vast majority of the African Instituted Churches have been "pace setters in regard to the question of women's involvement in the official priestly mediating ministry, a role which was totally curtailed in 'mainline' churches such as the Anglican and the Roman

Catholic church."²³ Another major work on a women's cult in South Togo has indicated how women, functioning as media of the spirit, link the world of the ancestors with the present in the "religion of everyday life."²⁴ What is striking is that there is continuity and transformation at two levels, the level of the "real and imagined" African heritage, and also at the level of the inherited missionary religion.

A parallel example can be found in terms of how health and healing has been understood. The Urhobo people in Nigeria understand health as encompassing "more than physical fitness, but wholeness experienced in the rapport with nature, in psychic and social integration in the world of cosmic forces and the level of human mortality."²⁵ Given this reality, and the fact that the rituals that accompanied the act of healing were not in consonance with the missionaries' stress on the Western germ theory of medicine, it is hardly surprising that the missionaries did all they could to discourage these traditional practices, which included incantations, sacrifices, and the use of ritual words and invocatory acts.²⁶

When it comes to healing, it is not surprising that down the ages people have tried to come to terms with the reality of suffering either by dealing with it in the existential present, or by warding it off by using magical methods, including the use of charms and amulets. Some of these involve the articulation of a combination of texts claimed to have ritualistic power, texts drawing from inherited religious traditions. These are combined with the use of mysterious, esoteric words, phrases, images, pictures, and objects claimed to unseal the door that stands at the interface between our worldly reality and otherworldly possibilities. All these factors have a bearing on how baptism has been understood over the centuries. For example, a protective "spell" from the world of Egyptian Christianity from the eighth or ninth century invokes not only the Holy Spirit, the 24 elders, the 144,000 of the book of Revelation, the young men of the book of Daniel, the confessors and the 12 apostles, but also other "powerful utterances." This reads in part:

> At the moment that N. child of N. will be anointed with
> this oil, you must take away from him all sickness and all
> illness and all magic and all potions and all mishaps and
> all pains and all male spirits and all female spirits,
> whether it has come from the east or the west, whether
> they have come from the four sides of the earth or the air.

> Let them be dispelled through the power of Eloei
> Elomas Sabaoth Abaktani Abanael Naflo AKRAMA'CHAMARI
> and the power of the one who has come down upon the altar
> on the 29th of Choiak [the Coptic date of Christmas], and the
> one who has come down upon the waters of the Jordan as a dove.
> He must come upon N. to protect him from all evil.
> Rule over N. who seals it.
> Apa Anoup has sealed this oil.
> Michael is the one who intercedes.
> Jesus Christ is the one who gives healing to N.,
> that he may be renewed in his whole body,
> like the tree of life that is in the middle of paradise,
> all the days of his life,
> yea, yea, at once, at once![27]

This is but one example from a long history of the fusing of traditional religious symbolism with words claimed to be bearers of mysterious but effective "power" and with figurative actions—all put at the service of either preventing or overcoming suffering.[28] It is perhaps not too farfetched to see the developments in the African Instituted Churches as a powerful reminder of the many layers that function in understanding what religion in general, and baptism in particular, means. Commenting on Christianity in Africa, Kwame Bediako notes that by "becoming a non-Western religion, Christianity has become a true world faith, and in the African context, the depth of the interpenetration between Christianity and Africa's primal religions points to the significance of the Christian factor."[29] But what is the *nature* of this Christian factor?

CONCLUSION: BAPTISMAL PRACTICES QUESTION THE UNASSAILABLE CORE

Slavoj Žižek writes:

> Insofar as the ultimate Other is God Himself, I should risk the claim that *it is the epochal achievement of Christianity to reduce its Otherness to Sameness*: God Himself is Man, "one of us." . . . The ultimate horizon of Christianity is thus not respect for the neighbor, for the abyss of its impenetrable Otherness; it is possible to go beyond—not of course, to penetrate the Other directly, to experience the Other as it is "in itself," but to become aware that there is no mystery, no hidden true content, behind the mask (deceptive surface) of the Other."[30]

However, both in the case of Dalit Christians and in the case of African Instituted Churches, we wonder whether the attempt to reduce "Otherness to Sameness" has really succeeded. In both cases, one thing that is being problematized is what Appiah identified as being at the core of Christian faith and practice—doctrines. Thus Appiah writes:

> The extraordinary importance attached to doctrine in the Christian churches is not a modern phenomenon; growing up between Roman and Hellenistic paganism, on the one side, and Judaism, on the other, and divided bitterly and regularly from the very beginning on topics that may seem to us wonderfully abstruse, the history of the church is, to a great extent, the history of doctrines. But, though doctrine is indeed central to Christianity in this way, it is important to remember what this means. "Doctrine" does not mean, precisely, belief . . . rather it means the verbal formulae that express belief. And this has proved something of an embarrassment for many Christians in the world since the scientific revolution.[31]

In many non-Western spaces, the unassailable doctrines of Christianity have been pushed to the limits and reformulated into the religion of everyday life. This is especially the case in populist forms of Christianity, including their baptismal practices. Probing the practices of Indian Ocean communities of Dalit Christians and those belonging to the African Instituted Churches will shatter the myth that all faith communities need doctrines to survive. I cannot imagine what methodological tools are needed for a study of these popular forms of belief, forms that have successfully transformed existing definitions of Christianity and pushed them beyond Christianity (as, for example, in the attempts to construct Dalit cosmology[32]). I can, however, suggest that a comparative study will need to look for new analytical frames for the study of these non-Western religious practices and spaces informed by Christianity. They are no doubt shaped by ingrained Christian doctrines; but, in the Indian Ocean context, they have transformed the religion of the Roman Mediterranean in ways beyond recognition.[33]

Notes
[1] Raimon Panikkar, "The Drop of Water: An Intercultural Metaphor," in *Samarasya: Studies in Indian Arts, Philosophy, and Interreligious Dialogue – in Honour*

of Bettina Bäumer, eds. Sadananda Das and Ernst Fürlinger (New Delhi: D. K. Printworld (P) Ltd., 2005), 585.

² Fernand Braudel, *Memory and the Mediterranean* (New York: Knopf, 2001), 314.

³ From the extensive literature see Stephen Benko, *Pagan Rome and the Early Christians* (Bloomington: Indiana University Press, 1984); Jaroslav Pelikan, *The Excellent Empire: The Fall of Rome and the Triumph of the Church* (San Francisco: Harper and Row, 1987); Paul Keresztes, *Imperial Rome and the Christians: Vol. I: From Herod the Great to about 200 A.D.; Vol. II: From the Severi to Constantine the Great* (Lanham: University Press of America, 1989); G. W. Bowersock, *Martyrdom and Rome* (Cambridge: Cambridge University Press, 1995); T. G. Elliott, *The Christianity of Constantine the Great* (Scranton, PA: University of Scranton Press, 1996); Allen Brent, *The Imperial Cult and the Development of Church Order: Concepts and Images of Authority in Paganism and Early Christianity before the Age of Cyprian* (Leiden: Brill, 1999); Aldo Schiavone, *The End of the Past: Ancient Rome and the Modern West* (Cambridge, MA: Harvard University Press, 2000); Elizabeth DePalma Digeser, *The Making of a Christian Empire: Lactantius and Rome* (Ithaca, NY: Cornell University Press, 2000); H. A. Drake, *Constantine and the Bishops: The Politics of Intolerance* (Baltimore, MD: Johns Hopkins University Press, 2000).

⁴ See A. Mathias Mundadan, *History of Christianity in India, Vol. I: From the Beginning up to the Middle of the Sixteenth Century* (Bangalore: Theological Publications in India, 1984); Joseph Thekkedath, *History of Christianity in India, Vol. II: From the Middle of the Sixteenth Century to the End of the Seventeenth Century* (Bangalore: Theological Publications in India, 1982); Brijraj Singh, *The First Protestant Missionary to India: Bartholomaeus Ziegenbalg (1683–1719)* (Delhi: Oxford University Press, 1999); D. Dennis Hudson, *Protestant Origins in India: Tamil Evangelical Christians, 1706–1835*, Studies in the History of Christian Missions (Grand Rapids, MI, and Richmond, Surrey, UK: Wm. B. Eerdmans Publishing Co. and Curzon Press Ltd., 2000).

⁵ Including those in S. N. Balagangadhara, *"The Heathen in His Blindness . . .": Asia, the West and the Dynamic of Religion* (Leiden: E. J. Brill, 1994).

⁶ See, for example, H. Kotani, ed., *Caste System, Untouchability and the Depressed*, Japanese Studies on South Asia No. 1 (New Delhi: Manohar, 1997), S. M. Michael, ed., *Dalits in Modern India: Vision and Values* (New Delhi: Vistaar Publications, 1999).

⁷ See Arvind P. Nirmal, "Towards a Christian Dalit Theology," in *Frontiers in Asian Christian Theology: Emerging Trends*, ed. R. S. Sugirtharajah (Maryknoll, NY: Orbis, 1994), 27–40; Sathianathan Clarke, *Dalits and Christianity: Subaltern Religion and Liberation Theology in India* (Delhi: Oxford University Press, 1998); John C. B. Webster, *Religion and Dalit Liberation: An Examination of Perspectives*, 2nd ed. (New Delhi: Manohar, 2002); Complete issue of *Religion and Society* 49, nos. 2 and 3 (June and September 2004), on the theme: "Dalit Concerns"; and the fine collection of essays in James Massey and Samson Prabhakar, eds., *Frontiers in Dalit Hermeneutics* (Bangalore and Delhi: BTESSC/SATHRI and CDSS, 2005).

[8] Homi K. Bhabah, "Signs taken for wonders: Questions of ambivalence and authority under a tree outside Delhi, May 1817," in *The Location of Culture* (London: Routledge, 1994), 121–22.

[9] On images and art see, for example, Thomas F. Mathews, *The Clash of Gods: A Reinterpretation of Early Christian Art* (Princeton, NJ: Princeton University Press, 1993).

[10] Clarke, *Dalits and Christianity*, 127–28.

[11] Among the important publications stemming from this Institute are: Roger E. Hedlund, ed., *Christianity Is Indian: The Emergence of an Indigenous Community* (Mylapore and Delhi: MIIS and ISPCK, 2000); O. L. Snaitang, ed., *Churches of Indigenous Origins in North East India* (Mylapore and Delhi: MIIS and ISPCK, 2000); Roger E. Hedlund, *Quest for Identity: India's Churches of Indigenous Origins, The "Little Tradition" in Indian Christianity* (Mylapore and Delhi: MIIS and ISPCK, 2000).

[12] Herbert E. Hoefer, *Churchless Christianity* (Pasadena, CA: William Carey Library, 2001).

[13] Timothy Bradshaw, "Baptism and Inclusivity in the Church," in *Baptism, the New Testament and the Church: Historical and Contemporary Studies in Honour of R. E. O. White*, eds. Stanley E. Porter and Anthony R. Cross, Journal for the Study of the New Testament Supplement Series 171 (Sheffield: Sheffield Academic Press, 1999): 466.

[14] Brian Heymes, in "The Moral Miracle of Faith," talks about baptism declaring "a deep relationship in God through Christ" that should lead to the crucial ecclesial dimension of "the more careful nurture of those who are baptized." In Stanley E. Porter and Anthony R. Cross, eds., *Dimensions of Baptism: Biblical and Theological Studies*, Journal for the Study of the New Testament Supplement Series 234 (Sheffield: Sheffield Academic Press, 2002): 332.

[15] Including R. S. Sugirtharajah, *The Bible and the Third World: Precolonial, Colonial and Postcolonial Encounters* (Cambridge: Cambridge University Press, 2001).

[16] R. S. Sugirtharajah, "Scripture, Scholarship, Empire: Putting the Discipline in Its Place," *The Expository Times*, 117, no. 1 (October 2005): 3.

[17] Ibid., 11. Sections of this article are also found in the "Afterword" of his *The Bible and Empire: Postcolonial Explorations* (Cambridge: Cambridge University Press, 2005).

[18] His doctoral thesis is now published as *The Self Understanding of African Instituted Churches: A Study Based on the Church of Apostles Founded by John of Marange in Zimbabwe*, Perspektiven der Weltmission, Band 29 (Aachen: Verlaghaus Mainz GmbH, Aachen, 1999).

[19] John Pobee, "Baptismal Recognition and African Instituted Churches," in *Baptism and the Unity of the Church*, eds. Michael Root and Risto Saarinen (Grand Rapids, MI/Cambridge, UK: Wm. B. Eerdmans Publishing Co.; Geneva: WCC Publications, 1998), 177.

[20] Ibid.

[21] John D. K. Ekem, "Priestly Meditation [sic] in a Ghanian Setting: The Case of the Musama Disco Christo Church," in *Neuere religiöse Bewegungen in internationaler Perspektive: Festschrift für Erhard Kamphausen*, eds. Andreas Heuser and Wolfram Weiße (Aachen: Verlaghaus Mainz GmbH, Aachen, 2005), 209–15. Pobee also offers a "snapshot" of this church in the article quoted above, 172–75. "The church name means 'The Army (musama) of the Cross (disco) of Christ,' and its battle is against all idols and ungodliness." See www.geocities.com/missionalia/ghanacon.htm, viewed on December 7, 2005.

[22] Ekem, "Priestly Meditation [sic] in a Ghanian Setting," 210.

[23] Ibid., 213–14.

[24] Amélé Ekué, *"Und sie denken, du bist eine mamissi . . .": Geistinhabitation in einem Frauenkult und ihre Adaptation im Kontext afrikanischer Christen in Süd-Togo*, Hamburger Theologische Studien, Band 9 (Hamburg: LIT Verlag, 1996).

[25] J. O. Ubrurhe, "African Concept of Health," in *Bangalore Theological Forum* 37, no. 1 (June 2005): 174.

[26] See J. O. Ubrurhe, "Missionaries' Attitude Towards African Traditional Medicine," in *Bangalore Theological Forum* 36, no. 2 (December 2004): 117–30.

[27] "Ritual spell to heal and protect (a woman and her children?)," in *Ancient Christian Magic: Coptic Texts of Ritual Power*, eds. Marvin W. Meyer and Richard Smith (Princeton, NJ: Princeton University Press, 1999), 117–19.

[28] See Daniel Ogden, *Magic, Witchcraft, and Ghosts in the Greek and Roman Worlds: A Sourcebook* (Oxford: Oxford University Press, 2002), for a vast variety and range of incantations and texts from the ancient Mediterranean world in which certain early forms of Christianity evolved.

[29] Kwame Bediako, *Christianity in Africa: The Renewal of a Non-Western Religion* (Edinburgh: Edinburgh University Press, 1995), 265.

[30] Slavoj Žižek, *The Puppet and the Dwarf: The Perverse Core of Christianity* (Cambridge, MA: MIT Press, 2003), 138. In his *On Belief* (London: Routledge, 2001), 110, he asks: "Is it not that ALL religion, ALL experience of the sacred, involves—or, rather, simply IS—an 'unplugging' from the daily routine? Is this 'unplugging' not simply the name for the basic ECSTATIC experience of entering the domain in which everyday rules are suspended, the domain of the sacred TRANSGRESSION?"

[31] Kwame Anthony Appiah, *In My Father's House: Africa in the Philosophy of Culture* (New York: Oxford University Press, 1992), 114.

[32] See M. C. Raj, *Dalitology: The Book of the Dalit People* (Tumkur: Ambedkar Resource Centre, 2001), and Jyothi and M. C. Raj, *Cosmosity: Cultural Discourse of the Unbroken People* (Tumkur: Ambedkar Resource Centre, 2005).

[33] Several ideas in this article were originally developed at a presentation made at an International Workshop in Bangalore on "Exploring the Indian Ocean as a Cultural Terrain," organized by the Centre for the Study of Culture and Society, Bangalore, with the University of Witwatersrand, Johannesburg, South Africa, December 9–10, 2005.

Part V

Baptismal Services

Chapter 1

Rite of Christian Initiation (Eastern Orthodox)*

Order That Takes Place before Holy Baptism

Prayer for making a catechumen

The Priest unties the girdle of the one who is about to be enlightened and divests them of outer clothing and shoes. He stands them facing East, wearing only a tunic, unbelted, bareheaded and unshod, with the hands down. He breathes on their face three times, signs the forehead and breast three times and places his hand on their head as he says the following Prayer:

In your name, Lord God of truth, and that of your Only-Begotten Son and your Holy Spirit, I place my hand on the head of your servant N., who has been counted worthy to take refuge in your holy Name and to be guarded under the shelter of your wings. Remove from him/her that ancient error and fill him/her with faith in you, and hope and love, so that he/she may know that you alone are God, true God, and your Only-Begotten Son, our Lord Jesus Christ, and your Holy Spirit. Grant that he/she may walk in your commandments and preserve those things that are pleasing to you, for if someone does them, they will live by them. Inscribe him/her in your book of life and unite him/her to the flock of your inheritance. Let your holy Name and that of your beloved Son, our Lord Jesus Christ and of your life-giving Spirit, be glorified in him/her. Let your eyes remain ever fixed in mercy on him/her, and your ears to hear the voice of his/her supplication. Make him/her glad in the works of his/her hands and in all his/her race, that he/she may confess you, worshipping and glorifying your great and most high Name, and may praise you throughout all the days of his/her life. For every power of heaven sings your praise, and yours is the glory, of the Father, the Son and the Holy Spirit, now and for ever, and to the ages of ages. Amen.

---

*Used in Eastern Orthodox Churches. Variations may be found between Greek, Russian, and other practices; these are mostly minor in character and, in any case, do not affect the fundamental theological understanding of baptism.

First exorcism

Deacon: Let us pray to the Lord.

People: **Lord, have mercy.**

Priest: **The Lord rebukes you, O Devil, the Lord who came into the world and dwelt among mortals so that he might destroy your tyranny and deliver humanity; the Lord who on the Tree crushed the hostile powers, when the sun was darkened, the earth shaken, the graves opened and the bodies of Saints arose; the Lord who by death abolished death and destroyed the one who had the power of death, that is you, the Devil. I adjure you by God, who revealed the tree of life and set in place the Cherubim and the flaming sword which turned this way and that to guard it: Be rebuked and withdraw! I adjure you by the One who walked on the surface of the sea as on dry land and rebuked the tempest of the winds, the One whose gaze dries up the deeps and whose curse melts mountains. For it is he who now commands you, through us: Be afraid, come out, withdraw from this creature and return no more. Do not hide in him/her, nor encounter him/her, nor influence him/her either by night or day, early or at noon. But go back to your own Tartarus until the great day of the judgement that has been prepared. Be afraid of God, who is seated upon the Cherubim and looks upon the deeps; before whom Angels, Archangels, Thrones, Dominions, Principalities, Authorities, Powers, the many-eyed Cherubim and the six-winged Seraphim tremble; before whom heaven and earth, the sea and all that is in them tremble. Come out, and withdraw from the sealed and newly-enlisted soldier of Christ our God. For it is by him that I adjure you, the One who walks on the wings of the winds, who makes his Angels spirits and his ministers a flaming fire. Come out, and withdraw from this creature with all your power and your angels. For the name of the Father and of the Son and of the Holy Spirit has been glorified, now and for ever, and to the ages of ages.**

People: **Amen.**

Second exorcism

Deacon: Let us pray to the Lord.

People: **Lord, have mercy.**

Priest: **It is God, the Holy One, who is beyond understanding and unsearchable in all his works and in his strength, the One who foreordained** for you, O Devil, the penalty of eternal damnation, that through us, his unprofitable servants, orders you, and every power that works with you, to depart from the one who has been newly sealed in the name of our Lord Jesus Christ, our true God. I adjure you, most evil, unclean, foul, abominable and alien spirit, by the power of Jesus Christ, who has all authority in heaven and on earth and who said to the deaf and dumb demon, 'Come out of the man, and enter him no more!' Depart! Acknowledge the futility of your power, which had no authority even over swine. Remember the One who ordered you, in accordance with your own request, to enter the herd of swine. Fear God, at whose command the earth was established upon the waters, who created the heavens and fixed the mountains with a king post and the valleys with a cross-beam, placed sand as a boundary for the sea and made a safe path through wild water; who touches the mountains and they smoke; who wraps himself in light as in a garment, stretching out the heavens like a tent cloth; who roofs his upper chambers with waters; who established the earth on its foundations; it will not be moved for to age on age; who summoned the water of the sea and poured it out upon the face of the earth. Come and depart from one who is being made ready for holy Enlightenment. I adjure you by the saving Passion of our Lord Jesus Christ, by his precious Body and Blood and his dread Coming; for he will come, and he will not delay, to judge the whole earth and he will condemn you and the power that works with you to the Gehenna of fire, handing you over to the exterior darkness, where the worm is unsleeping and the fire is not quenched. Because the might is Christ our God's, with the Father and the Holy Spirit, now and for ever, and to the ages of ages.

People: **Amen.**

Third exorcism

Deacon: **Let us pray to the Lord.**

People: **Lord, have mercy.**

Priest: **Lord Sabaoth, God of Israel, who heals every disease and every sickness, look upon your servant, search out, seek and drive from him/her all the activities of the devil. Rebuke the unclean spirits and expel them, and cleanse the work of your hands; and using your swift force, crush Satan speedily under his/her feet and grant him/her victories against him and all his unclean spirits, so that, obtaining mercy from you, he/she may be found worthy of your immortal and heav-**

enly Mysteries and may give glory to you, the Father, the Son and the Holy Spirit, now and for ever, and to the ages of ages.

People: **Amen.**

Deacon: **Let us pray to the Lord.**

People: **Lord, have mercy.**

Priest: **Master and Lord, the One who Is, who made man according to your image and likeness and gave him the power of eternal life; then, when he fell through sin, did not disdain him, but provided for the salvation of the world through the incarnation of your Christ, do you yourself receive also this creature of yours, whom you have redeemed from the slavery of the foe, into the heavenly Kingdom. Open the eyes of his/her mind so that the enlightenment of your Gospel may dawn on him/her. Yoke to his/her life an Angel of light, to deliver him/her from every attack of the adversary, from evil encounter, from the noon-day demon, from evil visions.**

Then the Priest breathes on the mouth, forehead and breast of the Catechumen, saying:

Drive out of him/her every evil and unclean spirit hiding and lurking in his/her heart. *(He says this three times)* The spirit of error, the spirit of wickedness, the spirit of idolatry and diabolic oppression; the spirit of lying and every uncleanness which operates in accordance with the teaching of the devil. And make him/her a rational sheep of the flock of your Christ, an honoured member of your Church, a vessel made holy, a child of light and an heir of your Kingdom. So that, having lived in accordance with your commandments, preserving the seal undamaged and keeping his/her garment undefiled, he/she may attain to the blessedness of the Saints in your Kingdom.

Aloud: By the grace and pity and love for mankind of your Only-Begotten Son, with whom you are blessed, together with your all-holy, good and life-giving Spirit, now and for ever, and to the ages of ages.

People: **Amen.**

When the Catechumen is undressed and unshod, the Priest turns him/her to the West with hands raised on high, and says: **Do you renounce Satan? And all his works? And all his angels? And all his worship? And all his solemn rites?**

And to each question the Catechumen, or the Godparent, if the catechumen is a barbarian or a child, answers and says: **I renounce them.**

And when he/she has said this three times, the Priest again asks the one to be baptized: **Have you renounced Satan?**

And the Catechumen, or the Godparent, answers: **I have renounced him.**

After he/she has said this three times the Priest says: **Then blow and spit on him.**

After this the Priest turns the Catechumen to the East with lowered hands and says to him/her three times: **Do you unite yourself to Christ?**

The Catechumen, or Godparent, answers three times: **I unite myself to him.**

And again the Priest asks three times: **Have you united yourself to Christ?**

And each time the Catechumen, or Godparent, answers: **I have united myself to him.**

And the Priest asks: **And do you believe in him?**

The Catechumen, or Godparent, answers: **I believe in him as King and God,** *and continues:* **I believe in one God, Father almighty, Maker of heaven and earth, and of all things visible and invisible.**

And in one Lord, Jesus Christ, the only-begotten Son of God, begotten from the Father before all ages. Light from Light, true God from true God, begotten not made, consubstantial with the Father; through him all things were made; for our sake and for our salvation he came down from heaven, and was incarnate from the Holy Spirit and the Virgin Mary and became man; he was crucified also for us under Pontius Pilate, and suffered and was buried; he rose again on the third day, in accordance with the Scriptures, and ascended into heaven and is seated at the right hand of the Father; he is coming again in glory to judge the living and the dead; and his kingdom will have no end.

And in the Holy Spirit, the Lord, the Giver of life, who proceeds from the Father, who together with Father and Son is worshipped and together glorified; who spoke through the Prophets. In one Holy, Catholic and Apostolic Church; I confess one Baptism for the forgiveness of sins; I await the resurrection of the dead and the life of the age to come. Amen.

When the holy Profession of faith has been completed [the Priest again asks three times: **Have you united yourself to Christ?** *and the rest. The Catechumen, or the Godparent, answers each time as before. After the third question and the third recitation of the Creed] the Priest asks three times:* **Have you united yourself to Christ?**

And the Catechumen, or the Godparent, answers: **I have united myself to him.**

And the Priest says: **Bow down also and worship him.**

The candidate makes a prostration, saying: **I worship Father, Son and Holy Spirit, Trinity consubstantial and undivided.**

The Priest says: **Blessed is God who wishes all to be saved and come to the knowledge of the truth, now and for ever, and to the ages of ages. Amen.**

Then he says this Prayer:

Deacon: **Let us pray to the Lord.**

People: **Lord, have mercy.**

Priest: **Master, Lord our God, call your servant N. to your holy Enlightenment and count him/her worthy of the great grace of your holy Baptism. Put off his/her old self and renew him/her for eternal life and fill him/her with the power of your Holy Spirit for union with your Christ, that he/she may no longer be a child of the body, but a child of your kingdom. Through the good pleasure and grace of your Only-begotten Son, with whom you are blessed, together with your all-holy, good and life-giving Spirit, now and for ever, and to the ages of ages.**

People: **Amen.**

Service of Holy Baptism

The Priest enters the Sanctuary and vests in white vestments and the cuffs. While all the candles are being lit he takes the censer, goes to the Font and censes it in a circle. He hands the censer away and makes a bow.

Then the Deacon says: **Master, give the blessing.**

The Priest, out loud: **Blessed is the Kingdom of the Father, and of the Son, and of the Holy Spirit, now and for ever, and to the ages of ages.**

People: **Amen.**

Deacon: **In peace, let us pray to the Lord.**

People: **Lord, have mercy.** *And so after each petition.*

Deacon: **For the peace from on high and for the salvation of our souls, let us pray to the Lord.**

For the peace of the whole world, for the welfare of the holy Churches of God, and for the union of all, let us pray to the Lord.

For this holy house, and for those who enter it with faith, reverence and the fear of God, let us pray to the Lord.

For our Archbishop (N.), for the honoured order of presbyters, for the diaconate in Christ, for all the clergy and the people, let us pray to the Lord.

For our Sovereign Lady, Queen Elizabeth, the Royal Family, her Government, and all in authority, let us pray to the Lord.*

That this water may be sanctified by the power, operation and descent of the Holy Spirit, let us pray to the Lord.

That there may be sent down upon it the grace of redemption, the blessing of Jordan, let us pray to the Lord.

That there may come down upon these waters the cleansing operation of the Trinity beyond being, let us pray to the Lord.

That we may be enlightened with the enlightenment of knowledge and true religion through the descent of the Holy Spirit, let us pray to the Lord.

That this water may be shown to be a protection against every assault of visible and invisible enemies, let us pray to the Lord.

That the one to be baptized in it may become worthy of the incorruptible Kingdom, let us pray to the Lord.

For the one who now draws near for holy Enlightenment and for his/her safety and salvation, let us pray to the Lord.

That he/she may be shown to be a child of light and heir of eternal blessings, let us pray to the Lord.

That he/she may be rooted in, and be a partaker in the death and resurrection of Christ our God, let us pray to the Lord.

That he/she may preserve the garment of Baptism and the pledge of the Holy Spirit unsullied and undefiled on the dread Day of Christ our God, let us pray to the Lord.

That this water may become for him/her a washing of rebirth for forgiveness of sins and a garment of incorruption, let us pray to the Lord.

* This reflects the use of this liturgy in the U.K. In other contexts other appropriate prayers for those in authority would be used.

275

That the Lord God would hearken to the voice of our supplication, let us pray to the Lord.

For our deliverance from all affliction, wrath, danger and constraint, let us pray to the Lord.

Help us, save us, have mercy on us, and keep us, O God, by your grace.

Commemorating our all-holy, pure, most blessed and glorious Lady, Mother of God and Ever-Virgin Mary, with all the Saints, let us entrust ourselves and one another and our whole life to Christ our God.

People: **To you, O Lord.**

While the Deacon is saying this the Priest says this prayer quietly: **Compassionate and merciful God, you test minds and hearts and alone know the secrets of mortals, for no deed is hidden in your sight, but everything is naked and exposed to your eyes. You know all about me; do not then despise me or turn your face from me, but overlook my offences at this hour, you who overlook the sins of mortals for their repentance. Wash away the filth of my body and the defilement of my soul by the power of your invisible and spiritual right hand, lest, as I proclaim freedom to others and grant it by the perfect faith of your ineffable love for mankind, I myself, as a slave of sin, become unworthy of it. May I not, Master, alone good and lover of mankind, may I not be turned away humiliated and put to shame, but from on high send power out to me and give me strength for your great and heavenly Mystery which lies before me, and through my miserable person form your Christ in the one who is about to be reborn. Build him/her up on the foundation of your Apostles and Prophets, and do not pull him/her down, but plant him/her as a plant of truth in your holy Catholic and Apostolic Church, and do not pull him/her out. So that by his/her progressing in true religion, your all-holy name, of Father, Son and Holy Spirit, may be glorified also through him/her, now and for ever, and to the ages of ages. Amen.**

It is to be noted that the Priest says none of this out loud, but he even says the Amen to himself.

Then he says the following prayer in a loud voice: **Great are you, O Lord, and wonderful are your works; and no word will be adequate to sing the praise of your wonders** *(x3)*. **For as by your will you brought the universe from non-existence into being, by your might you uphold crea-**

tion and by your providence you direct the world. From four elements you composed the world, with four seasons you crowned the circle of the year. All the spiritual Powers tremble before you. The sun sings your praise, the moon glorifies you, the stars entreat you, the light obeys you, the deeps tremble before you, the springs are your servants. You stretched out the heaven like a curtain; you established the earth on the waters; you walled in the sea with sand; you poured out the air for breathing. Angelic Powers minister to you, the choirs of Archangels worship you, the many-eyed Cherubim and the six-winged Seraphim, as they stand and fly around you, veil themselves in fear of your unapproachable glory. For you, God uncircumscribed, without beginning and ineffable, came upon earth taking the form of a slave, being found in the likeness of mortals. For through the compassion of your mercy, Master, you could not endure to watch the human race being tyrannized by the devil, but you came and saved us. We confess your grace, we proclaim your mercy, we do not conceal your benevolence. You set at liberty the generations of our nature, you sanctified a virgin womb by your birth. All creation sang your praise when you appeared. For you, our God, were seen on earth and lived among mortals. You also sanctified the streams of Jordan by sending down to them from heaven your all-holy Spirit, and you crushed the heads of the dragons that lurked their. Therefore, O King, lover of mankind, be present now too, through the visitation of your Holy Spirit, and sanctify this water *(x3)*. Give it the grace of redemption, the blessing of Jordan. Make it a source of incorruption, a gift of sanctification, an deliverance from sins, a destruction of demons. Make it unapproachable by hostile powers and filled with angelic strength. Let those that conspire against your creature flee from it, because I, Lord, have called upon your Name, which is wondrous and glorious and fearful to adversaries.

And breathing on the water three times, with two fingers he makes the sign of the Cross in it three times and prays over it, saying: **Let all adverse powers be crushed beneath the sign of the image of your Cross** *(x3)*. We pray you, Lord, let all airy and invisible spectres withdraw from us, and do not let a demon of darkness hide itself in this water, and do not let an evil spirit, bringing darkening of thoughts and disturbance of mind, go down into it with the one who is being baptized. But do you, Master of all things, declare this water to be water of redemption, water of sanctification, cleansing of flesh and spirit, untying of bonds, forgiveness of offences, enlightenment of soul, washing of rebirth, renewal of spirit, gift of adoption, garment of incorruption, source of life. For it was you, Lord, who said, 'Wash and be made clean, and put away evils from your souls'. It is you who have given us the grace of rebirth from on high through water and Spirit. Manifest yourself, Lord, in this water, and grant that the one being baptized in it may be transformed for the putting off of the old self that is corrupted after the desires of deception, and may put on the new that is renewed after the image of the One who created him/her. So that, planted in the likeness of your death through Baptism, he/she may also become a partaker in your Resurrection, and having guarded the gift of the Holy Spirit and increased the deposit of grace, may receive the prize of his/her high calling and be numbered with the firstborn, whose names are inscribed in heaven, in you our God and Lord, Jesus Christ. Because to you belong glory, might, honour and worship, together with your Father who is without beginning and your all-holy, good, and life-giving Spirit, now and for ever, and to the ages of ages.

People: **Amen.**

Priest: **Peace to all.**

People: **And to your spirit.**

Deacon: **Let us bow our heads to the Lord.**

People: **To you, O Lord.**

The Priest breathes on the container of oil three times and signs the oil three times as it is held by the Deacon [Godparent].

Deacon: **Let us pray to the Lord.**

People: **Lord, have mercy.**

The Priest says the following prayer quietly:

Master, Lord God of our fathers, who sent out a dove to those in Noë's ark, with a branch of olive in its beak as sign of reconciliation and salvation from the flood, and through these things prefigured the Mystery of grace; who have given the fruit of the olive for the completion of your holy Mysteries; who through it both filled those under the Law with the Holy Spirit, and make perfect those under grace; do you yourself bless this olive oil also by the power, operation and descent of your Holy Spirit, so that it may become an anointing of incorruption, a weapon of righteousness, renewal of soul and body, a driving away of every operation of the devil, for the removal of all evils from those who are anointed with it in faith, or who partake of it to your glory and that of your Only-Begotten Son and your all-holy, good, and life-giving Spirit, now and for ever, and to the ages of ages.

People: **Amen.**

Deacon: **Let us attend.**

The Priest, chanting Alleluia three times with the People, makes three Crosses with the oil in the water. Then he proclaims: **Blessed is God, who enlightens and sanctifies everyone who comes into the world, now and for ever, and to the ages of ages.**

People: **Amen.**

The one to be baptized is brought forward. The Priest takes some of the oil and makes the sign of the Cross on the forehead, breast and back of the candidate, saying: **The servant of God, N., is anointed with the oil of gladness, in the name of the Father, and of the Son, and of the Holy Spirit. Amen.**

As he signs their breast and back he says: **For healing of soul and body.**

On the ears: **For the hearing of faith.**

On the feet: **For your feet to walk.**

On the hands: **Your hands made me and fashioned me.**

And when the whole body has been anointed the Priest baptizes the person, holding them upright and facing East, as he says: **The servant of God N. is baptized, in the name of the Father. Amen. And of the Son. Amen. And of the Holy Spirit. Amen.**

At each invocation the Priest immerses them and raises them again. After the baptism the Priest washes, as he and the People chant (x3):

Psalm 31

Blessed are those whose iniquities have been forgiven and whose sins have been covered *(x3)*. Blessed is the one to whom the Lord imputes no sin and in whose mouth there is no guile. Because I kept silent my bones grew old from my crying out all day long. Because night and day your hand was heavy upon me; I was turned to wretchedness by a thorn's being fastened in me. I acknowledged my sin and did not hide my iniquity. I said, 'Against myself I will admit my iniquity to the Lord', and you forgave the ungodliness of my heart. For this every holy one will pray to you at a fitting moment. Except in a flood of many waters they will not come near him. For you are my refuge from the affliction which surrounds me, my joy to deliver me from those who have surrounded me. 'I will make you understand and guide you in the way in which you should go. I will fix my eyes upon you. Do not become like horse and mule, who have no understanding. With bit and bridle you must constrain their cheeks so that they do not come near you.' Many are the scourges of the sinner, but mercy will surround the one who hopes in the Lord. Rejoice in the Lord and be glad you righteous, and boast all you upright in heart.

And as he clothes the newly baptized, the Priest says: **The servant of God N. is clothed with a tunic of righteousness, in the name of the Father, and of the Son, and of the Holy Spirit. Amen.**

Then the following is chanted in Tone 8: **Grant me a tunic of light, O most merciful, Christ our God, who wrap yourself in light as in a garment.**

After the newly-baptized is clothed:

Deacon: **Let us pray to the Lord.**

People: **Lord, have mercy.**

And the Priest says this prayer: **Blessed are you, Lord God Almighty, the source of blessings, the Sun of righteousness, who have made the light of salvation shine for those in darkness through the appearing of your Only-Begotten Son and our God, and have granted us, unworthy though we are, the grace of blessed cleansing by holy Baptism, and divine sanctification by life-giving Anointing. And you have now been well-pleased to make your newly-enlightened servant to be born again through water and Spirit, and have granted him/her forgiveness of sins both voluntary and involuntary. Do you then, Master, compassionate, universal King, grant him/her also the Seal of the gift of your holy, all-powerful and adorable Spirit and the Communion of the holy Body and precious Blood of your Christ. Keep him/her in your sanctification; confirm him/her in the Orthodox Faith; deliver him/her from the evil one and all his devices, and by your saving fear guard his/her soul in purity and righteousness; so that being in every deed and word well-pleasing to you, he/she may become a child and heir of your heavenly Kingdom.**

Aloud: **Because you are our God, a God who has mercy and who saves, and to you we give glory, to the Father and to the Son and to the Holy Spirit, now and for ever, and to the ages of ages.**

People: **Amen.**

And after the Prayer he anoints the newly baptized with the holy Myron, making a sign of the Cross on the forehead, the eyes, the nostrils, the mouth, the two ears, the breast, the hands and the feet, and saying: **Seal of the gift of the Holy Spirit. Amen.**

[In many places it is the custom for the Priest to place the baptismal Cross, after blessing it in the Baptismal Water, round the neck of the newly baptized and to give them a lighted candle. See Appendix.]

Then the Priest, having washed his hands, censes the Font, going round it in a circle, with the Godparent and the Newly-baptized following and standing opposite him, while we chant:

As many of you as have been baptized into Christ have put on Christ. Alleluia.

As many of you as have been baptized into Christ have put on Christ. Alleluia.

As many of you as have been baptized into Christ have put on Christ. Alleluia.

Glory to the Father and to the Son and to the Holy Spirit.

Both now and for ever, and to the ages of ages. Amen.

Have put on Christ. Alleluia.

As many of you as were baptized into Christ have put on Christ. Alleluia.

[Deacon: **Let us attend.**

Priest: **Peace to all.**

Reader: **And to your spirit.**

Deacon: **Wisdom.**]

Reader: Prokeimenon in the 3rd Tone. [Psalm 26]

The Lord is my enlightenment and my Saviour; * whom shall I fear?

Verse: **The Lord is the defender of my life, of whom shall I be afraid?**

Deacon: **Wisdom.**

The Apostle

The Reading is from the Epistle of Paul to the Romans [6:3-11]

Deacon: **Let us attend.**

Reader: **Brethren, as many of us as were baptized into Christ were baptized into his death. We were buried then with him through baptism to death, so that, just as Christ was raised from the dead through the glory of the Father, we too might walk in newness of life. For if we have grown into union with him through a death like his, we shall also be united with him in the resurrection. For we know that our old self was crucified with him, so that our sinful body might be done away with, that we might no longer be in slavery to sin. For one who has died has been justified from sin. If then we died with Christ, we believe that we shall also live with him. For we know that Christ, being raised from the dead, dies no more; death no longer lords it over him. As to dying, he died once and for all; as to living, he lives for God. Consequently, you also must consider yourselves dead to sin, but alive to God in Christ Jesus our Lord.**

Priest: **Peace to you.**

Reader: **And to your spirit. Alleluia, Alleluia, Alleluia.**

The Gospel

Deacon: **Wisdom. Stand upright. Let us listen to the Holy Gospel.**

Priest: **Peace to all.**

People: **And to your spirit.**

Priest: **The Reading is from the holy Gospel according to Matthew.**

People: **Glory to you, Lord, glory to you.**

Deacon: **Let us attend.**

Priest: **At that time the eleven Disciples journeyed to Galilee, to the mountain which Jesus had commanded them. And when they saw him they worshipped him; but some doubted. And Jesus drew near and said to them, 'All authority has been given to me in heaven and on earth. Go therefore and make disciples of all the nations, baptizing them in the name of the Father and of the Son and of the Holy Spirit, teaching them to observe all the things that I have commanded you. And see, I am with you all days until the end of the age. Amen'.**

People: **Glory to you, Lord, glory to you.**

Then the Litany and Dismissal. [Frequently the Ablution and Tonsure are done before the Litany.]

Deacon: **Have mercy on us, O God, according to your great mercy, we pray you, hear and have mercy.**

People: **Lord, have mercy.** *(x3)*

Deacon: **Again we pray for mercy, life, peace, health, salvation and forgiveness of sins for the servant of God, the Sponsor** N.

Again we pray for the newly enlightened servant of God N.

That he/she may be kept in the faith of a pure confession, in all godliness and in the fulfilling of the commandments of Christ all the days of his/her life.

Priest: **For you, O God, are good and love mankind, and to you we give glory, to the Father and to the Son and to the Holy Spirit, now and for ever, and to the ages of ages.**

People: **Amen.**

Prayers of the ablution

After seven days they again bring the newly baptized to Church for the Ablution. The Priest loosens the linen cloth and girdle saying the following Prayers: **Master and Lord, who have granted your servant forgiveness of sins through holy Baptism, and given him/her the grace of a life of rebirth, be well pleased for the illumination of your face to shine for ever in his/her heart; keep the shield of his/her faith safe from attack by foes; preserve on him/her the garment of incorruption, which he/she has put on, undefiled and unstained; by your grace keeping the spiritual seal unbroken in him/her, and being merciful to him/her and to us. For blessed and glorified is your all-honoured and majestic Name, of the Father, the Son and the Holy Spirit, now and for ever, and to the ages of ages.**

People: **Amen.**

Deacon: **Let us pray to the Lord.**

People: **Lord, have mercy.**

Priest: **Master, Lord our God, who through the font grant heavenly radiance to those who are baptized, who have given your newly enlightened servant rebirth through water and Spirit, and granted him/her forgiveness of sins both voluntary and involuntary, lay your mighty hand on him/her and guard him/her by the power of your loving** kindness; preserve the pledge inviolate; and count him/her worthy of eternal life and your good pleasure. Because you are our sanctification, and to you we give glory, to the Father, the Son and the Holy Spirit, now and for ever, and to the ages of ages.

People: **Amen.**

Priest: **Peace to all.**

People: **And to your spirit.**

Deacon: **Let us bow our heads to the Lord.**

People: **To you, O Lord.**

Priest: **The one who has put you on, Christ our God, has bowed his/her head to you with us. Guard him/her always to remain an invincible warrior against those that in vain bear enmity against him/her and us, and with your incorruptible crown declare us all to be victors unto the end. Because yours it is to have mercy and to save us, and to you we give glory, with your Father who is without beginning and your all-holy, good and life-giving Spirit, now and for ever, and to the ages of ages.**

People: **Amen.**

And he unties the girdle and linen cloth of the newly baptized, and having joined their ends he wets them with water and sprinkles the newly baptized, saying: **You have been justified. You have been enlightened. You have been sanctified. You have been washed in the name of our Lord Jesus Christ and by the Spirit of God.**

And taking a new sponge with water he sponges the face of the newly baptized, together with his/her head, breast and the rest, saying: **You have been baptized. You have been enlightened. You have been anointed with chrism. You have been sanctified. You have been washed clean. In the name of the Father and of the Son and of the Holy Spirit. Amen.**

Prayers for the tonsure

Deacon: **Let us pray to the Lord.**

People: **Lord, have mercy.**

Priest: **Master, Lord our God, who honoured mortals with your image, furnishing them with a rational soul and a comely body, so that the body might serve the rational soul, you placed the head at the very top and in it you planted the majority of the senses, which do not interfere** with one another, while you covered the head with hair so as not to be harmed by the changes of the weather, and you fitted all the limbs most suitably to each one, so that through them all they might give thanks to you, the master craftsman. Do you yourself, Master, who through your vessel of election, the Apostle Paul, ordered us to do all things to your glory, bless your servant N. who has come to make a first offering by the cutting of the hair of his/her head. Bless his/her Sponsor also and grant that they may always meditate on your law and do what is well-pleasing to you. For you, O God, are merciful and love mankind, and to you we give glory, to the Father and to the Son and to the Holy Spirit, now and for ever, and to the ages of ages.

People: **Amen.**

Priest: **Peace to all.**

People: **And to your spirit.**

Deacon: **Let us bow our heads to the Lord.**

People: **To you, O Lord.**

Priest: **Lord our God, who through your loving kindness have sanctified from the fullness of the font those who believe in you, bless this child here present, and let your blessing come down upon his/her head. As you blessed King David through Samuel the Prophet, bless too the head of your servant N. through the hand of me, a sinner, visiting him/her with your Holy Spirit, so that as he/she advances to mature years and to the grey hairs of old age, he/she may give glory to you and see the good things of Jerusalem all the days of his/her life. For to you belong all glory, honour and worship, to the Father and to the Son and to the Holy Spirit, now and for ever, and to the ages of ages.**

People: **Amen.**

And the Priest tonsures him/her in the form of a cross, saying: **The servant of God N. is tonsured, in the name of the Father, and of the Son and of the Holy Spirit. Amen.**

Deacon: **Have mercy on us, O God, according to your great mercy, we pray you, hear and have mercy.**

People: **Lord, have mercy. Lord, have mercy. Lord, have mercy.**

Deacon: **Again we pray for mercy, life, peace, health, salvation, for the servants of God the Sponsor N. and the newly enlightened N.**

Priest: For you, O God, are merciful and love mankind, and to you we give glory, to the Father, the Son and the Holy Spirit, now and for ever, and to the ages of ages.

People: **Amen.**

And the Dismissal

Priest: Glory to you, Christ God, our hope, glory to you.

Reader: Glory to the Father, and to the Son, and to the Holy Spirit, both now and for ever, and to the ages of ages. Amen. Lord, have mercy. Lord, have mercy. Lord, have mercy. Holy Master, give the blessing.

Priest: May he who accepted to be baptized by John in the Jordan, Christ our true God, through the prayers of his all-pure and holy Mother, through the intercessions of the honoured, glorious Prophet, Forerunner and Baptist, John, of the holy, glorious and all-praised Apostles, of the holy and righteous forebears of God, Joachim and Anne, of Saint N. (the Saint of the Newly-baptized), of Saint N. (to whom the Church is dedicated), of Saint N., whose memory we keep today, and of all the Saints, have mercy on us and save us, for he is good and loves mankind.

Through the prayers of our holy Fathers, Lord Jesus Christ, our God, have mercy on us and save us.

People: **Amen.**

Appendix

The Small Euchologion has an Instruction at the end of the service which runs as follows:

Be careful, Priest, to instruct both the nurse and the mother not to bath or wash the face of the newly baptized until the seventh day. On the eighth day they are to wash and bath the child and they are to dispose of the water in a place where no one walks, or in a river, or in the piscina of the Church.

It also says that after the service the newly baptized and the Godparent are to go in procession to the former's house, with everyone carrying lamps and singing *As many of you as were baptized into Christ*.

At the giving of the Cross and the Candle many priests say, for the Cross, *If anyone would be my disciple, let them deny themselves, take up their cross and follow me*; for the Candle, *So let your light shine before your fellows, that they may see your good works, and glorify your Father in heaven.*

It is the custom in many places for the Godparent to return the newly baptized infant to its mother after the service. The mother should do a prostration before her newly enlightened child and then take it in her arms.

If it is not possible for the newly baptized to receive Holy Communion immediately after their Baptism, they should come, or be brought, to the Liturgy at the first opportunity in order to do so. Accompanied by their God-parent they should come with their baptismal candle and be the first of the congregation to receive Communion.

Chapter 2

The Canon of the Sacrament of Holy Baptism (Oriental Orthodox—Armenian)*

They shall enter into the chancel of the church saying:

Priest:

THE LORD'S PRAYER

Blessed be our Lord Jesus Christ. Amen.

Our Father who art in heaven, hallowed be Thy name, Thy kingdom come, Thy will be done on earth as it is in heaven. Give us this day our daily bread. And forgive us our trespasses, as we forgive those who trespass against us. And lead us not into temptation, but deliver us from evil. For Thine is the kingdom, and the power, and the glory, forever and ever, Amen.

Blessed be the Holy Spirit, the true God.

Congregation:

Psalm 51

Have mercy on me, O God, according to thy steadfast love; according to thy abundant mercy blot out my transgressions. Wash me thoroughly from my iniquity, and cleanse me from my sin! Purge me with hyssop, and I shall be clean; wash me, and I shall be whiter than snow.

Create in me a clean heart, O God, and renew a steadfast spirit within me.

Restore to me the joy of thy salvation, and uphold me with a willing spirit.

O Lord, open thou my lips, and my mouth shall show forth thy praise.

Glory to the Father and to the son and to the Holy Spirit; Now and always and forever and ever. Amen.

---

* Liturgy currently used in Armenian Apostolic Churches around the world.

Choir:

HYMN OF THE HOLY SPIRIT

The indivisible Trinity and the heavenly power shone forth as a light upon the world; Let us praise Him with song.

The very Holy Spirit came down from heaven and rested upon the Apostles; Let us praise Him with song.

Descending upon the Apostles the mystery of salvation manifested himself as having been known by the prophet; Let us praise Him with song.

Deacon:

BIDDING

Again in peace let us beseech the Lord.

For *the* expiation of sins and forgiveness of transgressions and for the mercy of God to be descended upon this child, Let us beseech the Lord.

Priest:

PRAYER

Lord have mercy, Lord have mercy, Lord have mercy.

O Lord God, great and *glorified* by all creatures, this your servant has bowed his/her head and has found refuge in your most powerful and holy name. Look with mercy, O Lord, upon this child, and by calling of your name expel and keep away the thoughts, the words, and the deeds, and all the deceptions of the evil one who is accustomed to deceive men and make them perish. Fill this child with your heavenly grace and grant him/her the joy to be named a Christian and make him/her worthy of Baptism of the second birth of the holy Font. And by receiving your Holy Spirit let him/her be body and member of your holy Church. And by leading a blameless Christian life in this world may he/she attain all the good things of the world to come with the help *of your* saints, glorifying your unchangeable dominion. Now and forever and ever. Amen.

Then the Godfather shall hold the child and bowing down three times shall say thrice:

Upon thee was I cast from my birth, and since my mother bore me thou hast been my God.

At this point everyone at the church will turn to the West for the renunciation.

Priest:

THE RENUNCIATION

We renounce Satan and his every deceit, his wiles, his deliberations, his course, his evil will, his evil angels, his evil ministers, his evil agents, and his every power renouncing, we renounce.

Then all shall turn toward the East and the priest shall say:
We turn to the light of the knowledge of God.

CONFESSION OF FAITH

We believe in the all-holy Trinity, in the Father and in the Son, and in the Holy Spirit.

We believe in the annunciation of Gabriel, in the Nativity of Christ, in His Baptism, in His Passion, in His Crucifixion, in His three day Entombment, in His resurrection, in His Ascension, in His sitting at the right hand of the Father and His awesome and glorious Second Coming,

We confess and we believe.

Deacon:
Alleluia. Orthi. (Praise the Lord. Arise)

Priest:
Peace be unto all.

Deacon:
And to your spirit Listen in awe.

Priest:
To the Holy Gospel of Jesus Christ according to St. Matthew. (28:16-20)

Deacon:
Glory to You, O Lord our God. Proschumen. (Let us attend). God speaks.

Priest:
After the Resurrection of our Lord Jesus Christ.

Now the eleven disciples went to Galilee, to the mountain to which Jesus had directed them. And when they saw Him they worshipped Him; but some doubted. And Jesus came and said to them, "All authority in heaven and earth has been given to me. Go therefore and make disciples of all nations, baptizing them in the name of the Father and of the Son and of the Holy Spirit, teaching them to observe all that I have commanded you; and lo, I am with you always, to the close of the age".

Then they shall enter the chancel and sing:

HYMN

Open the gate of your mercy, O Lord, and make us worthy of your luminous dwellings together with your saints.

Receive us, O Saviour, in the mansions prepared for your saints, inscribing our names in the book of life.

O formidable Judge, when you sit at the judgment seat, spare your creatures through the intercession and prayers of the holy ascetics.

Deacon:

BIDDING

Again in peace let us beseech the Lord.

Let us beseech the compassionate God, to have mercy upon this child according to his great mercy and make him/her worthy of the washing of the second birth and of the garment of purity. Let us beseech our Lord, to rank him/her among the faithful who believe in His name, and save him/her by the grace of His mercy. Almighty Lord, our God, save us and have mercy.

Priest:

PRAYER

Lord have mercy, Lord have mercy, Lord have mercy.

Receive, O compassionate God, this child who is being presented to you. Cleanse his/her mind and his/her thoughts from all the influences of the adversary; and make him/her worthy to be washed of our old sins through the holy Font and to be renewed by the light of Your grace, so that together with us he/she may glorify the Father and the Son and the Holy Spirit, now and forever and ever, Amen.

The Priest and the godfather holding the child, will walk towards the baptismal Font, singing:

HYMN

Christ, the sun of righteousness, rising over the world banished the darkness of ignorance; and after His death and resurrection ascended to the Father from whom He was begotten. Together with the Father and the Holy Spirit, He is worshipped by the heavenly and the terrestrial; and consequently we adore the Father in spirit and in truth.

Pouring water into the Font crosswise, the priest shall say:

Alleluia, Alleluia.

The voice of the Lord is upon the waters; the God of glory thunders, the Lord, upon many waters.

The voice of the Lord is powerful, the voice of the Lord is full of majesty (Ps. 29:3-4).

The reading is from the Epistle of St. Paul to the Galatians (3:24-29).

So that the law was our custodian until Christ came, that we might be justified by faith. But now that faith has come, we are no longer under a custodian; for in Christ Jesus you are sons of God, through faith. For as many of you as were baptized into Christ have put on Christ. There is neither Jew nor Greek, there is neither slave nor free, there is neither male nor female; for you are all one in Christ Jesus. And if you are Christ's, then you are Abraham's offspring heirs according to promise.

Deacon:
Alleluia, Alleluia. The Lord is my shepherd, I shall not want. (Ps. 23:1). Alleluia. Orthi. (Praise the Lord. Arise.)

Priest:
Peace be unto all

Deacon:
And to your spirit. Listen in awe.

Priest:
To the Holy Gospel of Jesus Christ according to St. John. (3:1-8)

Deacon:
Glory to You, O Lord our God. Proschumen. (Let us attend.) God speaks.

Priest:
To our Lord Jesus Christ.

Now there was a man of the Pharisees, named Nicodemus, a ruler of the Jews. This man came to Jesus by night and said to him, "Rabbi, we know that you are a teacher come from God; for no one can do these signs that you do, unless God is with him". Jesus answered him, "Truly, truly, I say to you, unless one is born anew, he cannot see the kingdom of

God". Nicodemus said to him, "How can a man be born when he is old? Can he enter a second time into his mother's womb and be born?" Jesus answered, "Truly, truly, I say to you, unless one is born of water and the Spirit, he cannot enter the kingdom of God. That which is born of the flesh is flesh, and which is born of the Spirit is spirit. Do not marvel that I said to you, 'You must be born anew', The wind blows where it wills, and you hear the sound of it, but you do not know from where it comes or where it goes; so it is with every one who is born of the Spirit".

Deacon:

BIDDING

- Again in peace let us beseech the Lord.
- Lord have mercy.
- For the cleansing of this water by the power of the Holy Spirit, let us beseech the Lord.
- Lord have mercy.
- For the reinstatement as the sons of light, those who are baptized in this, let us beseech the Lord.
- Lord have mercy.
- For the transformation of him/her to a vessel of Sacrament to contain the God given mysteries, let us beseech the Lord.
- Lord have mercy, Lord have mercy, Lord have mercy,

Priest:

PRAYER

Lord, our God, Jesus Christ, you who are the holiest and exempt from every sin, we beseech you, send your Holy Spirit to these Waters and cleanse them, as you have done to the waters of the Jordan River by your immersion in it, setting that as an example to this Baptismal Font of rebirth of all mankind. Grant through this water, where he/she is being baptized now, the forgiveness of sins and the acceptance of the Holy Spirit, so that he/she may be adopted by your heavenly Father and inherit the Kingdom of Heavens. Thus, being cleaned from all sins, he might live according to your will in this world, and in the after life enjoy your inexhaustible blessings with all your saints, joyfully giving thanks and always praising you, with the Father, and the Holy Spirit now and always, and forever and ever. Amen.

The Godfather shall take the baby to be undressed and shall bring him/her wrapped in a towel to the priest. The priest shall take the holy Muron and shall make the sign of the cross over the water, saying:

Deacon:
Amen. Alleluia, alleluia, alleluia.

Priest:
May this water be blessed and sanctified by the sign of the holy Cross and by the holy Gospel and by the holy Muron and by the grace of this day, in the name of the Father and of the Son and of the Holy Spirit, now and always and forever and ever. Amen.

(Repeat thrice and then say)

Blessing and glory to the Father and to the Son and to the Holy Spirit, now and always and forever and ever. Amen.

Then pouring the holy Muron crosswise into the font, the Priest shall sing:

HYMN

The dove (The Holy Spirit) sent from on high, descending with high sound and like flashing light, fortified the disciples with in-combustible fire while they were sitting at the holy upper chamber.

The dove is insubstantial and unsearchable; but he knows all the deep secrets of God and taking the same from the Father, tells us about the awesome second coming of Christ, He is consubstantial with the Father.

Blessing in the highest to the Holy Spirit that proceeded from the Father. The apostles drank from the immortal cup of graces and invited the earth to heaven.

The godfather holding the baby in his arms stands next to the baptismal Font, facing the priest.

Priest:

PRAYER

We beseech you, Lord, to call this your servant to the participation and enlightenment of the baptism. We beseech you, O Lord, to make this your servant worthy of your most precious grace whom you have called to the purification and enlightenment of the baptism. Cleanse him/her from old sins and renew him/her in a new life. Fill him/her with the power of the Holy Spirit so that he/she may have the renewal of the glory of your Christ. And to you, the Mighty One, and to your only begotten Son and to the liberating Holy Spirit is befitting dominion and honor, now and always and forever and ever. Amen.

Then the Priest shall ask the godfather:

Priest:
What is the request of this child?

Godfather:
Faith, hope, love and baptism. To be baptized and justified; to be cleansed of sins; to be freed from demons and to serve God. *(Repeat thrice)*

Priest:
Be it unto you according to your faith.

Then the Priest shall immerse the child three times into the water, in the name of the Father and of the Son and of the Holy Spirit, saying only once the following invocation:

(name) the servant of God, coming from the state of catechumen to baptism, is now being baptized in the name of the Father and of the Son and of the Holy Spirit. Redeemed by the blood of Christ from the servitude of sin, he/she becomes an adopted child of the heavenly Father, a co-heir with Christ and a temple of the Holy Spirit.

Then taking the child out of the Font, shall say:

Once you have been baptised to Christ, you have put on Christ. Alleluia.

Once you have been enlightened in the Father, the Holy Spirit shall rejoice in you. Alleluia:

Glory be to the Father, to the Son and to the Holy Spirit, now and always and forever and ever. Amen.

HYMN

Thou who art consubstantial with the Father and the Son, ineffable procession of the Eternal Being, this day Thou didst spring as living water in Jerusalem,
Spirit of God, have mercy.

Thou who art co-creator with the Father and the Son, by Thee we creatures were reborn in the waters, *this day Thou doest give* birth from the waters to the children of God,
Spirit of God have mercy.

Thou who share the glory of the Father and the Son, and doest search the depths of God, this day Thou didst turn the fools of the world into masters of wisdom,
Spirit of God have mercy.

THE CANON OF HOLY CONFIRMATION

PRAYER

Christ Our Lord, You have illuminated your creatures by shining the light of the knowledge of God upon us, and now you have redeemed this servant of yours, by making him/her clean and just and giving him/her the honour of adoption.

Lord, Omnipotent God, Father of our Lord Jesus Christ, Who granted the knowledge of your truth to all those who believe in you, and granted the power to become the Sons of God through the rebirth from the water and the Holy Spirit. You renewed this servant of yours (Name) through the atonement granted by the Holy Font. Clean him with your truth and by the shining grace of the Holy Spirit, in order that he may be a temple and the dwelling place of your divinity, so that he may walk in the paths of righteousness and be able to stand with courage in front of the awesome stage of Your Only Son, Our Lord Jesus Christ.

THE SACRAMENT OF CHRISMATION

The Priest pours holy Muron in his palm and starts to anoint, saying:

THE FOREHEAD: This sweet oil, which is poured upon your forehead in the name of Jesus Christ, be a seal of incorruptible heavenly gifts.

THE EYES: May this seal in the name of Jesus Christ enlighten your eyes, so that you may never sleep unto death.

THE EARS: May with this holy anointment you hear the divine commandments of God.

THE NOSTRILS: May this seal in the name of Jesus Christ be to you a sweet smell from life to life.

THE MOUTH: May this seal in the name of Jesus Christ guard your mouth and be a strong door for your lips.

THE HANDS: May this seal in the name of Jesus Christ be a cause for benevolence and for all virtuous deeds and behavior.

THE HEART: May this divine seal cleanse your heart and establish an upright spirit within you.

THE BACK: May this seal in the name of Jesus Christ be for you a shield of strength so that you may quell the fierce arrows of the evil.

THE FEET: May this divine seal direct your journey towards eternal life so that you may not be shaken.

Then the Priest says:
Peace unto you, O saved one of God. Peace unto you, O anointed one of God.

And the godfather answers:
And with your spirit.

Then the godparents shall dress the child with new white clothes and the priest shall tie the Narode around the neck of the child and shall give two lighted candles to the godfather and sing:

THE HYMN OF RESURRECTION

God spoke from on high, hear, O inhabitants of the earth, He came and saved all the creatures so that we may call upon the name of the Lord *and* praise Him *in* the highest.

By joining Christ we became the New Israel, the portion of God and co-heirs with Christ, so that we may call upon the name of the Lord and praise Him in the highest.

We have tasted from the table of life for the *Lord is* sweet; and we have been anointed with holy oil in faith, so that we may call upon the name of the Lord and praise the Lord in the highest.

We have put our trust in you, O Mother and maiden of Christ, intercede for us so that we may call upon the name of the Lord and venerate and honor you.

Priest:

PRAYER

Blessed are you, O provident God, that have clothed your servant with a garment of salvation and a robe of gladness, and placed upon his/her head a helmet of redemption and a crown of grace as an indestructible weapon against the adversary. Therefore we thankfully glorify you together with the Son and the Holy Spirit, now and always and forever and ever. Amen.

Peace unto all

O Lord, omnipotent God, the Father of our Lord Jesus Christ, the faithful gathered here bow down their heads before you. Stretch your invisible Hand and bless them and let the deeds of their hands prosper. And them who are in the state of virginity, fortify in their course with temperance and total godliness and keep them in peace. Nurture this child and make him/her reach to full stature and protect all and every one here present at their homes that they may have the joy and the gladness of our Lord Jesus Christ, with whom to you, the Father and to the Holy Spirit is befitting glory, dominion and honor, now and always and forever and ever. Amen.

The godparents will bring the child and stand at the chancel before the Sanctuary.

The Priest shall take the Neophyte up to the Sanctuary, reciting Ps. 43.

I will go to the altar of God, to God who makes my youth joyful. Vindicate me, O God, and defend my cause against an ungodly people.

Then the priest shall bow down and say thrice:

(Name), servant of Christ, coming from the state of catechumen to baptism, and from baptism to worship, now worships before this holy Table, before this holy Altar, and before this holy Font, for he/she has renounced iniquity and has put on the light of the knowledge of God.

Then the Priest gives the child to the godfather and shall administer the Holy Communion to the neophyte,

After the Holy Communion, the godfather shall give the child to the mother standing at the chancel, and the Priest shall sing the following hymn:

HYMN OF THE BAPTISM

O children of the New Zion born from the holy Font, you who are adorned with the gifts of the Holy Spirit, praise the heavenly Father on the day of the holy Virgin's birth. For it was because of the bearer-of-God in whom the curse of the foremother was changed into a blessing.

Priest:

PRAYER OF COMMUNION

Lord have mercy, Lord have mercy, Lord have mercy.

Glory to you, king eternal, that you have enlarged and replenished your church *with* the luminous *faith of the* innumerable souls redeemed through the true knowledge of God in Christ. Glory to you, that we were made worthy with a second birth for adoption and worthy to partake the Body and the Blood of your Only-begotten. And now, O Lord, keep this child in the purity of the Holy Spirit so that he/she may spotlessly do your will and sinlessly attain your eternal life. And now we beseech you, lead the course of this child and fortify him/her in your fear and keep him/her in the obedience of your luminous commandments. Keep him/her in peace and without sin through the grace and the loving kindness of our Lord and Savior Jesus Christ with whom to you God the Father and to your lifegiving Holy Spirit is befitting glory, dominion and honor, now and always and forever and ever, Amen.

BLESSING OF DISMISSAL

Deacon:

BIDDING

By the holy Cross let us beseech the Lord that he may thereby deliver us from our sins and save us by the grace of his mercy. Almighty Lord, our God, save us and have mercy.

THE PRAYER OF THE CROSS

Lord have mercy, Lord have mercy, Lord have mercy.

O Christ our God, guardian and hope of all your faithful, protect and keep your people and especially this child under the shadow of your holy and venerable Cross in peace. Deliver us from enemies visible and invisible. Make us worthy to thankfully glorify You with the Father and the Holy Spirit, now and always and forever and ever. Amen.

THE LORD'S PRAYER

Blessed be our Lord Jesus Christ. Amen.

Our Father who art in heaven, hallowed be Thy name. Thy kingdom come, Thy will be done on earth as it is in heaven. Give us this day our daily bread. And forgive us our trespasses, as we forgive those who trespass against us. And lead us not into temptation, but deliver us from evil. For Thine is the kingdom, and the power, and the glory, forever and ever. Amen.

Be you blessed by the graces of the Holy Spirit. Depart in peace and may the Lord be with you all. Amen.

* * *

Explanatory notes

MODES OF BAPTISM

The Armenian Church practices Baptism by Immersion. In case of adults and persons with physical illness baptism is performed by sprinkling the blessed water three times over the head of the person and repeating the same rites as in Immersion.

CATHECUMEN

In the Early Church the person who was not baptized and was under the instruction of the Church was called Cathecumen. The Armenian word for it is "Yerakha".

GODFATHER

Only a male person can perform the role of the Godfather in the Armenian Church. He should be an adult and not a child.

- A person who is not baptized Christian cannot become a Godfather.
- In case of adult baptism, a person cannot become Godfather of his own fiancee or wife.
- The role of the Godmother is to assist the Godfather in disrobing and dressing the child. She cannot assume the role of the Godfather.
- The Armenian Church forbids the marriage of a Godfather with his god-daughter.
- He should know the teachings of the Church in order to teach the same to his god-children.
- The Godfather is the spiritual parent of the child, and should see that the child receives the proper Christian education.
- Parents cannot become god-parents of their own children.
- There could be only one Godfather at one baptism.

HOLY MURON (CHRISM)

The Eastern Apostolic Churches have the custom of anointing and confirming the child with Holy Muron (*Chrism*). This custom dates back even before the Fourth Century. Muron is prepared with the oils of forty-three fragrant flowers and consecrated by the Catholicoses of the Armenian Church. This is done once in seven years, generally at the time of the Feast of Pentecost (Hoqeqaloosd).

BAPTISM

Christ Himself with His own baptism in the River Jordan instituted the Sacrament of Baptism. In Matt. 28:19, He instructed His disciples, telling them to "go forth, teach all nations, baptizing them in the name of the Father, and of the Son and of the Holy Spirit." In the pattern of the Early Christian Church, it has been the custom of the Armenian Church to baptize infants before they are forty days old. God receives His own at any age.

CONFIRMATION

In the Early Church the Confirmation was done by either laying of the hands or by anointing. The Armenian Church practices anointment. In some Christian churches Confirmation is done by a bishop. In our Church all duly ordained priests are able to perform the rite.

Chapter 3

Text of the Mystery of Holy Baptism (Oriental Orthodox—Syrian, India)*

(If the candidate for baptism is a child, there must be an orthodox godfather/godmother: for the male child a godfather and for the female child a godmother).

Priest (P): Glory be to the Father, and to the Son and to the Holy Spirit

Congregation (C): And upon us, weak and sinful. His mercy and compassion be showered in both worlds forever. Amen.

The Opening Prayer

P: Lord our God, make us worthy of this spiritual priestly ministry that was entrusted by You to your holy apostles to give baptism by fire and spirit. Lord, enable this soul, who draws near for baptism and for birth from above, through the mediation of us, sinners, to attain salvation, blessings and mercy.

Kukilion

(for males)

P: Give the male children to the Lord—Hallelujah
Give Honour and glory to the Lord.

C: Adore His name—Hallelujah;
Worship the Almighty in the holy Temple.

P: The voice of the Lord above the water—Hallelujah;
The Almighty God's sound echoed in the clouds.

C: The voice of the Lord—Hallelujah;
marvelously heard over the ocean.

(for females)

P: The royal daughter stood—Hallelujah;
Glorious queen at Thy right hand.

---

* Liturgy currently used in the Malankara Orthodox Church (Indian Orthodox Church) and other Syrian Orthodox churches around the world.

C: Thy father's folk and home leave thou—Hallelujah;
The King desires thy beauty now.

P&C: King David stands near the baptismal candidate and says in the Holy spirit, "Come those who are thirsty; be strengthened in the Lord's presence." The fallen Adam called the Lord, the Lord answered him in the river Jordan and renewed him from his desperate state.

Like the blood that smeared on the door delivered Israel, the divine and enlivening grace of new birth through baptism be the protecting sign for us believers. We behold the Holy Trinity through this eternal glory.

Prayer

P: O Lord, God of the holy hosts, bless this Your servant who is being given the divine instruction—Grant him (her) wisdom and enlighten his (her) mind, to realize the vanity of worldliness. May he (she) cast off all mortal acts and worship You, Lord—together with the Father and the Holy Spirit now and for ever more. Amen.

P: The Lord is my shepherd; I have everything I need. He lets me rest in fields of green grass.

P&C: John trembled; Jordan blushed; Seraphim sang: "God who comes for baptism is Holy, Holy, Holy."

P: He leads me to quiet pools of fresh water; He gives me new strength and guides me in the right path.

P&C: The one who gives sanctity to Seraphim arrived *for* baptism in order to bless the water and give new birth through baptism to the children of Adam.

Glory be to the Father, the only begotten Son and the Holy Spirit, who renews the children of Adam through baptism.

Prumion (Introductory Praise)

Glory be to the indescribable true Light who instituted and consecrated baptism for His spiritual sheepfold through His majestic and divine wisdom.

Sedro (A collection of petitions)

Christ our God, you turned us from sinful thoughts and invited us to observe the holy commandments. You gave us entry to Your spiritual sheepfold and attracted us to the fountains and waters of salvation and exhorted us in an enlivening voice to be cleansed in hearts from all wickedness. Bless this servant to receive the living sign of Your protection. Include him (her) in your fold; reflect in him (her) the glory of Your face. Make him (her) Your Father's child. Enable him (her) for the new birth. Throw away the old nature from him (her). Put on him (her) the garment of immortality. Lead him (her) to Christian perfection and good departure from this world through a life of peace and comfort, give him (her) Your protection and growth in all aspects of life, so that we along with him (her) glorify You and Your Father and the Holy Spirit for ever and ever. Amen.

Hymn

Lord, protect by your Cross children
who are to be baptised.
    Regarding this baptism, John the
    son of Zachariah already said,
    "I give you baptism of water,
    but He who is coming will give you
    baptism of the spirit."
John the son of Zachariah
Came to the banks of river.
He, the power that is hidden to the angels
Came to be baptised.
The Lord came for baptism
And John came for witnessing.
The Father in heaven declared,
"Behold my dear son."

Prayer of incense

Priests: Unto the abundance of Your mercies, O Lord, we offer this sweet incense on behalf of this Your servant who is prepared for this holy baptism. May he (she) be made eligible for life by Your seal. May he (she) inherit the gifts of Your House and observe Your divine commandments and offer glory and praise to you and Your Father and to Your Holy Spirit now and evermore. Amen.

Psalm

As a deer longs for a stream of cool water, so I long for You, O God.

Epistle
Romans 5:20-6:4

"So then, as the one sin condemned all mankind, in the same way the one righteous act sets all mankind free and gives them life. And just as all people were made sinners as the result of the disobedience of one man, in the same way they will all be put right with God as the result of the obedience of the one man.

Law was introduced in order to increase wrongdoing; but where sin increased, God's grace increased much more. So then, just as sin ruled by means of death, so also God's grace rules by means of righteousness, leading us to eternal life through Jesus Christ our Lord."

Psalm

Sprinkle me with hyssop, and I shall be clean;
Wash me, and I will be whiter than snow—Hallelujah.

Gospel
(Luke 3:15-16, John 3:5-6)

Deacon: With calmness, awe and modesty, let us give heed to the good tidings *of the* living words of the Holy Gospel of our Lord Jesus Christ, which is read for us.

Congregation: Make us worthy, O Lord God.

Priest: Peace be to all of you.

C: And with your spirit.

P: The Holy Gospel of our Lord Jesus Christ, the life-giving preaching from Luke and John who preach life and redemption to the world.

C: Blessed is He who has come and shall come. Praises be to Him who sent Him, and upon all of us be His mercy forever.

P: Now in the time of the incarnation of our Lord, our God, and our Redeemer Jesus Christ, the Word of Life. God who had taken flesh of the Holy Virgin Mary. These things thus came to pass.

C: We believe and confess.

(Priest reads the Gospel):

People's hopes began to rise, and they began to wonder whether John perhaps might be the Messiah. So John said to all of them, "I baptize you with water, but someone is coming who is much greater than I am. I am not good enough even to untie his sandals. He will baptize you with the Holy Spirit and fire."

"I am telling you the truth," replied Jesus, "that no one can enter the Kingdom of God unless he is born of water and the Spirit. A person is born physically of human parents, but he is born spiritually of the Spirit.

P: Peace be to all of you.

Antiphon: **Wash me thoroughly from mine iniquity, and cleanse me from my sins. Neither hyssop nor ordinary water have the power to cleanse and purify the sins which I have committed. They can only be blotted out by the multitude of Your tender mercies.**

C: **Kyrie eleison.***

Priest (facing east):

Silent Prayer

Giver of Light and Enlightener of body and spirit, You have commanded the creation of light from darkness. You have risen in our minds and gave us saving sanctity, through the blessed water, divine holiness through the holy anointment, and union with Lord Jesus Christ through the communion in the holy body and blood. Merciful Lord, write the name of this servant in the book of Life. You have called him/her, from darkness to the true wisdom through Your holy exhortation. Count him/her among those who worship You and reflect Your Glory in him/her. Imprint the Cross of Your Christ in his/her heart and mind. Protect him (her) from all evils of the enemy. May he (she) flee from the vanity of this world and tread on the path of Your holy commandments.

Priest: Prayer
Give on this servant the divine breath that Your only son breathed on the apostles. (+)

Take away from his/her mind all remains of idolatry and equip him/her for the gift of the Holy Spirit. Enable him/her for the baptism of new birth. Enable him/her for the remission of sins through Jesus Christ Your only Son. We give reverence to and acknowledge authority of Him and to Your Holy Spirit and to You Father for ever and ever. Amen.

* *To be repeated until the secret prayer is completed.*

(The celebrant marks on the forehead of the candidate three times without oil.)

In the name of the Father, the Son and the living Holy Spirit
. . . . (name) is marked for eternal life.

C: **Kyrie eleison** . . . *(repeatedly while the celebrant prays in silence the following prayer).*

P. *(Prays silently),*
Lord God Almighty, I call you through our Lord and God Jesus Christ, Your only Son for the exorcism of all evil spirits and for the casting off of all unseen and opposing influences. Accept with sanctity and purity this spirit, who draws near You by the indwelling of Your Holy Spirit. Lord reveal to us and empower us not with vain words but to speak with Your Grace and Power that saves the world from the evil one.

Prayer of exorcism

Priest (celebrant) addressing the candidate pledges him/her in the following way and signs nine times on him/her.

Lord God, Creator of the visible and the invisible. We lay hands on this creation of Yours and call you by stamping Your name on this creation and image of You for the casting off of all spirits that are evil and unholy from him/her. Lord hear us by saving this servant of Yours from and forbidding all association with the opponent.

- (+) Listen, you unholy and proud one who haunts this creation of God.
- (+) I pledge with the glory of the Great King, you who are the enemy of all righteousness and violator of Law,
- (+) Be subdued by the Awesome Lord who founded the earth on the waters by his commandant and flee away with trembling.
- (+) I pledge you by the Almighty One who reigns in heaven and earth and by whom everything is created and preserved and by whom the heavenly ones exist and the earthly ones are empowered.
- (+) I pledge you by the One who sent the legion of evil ones to the depths through the pigs and who drowned Pharaoh and his chariots and forces in water.
- (+) I pledge you by the One who commanded the deaf and dumb spirit to depart and who admonished him from an attempt to re-entry.

- (+) Be afraid of the awesome name of the God who chained and banished the first opponent to the abyss and in whose presence the Seraphim and the Cherubim tremble and all the creation including the angels, the archangel, the principalities and the ministrants stand with fear.
- (+) Move away fast being afraid of the impending judgment.
- (+) Do not draw near to the creation of God and do not trouble the creation of God and do not like to live in the creation of God.

    This is not the abode of devils. This is the abode of the living God. He has said, "I will live and move among them and I will be their God and they will be my holy people." You wicked and despicable evil spirit, You are destined to be devoured by fire.

I pledge you by the Triune God, Father, Son and Holy spirit, undefiled and victorious. Keep away from the servants of God. Move out to uninhabitable and barren areas. Quick. Don't protest. Let you be thoroughly perished. You cursed, unholy traitor and prey to fire, flee from the creation of God. The triune God, Father, Son and Holy Spirit will destroy you utterly and make you prey for Fire. God will preserve this handwork of His for the day of salvation. May the Power and Authority be to Him. We give glory to Him for ever and ever. Amen.

(An alternate smaller version of the above prayer)

- +++Lord God, I exorcise from your handwork, *this* creation, all evil spirits, by the seal of your name
- +++Liberate this servant of Yours from traitor spirits. Oh evil spirit, be afraid of the impending judgment
- +++O evil spirit, do not draw near to the creation of God because it is not the abode of devils but the temple of God.
- +++I pledge you by the Triune God, Father, Son and Holy Spirit. Flee away, O evil one, completely and quickly. Do not protest.

Denouncing of Satan

(Candidate and Godparent facing West; candidate/Godparent repeats the words as the priest utters as follows),

Candidate/Godparent: "I, ... (name), **denounce Satan and all his deeds, his services, his worship, his vanity, his worldly deceitfulness and all his followers and adherents**—*(to be repeated three times).*

Confession of faith

(Candidate and Godparent facing East)

(Candidate/Godparent repeats the words as the priest utters as follows)

Candidate/ Godparent: "I, ... (name), **commit myself to You Christ, our God, trusting all the doctrines which You divinely entrusted to the prophets, the disciples, and the holy fathers"** *(to be repeated three times)*. **I denounce Satan. I accept Jesus Christ** *(three times)*.

(Priest begins and the Congregation along with the candidate recites the Nicene Creed).

P: **We believe in one true God**

C: **The Father Almighty, maker of heaven and earth, and of all things visible and invisible, and in one Lord, Jesus Christ, the Only Begotten Son of God, who was begotten of the Father before all worlds;**

Light of Light, true God of true God, begotten and not made; being of one substance with His Father; by whom all things were made; who for us men and for our salvation came down from heaven and was incarnate by the Holy Spirit and of the Virgin Mary, the mother of God. He became man, and was crucified for us under Pontius Pilate and He suffered, died, and was buried, and the third day He rose according to His will, and ascended into heaven, and sits at the right hand of His Father; and He will come again with great glory to judge both the living and the dead; and His Kingdom shall have no end. And we believe in the Holy Spirit, the Lord, the giver of life to all, who proceeds from the Father; who together with the Father and the Son is worshipped and glorified. Who spoke *through* the prophets and the apostles. And in one Holy, Catholic and Apostolic Church. We confess one baptism for the remission of sins. And we look for the resurrection of the dead, and the new life in the world to come Amen.

Anointing with the oil of gladness

P *(says silently)*: **Lord who created this servant from non being and enabled his/her baptism by Your Holy Spirit, establish him/her on the foundation of the apostles. Make him/her a true vegetation in the Holy Church. Send Your Holy Spirit to enable him/her for the sacramental anointment. Fill him/her with the divine gifts. Enlighten with your light, the mind of this devotee to get freedom from the slavery to sin.**

(Priest dips finger in oil of anointment and marks on the forehead of the candidate and prays),

To enable his/her status by new birth, _____ (name) is anointed by the oil of gladness in the name of the Father, the Son and the Holy Spirit.

(Water is poured in the baptismal font; while the priest holds his arms in cross-form the assistant pours warm water on right arm and cold water on left arm)

P: Lord, God, by our weak mediatorship we beseech you to make this water a spiritual womb and the mould that shapes immortality through the indwelling and exercise of the Holy Spirit. Enable Your servant to experience this as the garment of immortality and the deliverance from the slavery to sin by the love of Your only begotten Son and the indwelling of Your Holy Spirit.

(The priest places a cross on the baptismal font and covers with a veil.)

P & C: (hymn)
Hear, O all people! John mixed the water for baptism, which Christ sanctified and went into the river to be baptized in it. At the moment he came out from the water, heaven and earth gave honour to Him. The sun submitted its dazzling light and the stars did obeisance to Him who sanctified all the rivers and springs—Hallelujah. Hallelujah.

Who has ever two noble sisters such as the pure baptism and the Holy Church; the one gives birth to the new and spiritual children and the other nurtures them; whomsoever the baptism bears from the water, the Holy Church receives and presents to the altar—Hallelujah, Hallelujah.

P: Glory be to the Father, and to the Son and to the Holy Spirit.

(Priest unveils the font and lifts the cross.)

P&C: How mysterious is the time, when the priest stretches out his hands and opens the baptismal font: The heavenly hosts are astounded to behold the mortal standing above the flame. He calls upon the Holy Spirit to descend from above. His desire is hastily fulfilled when the Holy Spirit sanctifies the baptismal font for the remission of sins—Hallelujah, Hallelujah.

P: From eternity to eternity, Amen.

P&C: When the baptismal font is sanctified by the Father, the Son and the Holy Spirit, it becomes a fountain of life. The Father's voice was heard saying: "This is my beloved son," the Son was bending His head to be baptised and the Holy Spirit descending upon Him like a dove, Holy Trinity by whom the worlds gained life—Hallelujah, Hallelujah.

Deacon/Assistant: O merciful Lord, have mercy upon us and help us.

Priest: (Prayer in silence)
Lord You gave us the springs of true sanctity that cleanse all impurities of sin. Lord by the prayers of us sinners grant the breath that Your only begotten Son breathed on the holy apostles.

P: Lord, You are the Saviour, the sanctifier and the giver of all good gifts: We offer glory to You and to Your only-begotten Son and to Your Holy Spirit, now and for evermore. Amen.

(Priest breathes three times crosswise on water from west to east and from south to north.)

P: Lord by Your mercy turn to this water and cleanse it.

Deacon/Assistant: Kyrie eleison.

Priest: (Prayer in silence)
Break in pieces the head of the dragon, the murderer of mankind, under the sign of Your Cross. Drive away from this water all the aerial and invisible demons. Let not the evil spirit of darkness be hidden in it, nor the unclean spirits of obscurity, that cause mortal troubles and mental disturbance, be allowed to go down into this water with this child to be baptized. Put away from him (her), Almighty God, all the operations of the adversary.

P: Your Church and Fold saved by Your Cross stand at the river-flow of Jordan and appeal to You and through You to the Father with a contrite heart.

C: Almighty God the Father, have mercy upon us.

P: Lord we the weak and sinful servants give You thanks and offer to Your Grace thanksgiving for all and on behalf of all.

Deacon/Assistant: How awful is this hour and how dreadful this time of my beloved ones, wherein the Holy Spirit from the topmost heights of heaven takes wing and descends, broods and rests upon the water of this baptismal font and hallows it. In calm and reverence, you keep standing and praying. Pray that peace may be with us and all of us may have tranquility.

C: May peace be with us and tranquility among us all.

The Invocation of the Holy Spirit

P: (Prayer in silence)

Almighty God, the Father have mercy upon us and send Your Holy Spirit from Your unlimited abode and bosom—He, the Spirit, is personal, Lord, esteemed one, life giving one, spoken through the prophets and apostles, omnipresent, perfector of everything, who brings out holiness not as a servant but as one with authority, and who is holy by nature and does works of holiness and who is with diverse activities. He is the source of divine gifts and one with the Lord in essence. He proceeds from the Father and takes from the Son. He is equal with you and Your Son in Glory.

P: Hear me, O Lord
Hear me, O Lord
Hear me, O Lord, and have mercy upon us.

C: **Kyrie eleison** (thrice)

P: (At every invocation, the priest makes a transverse line of a cross)
Almighty God, make these waters, waters of refreshment, waters of happiness and rejoicing, waters which symbolize the death and resurrection of Your only begotten Son, and the waters of sanctification.

C: **Amen.**

P: For the purification of the defilements of the body and soul, for the loosening of the bonds, for the remission of sins and for the enlightenment of the souls and bodies.

C: **Amen**

P: For the washing of regeneration, for the gift of the status of child of God, for the garment of immortality and for the renewal by the Holy Spirit.

C: **Amen**

(Priest takes the vessel of holy Myron and moves it thrice over the water crosswise saying)

The waters saw You, O God, the waters saw You; they were afraid.

D/C: **Hallelujah**

P: The Lord is upon the great waters.

D/C: **Hallelujah**

(The Priest pours the holy Myron into the water in the sign of the cross, saying)

We pour holy Myron into this water of baptism for the blessings of regeneration and incorruptibility.

Deacon: **Barekmor**

P: In the name of the Father +

D/C: **Amen**

P: And of the Son +

D/C: **Amen**

P: And of the living Holy Spirit + for life eternal

D/C: **Amen. Kyrie eleison**

(Prayer in silence)

P: Lord our God, You sent Your Holy Spirit in the likeness of a dove and sanctified the streams of Jordan. Even now, O Lord, be pleased to perfect this Your servant who receives baptism. Prove him (her) to be an associate of Your Christ through Your saving baptism.

P: May this child be renewed and uplifted, may he/she be filled with Your Grace and observe Your divine Commandments and we along with him/her offer thanks and praise to You and to Your Son and to the Holy Spirit.

C: **Amen**

P: Peace be unto you all.

C: And with your spirit

(The priest after waving hands over the font, stretches his right hand and signs crosswise on the edge of water).

May this water be blessed and sanctified so as to become a divine regenerating laver.

D: **Barekmor**

P: In the name of the ever-living Father + for life eternal

D/C: **Amen**

P: In the name of the ever-living Son + for life eternal

D/C: **Amen**

P: And of the ever-living Holy Spirit + for life eternal

D/C: Amen

(The deacon/assistant, presents the child to the priest and the priest lays his right hand upon the child's head and with his left hand he pours water upon the child's head, front, back, right side and left side, saying:)

(Name) . . . . is baptised in the hope of life and forgiveness of sins

D: Barekmor

P: In the name of the Father +

D/C: Amen

P: And of the Son +

D/C: Amen

P: And of the Holy Spirit + for life eternal

D/C: Amen.

(The candidate is handed over to the godfather/mother)

Godfather/mother receives the child in a new white garment

Hymn: The princess stood in glory . . .

P/C/D: Stretch out your arms, O Holy Church, and receive this guileless lamb who has been born through the Holy Spirit.

O my daughter *hear, see* and give heed

John the Son of Zachariah, prophesied about this baptism, saying "I am only baptising you with water, but He who is coming after me will baptize you with the Holy Spirit."

D: Barekmor

P: Glory be to the Father, and to the Son and to the Holy Spirit

P/C/D: O Lamb, child of baptism, Come. I welcome you who are born in baptism in the name of the Holy Trinity.

D/C: From eternity to eternity. Amen

P/C/D: Gideon selected his army from water. Messiah welcomes his devotees from the water of baptism.

P: (Holding the vessel of Myron in his hands): **May this Your servant, who in faith and baptism has been counted among Your servants, be worthy to receive this seal in Your Holy Name. Grant, O Lord, that when he (she) is spiritually filled with the sweet fragrance, through this Myron, he (she) may become unyielding to the hostile forces and henceforth, may not be afraid of the prince of this world and the rulers of darkness. Let him (her) walk in the light of Your Glory, become the child of light and reach Your presence by walking in You.**

(The Priest smears his right thumb with holy Myron and seals thrice upon the child's forehead crosswise).

P: By the holy Myron which is Christ's sweet fragrance, the seal of the true faith, and the perfection of the Holy Spirit's gifts . . . . (name) is sealed for eternal life.

C: Barekmor

P: In the name of the Father +

D/C: Amen

P: And of the Son +

D/C: Amen

P: And of the ever-living Holy Spirit + for life eternal

D/C: Amen.

(The Priest pours the holy Myron in his palm and anoints the child first on the forehead, hand, shoulder, leg, etc. on the right side and then similarly on the left side, and again on forehead, head, eyes, ears, chest and back until the child is fully anointed by the Myron)

Hymn: God said (to Moses) anoint Aaron with holy oil. Now the lamb that receives baptism is anointed with the holy oil.

D: Barekmor

P: Glory be to the Father, and to the Son and to the Holy Spirit

Hymn: This is the oil that anoints the lamb of baptism. The Spirit bless him/her by signing mysteriously.

Holy Communion

(Holy Communion is administered to the baptised)

Hymn: **The fruit of life untasted by Adam in Paradise is being given to your mouth today.**

(Entry to the Altar/Sanctuary)

(The baptised is taken to the Holy Sanctuary and he/she is made to bow before and kiss the four corners of the altar, the front of the altar and the gospel).

Crowning

(Crowning at the entry of the Sanctuary)

P: Crown, O Lord, this Your servant with the crown of glory and splendour. May his (her) life be for Your delight and for the glory of Your name, Father, Son and Holy Spirit now and evermore.

D/C: **Amen**

(When detaching the Crown)

P: By the grace of the spiritual mother of the adoption as child of God, You have, O Lord, perfected this Your servant to become a brother (sister) to Your Only begotten Son. We humbly beseech You to guide him (her) by Your life-giving wisdom to the godly life of Your gospel. May he (she) increase in wisdom and stature that he (she) may be worthy to receive the crown which You have prepared in Your heavenly Kingdom for those who have virtuously departed, and by laying aside of this crown, may he (she) not be deprived of the holding up of Your right hand, but may he (she) be therewith protected, strengthened and nourished and be worthy to receive the crown of the calling from above and offer praise to You, and to Your Only begotten son, and to Your Holy Spirit now and evermore. Amen.

Benediction and dismissal

We commend you to the Holy Trinity with the divine provisions that you have received from the baptism and the atoning altar of Christ our God forever and ever. May God the Father be with you, and the adorable Son protect You, and the Holy spirit which you have received bring you to perfection and deliver you from all deceit and may the baptism that you have received abide with you forever and ever.

Chapter 4

Rite of Christian Initiation of Adults and Rite of Baptism for Several Children (Catholic—Roman Rite)

[THIRD STEP:] CELEBRATION OF THE SACRAMENTS OF INITIATION*

*When we were baptized we joined Jesus in death
so that we might walk in the newness of his life*[1]

206 The third step in the Christian initiation of adults is the celebration of the sacraments of baptism, confirmation, and eucharist. Through this final step the elect, receiving pardon for their sins, are admitted into the people of God. They are graced with adoption as children of God and are led by the Holy Spirit into the promised fullness of time begun in Christ and, as they share in the eucharistic sacrifice and meal, even to a foretaste of the kingdom of God.

207 The usual time for the celebration of the sacraments of initiation is the Easter Vigil (see no. 23), at which preferably the bishop himself presides as celebrant, at least for the initiation of those who are fourteen years old or older (see no. 12). As indicated in the Roman Missal, "Easter Vigil" (no. 44), the conferral of the sacraments follows the blessing of the water.

208 When the celebration takes place outside the usual time (see nos. 26–27), care should be taken to ensure that it has a markedly paschal character (see *Christian Initiation*, General Introduction, no. 6). Thus the texts for one of the ritual Masses "Christian Initiation: Baptism" given in the Roman Missal are used and the readings are chosen from those given in the Lectionary for Mass, "Celebration of the Sacraments of Initiation apart from the Easter Vigil."

---

* Liturgy currently used in the Catholic Church (Roman Rite).
[1] See Vatican Council II, Dogmatic Constitution on the Church (*Lumen Gentium*), no. 48; also Ephesians 1:10.

CELEBRATION OF BAPTISM

209 The celebration of baptism has as its center and high point the baptismal washing and the invocation of the Holy Trinity. Beforehand there are rites that have an inherent relationship to the baptismal washing: first, the blessing of water, then the renunciation of sin by the elect, and their profession of faith. Following the baptismal washing, the effects received through this sacrament are given expression in the explanatory rites: the anointing with chrism (when confirmation does not immediately follow baptism), the clothing with a white garment, and the presentation of a lighted candle.

210 PRAYER OVER THE WATER: The celebration of baptism begins with the blessing of water, even when the sacraments of initiation are received outside the Easter season. Should the sacraments be celebrated outside the Easter Vigil but during the Easter season (see no. 26), the water blessed at the Vigil is used, but a prayer of thanksgiving, having the same themes as the blessing, is included. The blessing declares the religious meaning of water as God's creation and the sacramental use of water in the unfolding of the paschal mystery, and the blessing is also a remembrance of God's wonderful works in the history of salvation.

The blessing thus introduces an invocation of the Trinity at the very outset of the celebration of baptism. For it calls to mind the mystery of God's love from the beginning of the world and the creation of the human race; by invoking the Holy Spirit and proclaiming Christ's death and resurrection, it impresses on the mind the newness of Christian baptism, by which we share in his own death and resurrection and receive the holiness of God himself.

211 RENUNCIATION OF SIN AND PROFESSION OF FAITH: In their renunciation of sin and profession of faith those to be baptized express their explicit faith in the paschal mystery that has already been recalled in the blessing of water and that will be connoted by the words of the sacrament soon to be spoken by the baptizing minister. Adults are not saved unless they come forward of their own accord and with the will to accept God's gift through their own belief. The faith of those to be baptized is not simply the faith of the Church, but the personal faith of each one of them and each one of them is expected to keep it a living faith.

Therefore the renunciation of sin and the profession of faith are an apt prelude to baptism, the sacrament of that faith by which the elect hold fast to God and receive new birth from him. Because of the renunciation of sin and the profession of faith, which form the one rite, the elect will not be baptized merely passively but will receive this great sacrament with the active resolve to renounce error and to hold fast to God. By their own personal act in the rite of renouncing sin and professing their faith, the elect, as was prefigured in the first covenant with the patriarchs, renounce sin and Satan in order to commit themselves for ever to the promise of the Savior and to the mystery of the Trinity. By professing their faith before the celebrant and the entire community, the elect express the intention, developed to maturity during the preceding periods of initiation, to enter into a new covenant with Christ. Thus these adults embrace the faith that through divine help the Church has handed down, and are baptized in that faith.

212 BAPTISM: Immediately after their profession of living faith in Christ's paschal mystery, the elect come forward and receive that mystery as expressed in the washing with water; thus once the elect have professed faith in the Father, Son, and Holy Spirit, invoked by the celebrant, the divine persons act so that those they have chosen receive divine adoption and become members of the people of God.

213 Therefore in the celebration of baptism the washing with water should take on its full importance as the sign of that mystical sharing in Christ's death and resurrection through which those who believe in his name die to sin and rise to eternal life. Either immersion or the pouring of water should be chosen for the rite, whichever will serve in individual cases and in the various traditions and circumstances to ensure the clear understanding that this washing is not a mere purification rite but the sacrament of being joined to Christ.

214 EXPLANATORY RITES: The baptismal washing is followed by rites that give expression to the effects of the sacrament just received. The anointing with chrism is a sign of the royal priesthood of the baptized and that they are now numbered in the company of the people of God. The clothing with the baptismal garment signifies the new dignity they have received. The presentation of a lighted candle shows that they are called to walk as befits the children of the light.

CELEBRATION OF CONFIRMATION
215 In accord with the ancient practice followed in the Roman liturgy, adults are not to be baptized without receiving confirmation immediately afterward, unless some serious reason stands in the way. The conjunction of the two celebrations signifies the unity of the paschal

mystery, the close link between the mission of the Son and the outpouring of the Holy Spirit, and the connection between the two sacraments through which the Son and the Holy Spirit come with the Father to those who are baptized.

216 Accordingly, confirmation is conferred after the explanatory rites of baptism, the anointing after baptism (no. 228) being omitted.

The Neophytes' First Sharing in the Celebration of the Eucharist

217 Finally in the celebration of the eucharist, as they take part for the first time and with full right, the newly baptized reach the culminating point in their Christian initiation. In this eucharist the neophytes, now raised to the ranks of the royal priesthood, have an active part both in the general intercessions and, to the extent possible, in bringing the gifts to the altar. With the entire community they share in the offering of the sacrifice and say the Lord's Prayer, giving expression to the spirit of adoption as God's children that they have received in baptism. When in communion they receive the body that was given for us and the blood that was shed, the neophytes are strengthened in the gifts they have already received and are given a foretaste of the eternal banquet.

OUTLINE OF THE RITE
    SERVICE OF LIGHT
    LITURGY OF THE WORD
    CELEBRATION OF BAPTISM
        Presentation of the Candidates
        Invitation to Prayer
        Litany of the Saints
        Prayer over the Water
        Profession of Faith
            Renunciation of Sin
            Profession of Faith
        Baptism
        Explanatory Rites
            [Anointing after Baptism]
            [Clothing with a Baptismal Garment]
            Presentation of a Lighted Candle

CELEBRATION OF CONFIRMATION
  Invitation
  Laying on of Hands
  Anointing with Chrism
[RENEWAL OF BAPTISMAL PROMISES (AT THE EASTER VIGIL)]
  Invitation
  Renewal of Baptismal Promises
    Renunciation of Sin
    Profession of Faith
  Sprinkling with Baptismal Water
LITURGY OF THE EUCHARIST

CELEBRATION OF THE SACRAMENTS OF INITIATION
(Easter Vigil)

CELEBRATION OF BAPTISM

218 The celebration of baptism begins after the homily. It takes place at the baptismal font, if this is in view of the faithful; otherwise in the sanctuary, where a vessel of water for the rite should be prepared beforehand.

Presentation of the Candidates

219 Accordingly, one of the following procedures, options A, B, or C, is chosen for the presentation of the candidates.

A   *When Baptism Is Celebrated Immediately at the Baptismal Font*
The celebrant accompanied by the assisting ministers goes directly to the font. An assisting deacon or other minister calls the candidates forward and their godparents present them. Then the candidates and the godparents take their place around the font in such a way as not to block the view of the congregation. The invitation to prayer (no. 220) and the Litany of the Saints (no. 221) follow.

[If there are a great many candidates, they and their godparents simply take their place around the font during the singing of the Litany of the Saints.]

B   *When Baptism Is Celebrated after a Procession to the Font*
There may be a full procession to the baptismal font. In this case an assisting deacon or other minister calls the candidates forward and their godparents present them.

[If there are a great many candidates, they and their godparents simply take their place in the procession.]

The procession is formed in this order: a minister carries the Easter candle at the head of the procession (unless, outside the Easter Vigil, it already rests at the baptismal font), the candidates with their godparents come next, then the celebrant with the assisting ministers. The Litany of the Saints (no. 221) is sung during the procession. When the procession has reached the font, the candidates and their godparents take their place around the font in such a way as not to block the view of the congregation. The invitation to prayer (no. 220) precedes the blessing of the water.

C *When Baptism Is Celebrated in the Sanctuary*
An assisting deacon or other minister calls the candidates forward and their godparents present them. The candidates and their godparents take their place before the celebrant in the sanctuary in such a way as not to block the view of the congregation. The invitation to prayer (no. 220) and the Litany of the Saints (no. 221) follow.

[If there are a great many candidates, they and their godparents simply take their place in the sanctuary during the singing of the Litany of the Saints.]

INVITATION TO PRAYER

220 The celebrant addresses the following or a similar invitation for the assembly to join in prayer for the candidates.

Dear friends, let us pray to almighty God for our brothers and sisters, N. and N., who are asking for baptism. He has called them and brought them to this moment; may he grant them light and strength to follow Christ with resolute hearts and to profess the faith of the Church. May he give them the new life of the Holy Spirit, whom we are about to call down on this water.

LITANY OF THE SAINTS

221 The singing of the Litany of the Saints is led by cantors and may include, at the proper place, names of other saints (for example, the titular of the church, the patron saints of the place or of those to be baptized) or petitions suitable to the occasion.

Lord, have mercy	Lord, have mercy
Christ, have mercy	Christ, have mercy
Lord, have mercy	Lord, have mercy
Holy Mary, Mother of God	pray for us
Saint Michael	pray for us
Holy Angels of God	pray for us
Saint John the Baptist	pray for us
Saint Joseph	pray for us

Saint Peter and Saint Paul	pray for us
Saint Andrew	pray for us
Saint John	pray for us
Saint Mary Magdalene	pray for us
Saint Stephen	pray for us
Saint Ignatius	pray for us
Saint Lawrence	pray for us
Saint Perpetua and Saint Felicity	pray for us
Saint Agnes	pray for us
Saint Gregory	pray for us
Saint Augustine	pray for us
Saint Athanasius	pray for us
Saint Basil	pray for us
Saint Martin	pray for us
Saint Benedict	pray for us
Saint Francis and Saint Dominic	pray for us
Saint Francis Xavier	pray for us
Saint John Vianney	pray for us
Saint Catherine	pray for us
Saint Teresa	pray for us
All holy men and women	pray for us
Lord, be merciful	Lord, save your people
From all evil	Lord, save your people
From every sin	Lord, save your people
From everlasting death	Lord, save your people
By your coming as man	Lord, save your people
By your death and rising to new life	Lord, save your people
By your gift of the Holy Spirit	Lord, save your people
Be merciful to us sinners	Lord, hear our prayer
Give new life to these chosen ones by the grace of baptism	Lord, hear our prayer
Jesus, Son of the living God	Lord, hear our prayer
Christ, hear us	Christ, hear us
Lord Jesus, hear our prayer	Lord Jesus, hear our prayer

PRAYER OVER THE WATER

    222 After the Litany of the Saints, the celebrant blesses the water, using the blessing formulary given in option A.

When baptism is celebrated outside the Easter Vigil (see no. 26), the celebrant may use any of the blessing formularies given in options A, B, and C.

But when baptism is celebrated during the Easter season (see no. 26) and water already blessed at the Easter Vigil is available, the celebrant uses either option D or option E, so that this part of the celebration will retain the themes of thanksgiving and intercession.

A   BLESSING OF THE WATER: Facing the font (or vessel) containing the water, the celebrant sings the following.

Father,
you give us grace through sacramental signs,
which tell us of the wonders of your unseen power.

In baptism we use your gift of water,
which you have made a rich symbol of the grace
you give us in this sacrament.

At the very dawn of creation
your Spirit breathed on the waters,
making them the wellspring of all holiness.

The waters of the great flood
you made a sign of the waters of baptism
that make an end of sin
and a new beginning of goodness.

Through the waters of the Red Sea
you led Israel out of slavery
to be an image of God's holy people,
set free from sin by baptism.

In the waters of the Jordan
your Son was baptized by John
and anointed with the Spirit.

Your Son willed that water and blood should flow from his side
as he hung upon the cross.

After his resurrection he told the disciples:
"Go out and teach all nations,
baptizing them in the name of the Father, and of the Son, and of the Holy Spirit."

Father,
look now with love upon your Church
and unseal for it the fountain of baptism.

By the power of the Holy Spirit
give to this water the grace of your Son,
so that in the sacrament of baptism
all those whom you have created in your likeness
may be cleansed from sin
and rise to a new birth of innocence
by water and the Holy Spirit.

> Here, if this can be done conveniently, the celebrant before continuing lowers the Easter candle into the water once or three times, then holds it there until the acclamation at the end of the blessing.

> [Outside the Easter Vigil, the celebrant before continuing simply touches the water with his right hand.]

We ask you, Father, with your Son
to send the Holy Spirit upon the waters of this font.
May all who are buried with Christ in the death of baptism
rise also with him to newness of life.
We ask this through Christ our Lord.

> All:

Amen.

> The people sing the following or some other suitable acclamation.

Springs of water, bless the Lord.
Give him glory and praise for ever.

B BLESSING OF WATER: Facing the font (or vessel) containing the water, the celebrant says the following.

Praise to you, almighty God and Father,
for you have created water to cleanse and to give life.

> All sing or say the following or some other suitable acclamation.

Blessed be God.

> Celebrant:

Praise to you, Lord Jesus Christ, the Father's only Son,
for you offered yourself on the cross,
that in the blood and water flowing from your side
and through your death and resurrection
the Church might be born.

> All:

Blessed be God.

Celebrant:
Praise to you, God the Holy Spirit,
for you anointed Christ at his baptism in the waters of the Jordan,
that we might all be baptized in you.

All:
Blessed be God.

Celebrant:
Come to us, Lord, Father of all,
and make holy this water which you have created,
so that all who are baptized in it may be washed clean of sin
and be born again to live as your children.

All sing or say the following or some other suitable invocation.
Hear us, Lord.

Celebrant:
Make this water holy, Lord,
so that all who are baptized into Christ's death and resurrection by this water
may become more perfectly like your Son.

All:
Hear us, Lord.

The celebrant touches the water with his right hand and continues.
Lord,
make holy this water which you have created,
so that all those whom you have chosen
may be born again by the power of the Holy Spirit
and may take their place among your holy people.

All:
Hear us, Lord.

C BLESSING OF WATER: Facing the font (or vessel) containing the water, the celebrant says the following.
Father, God of mercy,
through these waters of baptism
you have filled us with new life as your very own children.

All sing or say the following or some other suitable acclamation.
Blessed be God.

Celebrant:
From all who are baptized in water and the Holy Spirit,
you have formed one people.
United in your Son, Jesus Christ.

All:
Blessed be God.

Celebrant:
You have set us free and filled our hearts with the Spirit of your love,
that we may live in your peace.

All:
Blessed be God.

Celebrant:
You call those who have been baptized
to announce the Good News of Jesus Christ to people everywhere.

All:
Blessed be God.

The celebrant concludes with the following.
You have called your children, N. and N.,
to this cleansing water and new birth,
that by sharing the faith of your Church they may have eternal life.
Bless ☩ this water in which they will be baptized.
We ask this in the name of Jesus the Lord.

All:
Amen.

D EASTER-SEASON THANKSGIVING OVER WATER ALREADY BLESSED: Facing the font (or vessel) containing the water, the celebrant says the following.

Praise to you, almighty God and Father,
for you have created water to cleanse and to give life.

All sing or say the following or some other suitable acclamation.
Blessed be God.

Celebrant:
Praise to you, Lord Jesus Christ, the Father's only Son,
for you offered yourself on the cross,
that in the blood and water flowing from your side
and through your death and resurrection
the Church might be born.

All:
Blessed be God.

Celebrant:
**Praise to you, God the Holy Spirit,
for you anointed Christ at his baptism in the waters of the Jordan,
that we might all be baptized in you.**

All:
Blessed be God.

The celebrant concludes with the following prayer.
**You have called your children, N. and N., to this cleansing water,
that they may share in the faith of your Church and have eternal life.
By the mystery of this consecrated water
lead them to a new and spiritual birth.
We ask this through Christ our Lord.**

All:
Amen.

E EASTER-SEASON THANKSGIVING OVER WATER ALREADY BLESSED: *Facing the font (or vessel) containing the blessed water, the celebrant says the following.*

**Father, God of mercy,
through these waters of baptism
you have filled us with new life as your very own children.**

All sing or say a suitable acclamation or the following.
Blessed be God.

Celebrant:
**From all who are baptized in water and the Holy Spirit,
you have formed one people,
united in your Son, Jesus Christ.**

All:
Blessed be God.

Celebrant:
**You have set us free and filled our hearts with the Spirit of your love,
that we may live in your peace.**

All:
Blessed be God.

Celebrant:
You call those who have been baptized
to announce the Good News of Jesus Christ to people everywhere.

All:
Blessed be God.

The celebrant concludes with the following.
You have called your children, N. and N., to this cleansing water,
that they may share in the faith of your Church and have eternal life.
By the mystery of this consecrated water
lead them to a new and spiritual birth.
We ask this through Christ our Lord.

All:
Amen.

PROFESSION OF FAITH

223 After the blessing of the water (or prayer of thanksgiving), the celebrant continues with the profession of faith, which includes the renunciation of sin and the profession itself.

RENUNCIATION OF SIN

224 Using one of the following formularies, the celebrant questions all the elect together; or, after being informed of each candidate's name by the godparents, he may use the same formularies to question the candidates individually.

[At the discretion of the diocesan bishop, the formularies for the renunciation of sin may be made more specific and detailed as circumstances might require (see no. 33.8).]

A   Celebrant:
Do you reject sin so as to live in the freedom of God's children?

Candidates:
I do.

Celebrant:
Do you reject the glamor of evil,
and refuse to be mastered by sin?

Candidates:
I do.

Celebrant:
Do you reject Satan, father of sin and prince of darkness?

> Candidates:
>
> I do.

B   Celebrant:

Do you reject Satan
and all his works,
and all his empty promises?

> Candidates:
>
> I do.

C   Celebrant:

Do you reject Satan?

> Candidates:
>
> I do.

> Celebrant:

And all his works?

> Candidates:
>
> I do.

> Celebrant:

And all his empty promises?

> Candidates:
>
> I do.

Profession of Faith

> 225 Then the celebrant, informed again of each candidate's name by the godparents, questions the candidates individually. Each candidate is baptized immediately after his or her profession of faith.
>
> [If there are a great many to be baptized, the profession of faith may be made simultaneously either by all together or group by group, then the baptism of each candidate follows.]

> Celebrant:

N., do you believe in God, the Father almighty, creator of heaven
    and earth?

> Candidate:

I do.

> Celebrant:

Do you believe in Jesus Christ, his only Son, our Lord,
    who was born of the Virgin Mary,

was crucified, died, and was buried,
rose from the dead,
and is now seated at the right hand of the Father?

Candidate:

I do.

Celebrant:

Do you believe in the Holy Spirit,
the holy catholic Church, the communion of saints,
the forgiveness of sins, the resurrection of the body,
and the life everlasting?

Candidate:

I do.

BAPTISM

226 The celebrant baptizes each candidate either by immersion, option A, or by the pouring of water, option B. Each baptism may be followed by a short acclamation (see Appendix II, no. 595), sung or said by the people.

[If there are a great number to be baptized, they may be divided into groups and baptized by assisting priests or deacons. In baptizing, either by immersion, option A, or by the pouring of water, option B, these ministers say the sacramental formulary for each candidate. During the baptisms, singing by the people is desirable or readings from Scripture or simply silent prayer.]

A   If baptism is by immersion, of the whole body or of the head only, decency and decorum should be preserved. Either or both godparents touch the candidate. The celebrant, immersing the candidate's whole body or head three times, baptizes the candidate in the name of the Trinity.

N., I baptize you in the name of the Father,

He immerses the candidate the first time.

and of the Son,

He immerses the candidate the second time.

and of the Holy Spirit.

He immerses the candidate the third time.

B   If baptism is by the pouring of water, either or both godparents place the right hand on the shoulder of the candidate, and the celebrant, taking baptismal water and pouring it three times on the candidate's bowed head, baptizes the candidate in the name of the Trinity.

N., **I baptize you in the name of the Father,**

He pours water the first time.

and of the Son,

He pours water the second time.

and of the Holy Spirit.

He pours water the third time.

Explanatory Rites

227 The celebration of baptism continues with the explanatory rites, after which the celebration of confirmation normally follows.

Anointing after Baptism

228 If the confirmation of those baptized is separated from their baptism, the celebrant anoints them with chrism immediately after baptism.

[When a great number have been baptized, assisting priests or deacons may help with the anointing.]

The celebrant first says the following over all the newly baptized before the anointing.

The God of power and Father of our Lord Jesus Christ has freed you from sin and brought you to new life through water and the Holy Spirit.

**He now anoints you with the chrism of salvation,
so that, united with his people,
you may remain for ever a member of Christ
who is Priest, Prophet, and King.**

Newly baptized:

Amen.

In silence each of the newly baptized is anointed with chrism on the crown of the head.

Clothing with a Baptismal Garment

229 The garment used in this rite may be white or of a color that conforms to local custom. If circumstances suggest, this rite may be omitted.

The celebrant says the following formulary, and at the words "Receive this baptismal garment" the godparents place the garment on the newly baptized.

N. and N., you have become a new creation
and have clothed yourselves in Christ.
Receive this baptismal garment
and bring it unstained to the judgment seat of our Lord Jesus Christ,
so that you may have everlasting life.

Newly baptized:

Amen.

Presentation of a Lighted Candle

230 The celebrant takes the Easter candle in his hands or touches it, saying to the godparents:

Godparents, please come forward to give to the newly baptized the light of Christ.

A godparent of each of the newly baptized goes to the celebrant, lights a candle from the Easter candle, then presents it to the newly baptized.

Then the celebrant says to the newly baptized:

**You have been enlightened by Christ.
Walk always as children of the light
and keep the flame of faith alive in your hearts.
When the Lord comes, may you go out to meet him
with all the saints in the heavenly kingdom.**

Newly baptized:

Amen.

[If the celebration of confirmation is to be deferred, the renewal of baptismal promises, as in the Roman Missal, "Easter Vigil" (no. 46), now takes place; then the neophytes are led back to their places among the faithful.]

[Outside the Easter Vigil, if confirmation is to be deferred, the neophytes are led back to their places among the faithful after the presentation of a lighted candle.]

CELEBRATION OF CONFIRMATION

231 Between the celebration of baptism and confirmation, the congregation may sing a suitable song.

The place for the celebration of confirmation is either at the baptismal font or in the sanctuary, depending on the place where, according to local conditions, baptism has been celebrated.

232 If the bishop has conferred baptism, he should now also confer confirmation. If the bishop is not present, the priest who conferred baptism is authorized to confirm.

[When there are a great many persons to be confirmed, the minister of confirmation may associate priests with himself as ministers of the sacrament (see no. 14).]

Invitation

233 The celebrant first speaks briefly to the newly baptized in these or similar words.

My dear newly baptized, born again in Christ by baptism, you have become members of Christ and of his priestly people. Now you are to share in the outpouring of the Holy Spirit among us, the Spirit sent by the Lord upon his apostles at Pentecost and given by them and their successors to the baptized.

The promised strength of the Holy Spirit, which you are to receive, will make you more like Christ and help you to be witnesses to his suffering, death, and resurrection. It will strengthen you to be active members of the Church and to build up the Body of Christ in faith and love.

[The priests who will be associated with the celebrant as ministers of the sacrament now stand next to him.]

With hands joined, the celebrant next addresses the people:

My dear friends, let us pray to God our Father, that he will pour out the Holy Spirit on these newly baptized to strengthen them with his gifts and anoint them to be more like Christ, the Son of God.

All pray briefly in silence.

Laying on of Hands

234 The celebrant holds his hands outstretched over the entire group of those to be confirmed and says the following prayer.

[In silence the priests associated as ministers of the sacrament also hold their hands outstretched over the candidates.]

All-powerful God, Father of our Lord Jesus Christ,
by water and the Holy Spirit
you freed your sons and daughters from sin
and gave them new life.

Send your Holy Spirit upon them
to be their helper and guide.

Give them the spirit of wisdom and understanding,
the spirit of right judgment and courage,
the spirit of knowledge and reverence.
Fill them with the spirit of wonder and awe in your presence.
We ask this through Christ our Lord.
R. Amen.

ANOINTING WITH CHRISM

235 A minister brings the chrism to the celebrant.

[When the celebrant is the bishop, priests who are associated as ministers of the sacrament receive the chrism from him.]

Each candidate, with godparent or godparents, goes to the celebrant (or to an associated minister of the sacrament); or, if circumstances require, the celebrant (associated ministers) may go to the candidates.

Either or both godparents place the right hand on the shoulder of the candidate and either a godparent or the candidate gives the candidate's name to the minister of the sacrament. During the conferral of the sacrament a suitable song may be sung.

The minister of the sacrament dips his right thumb in the chrism and makes the sign of the cross on the forehead of the one to be confirmed as he says:

N., **be sealed with the Gift of the Holy Spirit.**

Newly confirmed:

Amen.

The minister of the sacrament adds:

Peace be with you.

Newly confirmed:

And also with you.

236 At the Easter Vigil the renewal of baptismal promises by the congregation [nos. 237–240 below or in the Roman Missal, "Easter Vigil" (no. 46)] follows the celebration of confirmation. Then the neophytes are led to their places among the faithful.

[Outside the Easter Vigil, the neophytes are led to their places among the faithful immediately after confirmation. The general intercessions then begin (see no. 241).]

RENEWAL OF BAPTISMAL PROMISES (AT THE EASTER VIGIL)

INVITATION

237 After the celebration of baptism, the celebrant addresses the community, in order to invite those present to the renewal of their baptismal promises; the candidates for reception into full communion join the rest of the community in this renunciation of sin and profession of faith. All stand and hold lighted candles. The celebrant may use the following or similar words:

Dear friends, through the paschal mystery we have been buried with Christ in baptism, so that we may rise with him to newness of life. Now that we have completed our Lenten observance, let us renew the promises we made in baptism, when we rejected Satan and his works and promised to serve God faithfully in his holy catholic Church.

RENEWAL OF BAPTISMAL PROMISES

RENUNCIATION OF SIN

238 The celebrant continues with one of the following formularies of renunciation.

[If circumstances require, the conference of bishops may adapt formulary A in accord with local conditions.]

A   Celebrant:

Do you reject sin so as to live in the freedom of God's children?

All:

I do.

Celebrant:

Do you reject the glamor of evil,
and refuse to be mastered by sin?

All:

I do.

Celebrant:

Do you reject Satan, father of sin and prince of darkness?

All:

I do.

B   Celebrant:
Do you reject Satan?

All:
I do.

Celebrant:
And all his works?

All:
I do.

Celebrant:
And all his empty promises?

All:
I do.

Profession of Faith

239 Then the celebrant continues:
Do you believe in God, the Father Almighty,
creator of heaven and earth?

All:
I do.

Celebrant:
Do you believe in Jesus Christ, his only Son, our Lord,
who was born of the Virgin Mary,
was crucified, died, and was buried,
rose from the dead,
and is now seated at the right hand of the Father?

All:
I do.

Celebrant:
Do you believe in the Holy Spirit,
the holy catholic Church, the communion of saints,
the forgiveness of sins, the resurrection of the body,
and the life everlasting?

All:
I do.

Sprinkling with Baptismal Water

240 The celebrant sprinkles all the people with the blessed baptismal water, while all sing the following song or any other that is baptismal in character.

I saw water flowing
from the right side of the temple, alleluia.
It brought God's life and his salvation,
and the people sang in joyful praise:
alleluia, alleluia. (See Ezekiel 47:1-2, 9)

The celebrant then concludes with the following prayer.

God, the all-powerful Father of our Lord Jesus Christ, has given us a new birth by water and the Holy Spirit and forgiven all our sins.

May he also keep us faithful to our Lord Jesus Christ for ever and ever.

All:
Amen.

LITURGY OF THE EUCHARIST

241 Since the profession of faith is not said, the general intercessions begin immediately and for the first time the neophytes take part in them. Some of the neophytes also take part in the procession to the altar with the gifts.

242 With Eucharistic Prayers I, II, or III the special interpolations given in the Roman Missal, the ritual Masses, "Christian Initiation: Baptism" are used.

[Eucharistic Prayer IV, with its special interpolation indicated in the same ritual Masses, may also be used but outside the Easter Vigil.]

243 It is most desirable that the neophytes, together with their godparents, parents, spouses, and catechists, receive communion under both kinds.

Before saying "This is the Lamb of God," the celebrant may briefly remind the neophytes of the preeminence of the eucharist, which is the climax of their initiation and the center of the whole Christian life.

PERIOD OF POSTBAPTISMAL CATECHESIS OR MYSTAGOGY

You are a chosen race, a royal priesthood, a holy people; praise God who called you out of darkness and into his marvelous light

244 The third step of Christian initiation, the celebration of the sacraments, is followed by the final period, the period of postbaptismal catechesis or mystagogy. This is a time for the community and the neophytes together to grow in deepening their grasp of the paschal mystery and in making it part of their lives through meditation on the Gospel, sharing in the eucharist, and doing the works of charity. To strengthen the neophytes as they begin to walk in newness of life, the community of the faithful, their godparents, and their pastors should give them thoughtful and friendly help.

245 The neophytes are, as the term "mystagogy" suggests, introduced into a fuller and more effective understanding of mysteries through the Gospel message they have learned and above all through their experience of the sacraments they have received. For they have truly been renewed in mind, tasted more deeply the sweetness of God's word, received the fellowship of the Holy Spirit, and grown to know the goodness of the Lord. Out of this experience, which belongs to Christians and increases as it is lived, they derive a new perception of the faith, of the Church, and of the world.

246 Just as their new participation in the sacraments enlightens the neophytes' understanding of the Scriptures, so too it increases their contact with the rest of the faithful and has an impact on the experience of the community. As a result, interaction between the neophytes and the faithful is made easier and more beneficial. The period of postbaptismal catechesis is of great significance for both the neophytes and the rest of the faithful. Through it the neophytes, with the help of their godparents, should experience a full and joyful welcome into the community and enter into closer ties with the other faithful. The faithful, in turn, should derive from it a renewal of inspiration and of outlook.

247 Since the distinctive spirit and power of the period of postbaptismal catechesis or mystagogy derive from the new, personal experience of the sacraments and of the community, its main setting is the so-called Masses for neophytes, that is, the Sunday Masses of the Easter season. Besides being occasions for the newly baptized to gather with the community and share in the mysteries, these celebrations include particularly suitable readings from the Lectionary, especially the readings for Year A. Even when Christian initiation has been celebrated outside the usual times, the texts for these Sunday Masses of the Easter season may be used.

248 All the neophytes and their godparents should make an effort to take part in the Masses for the neophytes and the entire local community should be invited to participate with them. Special places in the congregation are to be reserved for the neophytes and their godparents. The homily and, as circumstances suggest, the general intercessions should take into account the presence and needs of the neophytes.

249 To close the period of postbaptismal catechesis, some sort of celebration should be held at the end of the Easter season near Pentecost Sunday; festivities in keeping with local custom may accompany the occasion.

250 On the anniversary of their baptism the neophytes should be brought together in order to give thanks to God, to share with one another their spiritual experiences, and to renew their commitment.

251 To show his pastoral concern for these new members of the Church, the bishop, particularly if he was unable to preside at the sacraments of initiation himself, should arrange, if possible, to meet the recently baptized at least once in the year and to preside at a celebration of the eucharist with them. At this Mass they may receive holy communion under both kinds.

* * *

[CHAPTER I]
RITE OF BAPTISM FOR SEVERAL CHILDREN*

RECEPTION OF THE CHILDREN

32. If possible, baptism should take place on Sunday, the day on which the Church celebrates the paschal mystery. It should be conferred in a communal celebration for all the recently born children, and in the presence of the faithful, or at least of relatives, friends, and neighbors, who are all to take an active part in the rite.

33. It is the role of the father and mother, accompanied by the godparents, to present the child to the Church for baptism.

34. If there are very many children, and if there are several priests or deacons present, these may help the celebrant in the parts referred to below.

35. The people may sing a psalm or hymn suitable for the occasion. Meanwhile the celebrating priest or deacon, vested in alb or surplice, with a stole (with or without a cope) of festive color, and accompanied

---

* Liturgy currently used in the Catholic Church [Roman Rite].

by the ministers, goes to the entrance of the church or to that part of the church where the parents and godparents are waiting with those who are to be baptized.

36. The celebrant greets all present, and especially the parents and godparents, reminding them briefly of the joy with which the parents welcomed their children as gifts from God, the source of life, who now wishes to bestow his own life on these little ones.

37. First the celebrant questions the parents of each child.

Celebrant:
What name do you give your child? (or: **have you given**?)

Parents:

N.

Celebrant:
What do you ask of God's Church for N.**?**

Parents:
Baptism.

The celebrant may choose other words for this dialogue. The first reply may be given by someone other than the parents if local custom gives him the right to name the child. In the second response the parents may use other words, e.g., **faith** or **the grace of Christ** or **entrance into the Church** or **eternal life**.

38. If there are many children to be baptized, the celebrant asks the names from all the parents together, and each family replies in turn. The second question may also be asked of all together.

Celebrant:
What name do you give each of these children? (or: **have you given?**)

Parents: N., N., etc.

Celebrant:
What do you ask of God's Church for your children?

All: **Baptism.**

39. The celebrant speaks to the parents in these or similar words:

You have asked to have your children baptized. In doing so you are accepting the responsibility of training them in the practice of the faith. It will be your duty to bring them up to keep God's commandments as Christ taught us, by loving God and our neighbor. Do you clearly understand what you are undertaking?

Parents: **We do.**

This response is given by each family individually. But if there are many children to be baptized, the response may be given by all together.

40. Then the celebrant turns to the godparents and addresses them in these or similar words:

Are you ready to help these parents in their duty as Christian mothers and fathers?

All the godparents: **We are.**

41. The celebrant continues:

N. and N. (or: **My dear children**), **the Christian community welcomes you with great joy. In its name I claim you for Christ our Savior by the sign of the cross. I now trace the cross on your foreheads, and invite your parents (and godparents) to do the same.**

He signs each child on the forehead, in silence. Then he invites the parents and (if it seems appropriate) the godparents to do the same.

42. The celebrant invites the parents, godparents, and the others to take part in the liturgy of the word. If circumstances permit, there is a procession to the place where this will be celebrated, during which a song is sung, e.g., Psalm 85:7, 8, 9ab:

Will you not give us life,
 and shall not your people rejoice in you?
Show us, O Lord, your kindness,
 and grant us your salvation.
I will hear what God proclaims;
 the Lord—for he proclaims peace to his people.

43. The children to be baptized may be carried to a separate place, where they remain until the end of the liturgy of the word.

LITURGY OF THE WORD

Scriptural Readings and Homily

44. One or even two of the following gospel passages are read, during which all may sit if convenient.

John 3:1-6 The meeting with Nicodemus.

Matthew 28:18-20 The apostles are sent to preach the gospel and to baptize.

Mark 1:9-11 The baptism of Jesus.

Mark 10:13-16 Let the little children come to me.

> The passages listed in nos. 186–194 and 204–215 may be chosen, or other passages which better meet the wishes or needs of the parents. Between the readings, responsorial psalms or verses may be sung as given in nos. 195–203.
>
> 45. After the reading, the celebrant gives a short homily, explaining to those present the significance of what has been read. His purpose will be to lead them to a deeper understanding of the mystery of baptism and to encourage the parents and godparents to a ready acceptance of the responsibilities which arise from the sacrament.
>
> 46. After the homily, or in the course of or after the litany, it is desirable to have a period of silence while all pray at the invitation of the celebrant. If convenient, a suitable song follows, e.g., one chosen from nos. 225–245.

GENERAL INTERCESSIONS [PRAYER OF THE FAITHFUL]

> 47. Then the general intercessions [prayer of the faithful] are said:

Celebrant:

My brothers and sisters,* let us ask our Lord Jesus Christ to look lovingly on these children who are to be baptized, on their parents and godparents, and on all the baptized.

Leader:

By the mystery of your death and resurrection, bathe these children in light, give them the new life of baptism and welcome them into your holy Church.

All: **Lord, hear our prayer.**

Leader:

Through baptism and confirmation, make them your faithful followers and witnesses to your gospel.

All: **Lord, hear our prayer.**

Leader:

Lead them by a holy life to the joys of God's kingdom.

---

* At the discretion of the priest, other words which seem more suitable under the circumstances, such as **friends** or **dearly beloved** or **brethren**, may be used. This also applies to parallel instances in the liturgy.

All: **Lord, hear our prayer.**

Leader:
Make the lives of their parents and godparents examples of faith to inspire these children.

All: **Lord, hear our prayer.**

Leader:
Keep their families always in your love.

All: **Lord, hear our prayer.**

Leader:
Renew the grace of our baptism in each one of us.

All: **Lord, hear our prayer.**

Other forms may be chosen from nos. 217–220.

48. The celebrant next invites all to invoke the saints. At this point, if the children have been taken out, they are brought back.

Holy Mary, Mother of God,	pray for us.
Saint John the Baptist,	pray for us.
Saint Joseph,	pray for us.
Saint Peter and Saint Paul,	pray for us.

The names of other saints may be added, especially the patrons of the children to be baptized, and of the church or locality. The litany concludes:

All holy men and women, pray for us.

Prayer of Exorcism and Anointing before Baptism

49. After the invocations, the celebrant says:

A

Almighty and ever-living God,
you sent your only Son into the world
to cast out the power of Satan, spirit of evil,
to rescue man from the kingdom of darkness,
and bring him into the splendor of your kingdom of light.
We pray for these children:
set them free from original sin,
make them temples of your glory,

and send your Holy Spirit to dwell within them.
(We ask this) through Christ our Lord.

> All: **Amen.**

> Another form of the prayer of exorcism:

B

Almighty God,
you sent your only Son
to rescue us from the slavery of sin,
and to give us the freedom
only your sons and daughters enjoy.
We now pray for these children
who will have to face the world with its temptations,
and fight the devil in all his cunning.
Your Son died and rose again to save us.
By his victory over sin and death,
cleanse these children from the stain of original sin.
Strengthen them with the grace of Christ,
and watch over them at every step in life's journey.
(We ask this) through Christ our Lord.

> All: **Amen.**

> 50. The celebrant continues:

We anoint you with the oil of salvation
in the name of Christ our Savior;
may he strengthen you
with his power,
who lives and reigns for ever and ever.

> All: **Amen.**

> He anoints each child on the breast with the oil of catechumens. If the number of children is large, the anointing may be done by several ministers.

> 51. If, for serious reasons, the conference of bishops so decides, the anointing before baptism may be omitted. [In the United States, it may be omitted only when the minister of baptism judges the omission to be pastorally necessary or desirable.] In that case the celebrant says once only:

May you have strength in the power of Christ our Savior, who lives and reigns for ever and ever.

> All: **Amen.**

And immediately he lays his hand on each child in silence.

52. If the baptistry is located outside the church or is not within view of the congregation, all go there in procession.

If the baptistry is located within view of the congregation, the celebrant, parents, and godparents go there with the children, while the others remain in their places.

If, however, the baptistry cannot accommodate the congregation, the baptism may be celebrated in a suitable place within the church, and the parents and godparents bring the child forward at the proper moment.

Meanwhile, if it can be done suitably, an appropriate song is sung, e.g., Psalm 23:

The Lord is my shepherd; I shall not want.
  In verdant pastures he gives me repose;
Beside restful waters he leads me;
  he refreshes my soul.
He guides me in right paths
  for his name's sake.
Even though I walk in the dark valley
  I fear no evil; for you are at my side
With your rod and your staff
  that give me courage.
You spread the table before me
  in the sight of my foes;
You anoint my head with oil,
  my cup overflows.
Only goodness and kindness follow me
  all the days of my life;
And I shall dwell in the house of the Lord
  for years to come.

CELEBRATION OF THE SACRAMENT

53. When they come to the font, the celebrant briefly reminds the congregation of the wonderful work of God whose plan it is to sanctify man, body and soul, through water. He may use these or similar words:

A

My dear brothers and sisters, we now ask God to give these children new life in abundance through water and the Holy Spirit.

B

My dear brothers and sisters, God uses the sacrament of water to give his divine life to those who believe in him. Let us turn to him, and ask him to pour his gift of life from this font on the children he has chosen.

BLESSING AND INVOCATION OF GOD
OVER BAPTISMAL WATER

> 54. Then, turning to the font, he says the following blessing (outside the Easter season):

A

Father, you give us grace through sacramental signs, which tell us of the wonders of your unseen power.

In baptism we use your gift of water, which you have made a rich symbol of the grace you give us in this sacrament.

At the very dawn of creation your Spirit breathed on the waters, making them the wellspring of all holiness.

The waters of the great flood you made a sign of the waters of baptism, that make an end of sin and a new beginning of goodness.

Through the waters of the Red Sea you led Israel out of slavery, to be an image of God's holy people, set free from sin by baptism.

In the waters of the Jordan your Son was baptized by John and anointed with the Spirit.

Your Son willed that water and blood should flow from his side as he hung upon the cross.

After his resurrection he told his disciples: "Go out and teach all nations, baptizing them in the name of the Father, and of the Son, and of the Holy Spirit."

Father, look now with love upon your Church, and unseal for her the fountain of baptism.

By the power of the Spirit give to the water of this font the grace of your Son.

You created man in your own likeness: cleanse him from sin in a new birth to innocence by water and the Spirit.

> The celebrant touches the water with his right hand and continues:

We ask you, Father, with your Son to send the Holy Spirit upon the water of this font. May all who are buried with Christ in the death of baptism rise also with him to newness of life. We ask this through Christ our Lord.

All:
Amen.

Other forms of the blessing, nos. 223–224, may be chosen.

55. During the Easter season, if there is baptismal water which was consecrated at the Easter Vigil, the blessing and invocation of God over the water are nevertheless included, so that this theme of thanksgiving and petition may find a place in the baptism. The forms of this blessing and invocation are those found in nos. 223–224, with the variation indicated at the end of each text.

RENUNCIATION OF SIN AND PROFESSION OF FAITH

56. The celebrant speaks to the parents and godparents in these words:

Dear parents and godparents: You have come here to present these children for baptism. By water and the Holy Spirit they are to receive the gift of new life from God, who is love.

On your part, you must make it your constant care to bring them up in the practice of the faith. See that the divine life which God gives them is kept safe from the poison of sin, to grow always stronger in their hearts.

If your faith makes you ready to accept this responsibility, renew now the vows of your own baptism. Reject sin; profess your faith in Christ Jesus. This is the faith of the Church. This is the faith in which these children are about to be baptized.

57. The celebrant questions the parents and godparents.

A

Celebrant:
Do you reject Satan?

Parents and godparents:
I do.

Celebrant:
And all his works?

Parents and godparents:

I do.

Celebrant:

And all his empty promises?

Parents and godparents:

I do.

or **B**

Celebrant:

Do you reject sin, so as to live in the freedom of God's children?

Parents and godparents:

I do.

Celebrant:

Do you reject the glamor of evil, and refuse to be mastered by sin?

Parents and godparents:

I do.

Celebrant:

Do you reject Satan, father of sin and prince of darkness?

Parents and godparents:

I do.

According to circumstances, this second form may be expressed with greater precision by the conferences of bishops, especially in places where it is necessary for the parents and godparents to reject superstitious and magical practices used with children.

58. Next the celebrant asks for the threefold profession of faith from the parents and godparents:

Celebrant:

Do you believe in God, the Father almighty, creator of heaven and earth?

Parents and godparents:

I do.

Celebrant:

Do you believe in Jesus Christ, his only Son, our Lord, who was born of the Virgin Mary, was crucified, died, and was buried, rose from the dead, and is now seated at the right hand of the Father?

Parents and godparents:

I do.

Celebrant:

Do you believe in the Holy Spirit, the holy catholic Church, the communion of saints, the forgiveness of sins, the resurrection of the body, and life everlasting?

Parents and godparents:

I do.

59. The celebrant and the congregation give their assent to the profession of faith:

Celebrant:

This is our faith. This is the faith of the Church. We are proud to profess it, in Christ Jesus our Lord.

All:

Amen.

If desired, some other formula may be used instead, or a suitable song by which the community expresses its faith with a single voice.

BAPTISM

60. The celebrant invites the first of the families to the font. Using the name of the individual child, he questions the parents and godparents.

Celebrant:

Is it your will that N. should be baptized in the faith of the Church, which we have all professed with you?

Parents and godparents:

It is.

He baptizes the child, saying:

N., I baptize you in the name of the Father,

He immerses the child or pours water upon it.

and of the Son,

He immerses the child or pours water upon it a second time.

and of the Holy Spirit.

He immerses the child or pours water upon it a third time.

He asks the same question and performs the same action for each child.

After each baptism it is appropriate for the people to sing a short acclamation. (See nos. 225–245.)

If the baptism is performed by the pouring of water, it is preferable that the child be held by the mother (or father). Where, however, it is felt that the existing custom should be retained, the godmother (or godfather) may hold the child. If baptism is by immersion, the mother or father (godmother or godfather) lifts the child out of the font.

61. If the number of children to be baptized is large, and other priests or deacons are present, these may baptize some of the children in the way described above, and with the same form.

EXPLANATORY RITES

Anointing after Baptism

62. Then the celebrant says:

God the Father of our Lord Jesus Christ has freed you from sin, given you a new birth by water and the Holy Spirit, and welcomed you into his holy people. He now anoints you with the chrism of salvation. As Christ was anointed Priest, Prophet, and King, so may you live always as members of his body, sharing everlasting life.

All:
Amen.

Next, the celebrant anoints each child on the crown of the head with chrism, in silence.

If the number of children is large and other priests or deacons are present, these may anoint some of the children with chrism.

Clothing with White Garment

63. The celebrant says:

(N. and N.,) **you have become a new creation, and have clothed yourselves in Christ.**

See in this white garment the outward sign of your Christian dignity. With your family and friends to help you by word and example, bring that dignity unstained into the everlasting life of heaven.

All:
Amen.

The white garments are put on the children. A different color is not permitted unless demanded by local custom. It is desirable that the families provide the garments.

Lighted Candle

64. The celebrant takes the Easter candle and says:

Receive the light of Christ.

Someone from each family (e.g., the father or godfather) lights the child's candle from the Easter candle.

The celebrant then says:

Parents and godparents, this light is entrusted to you to be kept burning brightly. These children of yours have been enlightened by Christ. They are to walk always as children of the light. May they keep the flame of faith alive in their hearts. When the Lord comes, may they go out to meet him with all the saints in the heavenly kingdom.

Ephphetha or Prayer over Ears and Mouth

65. If the conference of bishops decides to preserve the practice, the rite of *Ephphetha* follows. [In the United States it may be performed at the discretion of the minister.] The celebrant touches the ears and mouth of each child with his thumb, saying:

The Lord Jesus made the deaf hear and the dumb speak. May he soon touch your ears to receive his word, and your mouth to proclaim his faith, to the praise and glory of God the Father.

All:
Amen.

66. If the number of children is large, the celebrant says the formula once, but does not touch the ears and mouth.

CONCLUSION OF THE RITE

67. Next there is a procession to the altar, unless the baptism was performed in the sanctuary. The lighted candles are carried for the children.

A baptismal song is appropriate at this time, e.g.:

**You have put on Christ,
in him you have been baptized.
Alleluia, alleluia.**

Other songs may be chosen from nos. 225–245.

Lord's Prayer

68. The celebrant stands in front of the altar and addresses the parents, godparents, and the whole assembly in these or similar words:

Dearly beloved, these children have been reborn in baptism. They are now called children of God, for so indeed they are. In confirmation they will receive the fullness of God's Spirit. In holy communion they will share the banquet of Christ's sacrifice, calling God their Father in the midst of the Church. In their name, in the Spirit of our common sonship, let us pray together in the words our Lord has given us:

69. All present join the celebrant in singing or saying:

Our Father . . .

Blessing and Dismissal

70. The celebrant first blesses the mothers, who hold the children in their arms, then the fathers, and lastly the entire assembly:

A

Celebrant:

God the Father, through his Son, the Virgin Mary's child, has brought joy to all Christian mothers, as they see the hope of eternal life shine on their children. May he bless the mothers of these children. They now thank God for the gift of their children. May they be one with them in thanking him for ever in heaven, in Christ Jesus our Lord.

All:

Amen.

Celebrant:

God is the giver of all life, human and divine. May he bless the fathers of these children. With their wives they will be the first teachers of their children in the ways of faith. May they be also the best of teachers, bearing witness to the faith by what they say and do, in Christ Jesus our Lord.

All:

Amen.

Celebrant:

By God's gift, through water and the Holy Spirit, we are reborn to everlasting life. In his goodness, may he continue to pour out his blessings upon all present, who are his sons and daughters. May he make them always, wherever they may be, faithful members of his holy people. May he send his peace upon all who are gathered here, in Christ Jesus our Lord.

All:

Amen.

Celebrant:

May almighty God, the Father, and the Son, ✢ and the Holy Spirit, bless you.

All:

Amen.

Celebrant:

Go in peace.

All:

Thanks be to God.

Other forms of the final blessing, nos. 247, 248, and 249 may be chosen.

B

Celebrant:

May God the almighty Father, who filled the world with joy by giving us his only Son, bless these newly-baptized children. May they grow to be more fully like Jesus Christ our Lord.

All:

Amen.

Celebrant:

May almighty God, who gives life on earth and in heaven, bless the parents of these children. They thank him now for the gift he has given them. May they always show that gratitude in action by loving and caring for their children.

All:

Amen.

Celebrant:

May almighty God, who has given us a new birth by water and the Holy Spirit, generously bless all of us who are his faithful children.

May we always live as his people, and may he bless all here present with his peace.

All:
Amen.

Celebrant:
May almighty God, the Father, and the Son, ✢ and the Holy Spirit, bless you.

All:
Amen.

Celebrant:
Go in peace.

All:
Thanks be to God.

C

Celebrant:
May God, the source of life and love, who fills the hearts of mothers with love for their children, bless the mothers of these newly-baptized children. As they thank God for a safe delivery, may they find joy in the love, growth, and holiness of their children.

All:
Amen.

Celebrant:
May God, the Father and model of all fathers, help these fathers to give good example, so that their children will grow to be mature Christians in all the fullness of Jesus Christ.

All:
Amen.

Celebrant:
May God, who loves all people, bless all the relatives and friends who are gathered here. In his mercy, may he guard them from evil and give them his abundant peace.

All:
Amen.

Celebrant:

And may almighty God, the Father, and the Son, ✢ and the Holy Spirit, bless you.

All:

Amen.

Celebrant:

Go in peace.

All:

Thanks be to God.

D

Celebrant:

My brothers and sisters, we entrust you all to the mercy and help of God the almighty Father, his only Son, and the Holy Spirit. May he watch over your life, and may we all walk by the light of faith, and attain the good things he has promised us.

And may almighty God, the Father, and the Son, ✢ and the Holy Spirit, bless you.

All:

Amen.

Celebrant:

Go in peace.

All:

Thanks be to God.

> 71. After the blessing, all may sing a hymn which suitably expresses thanksgiving and Easter joy, or they may sing the song of the Blessed Virgin Mary, the Magnificat.
>
> Where there is the practice of bringing baptized infants to the altar of the Blessed Virgin Mary, this custom is observed if appropriate.

Chapter 5

Holy Baptism (Lutheran)*

1. While a baptismal hymn is sung the candidates, sponsors, and parents gather at the font.

2. The minister addresses the baptismal group and the congregation.

P̄ In Holy Baptism our gracious heavenly Father liberates us from sin and death by joining us to the death and resurrection of our Lord Jesus Christ. We are born children of a fallen humanity; in the waters of Baptism we are reborn children of God and inheritors of eternal life. By water and the Holy Spirit we are made members of the Church which is the body of Christ. As we live with him and with his people, we grow in faith, love, and obedience to the will of God.

3. A sponsor for each candidate, in turn, presents the candidate with these or similar words

I present _____name_____ to receive the Sacrament of Holy Baptism.

4. The minister addresses those candidates who are able to answer for themselves:

P̄ _____name_____, do you desire to be baptized?

R̄ I do.

5. The minister addresses the sponsors and parents.

---

* Liturgy widely used in the Evangelical Lutheran Church in America and in the Evangelical Lutheran Church in Canada (see above, note 9, page 52).

6. When only young children are baptized the minister says

P In Christian love you have presented *these children* for Holy Baptism. You should, therefore, faithfully bring *them* to the services of God's house, and teach *them* the Lord's Prayer, the Creed, and the Ten Commandments. As *they grow* in years, you should place in *their* hands the Holy Scriptures and provide for *their* instruction in the Christian faith, that, living in the covenant of their Baptism and in communion with the Church, *they* may lead *godly lives* until the day of Jesus Christ.

Do you promise to fulfill these obligations?

R I do.

OR

7. When older children and adults are baptized also, the minister says:

P In Christian love you have presented *these people* for Holy Baptism. You should, therefore, faithfully care for *them* and help *them* in every way as God gives you opportunity, that *they* may bear witness to the faith we profess, and that, living in the covenant of *their* Baptism and in communion with the Church, *they* may lead *godly lives* until the day of Jesus Christ.

Do you promise to fulfill these obligations?

R I do.

Stand

8. When baptisms are celebrated within the Holy Communion, The Prayers may be said at this time, with special reference to those baptized

After each portion of the prayers:

A Lord, in your mercy,

C hear our prayer

9. The minister begins the thanksgiving.

P The Lord be with you.

C And also with you.

P Let us give thanks to the Lord our God.

C It is right to give him thanks and praise.

P Holy God, mighty Lord, gracious Father: We give you thanks, for in the beginning your Spirit moved over the waters and you created heaven and earth. By the gift of water you nourish and sustain us and all living things.

By the waters of the flood you condemned the wicked and saved those whom you had chosen, Noah and his family. You led Israel by the pillar of cloud and fire through the sea, out of slavery into the freedom of the promised land. In the waters of the Jordan your Son was baptized by John and anointed with the Spirit. By the baptism of his own death and resurrection your beloved Son has set us free from the bondage to sin and death, and has opened the way to the joy and freedom of everlasting life. He made water a sign of the kingdom and of cleansing and rebirth. In obedience to his command, we make disciples of all nations, baptizing them in the name of the Father, and of the Son, and of the Holy Spirit.

Pour out your Holy Spirit, so that *those* who *are* here baptized may be given new life. Wash away the sin of *all those* who *are* cleansed by this water and bring *them* forth as *inheritors* of your glorious kingdom.

To you be given praise and honor and worship through your Son, Jesus Christ our Lord, in the unity of the Holy Spirit, now and forever. (245)

C Amen

10. The minister addresses the baptismal group and the congregation.

P I ask you to profess your faith in Christ Jesus, reject sin, and confess the faith of the Church, the faith in which we baptize.

P Do you renounce all the forces of evil, the devil, and all his empty promises?

R I do.

P Do you believe in God the Father?

C **I believe in God, the Father almighty, creator of heaven and earth.**

P Do you believe in Jesus Christ, the Son of God?

C **I believe in Jesus Christ, his only Son, our Lord.**
    He was conceived by the power of the Holy Spirit
        and born of the virgin Mary.

He suffered under Pontius Pilate,
　　was crucified, died, and was buried.
He descended into hell.*
On the third day he rose again.
He ascended into heaven,
　　and is seated at the right hand of the Father.
He will come again to judge the living and the dead.

P Do you believe in God the Holy Spirit?

C I believe in the Holy Spirit,
　　the holy catholic Church,
　　the communion of saints,
　　the forgiveness of sins,
　　the resurrection of the body,
　　and the life everlasting. Amen

11. The minister baptizes each candidate.

P _____name_____, I baptize you in the name of the Father,	OR	P _____name_____, is baptized in the name of the Father,
The minister pours water on the candidate's head.		*The minister pours water on the candidate's head.*
P and of the Son,		P and of the Son,
The minister pours water on the candidate's head a second time.		*The minister pours water on the candidate's head a second time.*
P and of the Holy Spirit. Amen		P and of the Holy Spirit. Amen
The minister pours water on the candidate's head a third time.		*The minister pours water on the candidate's head a third time.*

Sit

12. A psalm or hymn may be sung as the minister and the baptismal group go before the altar.

P The Lord be with you.

C And also with you.

　　* *Or,* He descended to the dead.

13. Those who have been baptized kneel. Sponsors or parents holding young children stand. The minister lays both hands on the head of each of the baptized and prays for the Holy Spirit:

P God, the father of our Lord Jesus Christ, we give you thanks for freeing your sons and daughters from the power of sin and for raising them up to a new life through this holy sacrament. Pour your Holy Spirit upon _____name_____: the spirit of wisdom and understanding, the spirit of counsel and might, the spirit of knowledge and the fear of the Lord, the spirit of joy in your presence. (246)

C Amen

14. The minister marks the sign of the cross on the forehead of each of the baptized. Oil prepared for this purpose may be used. As the sign of the cross is made, the minister says:

P _____name_____, child of God, you have been sealed by the Holy Spirit and marked with the cross of Christ forever.

The sponsor or the baptized responds: "Amen."

15. After all have received the sign of the cross, they stand.

16. A lighted candle may be given to each of the baptized (to the sponsor of a young child) by a representative of the congregation who says:

Let your light so shine before others that they may see your good works and glorify your Father in heaven.

17. When small children are baptized, this prayer may be said.

P O God, the giver of all life, look with kindness upon the *fathers* and *mothers* of *these children*. Let them ever rejoice in the gift you have given them. Make them teachers and examples of righteousness for their *children*. Strengthen them in their own Baptism so they may share eternally with their *children* the salvation you have given them, through Jesus Christ our Lord. (247)

C Amen

Stand

18. The ministers and the baptismal group turn toward the congregation; a representative of the congregation says:

Through Baptism God has made *these* new *sisters and brothers* members of the priesthood we all share in Christ Jesus, that we may proclaim the praise of God and bear his creative and redeeming Word to all the world.

C **We welcome you into the Lord's family. We receive you as fellow members of the body of Christ, children of the same heavenly Father, and workers with us in the kingdom of God.**

19. The ministers may exchange the peace with the baptized with their sponsors and parents, and with the congregation:

Peace be with you. ℞ Peace be with you.

20. All return to their places.

21. The service continues with the Offering.

Chapter 6

The Baptism of Children
(Lutheran—Sweden)*

Hymn

Introduction and Prayer of Thanks

P   In the name of the Father and the Son and the Holy Spirit.

It is God's will that we should live in fellowship with him.
Therefore he sent his Son, Jesus Christ,
to save us from evil.
Through baptism he brings us to new life in his Church,
a life in union with him
which he today offers to *the child* we bring to be baptized.

P   Let us pray.

God, we thank you for *this child*.
Bless those who bear responsibility for *him*
(parents, godparents and friends).
Fill them with your love,
so that they may tenderly care for *him*
and give *him* security.
Help us all, in our life together,
to rejoice in the gift of our own baptism.

All   Amen.

The Gospel

P   Let us now hear the words of the Gospel about Jesus and the children.

(P)   They brought children for him to touch. The disciples rebuked them, but when Jesus saw it he was indignant, and said to them: "Let the children come to me; do not try to stop them; for the kingdom of God belongs to such as these. Truly I tell you, whoever does not accept the kingdom of God like a child will never enter

---

* Liturgy currently used in the Church of Sweden.

it." And he put his arms round them, laid his hands upon them,
and blessed them.
(Mark 10:13-16 REB)

The priest may say these or similar words:

P   In the same way we now receive this child,
    whom we welcome by name.

Prayer of Deliverance

P   What is your child's name?

One of the parents answers: NN

P   God, you alone can save us from all evil.
    Deliver NN from the power of darkness,
    write *his* name in the Book of Life
    and keep *him* in your light
    now and always.

The priest may say:

P   Receive the sign of the cross
    (on your forehead
    on your mouth
    and on your heart).
    Jesus Christ, crucified and risen,
    calls you to be his disciple.
    Amen.

Bible Reading

P   Let us hear the words of Jesus about baptism and faith:

Jesus came near and said to them: "Full authority in heaven and
on earth has been committed to me. Go therefore to all nations and
make them my disciples; baptize them in the name of the Father and
the Son and the Holy Spirit, and teach them to observe all that I have
commanded you. I will be with you always, to the end of time."
(Matthew 28.18-20 REB)

or Acts 2.38 *or* Acts 19.5 *or* Rom 6.4-5
or Gal 3.27-28 *or* Tit 3.4-5

The Address
May be omitted.

Hymn
May be omitted.

Baptismal Prayer

P Let us pray.

Heavenly Father, through water and the Spirit
you have created one people,
united with you in Jesus Christ.

We thank you that to us this water is a fountain of grace, and that *those* who are to be baptized in it will share in the victorious death and resurrection of your Son, Jesus Christ our Lord.

All Amen.

* The Creed   [The * here and at "The Baptism" below means that the whole congregation shall rise and remain standing during this part of the service.]

P Let us together confess the faith
into which we were baptized.

All I believe in God, the Father almighty,
creator of heaven and earth.

I believe in Jesus Christ, his only Son, our Lord.
He was conceived by the power of the Holy Spirit and born of the Virgin Mary.
He suffered under Pontius Pilate,
was crucified, died, and was buried.
He descended to the dead.
On the third day he rose again.
He ascended into heaven,
and is seated at the right hand of the Father.
He will come again to judge the living and the dead.

I believe in the Holy Spirit,
the holy catholic Church,
the communion of saints,
the forgiveness of sins,
the resurrection of the body,
and the life everlasting. Amen.

The priest may ask:

P Do you wish your child to be baptized into this faith and to live in fellowship with Christ in his Church?

The parents answer:
We do.

* The Baptism

P NN, I baptize you
in the name of the Father
and the Son
and the Holy Spirit.

P God of life,
fill NN with your Spirit
and help *him* day by day
to live as your child.

The Welcome *(and the giving of the candle)*

P Jesus said:
He who receives such a child in my name receives me.

(P) NN, we welcome you into the family of God and receive you in love and hope.

The lighting of the candle may take place here or during the baptism. At the handing over of the candle the following or similar words may be said:

(P) Receive this candle.
Its light reminds us that
Jesus said:
"I am the light of the world:
those who follow me shall not walk in darkness
but shall have the light of life."

P Dear Christian people,
through baptism *your child* has been made
a member of Christ's Church.
It is now your duty as parents (and godparents),
by your example and your prayers,
to lead *him* in the path of faith,
in fellowship with God's people.

Intercession

P Let us pray.

(P) Merciful God and Father
 our children are our future, our responsibility and our joy.
 Therefore we pray for *this child* (NN).
 May *he* grow in security,
 freedom and fellowship with others.
 Give *him* inner strength to sustain *him* in times of trial.
 Help us to live in the joy of our own baptism,
 and to grow in faith,
 until the day we share the full joy of your presence.

All Amen.

or

(P) God, the Creator of heaven and earth,
 by your Spirit you give life.
 We pray for *this child* (NN)
 whom you have received in baptism.
 Help us with joyful trust in you
 to give *him* security and confidence.
 Sustain *him* in the strength of your Spirit
 in a dangerous world,
 so that *he* may come to know the secret of your kingdom.
 So shield *him*, your *child*, in life and death
 and for all eternity.

All Amen.

The Lord's Prayer

All Our Father in heaven,
 hallowed be your name,
 your kingdom come,
 your will be done
 on earth as in heaven.
 Give us today our daily bread.
 Forgive us our sins
 as we forgive those who sin against us.
 Lead us not into temptation
 but deliver us from evil.

For the kingdom, the power, and the glory
are yours now and for ever.
Amen.

The Blessing

P   The Lord bless you and watch over you.
The Lord make his face shine upon you
and be gracious to you.
The Lord look kindly on you and give you peace.
In the name of the Father and the Son
and the Holy Spirit.

All   Amen.

Hymn

The Dismissal

P   Go in peace to serve the Lord with joy.

Chapter 7

An Anglican Service of Baptism and Confirmation (Anglican)*

¶ Preparation

At the entry of the ministers, a hymn may be sung.

The Greeting

The bishop greets the people, using these or other suitable words
Blessed be God, Father, Son and Holy Spirit.
Blessed be his kingdom, now and for ever. Amen.

or from Easter Day to Pentecost
Alleluia Christ is risen.
He is risen indeed. Alleluia.

There is one body and one spirit.
There is one hope to which we were called;
one Lord, one faith, one baptism,
one God and Father of all.

Peace be with you
And also with you.

The bishop may introduce the service.

The Gloria in excelsis may be used.

The Collect

The bishop introduces a period of silent prayer with the words Let us pray or a more specific bidding.

The Collect of the Day is normally used on Sundays and on Principal Festivals. On other occasions a seasonal Collect from the service for Holy Baptism or this prayer is used

Heavenly Father,
by the power of your Holy Spirit
you give to your faithful people new life in the water of baptism.

---

* Liturgy currently used in the majority of churches in the Church of England.

Guide and strengthen us by the same Spirit,
that we who are born again may serve you in faith and love,
and grow into the full stature of your Son, Jesus Christ,
who is alive and reigns with you in the unity of the Holy Spirit
now and for ever. **Amen.**

¶ The Liturgy of the Word

Readings

The readings of the day are normally used on Sundays and Principal Festivals. For other occasions a Table of Readings is provided.

Either one or two readings from Scripture may precede the Gospel reading.

At the end of each the reader may say
This is the word of the Lord.
Thanks be to God.

The psalm or canticle follows the first reading; other hymns and songs may be used between the readings.

Gospel Reading

An acclamation may herald the Gospel reading.

When the Gospel is announced the reader says
Hear the Gospel of our Lord Jesus Christ according to N.
Glory to you, O Lord.

At the end
This is the Gospel of the Lord.
Praise to you, O Christ.

Sermon

¶ The Liturgy of Initiation

Presentation of the Candidates

The candidates may be presented to the congregation. Where appropriate, they may be presented by their godparents or sponsors.

The bishop asks those who are candidates for baptism
Do you wish to be baptized?
I do.

The bishop asks the candidates for confirmation who have been baptized

Have you been baptized in the name of the Father, and of the Son, and of the Holy Spirit?
I have.

The bishop asks all the candidates

Are you ready with your own mouth and from your own heart to affirm your faith in Jesus Christ?
I am.

Testimony by the candidates may follow.

The bishop addresses the whole congregation

Faith is the gift of God to his people.
In baptism the Lord is adding to our number those whom he is calling.
People of God, will you welcome *these candidates* and uphold *them* in *their* life in Christ?

With the help of God, we will.

If children are to be baptized, the questions to parents and godparents in the service for Holy Baptism are used.

The Decision

A large candle may be lit. The bishop addresses all the candidates

In baptism, God calls us out of darkness into his marvellous light.
To follow Christ means dying to sin and rising to new life with him.
Therefore I ask:

Do you reject the devil and all rebellion against God?
I reject them.
Do you renounce the deceit and corruption of evil?
I renounce them.
Do you repent of the sins that separate us from God and neighbour?
I repent of them.

Do you turn to Christ as Saviour?
I turn to Christ.
Do you submit to Christ as Lord?
I submit to Christ.
Do you come to Christ, the way, the truth and the life?
I come to Christ.

Where there are strong pastoral reasons, the alternative form of the Decision may be used.

Signing with the Cross

The bishop or another minister makes the sign of the cross on the forehead of each candidate for baptism, saying

Christ claims you for his own.
Receive the sign of his cross.

The bishop may invite their sponsors to sign the candidates with the sign of the cross.

When all the candidates for baptism have been signed, the bishop says to them

Do not be ashamed to confess the faith of Christ crucified.
Fight valiantly as a disciple of Christ
against sin, the world and the devil,
and remain faithful to Christ to the end of your life.

The bishop says

May almighty God deliver you from the powers of darkness,
restore in you the image of his glory,
and lead you in the light and obedience of Christ. **Amen.**

Prayer over the Water

The ministers and candidates for baptism and confirmation gather at the baptismal font. A canticle, psalm, hymn or a litany may be used.

The bishop stands before the water of baptism and says (optional seasonal and responsive forms are provided in the service for Holy Baptism)

Praise God who made heaven and earth,
who keeps his promise for ever.

Let us give thanks to the Lord our God
It is right to give him thanks and praise.

We thank you, almighty God, for the gift of water
to sustain, refresh and cleanse all life.
Over water the Holy Spirit moved in the beginning of creation.
Through water you led the children of Israel
from slavery in Egypt to freedom in the promised land.
In water your Son Jesus received the baptism of John
and was anointed by the Holy Spirit as the Messiah, the Christ,
to lead us from the death of sin to newness of life.

We thank you, Father, for the water of baptism.
In it we are buried with Christ in his death.
By it we share in his resurrection.

Through it we are reborn by the Holy Spirit.
Therefore, in joyful obedience to your Son,
we baptize into his fellowship those who come to him in faith.

Now sanctify this water that, by the power of your Holy Spirit,
they may be cleansed from sin and born again.
Renewed in your image, may they walk by the light of faith
and continue for ever in the risen life of Jesus Christ our Lord;
to whom with you and the Holy Spirit
be all honour and glory, now and for ever. **Amen.**

Profession of Faith

The bishop addresses the congregation
Brothers and sisters, I ask you to profess
together with *these candidates*
the faith of the Church.

Do you believe and trust in God the Father?
I believe in God, the Father almighty,
creator of heaven and earth.

Do you believe and trust in his Son Jesus Christ?
I believe in Jesus Christ, his only Son, our Lord,
who was conceived by the Holy Spirit,
born of the Virgin Mary,
suffered under Pontius Pilate,
was crucified, died, and was buried;
he descended to the dead.
On the third day he rose again;
he ascended into heaven,
he is seated at the right hand of the Father,
and he will come to judge the living and the dead.

Do you believe and trust in the Holy Spirit?
I believe in the Holy Spirit,
the holy catholic Church,
the communion of saints,
the forgiveness of sins,
the resurrection of the body,
and the life everlasting. Amen.

Where there are strong pastoral reasons the Alternative Profession of Faith may be used.

Baptism

The bishop may address each candidate for baptism by name, saying
N, is this your faith?

and candidates answer in their own words, or
This is my faith.

The bishop or another minister dips each candidate in water, or pours water on them, saying
N, I baptize you
in the name of the Father,
and of the Son
and of the Holy Spirit. **Amen.**

If the newly baptized are clothed with a white robe, a hymn or song may be used, and a minister may say
You have been clothed with Christ.
As many as are baptized into Christ have put on Christ.

If those who have been baptized were not signed with the cross immediately after the Decision, the bishop signs each one now.

The bishop says
May God, who has received you by baptism into his Church,
pour upon you the riches of his grace,
that within the company of Christ's pilgrim people
you may daily be renewed by his anointing Spirit,
and come to the inheritance of the saints in glory. **Amen.**

The candidates for confirmation who have previously been baptized may come forward to the font and sign themselves with water, or the bishop may sprinkle them.

Then the bishop says
Almighty God,
we thank you for our fellowship in the household of faith
with all who have been baptized into your name.
Keep us faithful to our baptism,
and so make us ready for that day
when the whole creation shall be made perfect in your Son,
our Saviour Jesus Christ. **Amen.**

The bishop and the candidates gather at the place of confirmation. A hymn, chant or litany may be used.

Confirmation

The bishop stands before those who are to be confirmed, and says

Our help is in the name of the Lord
who has made heaven and earth.

Blessed be the name of the Lord
now and for ever. Amen.

The bishop extends his hands towards those to be confirmed and says
Almighty and ever-living God,
you have given these your servants new birth
in baptism by water and the Spirit,
and have forgiven them all their sins.
Let your Holy Spirit rest upon them:
the Spirit of wisdom and understanding;
the Spirit of counsel and inward strength;
the Spirit of knowledge and true godliness;
and let their delight be in the fear of the Lord. **Amen.**

The bishop addresses each candidate by name
N, God has called you by name and made you his own.

He then lays his hand on the head of each, saying
Confirm, O Lord, your servant with your Holy Spirit. **Amen.**

The bishop invites the congregation to pray for all those on whom hands have been laid
Defend, O Lord, these your servants with your heavenly grace,
that they may continue yours for ever,
and daily increase in your Holy Spirit more and more
until they come to your everlasting kingdom. Amen.

Commission

The bishop may use this Commission
Those who are baptized are called to worship and serve God.
Will you continue in the apostles' teaching and fellowship,
in the breaking of bread, and in the prayers?
With the help of God, I will.

Will you persevere in resisting evil,
and, whenever you fall into sin, repent and return to the Lord?
With the help of God, I will.

Will you proclaim by word and example
the good news of God in Christ?
With the help of God, I will.

Will you seek and serve Christ in all people,
loving your neighbour as yourself?
With the help of God, I will.

Will you acknowledge Christ's authority over human society,
by prayer for the world and its leaders,
by defending the weak, and by seeking peace and justice?
With the help of God, I will

May Christ dwell in your hearts through faith,
that you may be rooted and grounded in love
and bring forth the fruit of the Spirit. **Amen.**

The Prayers of Intercession may follow. It is appropriate that the newly baptized and confirmed take their part in leading the prayers. The prayers provided in the service for Holy Baptism may be used. If the rest of the Holy Communion does not follow, these prayers may be used after the Welcome and Peace.

The Welcome and Peace

The bishop may address the newly baptized

There is one Lord, one faith, one baptism.
N *and* N, by one Spirit we are all baptized into one body.
**We welcome you in the fellowship of faith;
we are children of the same heavenly Father;
we welcome you.**

The congregation may greet the newly baptized.

The bishop introduces the Peace in these or other suitable words (seasonal forms are provided in the service for Holy Baptism)

God has made us one in Christ.
He has set his seal upon us
and, as a pledge of what is to come,
has given the Spirit to dwell in our hearts.

The peace of the Lord be always with you.
And also with you.

A minister may say
Let us offer one another a sign of peace.

All may exchange a sign of peace.

If the Liturgy of the Eucharist does not follow immediately, the service concludes with suitable prayers, ending with the Lord's Prayer and the Sending Out.

¶ The Sending Out

The Blessing

The bishop may use a seasonal blessing from the service for Holy Baptism, or another suitable blessing, or

The God of all grace,
who called you to his eternal glory in Christ Jesus,
establish, strengthen and settle you in the faith;
and the blessing of God almighty,
the Father, the Son and the Holy Spirit,
be upon you and remain with you always. **Amen.**

Giving of a Lighted Candle

A hymn may be sung.

The bishop or another person may give all candidates a lighted candle. These candles may be lit from the candle used at the Decision.

When all have received a candle, the bishop says

God has delivered us from the dominion of darkness
and has given us a place with the saints in light.

You have received the light of Christ;
walk in this light all the days of your life.
Shine as a light in the world
to the glory of God the Father.

The Dismissal

Go in the light and peace of Christ.
Thanks be to God.

From Easter Day to Pentecost Alleluia Alleluia may be added to both the versicle and the response.

The bishop may lead the newly baptized and confirmed through the church.

Chapter 8

The Sacrament of Baptism (Presbyterian)*

Baptism is ordinarily celebrated as part of the worship of the congregation on the Lord's Day. It appropriately follows the reading and proclaiming of the Word.

If the liturgical practice of the congregation includes use of a paschal candle, it is lighted before the service begins.

After the sermon, an appropriate hymn, canticle, psalm, or spiritual may be sung while the candidates, sponsors, and parents assemble at the baptismal font or pool. Care should be taken to ensure that the baptism is fully visible to the congregation. An elder or a representative of the congregation may lead a procession to the place of baptism, carrying a large pitcher of water.

An Outline of the Service for the Lord's Day Including the Sacrament of Baptism

Gathering
    Call to Worship
    Prayer of the Day or Opening Prayer
    Hymn of Praise, Psalm, or Spiritual
    Confession and Pardon
    Canticle, Psalm, Hymn, or Spiritual

The Word
    Prayer for Illumination
    First Reading
    Psalm
    Second Reading
    Anthem, Hymn, Psalm, Canticle, or Spiritual
    Gospel Reading
    Sermon
    Hymn, Canticle, Psalm, or Spiritual

* Liturgy currently used in The Presbyterian Church (USA) and the Cumberland Presbyterian Church.

Baptism
  Presentation
  Profession of Faith
  Thanksgiving Over the Water
  The Baptism
  Laying On of Hands
  Welcome
  The Peace
  Hymn, Psalm, or Spiritual
  Prayers of the People

The Eucharist
  Offering
  Invitation to the Lord's Table
  Great Thanksgiving
  Lord's Prayer
  Breaking of the Bread
  Communion of the People

If the Eucharist is not celebrated:

  Offering
  Prayer of Thanksgiving
  Lord's Prayer

Sending
  Hymn, Spiritual, Canticle, or Psalm
  Charge and Blessing

Texts of the sacrament of baptism:

Presentation

The minister addresses all present:

Hear the words of our Lord Jesus Christ:
All authority in heaven and on earth
has been given to me.
Go therefore and make disciples of all nations,
baptizing them in the name of the Father,
and of the Son,

and of the Holy Spirit,
and teaching them to obey everything that I have commanded you.
And remember, I am with you always,
to the end of the age. [Matt 28:18-20]

Hear also these words from Holy Scripture:

The minister then continues, using one or more of the following:

There is one body and one Spirit,
just as you were called
to the one hope of your calling,
one Lord, one faith, one baptism,
one God and Father of all,
who is above all and through all and in all. [Eph 4:4-6]

As many of you as were baptized into Christ
have clothed yourselves with Christ.
There is no longer Jew or Greek,
there is no longer slave or free,
there is no longer male and female;
for all of you are one in Christ Jesus. [Gal 3:27, 28]

You are a chosen race, a royal priesthood,
a holy nation, God's own people,
in order that you may proclaim the mighty acts
of the One who called you out of darkness
into God's marvelous light. [1 Pet 2:9]

Do you not know
that all of us who have been baptized into Christ Jesus
were baptized into his death?
Therefore we have been buried with him by baptism into death,
so that, just as Christ was raised from the dead
by the glory of the Father,
so we too might walk in newness of life. [Rom 6:3, 4]

The promise is for you, for your children
and for all who are far away,
everyone whom the Lord our God calls. [Acts 2:39]

The minister continues:

Obeying the word of our Lord Jesus,
and confident of his promises,

we baptize those whom God has called.
In baptism God claims us,
and seals us to show that we belong to God.
God frees us from sin and death,
uniting us with Jesus Christ in his death and resurrection.
By water and the Holy Spirit,
we are made members of the church, the body of Christ,
and joined to Christ's ministry of love, peace, and justice.
Let us remember with joy our own baptism,
as we celebrate this sacrament.

An elder presents each candidate for baptism, using the appropriate forms:

For adults and older children
On behalf of the session,
I present N. and N. to receive the sacrament of Baptism.

For infants and younger children
On behalf of the session,
I present N., (son, daughter) of N. and N.,
to receive the sacrament of Baptism.

The minister addresses, in turn, candidates for baptism, parents bringing children for baptism, sponsors, and the congregation:

Adults and older children

The minister addresses the candidates for baptism:

N. and N., do you desire to be baptized?

The candidates respond:

I do.

Parent(s) of infants and younger children

The minister addresses parents presenting children for baptism:

Do you desire that N. and N. be baptized?

The parent(s) respond:

I do.

Minister:

Relying on God's grace,
do you promise to live the Christian faith,
and to teach that faith to your child?

The parent(s) respond:

I do.

Sponsors (if any are present)

The minister addresses the sponsors, if any are present:
Do you promise, through prayer and example,
to support and encourage N.
to be a faithful Christian?

The sponsors respond:
I do.

Congregation

The minister addresses the congregation:
Do you, as members of the church of Jesus Christ,
promise to guide and nurture N. and N.
by word and deed,
with love and prayer,
encouraging them to know and follow Christ
and to be faithful members of his church?

The people respond:
We do.

Profession of Faith
Through baptism we enter the covenant God has established.
Within this covenant God gives us new life,
guards us from evil,
and nurtures us in love.
In embracing that covenant, we choose whom we will serve,
by turning from evil
and turning to Jesus Christ.

The minister then asks the following questions of the candidates for baptism and/or the parents or guardians of children being presented for baptism.
As God embraces you within the covenant, I ask you
to reject sin,
to profess your faith in Christ Jesus,
and to confess the faith of the church,
the faith in which we baptize.

Renunciations

The minister continues, using one of the following:

1
Trusting in the gracious mercy of God,

do you turn from the ways of sin
and renounce evil and its power in the world?
I do.
Do you turn to Jesus Christ
and accept him as your Lord and Savior,
trusting in his grace and love?
I do.
Will you be Christ's faithful disciple,
obeying his Word and showing his love?
I will, with God's help.

2

Do you renounce all evil,
and powers in the world
which defy God's righteousness and love?
I renounce them.
Do you renounce the ways of sin
that separate you from the love of God?
I renounce them.
Do you turn to Jesus Christ
and accept him as your Lord and Savior?
I do.
Will you be Christ's faithful disciple,
obeying his Word and showing his love,
to your life's end?
I will, with God's help.

3

Trusting in the gracious mercy of God,
do you turn from the ways of sin
and renounce evil and its power in the world?
I do.
Who is your Lord and Savior?
Jesus Christ is my Lord and Savior.
Will you be Christ's faithful disciple,
obeying his Word and showing his love?
I will, with God's help.

Profession

The minister continues:
With the whole church,
let us confess our faith.

The people may stand.

All present profess their faith in the words of the Apostles' Creed, using the question and answer form (A) or reciting it directly (B).

A
Do you believe in God, the Father almighty?
I believe in God, the Father almighty,
creator of heaven and earth.
Do you believe in Jesus Christ?
I believe in Jesus Christ, God's only Son, our Lord,
who was conceived by the Holy Spirit,
born of the Virgin Mary,
suffered under Pontius Pilate,
was crucified, died, and was buried;
he descended to the dead.
On the third day he rose again;
he ascended into heaven,
he is seated at the right hand of the Father,
and he will come to judge the living and the dead.
Do you believe in the Holy Spirit?
I believe in the Holy Spirit,
the holy catholic church,
the communion of saints,
the forgiveness of sins,
the resurrection of the body,
and the life everlasting. Amen.

B
I believe in God, the Father almighty,
creator of heaven and earth.
I believe in Jesus Christ, God's only Son, our Lord,
who was conceived by the Holy Spirit,
born of the Virgin Mary,
suffered under Pontius Pilate,
was crucified, died, and was buried;
he descended to the dead.
On the third day he rose again;
he ascended into heaven,
he is seated at the right hand of the Father,
and he will come to judge the living and the dead.

I believe in the Holy Spirit,
the holy catholic church,
the communion of saints,
the forgiveness of sins,
the resurrection of the body,
and the life everlasting. Amen.

The minister asks one of the following questions of those being baptized on profession of their faith:

1

Will you be a faithful member of this congregation,
share in its worship and ministry
through your prayers and gifts,
your study and service,
and so fulfill your calling to be a disciple of Jesus Christ?
I will, with God's help.

2

Will you devote yourself to the church's teaching and fellowship,
to the breaking of bread and the prayers?
I will, with God's help.

Water is poured visibly and audibly into the font.

Thanksgiving Over the Water

One of the following prayers is said by the minister.

1

The Lord be with you.
And also with you.
Let us give thanks to the Lord our God.
It is right to give our thanks and praise.
We give you thanks, Eternal God,
for you nourish and sustain all living things
by the gift of water.
In the beginning of time,
your Spirit moved over the watery chaos,
calling forth order and life.
In the time of Noah,
you destroyed evil by the waters of the flood,
giving righteousness a new beginning.
You led Israel out of slavery,

through the waters of the sea,
into the freedom of the promised land.
In the waters of Jordan
Jesus was baptized by John
and anointed with your Spirit.
By the baptism of his own death and resurrection,
Christ set us free from sin and death,
and opened the way to eternal life.
We thank you, O God, for the water of baptism.
In it we are buried with Christ in his death.
From it we are raised to share in his resurrection,
Through it we are reborn by the power of the Holy Spirit.

The minister may touch the water.

Send your Spirit to move over this water
that it may be a fountain of deliverance and rebirth.
Wash away the sin of all who are cleansed by it.
Raise them to new life,
and graft them to the body of Christ.
Pour out your Holy Spirit upon them,
that they may have power to do your will,
and continue forever in the risen life of Christ.
To you, Father, Son, and Holy Spirit, one God,
be all praise, honor, and glory,
now and forever.
Amen.

2
The Lord be with you.
And also with you.
Let us give thanks to the Lord our God.
It is right to give our thanks and praise.
Eternal and gracious God, we give you thanks.
In countless ways you have revealed yourself in ages past,
and have blessed us with signs of your grace.
We praise you that through the waters of the sea,
you led your people Israel out of bondage,
into freedom in the land of your promise.
We praise you for sending Jesus your Son,
who for us was baptized in the waters of the Jordan,
and was anointed as the Christ by your Holy Spirit.

Through the baptism of his death and resurrection,
you set us free from the bondage of sin and death,
and give us cleansing and rebirth.
We praise you that in baptism
you give us your Holy Spirit,
who teaches us and leads us into all truth,
filling us with a variety of gifts,
that we might proclaim the gospel to all nations
and serve you as a royal priesthood.

The minister may touch the water.
Pour out your Spirit upon us
and upon this water,
that this font may be your womb of new birth.
May all who now pass through these waters
be delivered from death to life,
from bondage to freedom,
from sin to righteousness.
Bind them to the household of faith,
guard them from all evil.
Strengthen them to serve you with joy
until the day you make all things new.
To you be all praise, honor, and glory;
through Jesus Christ our Savior,
who, with you and the Holy Spirit,
lives and reigns forever.
Amen.

3

The minister may give thanks over the water in his or her own words:

a. praising God for God's faithfulness in the covenant;

b. thankfully remembering God's reconciling acts such as:
   the cleansing and rebirth in the flood in the time of Noah;
   the exodus through the waters of the sea;
   Jesus' baptism in the Jordan;
   the baptism of Jesus' death and his resurrection.

c. invoking the Holy Spirit
   to attend and empower the baptism;
   to make the water a water of redemption and rebirth;
   to equip the church for faithfulness.

The prayer concludes with an ascription of praise to the triune God.

The Baptism

The candidates, other than infants, who are to be baptized by pouring or sprinkling may kneel. Or if there are candidates to be immersed, they walk down into the water.

Calling each candidate by his or her Christian (given) name or names only, the minister shall pour or sprinkle water visibly and generously on the candidate's head, or immerse the candidate in the water, while saying:

N., I baptize you
in the name of the Father,
and of the Son,
and of the Holy Spirit.
Amen.

Laying On of Hands

The minister lays hands on the head of each person baptized, while saying one of the following:

1

O Lord, uphold N. by your Holy Spirit.
Give him/her the spirit of wisdom and understanding,
the spirit of counsel and might,
the spirit of knowledge and the fear of the Lord,
the spirit of joy in your presence,
both now and forever.
Amen.

2

Defend, O Lord, your servant N.
with your heavenly grace,
that he/she may continue yours forever,
and daily increase in your Holy Spirit more and more,
until he/she comes to your everlasting kingdom.
Amen.

The minister may mark the sign of the cross on the forehead of each of the newly baptized, while saying one of the following. Oil prepared for this purpose may be used.

1

N., child of the covenant,
you have been sealed by the Holy Spirit in baptism,
and marked as Christ's own forever.
Amen.

2

N., child of God,
you have been sealed by the Holy Spirit in baptism,
and grafted into Christ forever.
Amen.

Welcome

Candidates who have been kneeling will stand.

A representative of the session, or the minister, addresses the congregation in these or similar words:

N. and N. have been received into the one holy catholic and apostolic
    church through baptism.
God has made them members of the household of God,
to share with us in the priesthood of Christ.
Let us welcome the newly baptized.

Welcome is extended, using (A) or (B):

A

The people respond, saying:

With joy and thanksgiving
we welcome you into Christ's church
to share with us in his ministry,
for we are all one in Christ.

B

Those who have been baptized are welcomed in a manner appropriate to the particular congregation.

The Peace

The minister then says to all assembled at the font:

The peace of Christ be with you.

They respond:

And also with you.

The people may exchange signs of God's peace, greeting those who have been baptized.

All return to their places. An appropriate hymn, psalm, or spiritual may be sung.

The service continues with the prayers of the people, which will include petitions for the newly baptized and for those who will nurture them.

When the Lord's Supper is celebrated, it is appropriate for the newly baptized to receive Communion first.

Chapter 9

The Baptism of Believers (Baptist)*

Call to worship

Hymn

Prayer of praise and confession

Reading of scripture

Because baptism is a unique event in the life of a Christian and may be new to many members of the congregation, explanation and teaching will be an important part of the service. Suggested readings include: Isaiah 6:1-9a; Matthew 3:1-12; 3:13-17; Mark 1:1-13; John 3:1-8; Acts 2:38-42; 8:26-39; 9:1-19; 10:34-38; 16:11-15; 16:25-34; 19:1-7; Romans 6:3-11; Ephesians 4:1-6; Colossians 3:1-17; 1 Timothy 6:12; Titus 3:3-7; Hebrews 10:19-25.

Sermon

Hymn

Introduction to baptism

The following statement might be used as an introduction to baptism, or as the basis for teaching or preaching.

On the day of Pentecost, the Apostle Peter proclaimed the good news of God and called his hearers to repent and be baptized in the name of Jesus Christ. Following in that tradition, we baptize those whom Jesus Christ has led to repentance and new life in faith.

Jesus was baptized in the river Jordan by John. In baptism, believers take their stand in union with him, and declare their faith in his death and resurrection. Their baptism marks an ending and a beginning in life: they are washed free of sin to begin a new life in the power and joy of the Spirit. The public confession of faith in Christ is also an act of obedience to God, and the means of entry into his Church.

---

* Liturgy currently used widely among Baptist ministers in Great Britain and also adopted by English-speaking ministers in other Unions and Conventions throughout the world.

Baptism is our response to all that God has done for us in Christ, and a celebration of all that he gives of himself in his Spirit. The initiative is God's, and in baptism his grace is displayed.

'Baptized into union with him, you have all put on Christ like a garment'. *(Galatians 3: 27)*

Or the following may be used (and adapted if only one person is to be baptized):
My friends, you have heard NN tell of the pilgrimages of faith that *have* brought *them* to this point today. *They are* here because in Jesus Christ *they have* found a living Lord. *They have* met him in a personal way, and *know* that Jesus, the Son of God, loves *them*, and that he gave himself to die for *them* on a cross. *Each* knows that Jesus, the Son of God, was not defeated by death but was raised to life, and calls us to accept his forgiveness and hope, and to share in his resurrection life.

In baptism *they express* this belief, consecrating *themselves* in a special way to commitment and service. *They* will enter the water in obedience, believing that baptism is commanded by Christ himself. As *they go* under the water and *rise* from it, *they give* witness to *their* desire to die to self and rise with Christ to new life.

They come surrounded by the love and prayers of this church family and upheld by the great continuous prayer that unites us with the universal Church of Christ in heaven and on earth.

They come as much loved children of a Father who welcomes *them* here. Jesus is *their* brother, and *they are* bound to him by his Holy Spirit. God is glad, and we are glad, that *they have* come. This is a special moment—let us pray for *them*.

Prayer

Almighty God, we give you thanks that at the beginning your Spirit moved upon the face of the waters and you said, 'Let there be light'. We give you thanks that you led your people through the water of the Red Sea, out of slavery, and into the freedom of the Promised Land.

We give you thanks for your Son, Jesus Christ, who was baptized in the river Jordan. We thank you that he passed through the deep waters of his death on the cross and was raised to life in triumph. Send your Holy Spirit that this baptism may be for your servants a union with Christ in his death and resurrection that, as Christ was raised from death through the glory of the Father, *they* also might live new *lives*.

Send your Holy Spirit anew upon *them* that *they* may be brought into the fellowship of the Body of Christ and may grow in Christ's likeness.

Or:

Lord God, you know each one of us better than we know ourselves. In your Son you have shown us love that is greater than we can ever appreciate. In your Spirit we are bound closer to you and to each other.

We pray especially for your servants NN. We ask that *they* may know the fullness of your love and the filling of your Spirit as in baptism *they signify their* desire to follow your Son.

May this important step on *their lives' journeys* wash away the fears and sins of the past. May all *they know* of you be enhanced and magnified, and may what happens today underline *their* progress towards a future of sure and certain hope.

This we ask through Jesus Christ our Lord.

Declaration of Faith

This is an integral part of the act of worship and it is important that the congregation can hear what is happening. It is good to be in or near the baptistry at this point.

LEADER	N, do you believe in one God, Father, Son and Holy Spirit?
CANDIDATE	I do.
LEADER	In obedience to the call of our risen Lord Jesus Christ, do you repent of your sins and come to be baptized?
CANDIDATE	I do.
LEADER	With the help of the Holy Spirit, do you offer your life in service to God wherever he may call you to go?
CANDIDATE	I do.
LEADER	Then come and be baptized.

Or:

LEADER	Do you confess Jesus Christ as your Lord and Saviour?
CANDIDATE	I do.
LEADER	Do you turn from sin, renounce evil, and intend to follow Christ?
CANDIDATE	I do.

LEADER   Will you seek to live within the fellowship of his Church, and to serve him in the world?

CANDIDATE   With the Lord's help, I will.

Immediately before baptism, the candidate(s) may be given a text chosen for them by their minister.

The Baptism

Each candidate then enters the baptistry, to be baptized with the following words:

Having heard of your repentance and your faith, I now baptize you, N, my brother/sister, in the name of God the Father, God the Son, and God the Holy Spirit.

Or:

N, on your profession of faith and pledge of allegiance I gladly baptize you in the name of the Father, the Son, and the Holy Spirit.

As they emerge from the water the candidates may align themselves with the Church through the ages by making aloud the profession of faith:

CANDIDATE   Jesus is Lord!

CONGREGATION Hallelujah!

Baptism may be followed by the singing of a hymn. If there are a number of candidates, a verse may be sung between each baptism.

Words of Appeal

The challenge and witness of baptism may be followed by inviting others to respond to the Gospel.

The Leader and newly baptized leave to change.

Prayers of response and intercession

Offering

The leader and the newly baptized re-enter.

The newly baptized may bring bread and wine to the Table.

Invitation to the Lord's Supper

Hymn

Prayer of approach and sharing of the peace

The Laying on of Hands

Like baptism, the laying on of hands requires some explanation. Appropriate readings and verses are: Acts 8:14-17; 9:17-19; 13:1-3; 19:1-6; 1 Timothy 4:14; Revelation 1:17.

Words of introduction:

The New Testament records that those who were baptized often received the laying on of hands as a sign of commissioning for service.

We are now to lay hands on *NN*, who *have* been baptized, as a sign of blessing and an act of commissioning, and to ask that *they* may be fully equipped for *their* vocation as *servants* of Jesus Christ in the Church and in the world.

The candidate(s) may be addressed with words of scripture:

You are a chosen race, a royal priesthood, a dedicated nation, a people claimed by God for his own, to proclaim the glorious deeds of him who has called you out of darkness into his marvellous light.
1 Peter 2:9

You are light for all the world. You must shed light among your fellows, so that, when they see the good you do, they may give praise to your Father in heaven.
Matthew 5:14a, 16

Each candidate kneels and the leader(s) lay(s) hands on each, offering prayer such as:
Lord, bless *these* your servants and strengthen *them by* your Holy Spirit as we commission *them* for service in the Church and the world in the name of the Lord Jesus Christ.

The candidate(s) stand(s) as the leader says:
You are no longer aliens in a foreign land, but fellow-citizens with God's people, members of God's household. You are built on the foundation of the apostles and prophets, with Christ Jesus himself as the cornerstone. *Ephesians 2:19–20*

Reception into Membership

We are now to receive *NN* into the membership of — Baptist Church. We enter into a covenant with *them* to share with each other in building up the Church to the glory of God, working alongside one another in his service in the world, and encouraging one another in the love of God.

Questions to the newly baptized

LEADER   *N*, do you believe God has called you to serve Christ as part of this local Baptist church?

CANDIDATE   I do.

LEADER	Do you commit yourself to love and serve the Lord within this church community and in the world; and being filled with the Holy Spirit, to fulfil your ministry in the Body of Christ?
CANDIDATE	I do.

Or:

LEADER	N, do you believe that as a follower of Christ you are called to band together with other believers in his Church? Do you now believe that you are called to be part of this church community in —, and do you accept the Baptist principles to which we give expression?
CANDIDATE	I do.
LEADER	Do you now commit yourself to love and to work, to share and to serve within this church community and within our world? Do you believe that here you may learn and grow and do you accept the responsibility of being a member of this church?
CANDIDATE	I do.

Response of Church

Inviting church members to stand, the leader asks them:

LEADER	Do you welcome N into the family of God in this local church?
MEMBERS	We do.
LEADER	Do you promise to love, encourage, strengthen, guide, pray for, and care for N as an equal partner in the Body of Christ?
MEMBERS	We do.

Or:

LEADER	Do you commit yourselves to receive N as a member of this church, offering to *him/her* your friendship and love?
MEMBERS	We do.

LEADER	Do you receive N as a *brother/sister* in Christ, being ready to hear and serve the Lord in *him/her*, and to serve the Lord with *him/her*?
MEMBERS	We do.

Right hand of fellowship

Offering the hand of fellowship to the new member(s), the leader says, for example:

In the name of the Lord Jesus Christ, and on behalf of this fellowship, I welcome you into our membership.

The new member(s) may be invited to sign the church roll.

Prayer *such as:*

Lord our God, you have joined us together in Christ, and from each to the other you will speak your Word of comfort and challenge. Make us ready to listen and swift to act, both church and new member(s). May *they* not fail you, nor we fail *them*.

Or:

Lord God, we praise you for the ways you guide our lives and give sense and purpose to them, and thank you for all the direction and purpose that you have given in the lives of *NN*. We are grateful that in this church *they have* found a home. We pray that the sense of your direction and purpose may not leave *them* but may grow and mature and bear fruit in *their lives* and the life of the church. Send your blessing on our life together; through Jesus Christ our Lord.

The Order for the Lord's Supper

Hymn

Blessing

Chapter 10

The Rite of Baptism (Mennonite)*

Opening Remarks
Jesus said, "All authority in heaven and on earth has been given to me. Go therefore and make disciples of all nations, baptizing them in the name of the Father and of the Son and of the Holy Spirit, and teaching them to obey everything that I have commanded you. And remember, I am with you always, to the end of the age" (Mt. 28:18-20).

Because of Jesus' commandment and promise, we are here today. For this reason people make the covenant of baptism with God and the church. We are witnesses to their choice and companions to it.

Baptism is an act of God, of the church, and of the believer. In baptism, God gives us a good conscience and the seal of the Holy Spirit. Baptism enacts what God has done with us: made us dead to sin and alive to Christ. As an act of the church, baptism vouches for the faith of the believer and affirms the work of grace in her/his life. As an act of the individual, baptism enacts her/his surrender of the old self and the embrace of a new self, born in the image of Christ.

Questions
_____, do you renounce the evil powers of this world and turn to Jesus Christ as your savior? Do you put your trust in his grace and love and promise to obey him as your Lord?
Answer: I do.

Do you believe in God, the Father Almighty, maker of heaven and earth; in Jesus Christ, God's Son, our Lord; and in the Holy Spirit, the giver of life?
Answer: I do.

---

* Liturgy currently used by most congregations of Mennonite Church Canada and Mennonite Church USA.

Do you accept the Word of God as guide and authority for your life?
Answer: I do.

Are you willing to give and receive counsel in the congregation?
Answer: I am.

Are you ready to participate in the mission of the church?
Answer: I am.

Personal address to each candidate (affirmation of gifts, expression of hope)

Baptism
On your confession of faith in Jesus Christ *[pour or sprinkle water, or immerse candidate]* I baptize you with water in the name of the Father, the Son, and the Holy Spirit. May God baptize you with the Holy Spirit from above. Amen.

All-powerful God, grant _____ the fullness of the Holy Spirit:
 a clean heart, a right spirit, the joy of salvation.
Make her/him one in whom Christ is seen to live again.
Release the gifts you gave her/him in creation and redeemed in Christ.

 _____, may the God of peace sanctify you wholly.
 May your spirit and soul and body be kept sound and blameless
  until the coming of our Lord Jesus Christ.
 The One who calls you is faithful and will do it. Amen.

Reception
_____, in the name of Christ and the church,
I give you my hand and bid you to rise and walk in newness of life by
 the same power that raised Christ from the dead.
As long as you abide in his Word, you are Christ's disciple indeed and
 shall be acknowledged as a brother/sister in the church.

[Giving of a baptismal verse to each candidate]

You have made the good confession of Jesus Christ and offered yourself to be our companion in obeying him.
May God bless you and make you a blessing in our midst.
The peace of Christ be with you. (kiss of peace/right hand of fellowship)

Congregational Response
We welcome you, _____,
 as a brother/sister in this congregation.

We join together as companions seeking the way of Christ,
> bearing one another's burdens,
> and sharing our gifts with the world.

* * *

[Alternate Forms and Wording]

Other Baptismal Questions

(a)
Are you sorry for your sins?
Answer: I am.

Do you believe in God the Father, in Jesus Christ the Son, and in the Holy Spirit, the Giver of Life?
Answer: I do.

Do you promise, by God's grace, to follow Jesus, the Lamb, all the days of your life, ready to love your enemies and suffer wrong nonresistantly?
Answer: I do.

Do you accept the way of life set forth in our confession of faith?
Answer: I do.[1]

(b)
Let me ask you, in the hearing of this congregation, and in the name of the Lord and of his church, for a public confession of your faith:

Do you, in the presence of God and this assembly, solemnly renounce the Devil and all his works and declare the Lord to be your God?
Answer: I do.

Do you confess the Lord Jesus Christ as your Redeemer, trusting alone in the merits of his death and resurrection for the forgiveness of your sins, the sanctification of your fallen but now redeemed nature, the resurrection of your body, and everlasting salvation in heaven?
Answer: I do.

Do you solemnly pledge yourself to Christ and his service, and will you by the power of the Holy Spirit shun the ways of sin, seek communion with God, and abide by his Word?
Answer: I will.

May God ratify this covenant and give you grace to be steadfast in faith and love.[2]

(c) *(For situations in which very simple wording is required)*
Do you believe that Jesus loves you?
Answer: I do.

Do you believe that Jesus forgives you of all your sins?
Answer: I do.

Do you love Jesus and want to live by his teachings?
Answer: I do.

Do you want to be a member of this church?
Answer: I do.

Other Baptismal Forms

(a)
Upon your confession of faith, I baptize you with water in the name of God the Creator, Redeemer, and Sustainer. May God baptize you with the Holy Spirit.

(b)
Upon your confession of faith, I baptize you in the name of God, in the name of Christ Jesus, and in the name of the Holy Spirit, the holy Trinity.

Other Prayers of Blessing

Concluding Baptism

(a)
Almighty God,
    we give you thanks that in the beginning
    your Spirit moved upon the face of the waters
    and you said, "Let there be light."
We give you thanks that you led your people through the waters of the
    Red Sea, out of slavery, and into the freedom of the Promised Land.
We give you thanks for your Son, Jesus Christ, who was baptized in
    the river Jordan.
We thank you that he passed through the deep water of death on
    the cross
        and was raised to life in triumph.

Send us your Holy Spirit,
> that this baptism may manifest for your servants
> their union with Christ in his death and resurrection,
> and that, as Christ was raised from death
> through the glory of the Father, they also might live new lives.

Send your Holy Spirit anew upon them
> that they may be brought into the fellowship of the body of Christ
> and may grow in Christ's likeness.

Hear us, for his sake. Amen.[3]

(b)
O God, creator of all things visible and invisible,
for the gift of _____'s life and for your
saving presence in it,
> we give you thanks.

Be present in the trials and joys of his/her life that he/she may always trust your love.
O Jesus, perfect image of God and perfect image of humanity,
for your life of faithfulness we give thanks.
Guide _____ so that he/she may always trust your grace.
O Holy Spirit, sustainer and teacher,
for your energy moving in and around _____, we give thanks.
Strengthen him/her so that he/she may always trust your promises.
Amen.[4]

(c)
Following an ancient practice of the church, we are now to commission those who have been baptized to ministry as priests and servants of Jesus Christ. Let us as members of this congregation join with them and renew our commitment to the servant ministry of Christ.

You are a chosen race, a royal priesthood, a holy nation, God's own people, in order that you may proclaim the mighty acts of the one who called you out of darkness into light. (1 Pet. 2:9)

(Those who have been baptized kneel before the table, while the minister lays hands on them and prays freely or as follows:)

Eternal God, cause your Spirit to come upon these your servants to confirm them in ministry for the church and the world. May they be so filled with your love that as they live in the world, the world may know the love of Christ. Amen.

(The newly commissioned ones stand, and the minister says:)
You are no longer strangers and aliens, but you are members of the household of God. On behalf of this congregation, I welcome you. May the peace of God go with you always. Amen.[5]

Other Words of Reception

(a)
As brothers and sisters in the body of Christ and members
    of this congregation,
    we welcome you, _____, as a brother/sister
    into Christ's church.
We witness to the work of the Holy Spirit who has led you
    to Jesus as Savior and to God as the source of your life.
We promise to encourage you in faith,
    to rejoice with you in joy,
    to support you in suffering,
    to guide you in confusion,
    to listen to the word God speaks in you,
    and to call out the gifts the Holy Spirit is creating in you.
We thank God for your presence in the body of Christ,
    and we ask God's blessing on you all the days of your life.[6]

(b)
Arise, shine, for your light has come
    and the glory of the Lord is upon you.
Stand up in the name of the Lord Jesus Christ;
    be steadfast in the path he has set you upon.
I give you the hand of fellowship:
    welcome into the church of Jesus Christ.

(c)
In the name of Christ and the church, I now extend
    to you the right hand of fellowship
and welcome you, _____, as a brother/sister
    into the church of Christ.

Notes

[1] Simeon Rues, *Aufrichtige Nachrichten von dem Gegenwartigen Zustande der Mennoniten* (Jena: Johann Rudolph Kroker, 1743), 132–134. Translated and adapted by John Rempel, *Minister's Manual* (Winnipeg: Herald Press, 1998).

[2] *Minister's Manual*, 1950. Adapted by Rempel, *Minister's Manual*, 1998.

[3] *Patterns and Prayers for Christian Worship* (Oxford, England: Oxford University Press, 1991), 99–100. Cited in Rempel, *Minister's Manual*, 1998.

[4] Rebecca Slough. Adapted by Rempel, *Minister's Manual*, 1998.

[5] John E. Skoglund and Nancy E. Hall, *A Manual of Worship, New Edition* (Valley Forge, Judson Press, 1993), 200–202. Adapted by Rempel, *Minister's Manual*, 1998.

[6] Charlotte Holsopple Glick, in Rempel, *Minister's Manual*, 1998.

Chapter 11

The Baptismal Covenant I (Methodist)*

INTRODUCTION TO THE SERVICE

As persons come forward, an appropriate baptismal or confirmation hymn may be sung.

1. *The pastor makes the following statement to the congregation:*

    Brothers and sisters in Christ:
    Through the Sacrament of Baptism
        we are initiated into Christ's holy Church.
    We are incorporated into God's mighty acts of salvation
        and given new birth through water and the Spirit.
    All this is God's gift, offered to us without price.

2. *If there are confirmations or reaffirmations, the pastor continues:*

    Through confirmation,
    and through the reaffirmation of our faith,
    we renew the covenant declared at our baptism,
    acknowledge what God is doing for us,
    and affirm our commitment to Christ's holy Church.

PRESENTATION OF CANDIDATES

3. *A representative of the congregation presents the candidates with the appropriate statements:*

    I present *Name(s)* for baptism.
    I present *Name(s)* for confirmation.
    I present *Name(s)* to reaffirm *their* faith.
    I present *Name(s)* who come(s) to this congregation from the _____ Church.

---

* Liturgy illustrating the understanding and practice of baptism within the United Methodist Church, a global denomination, with congregations in North America, Europe, Africa, and Asia. *The United Methodist Book of Worship* is the official resource for all those congregations, but conferences (the Methodist equivalent of dioceses/synods/presbyteries) outside of the United States are at liberty to develop regional liturgies. Other denominations in the Methodist family also use the United Methodist Church's liturgical resources, such as the Methodist Church of Malaysia and the Methodist Church of Singapore.

If desired, Thanksgiving over the Water (section 10) may precede the Renunciation of Sin and Profession of Faith.

At this or some later point in the service, persons may add to their vows a personal witness to their Christian faith and experience.

RENUNCIATION OF SIN AND PROFESSION OF FAITH

4. Since the earliest times, the vows of Christian baptism have consisted first of the renunciation of all that is evil and then the profession of faith and loyalty to Christ. Parents or other sponsors reaffirm these vows for themselves while taking the responsibilities of sponsorship. Candidates for confirmation profess for themselves the solemn vows that were made at their baptism. The pastor addresses parents or other sponsors and those candidates who can answer for themselves.

On behalf of the whole Church, I ask you:
Do you renounce the spiritual forces of wickedness,
    reject the evil powers of this world,
    and repent of your sin?

I do.

Do you accept the freedom and power God gives you
    to resist evil, injustice, and oppression
    in whatever forms they present themselves?

I do.

Do you confess Jesus Christ as your Savior,
put your whole trust in his grace,
and promise to serve him as your Lord,
in union with the Church which Christ has opened
    to people of all ages, nations, and races?

I do.

5. The pastor addresses parents or other sponsors of candidates not able to answer for themselves:

Will you nurture *these children (persons)*
in Christ's holy church,
that by your teaching and example *they* may be guided
    to accept God's grace for themselves,
    to profess their faith openly,
    and to lead a Christian life?

I will.

6. The pastor addresses candidates who can answer for themselves.

According to the grace given to you,
will you remain *faithful members* of Christ's holy Church
and serve as Christ's *representatives* in the world?

I will.

7. If those who have answered for themselves have sponsors, the pastor addresses the sponsors:

> Will you who sponsor *these candidates*
> support and encourage *them* in *their* Christian life?
> **I will.**

8. The pastor addresses the congregation, and the congregation responds:

> Do you, as Christ's body, the Church,
> reaffirm both your rejection of sin
> and your commitment to Christ?
> **We do.**
> Will you nurture one another in the Christian faith and life
> and include *these* persons now before you in your care?
> **With God's help we will proclaim the good news**
> **and live according to the example of Christ.**
> **We will surround *these persons***
> **with a community of love and forgiveness,**
> **that they may grow in *their* trust of God,**
> **and be found faithful in *their* service to others.**
> **We will pray for *them*,**
> **that *they* may be *true disciples***
> **who *walk* in the way that leads to life.**

9. The Apostles' Creed in threefold question-and-answer form appeared at least as early as the third century as a statement of faith used in baptisms and has been widely used in baptisms ever since. The candidate(s), sponsor(s), and local congregation join with the universal Church across the ages in this historic affirmation of the Christian faith. The pastor addresses all, and the congregation joins the candidates and their parents and sponsors in responding:

> Let us join together in professing the Christian faith
> as contained in the Scriptures of the Old and New Testaments.
> Do you believe in God the Father?
> **I believe in God, the Father Almighty,**
> **creator of heaven and earth.**
> Do you believe in Jesus Christ?
> **I believe in Jesus Christ, his only Son, our Lord,**
> **[who was conceived by the Holy Spirit,**
> **born of the Virgin Mary,**
> **suffered under Pontius Pilate,**
> **was crucified, died, and was buried;**
> **he descended to the dead.**
> **On the third day he rose again;**
> **he ascended into heaven,**

> is seated at the right hand of the Father,
> and will come again to judge the living and the dead.]

Do you believe in the Holy Spirit?

I believe in the Holy Spirit,
> **[the holy catholic* church,**
> **the communion of saints,**
> **the forgiveness of sins,**
> **the resurrection of the body,**
> **and the life everlasting.]**

THANKSGIVING OVER THE WATER

10. If there are baptisms, or if water is to be used for reaffirmation, the water may be poured ceremonially into the font at this time in such a way that the congregation can see and hear the water. This prayer recalls scriptural images and meanings of Holy Baptism and is comparable to the Great Thanksgiving at Holy Communion:

The Lord be with you.

And also with you.

Let us pray.

Eternal Father:

When nothing existed but chaos,
> you swept across the dark waters
> and brought forth light.

In the days of Noah
> you saved those on the ark through water.

After the flood you set in the clouds a rainbow.

When you saw your people as slaves in Egypt,
> you led them to freedom through the sea.

Their children you brought through the Jordan
> to the land which you promised.

Sing to the Lord, all the earth.

Tell of God's mercy each day.

In the fullness of time you sent Jesus,
> nurtured in the water of a womb.

He was baptized by John and anointed by your Spirit.

He called his disciples
> to share in the baptism of his death and resurrection
> and to make disciples of all nations.

Declare his works to the nations,

His glory among all the people.

* *universal*

Pour out your Holy Spirit,
to bless this gift of water and *those* who *receive* it,
to wash away *their* sin
> and clothe *them* in righteousness
> throughout *their lives*,
that, dying and being raised with Christ,
> *they* may share in his final victory.
All praise to you, Eternal Father,
through your Son Jesus Christ,
who with you and the Holy Spirit
lives and reigns for ever. Amen.

BAPTISM WITH LAYING ON OF HANDS

11. As each candidate is baptized, the pastor uses the Christian name(s), but not the surname:

Christian Name(s), I baptize you in the name of the Father,
> and of the Son,
> and of the Holy Spirit. **Amen.**

Immediately after the administration of the water, the pastor places hands on the candidate's head and invokes the work of the Holy Spirit. Other persons, including baptized members of the candidate's family, may join the pastor in this action. During the Laying on of Hands, the pastor says:

The Holy Spirit work within you,
> that being born through water and the Spirit,
> you may be a faithful disciple of Jesus Christ. **Amen.**

If desired, one or more of the following acts may be added; but these should not be so emphasized as to seem as important as, or more important than, God's sign given in the water itself.

a) *The pastor may trace on the forehead of each newly baptized person the sign of the cross in silence or with the words:* **"Name, [child of God], you are sealed by the Holy Spirit in baptism and marked as Christ's own forever."** *Olive oil may be used in this action, following the biblical custom of anointing prophets (1 Kings 19:16), priests (Exodus 29:7), and kings (1 Kings 1:39). Jesus' titles* **Christ** *and* **Messiah** *both mean "Anointed One," and the New Testament repeatedly calls Christ our High Priest and King. Christians in baptism become members of the body of Christ (1 Corinthians 12:13), which is a "royal priesthood" (1 Peter 2:9). Anointing at baptism is a reminder that all Christians are anointed into this royal priesthood.*

b) *New clothing is sometimes presented to those just baptized, particularly in the case of infants, as a symbol that we "have put on Christ" (Galatians 3:27) as one would put on new clothing. Such clothing is traditionally white, suggesting the "white* robes" in Revelation 7:9-14. Words such as these may be used: **"Receive these new clothes as a token of the new life that is given in Christ Jesus."**

c) *A lighted baptismal candle may be presented to the newly baptized, with such words as:* **"Let your light so shine that others, seeing your good works, may glorify your Father in heaven."** *The candle may be presented to the parents or sponsors of baptized children, in which case "others" may be changed to "this child" or "these children." It is appropriate to light the baptismal candle in the home each year on the anniversary of baptism as a reminder of the grace of God offered through baptism. A baptismal candle bears either a Christian symbol or no decoration at all; it should not be confused with ornate birthday candles sold commercially to mark a child's birthdays. The candle may be lighted from the paschal candle or from one of the candles on or near the Lord's table.*

d) *A certificate of baptism may be presented to the newly baptized.*

When all candidates have been baptized, the pastor invites the congregation to welcome them:

Now it is our joy to welcome
> Our new *sisters* and *brothers* in Christ.

Through baptism
you are incorporated by the Holy Spirit
> **into God's new creation**

and made to share in Christ's royal priesthood.
We are all one in Christ Jesus.
With joy and thanksgiving we welcome you
> **as *members* of the family of Christ.**

CONFIRMATION OR REAFFIRMATION OF FAITH

12. *Here water may be used symbolically in ways that cannot be interpreted as baptism, as the pastor says:*

> Remember your baptism and be thankful. **Amen.**

Such ways of using water include the following:

a) *Persons being confirmed or reaffirming faith may be invited to touch the water and, if desired, touch their foreheads with a moistened finger.*

b) *The pastor may scoop up a handful of water and let it flow back into the font so that it is heard and seen.*

c) *The pastor may touch the water and mark each person on the forehead with the sign of the cross.*

As the pastor, and other if desired, place hands on the head of each person being confirmed or reaffirming faith, the pastor says to each:

Name, the Holy Spirit work within you,

that having been born through water and the Spirit,
you may live as a faithful disciple of Jesus Christ. **Amen.**

13. When there is a congregational reaffirmation of the Baptismal Covenant, water may be used symbolically in ways that cannot be interpreted as baptism, as the pastor says:

Remember your baptism and be thankful. **Amen.**

Such ways of using water include the following:

a) *Members of the congregation may be invited to touch the water and, if desired, touch their foreheads with a moistened finger.*

b) *The pastor may scoop up a handful of water and let it flow back into the font so that it is heard and seen.*

c) *A very small amount of water may be sprinkled toward the congregation, not falling directly on them as would be the case in baptism by sprinkling. This may be done by dipping the end of a small evergreen branch into the font and shaking it toward the congregation. It may be seen as representing biblical sprinkling with hyssop for purification (Exodus 12:22; Psalm 51:7) and sprinkling as a sign of renewal (Ezekiel 36:25-26).*

d) *The pastor may touch the water and mark each person on the forehead with the sign of the cross.*

RECEPTION INTO THE UNITED METHODIST CHURCH

14. If there are persons coming into membership in The United Methodist Church from other denominations who have not yet been presented, they may be presented at this time.

The pastor addresses all those transferring their membership into The United Methodist Church, together with those who, through baptism or confirmation, have just professed their own faith:

As *members* of Christ's universal Church,
will you be loyal to The United Methodist Church,
and do all in your power to strengthen its ministries?
I will.

RECEPTION INTO THE LOCAL CONGREGATION

15. If there are persons joining this congregation from other United Methodist congregations who have not yet been presented, they may be presented at this time.

The pastor addresses all those transferring membership into the congregation, together with those who, through baptism or confirmation, have just professed their own faith:

As *members* of this congregation,
will you faithfully participate in its ministries
    by your prayers, your presence,
        your gifts, and your service?
I will.

COMMENDATION AND WELCOME

16. The pastor addresses the congregation:
Members of the household of God,
I commend *these persons* to your love and care.
Do all in your power to increase *their* faith,
    confirm *their* hope, and perfect *them* in love.

The congregation responds:
We give thanks for all that God has already given you
    and we welcome you in Christian love.
As members together with you
    in the body of Christ
    and in this congregation
    of The United Methodist Church,
we renew our covenant
    faithfully to participate
    in the ministries of the Church
    by our prayers, our presence,
    our gifts, and our service,
that in everything God may be glorified
    through Jesus Christ.

The pastor addresses those baptized, confirmed, or received:
The God of all grace,
    who has called us to eternal glory in Christ,
establish you and strengthen you
    by the power of the Holy Spirit,
that you may live in grace and peace.

One or more laypersons, including children, may join the pastor in acts of welcome and peace. Baptized children may be welcomed by a kiss of peace or other acts or words immediately following Baptism with Laying on of Hands.

An appropriate hymn, stanza, or response may be sung.

Appropriate thanksgivings and intercessions for those who have participated in these acts should be included in the Concerns and Prayers that follow.

It is most fitting that the service continue with Holy Communion, in which the union of the new members with the body of Christ is most fully expressed. The new members, including children, may receive first.

Chapter 12

A Representative Disciples Rite of Christian Baptism (Christian Church [Disciples of Christ])*

The Invitation
The pastor shall say:
The apostle Peter said to the people on the Day of Pentecost, "You must repent, and every one of you must be baptized in the name of Jesus Christ for the forgiveness of sins, and you will receive the gift of the Holy Spirit" (Acts 2:38, *Jerusalem Bible*);

or

Jesus said, "Come to me, all you that are weary and are carrying heavy burdens, and I will give you rest. Take my yoke upon you and learn from me; for I am gentle in heart, and you will find rest for your souls. For my yoke is easy, and my burden is light" (Matthew 11:28-30);

or

"What is good has been explained to you. . . . This is what Yahweh asks of you: only this, to act justly, to love tenderly and to walk humbly with your God" (Micah 6:8, *Jerusalem Bible*).

The Call
The pastor issues the call to Christian discipleship. Included in the call will be the invitation (1) to confess faith in Christ and for acceptance into candidacy for Christian baptism; (2) to join the congregation by transfer from another congregation; and (3) to reaffirm one's baptismal vows by public rededication of faith. Each of these opportunities for response to God should be clearly stated at each invitation.

The pastor shall say words to this effect:
God is calling some of you to claim the promise that was made to generations past, the promise that is now, by the power of the Holy Spirit, offered to you. That promise is new life in Jesus Christ. Today

---

* Liturgy currently used in many congregations of the Christian Church (Disciples of Christ).

we appeal to all who desire this new life to confess your faith in Jesus who died that we may live. As scripture says, "If your lips confess that Jesus is Lord and if you believe in your heart that God raised him from the dead, then you will be saved. By believing from the heart you are made righteous; by confessing with your lips you are saved" (Romans 10:9–10, *Jerusalem Bible*). God calls you now to express this faith by being baptized into Christ. In baptism you are buried with him and emerge to live a new life (see Romans 6:3–11; Galatians 2:16–20; Colossians 2:12; 2 Corinthians 5:17; and Ephesians 2:15).

God is calling others of you to join the full life of this congregation by coming forward to transfer your church membership. You have already confessed Christ and been baptized. Your place in the family of God awaits you here, with sincere love and hospitality (see Romans 12:13; and Hebrews 13:1–2).

God is calling still others of you to reaffirm your Christian faith in a public way by rededicating yourself to Christian discipleship. For, as God has spoken, "I live in a high and holy place, but I am also with the contrite and humbled spirit, to give the humbled spirit new life, to revive contrite hearts" (Isaiah 57:15, *Jerusalem Bible*).

On God's behalf, we appeal to you to respond to God, as the congregation stands and sings the hymn of invitation.

Confession of Faith

Upon determining that a respondent has come forward to confess faith in Jesus Christ, the pastor calls the name of the person out clearly to the congregation and says:

Name comes before God and this congregation today to confess Jesus Christ as Lord and Savior.

Turning toward the respondent, the pastor says:

Name, do you, with Christians of every time and place, confess that Jesus is the Christ, the Son of the living God (Matthew 16:16)? Do you further commit yourself to live a life pleasing to God, and to remain faithful to your confession so long as you live? If these are your intentions, you shall answer, "I do."

The pastor offers the new believer a sign of acceptance and Christian affection, such as a handshake or embrace, and says:

On behalf of this congregation, I receive you as a candidate for Christian baptism, and I rejoice with you in your faith and trust in God. May God who has called you to this commitment grant you the courage to keep your vows and grow in grace. Amen.

Rededication of Faith or Renewal of Baptismal Vows
Upon determining that a respondent has come forward to renew a commitment to the Christian life, the pastor declares the name of the person and the person's desires to the congregation.

Then the pastor says:

Name, you come before God and this congregation today as a baptized believer in Jesus Christ, and a member of the body of Christ. Do you reaffirm that Jesus is the Christ, the Son of the living God, and renew your trust in his lordship and his saving work? Do you further rededicate yourself to a life pleasing to God and declare your intent to remain true to your confession as long as you live? If these are your intentions, you shall answer, "I do."

As at a confession of faith, the pastor greets the respondent with affection and says:

May God, who has called you to renew your vows, grant you the grace to keep true to your commitment and grow in grace. Amen.

Transfer of Membership from Another Congregation
If the respondent(s) come forward to join the congregation by transfer of membership, the pastor announces the name(s) of the respondent(s), and, when appropriate, the congregation(s) from which they come. Then the pastor says:

Name, you come before God and this congregation today to join us in service to God and the whole creation in love and justice. To seal this decision, I ask you to reaffirm the faith you confessed at your baptism. Do you believe that Jesus is the Christ, the Son of the living God, and do you accept him as your Lord and Savior, as he is the Lord and Savior of the world? Do you declare your recommitment to a life pleasing to God and to God's purpose in the world, so long as you live? If these are your intentions, you shall answer, "I do."

Then, greeting the new transfers with warmth and affection, the pastor says:

On behalf of the spirit of the risen Christ and this congregation, I welcome you to a new life of witness and service among us. May God, who has called you to this decision, grant you courage to keep true to your vows and to grow in grace. Amen.

The congregation may say:

With joy and thanksgiving, we welcome you into Christ's church; for we are all one in Christ. We promise to love, encourage, and support you, to share the good news of the gospel with you, and to help you know and follow Christ.

The pastor normally concludes the service with a prayer to God to send the Holy Spirit upon each person as is appropriate to the commitment each has made. Also the prayer invokes the Spirit upon the whole congregation as they receive these newly committed persons into their worship and witness.

It is also appropriate at this time to lead the congregation into an affirmation of their faith, such as the Preamble to Design for the Christian Church (Disciples of Christ), or some other affirmation, such as the Apostles' or Nicene Creeds, or the Affirmation of Faith of the United Church of Christ. The pastor may also wish to call upon the congregation to conclude this segment of worship with a verse from a hymn, such as, "Blest Be the Tie That Binds," or "Now Thank We All our God."

Baptism
Standing near the baptistery, or in the water, the pastor or other worship leader leads the congregation in sentences of worship and a reading from the Bible.
God be with you.
Response: **And also with you.**

Sisters and brothers, there is one body, and one Spirit, just as you were summoned into one and the same hope when you were called.
Response: **There is one Lord, one faith, one baptism, one God and Father of all** (Ephesians 4:5–6).

A reading from the Bible: Romans 6:3–11

Standing in the water, the pastor says:
Lift up your hearts.
Response: **We lift them up to God.**

Let us pray.

Holding a vessel of water, the pastor says:
We praise you and thank you, God.
You have led us to the water of life.
Before the world was made, you breathed
upon the face of the deep.
You made dry land appear.
You bless the earth with life-giving rain.
You make the wasteland bloom.
You are the Lord of the storm and the flood.
You speak and they are still.
Send now your Holy Spirit upon this water,
that it may become your servant in the mystery of baptism.

The pastor pours a generous stream into the baptistery.
You cleanse us with the waters of forgiveness.

You wash away our sins.
From the rock you make living water spring.
You quench the thirst of your people.
Send now your Holy Spirit upon this water,
that it may bathe your children clean of sin and death,
and satisfy all who thirst for your righteousness.

The pastor pours a second generous stream into the baptistery.
We praise you, O God, for your Son, Jesus Christ.
He is the Lord of the waves.
He speaks and they subside.
By the waters of regeneration he cleanses our iniquities.
He gives us new life.
He is the rock from whom living waters flow.
He died for us because he loved us.
But you raised him from death and revealed him
as Lord and Savior of the world.
Teach us to die with him that we may share
in the fullness of his life.
Baptize us in the living water of his Spirit
and unite us and all women and men in his peace. Amen.

The pastor pours the rest of the water into the baptistery.

One by one the candidates enter the baptistery and are positioned by the pastor who then asks:
Name, do you turn from your sin and renounce all manner of evil and injustice? Do you turn to Christ Jesus as your Lord and Savior?
The candidate says: I do.
Name, upon your confession of faith in Jesus Christ, I baptize you in the name of the Father and of the Son and of the Holy Spirit. Amen.

or

Name, upon your confession of faith in Jesus Christ, you are now baptized into the name of the Father and of the Son and of the Holy Spirit. Amen.

The candidate is immersed. Then, immediately after the baptized has recovered stable footing, the pastor places his or her hands on the head of the new Christian and says:
Dying, Christ destroyed your death;
Rising, Christ restored your life.
Receive the gift of the Holy Spirit.

The newly baptized Christian is led out of the baptistery.

The pastor says:
Let us give thanks to the Lord our God.
Response: **It is right to give God thanks and praise.**
Let us pray:

The pastor then prays for the growth in faith of the newly baptized Christians.

An appropriate hymn concludes the service of baptism and allows the pastor and the newly baptized Christians to meet in the sanctuary for the Lord's Supper, which is the culmination of the day's worship. Before the benediction, the pastor gives each new Christian the handshake or embrace of fellowship, and welcomes each one into the membership of the church. In the event that the newly baptized have sponsors and/ or family members present, they are all invited to stand with the pastor at the exit (if space permits), and the congregation is encouraged to welcome them and congratulate them personally.

Chapter 13

Order of Holy Baptism and Chrismation (Mar Thoma)*

INITIAL PRAYER

Priest: Glory to the Father and to the Son, and to the Holy Spirit

Congregation: Shower upon us, weak and sinful as we are, O' Lord, your blessings and mercies in this world and in the world to come now and forever. Amen

P. Make us worthy, O' Lord, for this ministration of Holy Baptism which you have commanded through your Holy Apostles. Grant salvation to this child who has come now for Baptism, through the mediation of us your sinful servants, and may we all obtain blessings and mercy, now and forever.

C. Amen.

KUKLYON

Psalm 23

EKBA

P. O' Lord, may the seal of your grace guard us your faithful people. Help us, who trust in the life-giving and divine grace of Holy Baptism to obtain salvation, as the Hebrews were saved from the Destroyer by the blood smeared on the door-post and the lintel; and by the unfading light of that salvation may we see the Holy Trinity.

C. Amen.

P. O' Lord God of the heavenly hosts, bless this your servant who now joins your Holy Church. Enlighten his mind that he may see the vanity

---

* Liturgy currently used in the Mar Thoma Church.

of this world and renounce all the works of death, and so offer to you, Father, Son and Holy Spirit praise and glory now and forever.

C. Amen.

Deacon. *Stomen Kalos* or Let us stand and attend

C. Kyrie eleison or Lord have mercy

PROMION

P. Let us pray to the Lord for his grace and mercy.

C. Merciful Lord, have mercy and help us.

P. Help us, O' Lord, continually to offer to you praise, adoration, worship, thanksgiving and glory.

To our Lord Christ, who is the true and indescribable Light, and who in His divine wisdom has instituted this Holy Baptism for His spiritual flock, be honour, praise and adoration, now at the Baptism of this your servant and all the days of our life.

C. Amen.

SEDRA

P. O' Lord Jesus Christ! You have gathered us from straying in sin. You have invited us to observe Your Holy Commandment and admitted us to your spiritual fold. You have called us to the streams of salvation and the fountain of eternal life, and with your life-giving voice have offered to cleanse us from our heart's defilement. Lord, bless this your servant who has come to receive the seal of life. Accept him/her into your fold. Number him/her among your sheep. May your countenance shine upon him/her. Make him/her worthy of regeneration to become a child of your Father. Enable him/her to put off the old man to put on the imperishable new man. Help him/her to grow to the full stature of Christian perfection and after a peaceful and holy life, bring him/her to eternal glory. We praise you, with the Father, Son, and the Holy Spirit, now and forever.

C. Amen.

Chant

O' Lord, Protect with your Cross this person who has come for Baptism. Zechariah's son said that he baptised with water, but the One who comes after him would baptise with the Holy Spirit.

John the Baptist came to the river Jordan. The Mighty One hidden to the angels drew near to be baptised by him. Our Lord came for baptism, and John witnessed to him. The voice of the Heavenly Father from above said, "This is my beloved Son."

P. O' Lord abundant in blessings, we pray for this your servant who has come prepared for holy baptism. May he be sealed for eternal life, may he or she become an heir in your household, may he/she be bound by your holy commandments and offer praise and thanksgiving to you, Father, Son and Holy Spirit.

C. Amen.

SCRIPTURE READINGS

Psalm: 42:1

D. As the deer longs for the running brooks; so longs my soul for you, O' God. Hallelujah. (Psalm 42:1)

D. From the Epistle of St. Paul to the Romans.

C. Praise to you, O' Lord of the Apostles. O' Lord, grant us grace to discern your word.

Epistle: Romans 5:20–6:8

Law was introduced in order to increase wrongdoing; but where sin increased, God's grace increased much more. So then, just as sin ruled by means of death, so also God's grace rules by means of righteousness, leading us to eternal life through Jesus Christ our Lord.

What shall we say, then? Should we continue to live in sin so that God's grace will increase? Certainly not; we have died to sin—how then can we go on living in it? For surely you know that when we were baptised into union with Christ Jesus, we were baptised into union with his death. By our baptism, we were buried with him and shared his death, in order that just as Christ was raised from death by the glorious power of the Father, so also we might live a new life. For since we have become one with Him in dying as He did, in the same way we shall be one with Him by being raised to life as He was. And we know that our old being has been put to death with Christ on His Cross, in order that the power of the sinful self might be destroyed so that we should no longer be the slaves of sin. For when a person dies, he is set free from the power of sin. Since we have died with Christ, we believe that we will also live with Him.

D. Purge me with hyssop and I shall be clean; wash me and I shall be whiter than snow. Make me hear of joy and gladness; let the bones which have broken rejoice.

D. Brethren, let us stand in silence and reverence and listen to the proclamation of the living word of God from the Gospel of our Lord Jesus Christ.

P. Peace be with you all. +

C. May the Lord make us all worthy to listen to His Word.

P. The Holy Gospel of our Lord Jesus Christ, which proclaims life and salvation to the world as recorded by the evangelists Luke and John.

C. Blessed is he that has come and will come again. Praise to the Father who sent him for our salvation. May His blessings be ever upon us.

P. In the days of Jesus the Christ, Our Lord and Saviour, the Word of life, God incarnate of the Blessed Virgin Mary, it happened in this way . . .

C. So we believe and affirm.

Gospel: Luke 3:15-16

P. As the people were in expectation and all the men questioned in their hearts concerning John, whether perhaps he were the Christ, John answered them all, "I baptise you with water; but he who is mightier than I is coming, the thong of whose sandal I am not worthy to untie; he will baptise you with the Holy Spirit and fire."

Gospel: John 3:5-6

Jesus answered Nicodimus, "Truly, truly, I say to you; unless one is born of water and the Spirit, he can not enter the Kingdom of God. That which is born of the flesh is flesh and that which is born of the Spirit is spirit."

[ENROLLMENT OF THE CANDIDATE]
CONSIGNATION

Peace be with you all. +

C. And also with you.

The priest makes the sign of the cross with his thumb on the forehead of those who are to be baptised, saying:

(Name) is sealed in the Name of the Father + and of the Son + and of the Holy Spirit +.

C. Amen.

EXORCISM

P. O' Lord God, cast out all the wicked dealings of the evil One from this your creation and handiwork, who has been sealed in your holy name + Rebuke the rebellious Traitor + Cleanse him from the spirit of deceit + May he not be the dwelling place of Satan but the sanctuary of God.

C. Amen.

Then one of the Godparents (the Godfather in the case of a boy, the Godmother in the case of a girl) holding the left hand of the child with his/her left hand, repeats thrice the words of renunciation after the priest.

I, who am being baptised—renounce Satan—all his angels—all his hosts—all his worship—and all his deceits.

Then, holding the right hand of the child with his/her right hand, the Godparents repeat thrice:

I, who am being baptised—believe and accept Jesus Christ—and all the divine teachings—entrusted to our Holy Fathers—through apostles and prophets.

Then the Godparents place his/her hand on the child's head and repeats:

I renounce Satan
I believe in Christ
I renounce Satan
I believe in Christ
Renouncing Satan, I fully believe in Christ.

THE CONFESSION OF FAITH

P. Let us affirm our faith:
We believe in the one true God, the Father Almighty.

C. Maker of heaven and earth and of all that is seen and unseen. We believe in one Lord Jesus Christ, the Only Son of God eternally begotten of the Father. Light from light, true God from the true God, begotten not made, of one Being with the Father. Through him all beings were made.

For us and for our salvation He came down from heaven by the power of the Holy Spirit, He became incarnate of the Virgin Mary, and was made man.

For our sake He was crucified under Pontius Pilate; He suffered death and was buried. On the third day, He rose again by His father's holy will, He ascended into heaven and is seated at the right hand of the Father. He will come again with glory to judge the living and the dead and His Kingdom will have no end.

We believe in the Holy Spirit, the Lord, the giver of life, who proceeds from the Father. With the Father and the Son, he is worshipped and glorified. He has spoken through the prophets and apostles. We believe in one holy, catholic and apostolic Church. We acknowledge one baptism for the remission of sins. We look for the resurrection of the dead and the life of the world to come. Amen.

[UNCTION]

D. *Stomen Kalos* or Let us stand and attend.

C. Kyrie eleison or Lord have mercy.

P. Lord, by sending your Holy Spirit out of nothing you have created this child as a living being, and by your love you have made him worthy of holy baptism. O' Lord build him upon the foundation of your holy apostles. Plant him to grow and flourish in your Church. Make him open to the mystery of the anointing of the Holy Spirit. Perfect him with your divine gifts. May the hearts of these, your worshippers, be kindled with your light that they may be free from the bondage of sin.

C. Amen.

The priest anoints the forehead of the candidate with Syth and says:

As a token of being born anew as child of God (Name) is sealed with Holy oil, in the name of the Father + and of the Son + and of the Holy Spirit +

C. Amen.

[STRIPPING OF THE CANDIDATE]

[MIXING AND BLESSING OF THE WATER]

Then the priest, mixing hot and cold water in the font, blesses the water:

O' Lord, accept our humble prayers by the mercies, grace and love for mankind of our Lord Jesus the Messiah, and sanctify this water. O' Lord, You have given us the fountain that truly cleanses us from all the defilement of sin. As you are the one who saves us, washes us clean and grants us all good gifts, we offer praise and thanksgiving to you and to your only Son and to the Holy Spirit.

C. Amen.

[*Kukaya:*] Chant

Hear this, all you nations. John stood in the river Jordan. The Messiah entered the water, sanctified it and was baptised in it. When He came up out of the water, heaven and earth honoured Him; sun, moon, stars and clouds praised Him who sanctified all rivers and streams.

Barek Mor

[INSUFFLATION]

Glory be to the Father and to the Son and to the Holy Spirit. As it was in the beginning, is now and shall be forever. Amen.

Baptism is given to us, a sign of the fountain of life. God the Father, Son and Holy Spirit has sanctified it:

The Father says, "This is my beloved Son." The Son bowed his head and received baptism. The Holy Spirit descended upon Him like a dove. We believe in the Holy Trinity through whom the world came to life.

C. O' Lord bless us and help us.

[EPICLESIS]

P. We beseech you, O' Lord, sanctify this water by your mercy and abundant grace. Grant that those who are baptised in this water may put off the defiling lusts of the old man and put on the new man that recreates them into the image of the Creator. We offer praise and thanksgiving to you, to your only Son and your Holy Spirit

C. Amen.

[INVOCATION OF THE HOLY SPIRIT]

The Priest beats his hands upon his chests thrice and says:

Answer unto us, O' Lord; answer unto us, O' Lord; answer unto us, O' Lord; and by your grace, have mercy upon us.

C. Kyrie eleison, Kyrie eleison, Kyrie eleison,

or

Lord have mercy, Lord have mercy, Lord have mercy

The priest makes the sign of the cross three times on the water and says:

Almighty God, grant those who are baptised in this water cleansing from defilement, freedom from bondage, remission of sins, forgiveness of trespasses, + a holy inheritance, imperishable garments, newness of the Holy Spirit + and identification with the death and resurrection of your only begotten Son.

C. Amen.

[THE INFUSION OF MURON]

The priest holds up the container of Muron and says:

Glory to the Father and to the Son and to the Holy Spirit:

C. As it was in the beginning, is now and shall be forever. Amen.

P. We pour the holy oil upon this water in the name of the Father + and the Son + and the Holy Spirit +

C. Amen.

P. O' Lord, perfect him who is now being baptised. Cleanse this your servant by your saving baptism and make him a fellow-heir with your Messiah. Let him be renewed and dignified through the fullness of your grace. May he use the gifts that you bestow upon him. We will offer praise and thanksgiving to you and to your Son and to the Holy Spirit, now and forever.

C. Amen.

[BAPTISM]

The candidate is placed in the water facing east and water is poured thrice over his head by the priest.

P. (Name) is baptised in the hope of the remission of sin and eternal life. In the name of the Father + the Son + and the Holy Spirit +

C. Amen.

Chant

Lord, bless us and accept our worship. Lord, stretch forth your right hand and bless this your servant. Give him grace from above to glorify your majesty. Grant him your Holy Spirit that he may do your will and praise your holy name. O' Lord, who hears our prayer and answers our supplications, hear our prayer now, forgive us and grant us your blessings.

EXHORTATION

You, who by baptism are the light of the world, be strong by the Holy Spirit with power from on high. Renounce the transient and deceitful lusts of fallen humanity and turn your face away from them. May you be strengthened by the Holy Spirit to hold forth the Word of God in the midst of unbelievers, always conscious that you are striving towards the eternal life promised to the faithful. May you be made worthy to reign with the Messiah forever, according to the riches of His grace.

C. Amen.

[ANOINTING WITH HOLY MURON]

Then the priest anoints the baptised person with Muron, saying:

(Name) is anointed with holy oil as a sign of the gift of the Holy Spirit given to true believers. In the name of the Father + and of the Son + and of the Holy Spirit + *Basamo dabo, udabero, wede ruho hayo quadish leolam, olmeen.* Amen.

C. Amen.

[CROWNING]

P. O' Lord God, adorn your servant with the crown of the radiance and glory of your holy name. May his life be subject to your sovereignty and reflect the glory of your majesty. May he show forth the grace of sonship, be adorned with the crown of glory, and be worthy to offer praise and thanksgiving to you, to your Father and the Holy Spirit, now and forever.

C. Amen.

Chant

Brethren, sing praise to the Son of Almighty God who adorns you with the crowns desired by kings. In paradise, Adam earned a curse. But you have received glory by water. In your chambers the angels rejoice and the spiritual ones are happy. Brethren, you have received heavenly treasure. Take care that you are not robbed by the evil one. He has made you sheep of his heavenly pastures; sing praises to the heavenly King. Unfading crowns have been placed on your heads. Let your lips sing His praises. Children through baptism depart in peace and worship the crucified Christ.

[EXHORTATION TO PARENTS AND GODPARENTS]

The following exhortation is given to the parents and Godparents before the final blessings of the Holy Baptism services:

On behalf of this child you have declared today the baptismal oath, "I renounce Satan and believe in Jesus Christ," before God and His Holy Church. Thus, you have taken a great responsibility upon yourselves. It is your responsibility to bring up this child in Christian faith. You should pray for him/her regularly. You must be an example for this child in every respect. As the child grows he/she should come to believe Jesus Christ as his/her own Lord and Saviour. It is your responsibility to train the child in such a way that he/she will make his own declaration of faith in public, "I renounce Satan and I believe in Jesus Christ," as he/she will reach the age of understanding. The Church entrusts you with this great responsibility and may the Lord Almighty enable you to be diligent in this task.

BLESSINGS

P. My beloved, depart in peace as I commend you to the grace and blessings of the Holy Trinity. +

C. Amen.

P. May God the Father be with you, the Holy Son keep you, and the Holy Spirit make you perfect. +

C. Amen.

P. May the Holy Trinity guard you from the damnation of sin and save you from all evil, now and forever. +

C. Amen.

List of Contributors

Albrecht—Dr. Daniel E. Albrecht (The Assemblies of God), PhD, Graduate Theological Union, Berkeley, CA, USA, is professor of Christian history and Christian spirituality in the School of Theological Studies at Bethany University, Scotts Valley, CA. He is the author of *Rites in the Spirit: A Ritual Approach to Pentecostal/Charismatic Spirituality,* JPT Supplement (Sheffield and London: Sheffield Academic and Continuum, 1999).

Beach—Dr. Bert B. Beach (Seventh-day Adventist Church) is former general secretary of the Council on Inter Church/Faith Relations, General Conference of Seventh-day Adventists. He served for thirty-two years as the secretary of the Conference of Secretaries of Christian World Communions and was secretary general of the International Religious Liberty Association.

Best—Rev. Dr. Thomas F. Best, a pastor of the Christian Church (Disciples of Christ), has recently retired as director of the Commission on Faith and Order, World Council of Churches. He has written and edited extensively on issues of worship and ecclesiology, including for *The New SCM Press Dictionary of Liturgy and Worship, The Oxford Dictionary of the Christian Church,* 3rd edition, and *Die Religion in Geschichte und Gegenwart,* 4th edition.

Bobrinskoy—Protopresbyter Boris Bobrinskoy (Eastern Orthodox [Russian]) is Honorary Dean and Emeritus Professor of St. Sergius Theological Orthodox Institute, Paris, where he taught Dogmatic Theology from 1954 to 2006, and Rector of Most Holy Trinity Orthodox Church in Paris, France. The author of many books and articles on Trinitarian and sacramental theology and spirituality, he has served on various Commissions of Faith and Order and holds honorary doctorates from universities in Switzerland, Romania, and the United States.

Bradshaw—Rev. Dr. Paul Frederick Bradshaw (Church of England) is professor of liturgical studies, University of Notre Dame, USA, and currently director of its London Undergraduate Program. He is a priest-vicar at Westminster Abbey, a member of the Church of England Liturgical Commission, and a former chairman of the International Anglican Liturgical Consultation.

Ephrem—The Very Revd. Ephrem Lash, Archimandrite of the Oecumenical Throne (Ecumenical Patriarchate, Archdiocese of Thyateira and Great Britain), England, is an authority on and translator of Byzantine liturgical and patristic texts as well as related works such as *On the Life of Christ* by Romanos the Melodist and the *Homiliae Cathedrales* of Severus of Antioch.

Fiddes—Rev. Dr. Paul Fiddes (Baptist) has been professor of systematic theology at the University of Oxford since 2002. He has been at Regent's Park College, Oxford, since 1977; he was principal there from 1989–2007 and is currently professorial research fellow and director of research at Regent's.

Gribben—Rev. Dr. Robert William Gribben (The Uniting Church in Australia) is professor of worship and mission, Uniting Church Theological College, and president of the United Faculty of Theology, Melbourne, Australia. He was a tutor in the Graduate School of Ecumenical Studies at Bossey in 1983–84, and general secretary of the Victorian Council of Churches 1989–1995. He participated in the series of consultations on worship in relation to the search for Christian unity conducted by the Commission on Faith and Order, WCC, is a member of Societas Liturgica, and is chair of the Standing Committee on Ecumenics and Dialogues, World Methodist Council.

Kurien—Fr. Dr. Jacob Kurien (Malankara Orthodox Syrian Church) is vice principal and professor of theology and world religions at the Orthodox Seminary, Kottayam, India, since 1978. Active in interreligious and ecumenical relations, he has been a member of the Standing Commission of Faith and Order and a speaker at the Faith and Order Plenary Commission, Kuala Lumpur, in 2004 and at the ninth WCC Assembly in Porto Alegre, Brazil, in 2006.

Larsson—Rev. Dr. Bo Larsson (Church of Sweden) has been director of the Pastoral Institute of the Church of Sweden in Uppsala since 2001. Ordained in 1974, he has served in many parishes. He received his doctorate in 1990.

Mathew—Rev. Dr. George Mathew is vicar of the Salem Mar Thoma Church, Pathanamthitta, and member of the Liturgical Commission and Lectionary Committee of the Mar Thoma Church. He holds a doctorate in liturgical theology from Pontifical Oriental Institute, Vadavathoor, Kerala, and is a former lecturer on liturgy at the Mar Thoma Theological Seminary, Kottayam.

Meyendorff—Prof. Dr. Paul Meyendorff (Orthodox Church in America) is the Father Alexander Schmemann Professor of Liturgical Theology at St. Vladimir's Orthodox Theological Seminary, Crestwood, NY, USA, and editor of St. Vladimir's Theological Quarterly. He has published and worked extensively on issues of worship, both within his church and in the ecumenical context.

Moore-Keish—Dr. Martha L. Moore-Keish (Presbyterian Church [USA]) is assistant professor of theology, Columbia Theological Seminary, Decatur, Georgia, USA. She holds a PhD in theology from Emory University and has worked in the Office of Theology and Worship of her church as well as at the Institute of Sacred Music at Yale Divinity School and Columbia Theological Seminary.

Oduro—Rev. Dr. Thomas Asante Oduro (Calvary Baptist Church, Accra, Ghana) is principal of Good News Theological College and Seminary in Accra,

Ghana, a tertiary ministerial seminary for African Instituted Churches. He holds a doctorate in the history of Christianity from Luther Seminary, St. Paul, MN, USA, and has been working with African Instituted Churches for almost three decades.

Puglisi—Rev. Dr. James F. Puglisi, SA, (Catholic Church) is director of the Centro Pro Unione (Rome); professor of ecclesiology, ecumenism, and sacraments at the Pontifical Ateneo Sant'Anselmo and the Pontifical University St. Thomas Aquinas ("Angelicum") (Rome). A member of the Franciscan Friars of the Atonement, he holds graduate degrees in liturgy from Catholic University of America, systematic theology from Institut catholique-Paris, religious anthropology and history from the Sorbonne-Paris, and a certificate in ecumenical studies from Boston University. He has served as president of *Societas Liturgica*.

Reid—Dr. George Reid (Seventh-day Adventist Church) was, prior to his retirement, for eighteen years the director of the Biblical Research Institute of the General Conference of Seventh-day Adventists. He also served as head of the religion department of Southwestern Adventist University and associate editor of the *Adventist Review*.

Robinson—Colonel Earl Robinson (The Salvation Army) has recently retired as secretary for spiritual life development and international external relations, The Salvation Army International Headquarters. He was a coauthor of the 1998 Salvation Army Handbook of Doctrine, and at the time of writing for this volume was chair of the International Doctrine Council of his church.

Scott—Dr. Janet Rosemary Scott (Britain Yearly Meeting of the Religious Society of Friends [Quakers]) is the clerk of Britain Yearly Meeting's Committee on Christian and Interfaith Relations. A director of Churches Together in England, of the Centre for Ecumenical Studies, Cambridge Theological Federation, and of religious studies, Homerton College, Cambridge, United Kingdom, she has represented Friends worldwide at WCC events and on the Faith and Order Commission.

Sebastian—The Rev. Dr. J. Jayakiran Sebastian is a presbyter of the Church of South India and professor in the Department of Theology and Ethics at the United Theological College, Bangalore, India. He is currently H. George Anderson Professor of Mission and Cultures and Director of the Multicultural Mission Resource Center at the Lutheran Theological Seminary in Philadelphia, USA.

Slough—Dr. Rebecca Slough (Mennonite) is dean of the Associated Mennonite Biblical Seminary, Elkhart, IN, USA, and the author of many contributions to the liturgical practice and theological understanding of Mennonite churches. A member of the Hymn Society of the United States and Canada and the North

American Academy of Liturgy, she served as managing editor for *Hymnal: A Worship Book* (Elgin, IL: Brethren Press; Newton, KS: Faith and Life Press; Scottsdale, PA: Mennonite Publishing House) from 1989–92.

Tashjian—Archpriest Dr. Mesrob Tashjian (Armenian Apostolic and Orthodox Church), is an educator, theologian, and author. Born in 1924 in Aleppo, Syria, he graduated from St. James Armenian Seminary in Jerusalem in 1943, was ordained into the priesthood in 1961, and holds an MA in biblical studies from Providence College and a DM from Boston University. He made weekly presentations for the Voice of America from 1983–93. Recently retired, he was pastor of Sts. Vartanantz Church in Providence, RI, for forty-five years.

Truscott—Rev. Dr. Jeffrey A. Truscott (Evangelical Lutheran Church in America) is chaplain and lecturer in liturgy and worship, Trinity Theological College, Singapore. He has written extensively on Christian initiation. Formerly, he taught at Japan Lutheran Theological Seminary in Tokyo.

Watkins—Rev. Dr. Keith Watkins (Christian Church, Disciples of Christ) is professor of practical parish ministry, emeritus, Christian Theological Seminary, Indianapolis, IN, USA, where he also taught worship. He has produced many publications on worship, particularly on baptism and the eucharist. He is currently doing research on a history of the Yakama Christian Mission in the western part of the United States.

Westerfield Tucker—Dr. Karen B. Westerfield Tucker, an elder (presbyter) of the United Methodist Church, is professor of worship, Boston University School of Theology. She is president-elect of the international and ecumenical *Societas Liturgica* and editor in chief of *Studia Liturgica*, is a member of the bilateral dialogue between the World Methodist Council and the Roman Catholic Church, and has been a consultant to the Faith and Order Commission of the WCC.

White—Rev. K. Gordon White (Episcopalian) is a retired priest who served as the executive secretary of the Massachusetts Commission on Christian Unity (MCCU) from 1984 until his retirement in 2004. During that period he oversaw the production of the MCCU document "Baptismal Practice in an Ecumenical Context."

* * *

Indexer

Flanagan—Brian P. Flanagan wrote his 2007 PhD dissertation on communion and ecclesiological method in the work of the late theologian and ecumenist Jean-Marie-Roger Tillard, OP. He is currently a visiting assistant professor in the Department of Religious Studies at the College of the Holy Cross in Worcester, Massachusetts, and the editor of *New Horizons in Faith and Order*, an electronic journal written and edited by younger theologians.

Acknowledgments

PART I: COMMENTARIES
"Baptism: Sacrament of the Kingdom." The original of this article was delivered at St. Vladimir's Seminary, Crestwood, NY, USA as a tribute to Fr. Alexander Schmemann on the anniversary of his passing.

PART III: SIGNS OF RECOGNITION
Mutual Recognition of Baptism Agreement, Germany. Text reprinted by permission of the *Arbeitsgemeinschaft Christlicher Kirchen in Deutschland*.

Common Baptismal Certificate, Australia. Text reprinted by permission of the Australian Consultation on Liturgy. Illustration reprinted by permission of the Joint Board of Christian Education.

Text on Baptismal Practice in an Ecumenical Context, Massachusetts, USA. Reprinted by permission of Massachusetts Council of Churches.

PART V: BAPTISMAL SERVICES
Eastern Orthodox: Translation from Greek sources by Archimandrite Ephrem (Ecumenical Patriarchate, Archdiocese of Thyateira and Great Britain). See http://www.anastasis.org.uk/baptism.htm. Translation copyright © Archimandrite Ephrem. Reprinted by permission.

Oriental Orthodox (Armenian): Reprinted with permission from *The Rituals of the Armenian Apostolic Church*, copyright 1992 by the Eastern Prelacy of the Armenian Apostolic Church of America.

Orthodox (Syrian, India): Father Abraham Konat. *Baptismal Liturgy of the Syrian Orthodox Church*. Pampakuda: Mar Julius Press, 1964. (Syriac text and Malayalam translation). Certain sections of this baptismal liturgy are a reproduction or adaptation from Murad Saliba Barsom, Athanasius Yeshue Samuel, Syrian Orthodox Eastern Church, *The Sacrament of Holy Baptism According to the Ancient Rite of the Syrian Orthodox Church of Antioch*. Hackensack, NJ: A.Y. Samuel, 1974. (Syriac text and English translation). Certain sections are a free English translation by Fr. Dr. Jacob Kurien of the currently used Malayalam text.

Catholic (for adults): Excerpts from the English translation of *Rite of Christian Initiation of Adults* © 1985, International Committee on English in the Liturgy, Inc. (ICEL). All rights reserved.

Catholic (for children): Excerpts from the English translation of *Rite of Baptism for Children* © 1969, International Committee on English in the Liturgy, Inc. (ICEL). All rights reserved.

Excerpt from Psalm 23 is taken from the *New American Bible with Revised New Testament and Revised Psalms* © 1991, 1986, 1970 Confraternity of Christian Doctrine, Washington, DC, and is used by permission of the copyright owner. All Rights Reserved. No part of the *New American Bible* may be reproduced in any form without permission in writing from the copyright owner.

Lutheran: Holy Baptism liturgy taken from Lutheran Book of Worship © copyright 1978. Used by permission of Augsburg Fortress.

Lutheran (Sweden): Svenska Kyrkans Församlingsnämnd. From *Den Svenska Kyrkohandboken* (Official Handbook for Church of Sweden). Reprinted by permission.

Anglican: From *Common Worship: Initiation Services*. London: Church House Publishing, 1998, 103–17. Some small changes were subsequently made to the rite in February 2000. These are listed at http://www.cofe.anglican.org/worship/liturgy/commonworship/texts/initiation/changes.html, and are included in a revised edition published in 2006: An Anglican Service of Baptism and Confirmation (Church of England) from *Common Worship: Christian Initiation*. Copyright © The Archbishops' Council, 2006. Reprinted by permission.

Presbyterian: From Theology and Worship Ministry Unit for the Presbyterian Church (USA) and the Cumberland Presbyterian Church. *Book of Common Worship*. Louisville, KY: Westminster/John Knox Press, 1993, 402–15. Reprinted by permission.

Baptist: From the first pattern for a service of baptism provided in *Patterns and Prayers for Christian Worship: A Guidebook for Worship Leaders*. The Baptist Union of Great Britain. Oxford: Oxford University Press, 1991, 93–107. Reprinted by permission of Baptist Union of Great Britain. (To accommodate variations in practice, this section as printed offers two patterns for the whole sequence of initiation through Baptism, Laying on of Hands, and the Lord's Supper, followed separately by material for each of the elements. For the purpose of the present book, this material has been integrated into one of the outline patterns.)

Mennonite: From *Minister's Manual*, edited by John Rempel. Copyright © 1998 by Faith & Life Press and Herald Press. Used by permission.

Methodist: From *The United Methodist Hymnal*. Baptismal Covenant I © 1976, 1980, 1985, 1989 The United Methodist Publishing House. Used by permission.

Christian Church (Disciples of Christ): From Stephen V. Sprinkle. "A Representative Disciples Rite of Christian Baptism." In Keith Watkins, ed. *A Resource for Christian Worship*, prepared for use of the Christian Church (Disciples of Christ) by the Division of Homeland Ministries. St. Louis: Chalice Press, 1991. Reprinted by permission of Stephen V. Sprinkle.

Mar Thoma: "The Order of Thanksgiving After Childbirth and Holy Baptism" from *Order of Services, Baptism, Matrimony, Prayer for Sick, House Dedication and Funeral*. Reprinted by permission of Mar Thoma Syrian Church.

Index

NOTE: Numbers in *italics* refer to the baptismal services collected in Section V of this book.

A

African Independent Churches baptism, 181–91, 260–62; as African Instituted Churches, 219; blessing of water in, 188; confession of faith in, 185, 188; creed in, 57; and Holy Spirit, 189; infant, 183, 187; laying on of hands in, 189; mode of, 185, 188; preparation of candidates for, 184

Ambrose, 20

Anabaptists, on baptism, 89–91. *See also* Mennonite baptism

Anglican baptism, 55–61, *371–79*; blessing of water in, 57, *374–75*; candle in, 58, *379*; confession of faith in, *375*; confirmation and, 55–56, 58, 60, *376–77*; of infants, 58–59; mode of, 58; oil in, 57, 58; preparation of candidates for, 59; renunciation of evil in, 57, *373*; white garment in, 58

Appiah, Kwame Anthony, 263

Armenian Apostolic baptism, 15–21, *289–302*; blessing of water in, 17–18, *294–95*; confession of faith in, 17, *291*; confirmation and, 19–20, *297–98, 302*; Eucharist and, 21, *299–300*; godfather in, 16–17, *301*; mode of, 19, *296, 301*; oil in, 18, 20, *295, 297–98, 301–2*; preparation of candidates for, 16–17; presentation to altar in, 21; renunciation of evil in, 17, *291*

Augustine, 37–38, 39

Australia, Common Baptismal Certificate of, 231–33

Australia, Uniting Church in. *See* Uniting Church in Australia

B

Bäckström, Anders, 250

baptism: in African Independent churches, 181–91, 260–62; in Anabaptist churches, 89–91; in Anglican Communion, 55–61, *371–79*; in Armenian Apostolic church, 15–21, *289–302*; in Baptist churches, 73–80, *393–99*; believers', 68–69, 74, 78–79, 89–91, 109, 148, 158, 161–62, 171, 200–2; in Catholic church, 29–43, *319–58*; in Christian Church (Disciples of Christ), 109–14, *417–22*; and church, 6–7, 26, 68, 202–3, 210, 215, 239; and church membership, 74, 77–78, 202–3, 210, 218, 397–99, 415–16; common certificate of, in Australia, 231–33; and Dalit communities, 256–60; and death, 10; in Eastern Orthodox churches, 3–14, *269–87*; ecumenical practice document, in Massachusetts, 221, 235–243; emergency, 45, 241; and evangelization, 214–17; and faith, 27, 39–40, 68–69, 74, 201; godparents and, 11, 16–17, 27, *301*; and Holy Spirit, 6, 10–11, 26, 85–87,

441

155–56, 189, 209, 210–11; in the Holy Spirit, 85–87, 159, 163–65, 189; of infants, 26–27, 38–40, 45, 50–51, 58–59, 66–67, 127–29, 158, 161–62, 178, 183, 187, 200–2, 214; in Jesus' name, 158–60, 217–18; in Lutheran tradition, 45–54, *359–70*; in Malankara Orthodox Syrian church, 23–27, *303–17*; in Mar Thoma Syrian Church, 115–32, *423–32*; in Mennonite churches, 89–98, *401–7*; in Methodist church, 99–107, *409–16*; mutual recognition agreement of, in Germany, 227–29; in Pentecostal tradition, 147–68; in Presbyterian/Reformed tradition, 63–71, *381–92*; and Quaker tradition, 81–88; recognition of, viii–ix, 203–4; repetition of, 78–79, 95, 158, 161, 238; as rite of passage, 150–51, 208–9, 216–17; and Salvation Army, 173–80; in Seventh-day Adventist church, 169–72; sponsors and, 46–47, 129–30, 240; in Sweden, 247–53, *365–70*; and testimony, 151, 153–54; time of, 33–34, 48–49; Trinitarian formula and, 36, 64, 142, 158–60, 217–18, 231–32, 237–38; in Uniting Church in Australia, 133–45. *See also specific practices related to baptism*

Baptism, Eucharist and Ministry (BEM), vii, 51, 142, 195, 208, 214, 219, 221, 228, 237, 242–43

baptismal certificate, common, Australian, 231–33

baptismal practice document, ecumenical, Massachusetts, 221, 235–43

"Baptismal Practice in an Ecumenical Context" (Massachusetts Commission on Christian Unity), 221, 235–43

baptismal recognition agreement, mutual, German, 227–29

Baptist baptism, 73–80, 215, *393–99*; as believers' baptism, 74, 78–79; and church membership, 74, 77–78, *397–99*; confession of faith in, *395–96*; faith and, 74; laying on of hands in, *396–97*; mode of, 75; and rebaptism, 78–79; and sacramentality, 76–77

Bar Kepha, Moses, 124

Barclay, Robert, 83

Basil of Caesarea, 5–6

believers' baptism, 200–2; in Baptist churches, 74, 78–79; in Disciples baptism, 109; in Mennonite churches, 89–91; in Pentecostal tradition, 148, 158, 161–62; in Presbyterian/Reformed tradition, 68–69; in Seventh-day Adventist church, 171

BEM. See Baptism, Eucharist and Ministry

Bhabha, Homi, 257

blessing of water, baptism and, 197; in African Independent churches baptism, 188; in Anglican baptism, 57, *374–75*; in Armenian Apostolic baptism, 17–18, *294–95*; in Catholic baptism, 34–35, *320, 325–31, 349–50*; in Disciples baptism, 111, *420–21*; in Eastern Orthodox baptism, 274–79; in Lutheran baptism, 47, *361, 367*; in Malankara Syrian Orthodox baptism, *310–15*; in Mar Thoma Syrian baptism, 123–35, *428–30*; in Methodist baptism, *412–13*; in Presbyterian/Reformed baptism, 64, *388–90*; in Uniting Church in Australia baptism, 136–37

Braudel, Fernand, 255

C

"Called to be the One Church," vii

Camelot, Pierre-Thomas, 8

candle: in Anglican baptism, 58, *379*; in Catholic baptism, 36, *335, 354*; in Lutheran baptism, 48, *368*; in Methodist baptism, *414*; in Presbyterian/Reformed baptism, 65, 67

catechumenate, in Catholic baptism, 31–32

Catholic baptism, 29–43, *319–58*; blessing of water in, 34–35, *320, 325–31, 349–50*; candle in, 36, *335, 354*; catechumenate in, 31–32; chrism in, 36, 37; confession of faith in, 35, *320–21, 332–33, 351–52*; confirmation and, 36–37, *321–22, 335–37*; and Eucharist, 37–38, 40, *322, 340*; exorcisms in, 32, *346–37*; of infants, 38–40; laying on of hands and, 36–37, *336–37*; mode of, 35–36, *321*; and mystagogy, 38, *340–42*; oil in, 36, 37, *334, 337, 347, 353*; preparation of candidates for, 31–33; renunciation of evil in, 35, *320–21, 331–32, 350–51*; white garment in, 36, *334–35, 353–54*

chrism. *See* oil

chrismation: and Armenian Apostolic baptism, *297–98*; in Eastern Orthodox baptism, 10–11, *280*; and Holy Spirit, 10–11, 26, 126; in Malankara Orthodox Syrian baptism, 25, *316*; in Mar Thoma Syrian baptism, 126, *431*. *See also* confirmation

Christian Church (Disciples of Christ) baptism, 109–14, *417–22*; as believers' baptism, 109; blessing of water in, 111, *420–21*; confession of faith in, 110, *418*; and Eucharist, 113; and rebaptism, 112–13

church: baptism and, 6–7, 26, 68, 77–78, 202–3, 210, 215, 239. *See also* membership

confession of faith: in African Independent churches baptism, 185, 188; in Anglican baptism, *375*; in Armenian Apostolic baptism, 17, *291*; in Baptist baptism, *395–96*; in Catholic baptism, 35, *320–21, 332–33, 351–52*; in Disciples baptism, 110, *418*; in Eastern Orthodox baptism, 9–10, *273–74*; in Lutheran baptism, 47, *361–62, 367*; in Malankara Orthodox Syrian baptism, 25, *310*; in Mar Thoma Syrian baptism, 121–22, *427–28*; in Mennonite baptism, 93, *401, 403–4*; in Methodist baptism, 105, *410–12*; in Presbyterian/Reformed tradition, 63–64, *386–88*; in Uniting Church in Australia baptism, 136. *See also* creeds

confirmation, baptism and, 219–20; and Anglican baptism, 55–56, 58, 60, *376–77*; and Armenian Apostolic baptism, 19–20, *297–98*, 302; and Catholic baptism, 36–37, *321–22, 335–37*; and Methodist baptism, 102–3; and Presbyterian/Reformed baptism, 69–70; and Uniting Church in Australia baptism, 134, 138, 142. *See also* chrismation; laying on of hands

convincement, in Quaker tradition, 82–84

creeds, baptism and, 201, 241; in Anglican baptism, 57; in Eastern Orthodox baptism, 9–10; in Lutheran baptism, 47; in Malankara Orthodox Syrian baptism, 25; in Mar Thoma Syrian baptism, 122; in Methodist baptism, 103, 105, *412–13*; in Presbyterian/Reformed baptism, 63–64, 65; in Uniting Church in Australia baptism, 136, 141. *See also* confession of faith

Cyprian, 16, 39
Cyril of Jerusalem, 19

D
Dalit communities, baptism and, 256–60
Didache, 9, 15
Disciples of Christ baptism. *See* Christian Church (Disciples of Christ) baptism

E
Eastern Orthodox baptism, 3–14, 269–87; blessing of water in, 274–79; chrismation in, 10–11, 280; confession of faith in, 9–10, 273–74; Eucharist and, 11, 12–13, 287; exorcism in, 270–72; godparents in, 11; mode of, 10, 274–79; oil in, 10–11, 277–79, 281; renunciation of evil in, 9, 272–73
"Ecclesiological and Ecumenical Implications of a Common Baptism," vii, xiiin7, 80n8, 214, 222n2
Elenjikal, Matthew, 116, 119, 120, 122, 125
Ellwood, Thomas, 86
Ephraim, 19–20
Eucharist, baptism and, xi, 221–22; and Armenian Apostolic baptism, 21, 299–300; baptism and, 11, 12–13; and Catholic baptism, 37–38, 40, 322, 340; and Disciples baptism, 113; and Eastern Orthodox baptism, 11, 12–13, 287; and Lutheran baptism, 49, 51; and Malankara Orthodox Syrian baptism, 24, 316–17; and Mar Thoma Syrian baptism, 129; and Methodist baptism, 103, 106; and Presbyterian/Reformed baptism, 69–70
evangelization, baptism, and, 214–17
evil, renunciation. *See* renunciation of evil

exorcism: in Catholic baptism, 32, 346–47; in Eastern Orthodox baptism, 270–72; in Malankara Orthodox Syrian baptism, 24, 308–9; in Mar Thoma Syrian baptism, 120–21, 427. *See also* renunciation of evil

F
faith, baptism and, 27, 39–40, 68–69, 74, 201
faith, confession of. *See* confession of faith
Fiddes, Paul, 219
Florovsky, Georges, 5
Fox, George, 86

G
Gehman, Henry S., 15
Germany, Mutual Baptismal Recognition Agreement in, 227–29
godparents: in Armenian Apostolic baptism, 16–17, 301; in Eastern Orthodox baptism, 11; in Malankara Orthodox Syrian baptism, 27. *See also* sponsors
Gregory the Illuminator, 19

H
Hippolytus, 9
Holy Spirit: baptism and, 6, 10–11, 26, 85–87, 155–56, 189, 209, 210–11; baptism in, 85–87, 159, 163–65, 189; chrismation and, 10–11, 26, 126

I
India, baptism in, 256–60
infant baptism, 200–2, 214; in African Independent churches, 183, 187; in Anglican communion, 58–59; in Catholic church, 38–40; in Lutheran tradition, 45, 50–51;

in Malankara Orthodox Syrian church, 26–27, *303–17*; in Mar Thoma Syrian church, 127–29; in Pentecostal tradition, 158, 161–62; in Presbyterian/Reformed tradition, 66–67; and Salvation Army, 178

J
Jacob of Edessa, 23
Jenkins, Philip, 181
Jesus' name, baptism in, 158, 161–62, 217–18
John Chrysostom, 9
Justin Martyr, 9

L
Larsson, Bo, 216
laying on of hands: and African Independent churches baptism, 189; and Baptist baptism, *396–97*; and Catholic baptism, 36–37, *336–37*; and Lutheran baptism, 48, *363*; in Mennonite baptism, *405*; in Presbyterian/Reformed baptism, 64, *391–92*; in Uniting Church in Australia baptism, 138. *See also* confirmation
Lima document. See *Baptism, Eucharist and Ministry*
Lord's Supper. *See* Eucharist
Luther, Martin, 45–46
Lutheran baptism, 45–54, *359–70*; blessing of water in, 47, *361, 367*; candle in, 48, *368*; confession of faith in, 47, *361–62, 367*; creed in, 47; and Eucharist, 49, 51; of infants, 45, 50–51; laying on of hands and, 48, *363*; mode of, 47–48; oil in, 48; preparation of candidates for, 50; renunciation of evil in, 47, *361*; sponsors in, 46–47; white garment in, 48

M
Malankara Orthodox Syrian baptism, 23–27; blessing of water in, *310–15*; chrismation in, 25, *316*; confession of faith in, 25, *310*; creed in, 25; crowning in, 25, *317*; Eucharist and, 24, *316–17*; exorcism in, 24, *308–9*; godparents in, 27; of infants, 26–27; mode of, 25; oil in, 25, 26, *314, 316*; preparation of candidates for, 50; presentation to altar in, 25; renunciation of evil in, 24, *309*
Mar Thoma Syrian baptism, 115–32, 215, *423–32*; blessing of water in, 123–25, *428–30*; chrismation in, 126, *431*; confession of faith in, 121–22, *427–28*; creed in, 122; crowning in, 126–27, *431*; Eucharist and, 129; exorcism in, 120–21, *427*; of infants, 127–29; mode of, 125–26; oil in, 122–23, 125, 126, *428, 430, 431*; renunciation of evil in, 121; sponsors in, 129–30
Massachusetts, Baptismal Ecumenical Practice Document of, 221, 235–43
Massachusetts Commission on Christian Unity, 221, 235–43
Matthew 28:16–20 (the "Great Commission"), 17, 63, 89, 116, 135, 159, 213, 217, 222, 237, *282, 291–92, 344, 366, 382–83, 401*
Mazambara, Phillip, 260
membership, church, baptism and, 202–3, 210, 218; Baptist baptism and, 74, 77–78, *397–99*; Methodist baptism and, *415–16*; Quaker tradition and, 81–84
Mennonite baptism, 89–98, *401–7*; as believers' baptism, 89–91; confession of faith in, 93, *401, 403–4*; laying on of hands in, *405*; mode of,

445

94; and rebaptism, 95; renunciation of evil in, *401, 403–4*

Methodist baptism, 99–107, *409–16*; blessing of water in, *412–13*; candle in, *414*; and church membership, *415–16*; confession of faith in, 105, *410–12*; and confirmation, 102–3; creed in, 103, 105, *411–12*; and Eucharist, 103, 106; mode of, 105; oil in, *413*; renunciation of evil in, *410*; white garment in, *413–14*

mode of baptism, 219; in African Independent churches, 185, 188; in Anglican baptism, 58; in Armenian Apostolic baptism, 19, *296, 301*; in Baptist baptism, 75; in Catholic baptism, 35–36, *321*; in Eastern Orthodox baptism, 10, 274–79; in Lutheran baptism, 47–48; in Malankara Orthodox Syrian baptism, 25; in Mar Thoma Syrian baptism, 125–26; in Mennonite baptism, 94; in Methodist baptism, 105; in Pentecostal tradition, 154–55, 158; in Presbyterian/Reformed baptism, 64; in Uniting Church in Australia baptism, 137

Moore-Keish, Martha, 218

Muron/Myron. *See* oil

O

Of Water and the Spirit (Schmemann), 3–4

oil: in Anglican baptism, 57, 58; in Armenian Apostolic baptism, 18, 20, *295, 297–98, 301–2*; in Catholic baptism, 36, 37, *334, 337, 347, 353*; in Eastern Orthodox baptism, 10–11, *277–79, 281*; in Lutheran baptism, 48; in Malankara Orthodox Syrian baptism, 25, 26, *314, 316*; in Mar Thoma Syrian baptism, 122–23, 125, 126, *428, 430, 431*; in Methodist baptism, *413*; in Presbyterian/Reformed baptism, 64, 67, *391*; in Uniting Church in Australia baptism, 142; and healing, 123, 145n17, 262

Okoh, Agnes, 181–82, 185–86

Okoh, Marius, 186–87

"One Baptism: Towards Mutual Recognition," vii–viii, xiiinn7, 9, 80n8, 211, 212n5, 223n11

Origen, 16, 38–39

P

Pentecostal baptism, 147–68; and baptism in the Sprit, 159, 163–65; as believers' baptism, 148, 158, 161–62; of infants, 158, 161–62; mode of, 154–55, 158; as oral tradition, 147–48; and rebaptism, 158, 161; as rite of passage, 150–51; and testimony, 151, 153–54

preparation of candidates, 239–40; for African Independent churches baptism, 184; for Anglican baptism, 59; for Armenian Apostolic baptism, 16–17; for Catholic baptism, 31–33; for Lutheran baptism, 50; for Malankara Orthodox Syrian baptism, 24; in Presbyterian/Reformed baptism, 66

Presbyterian/Reformed baptism, 63–71, *381–92*; as believers' baptism, 68–69; blessing of water, 64, *388–90*; candle in, 65, 67; confession of faith in, 63–64, *386–88*; and confirmation, 69–70; creed in, 63–64, 65; and Eucharist, 69–70; of infants, 66–67; laying on of hands in, 64, *391–92*; mode of, 64; oil in, 64, 67, *391*; preparation of candidates in, 66; renunciation of evil in, *385–86*; white garment in, 65, 67 profession of faith. *See* confession of faith

Puglisi, James F., 218

Q

Quaker tradition, 81–88; baptism in the Spirit in, 85–87, 215, 216; and membership, 81–84

R

rebaptism, 238; Baptist churches and, 78–79; Disciples churches and, 112–13; Mennonite churches and, 95; Pentecostal tradition and, 158, 161

recognition, of baptism, viii–ix, 203–4, 227–29

Reformed baptism. *See* Presbyterian/Reformed baptism

Reimers, Eva, 249–50, 251

renunciation of evil: in Anglican baptism, 57, *373*; in Armenian Apostolic baptism, 17, *291*; in Catholic baptism, 35, *320–21, 331–32, 350–51*; in Eastern Orthodox baptism, 9, *272–73*; in Lutheran baptism, 47, *361*; in Malankara Orthodox Syrian baptism, 24, *309*; in Mar Thoma Syrian baptism, 121; in Mennonite baptism, *401, 403–4*; in Methodist baptism, *410*; in Presbyterian/Reformed baptism, *385–86*; in Uniting Church in Australia baptism, 135–36. *See also* exorcism

Rite of Christian Initiation of Adults (*RCIA*, Catholic), 30–31, 59, 195, 197, 214

rite of passage, baptism as, 150–51, 208–9, 216–17

Roman Catholic baptism. *See* Catholic baptism

S

Salvation Army, 173–80; initiation in, 173–75

Satan, renunciation of. *See* renunciation of evil

Schmemann, Alexander, 3–4, 12–13

Seventh-day Adventist baptism, 169–72; as believers' baptism, 171; and infant baptism, 178

Severus of Antioch, 23

Spirituality of Baptism, The (Camelot), 8

sponsors, 240; in Lutheran baptism, 46–47; in Mar Thoma Syrian baptism, 129–30. *See also* godparents

Sugirtharajah, R. S., 259–60

Sweden, baptism in, 247–53

T

Tertullian, 19, 20, 39

testimony: and Pentecostal baptism, 151, 153–54

Tovey, Philip, 124–25

Trinitarian formula, baptism and, 36, 64, 142, 158–60, 217–18, 231–32, 237–38

Turner, Harold, 181

U

Udemba, Nicholas, 186

United Methodist baptism. *See* Methodist baptism

Uniting Church in Australia baptism, 133–45, 215; blessing of water in, 136–37; confession of faith in, 136; and confirmation, 134, 138, 142; creed in, 136, 141; mode of, 137; oil in, 142; renunciation of evil in, 135–36

V

Varghese, Baby, 120

W

water, blessing of. *See* blessing of water
Wesley, John, 99–100
white garment: in Anglican baptism, 58; in Catholic baptism, 36, *334–35, 353–54*; in Lutheran baptism, 48; in Methodist baptism, *413–14*; in Presbyterian/Reformed baptism, 65, 67
Woolman, John, 86

Z

Zizek, Slavoj, 262